EVENT MANAGEMENT

BLUEPRINT

Creating
and
Managing
Successful
Sports
Events

EDITED BY
Heather Lawrence • Michelle Wells

Kendall Hunt

publishing company

4050 Westmark Drive • P O Box 1840 • Dubuque IA 52004-1840

Front cover center image © Rob Wilson, 2009
Used under License from Shutterstock, Inc.

Front cover upper right image © Stephen Stratudee, 2009
Used under License from Shutterstock, Inc.

Front cover lower left image courtesy of New York Road Runners.

Back cover far left image courtesy of New York Road Runners.

Kendall Hunt
publishing company

www.kendallhunt.com
Send all inquiries to:
4050 Westmark Drive
Dubuque, IA 52004-1840

Copyright © 2009 by Kendall Hunt Publishing Company

ISBN 978-0-7575-7933-2

Printed in the United States of America
10 9 8 7 6 5 4

This book is dedicated to all of our event management mentors, professors, and colleagues.

CONTENTS

Preface ix

Foreword xiii

Acknowledgments xv

About the Editors/Authors xvii

SECTION I   EVENT CONCEPTUALIZATION 1

    Chapter 1   Event Management and the Event Manager 3

        The Harlem Globetrotters 8

        An Interview with Paul Ortolano 13

        Sample Job Description for a University
        Event Management Position 16

    Chapter 2   Event Feasibility 23

        Sample Bid Requirements 26

        The Principles of Universal Design 29

        The Olympic Bid Process 32

    Chapter 3   Event and Facility Contracts 41

        What I Wish I had Known 41

        Ohio University Game Contract 51

        Harlem Globetrotters Standard Co-Promotion Agreement 54

        Ohio University Facility Rental Agreement 64

        Sample Sponsorship Contract 66

    Chapter 4   Technology and Event Planning 71

        Q&A with the Montreal Canadiens 75

        The Power of Twitter 76

        Tickets and Technology—Flash Seats 80

        USA Swimming and Blogs 81

SECTION II   EVENT DEVELOPMENT 89

    Chapter 5   Event Budget 90

    Chapter 6   Event Marketing 107

        From Personal Experience 109

        Radio Advertising Glossary of Terms 112

    Chapter 7   Event Sponsorship 119

        Creativity with Caution 120

        National Sports Forum, Corporate & Industry Survey Results 122

        Proactive Communication with Sponsors 126

Chapter 8   **Participant Registration for Events** **131**

         Web Registration Made Easy..*133*

         Sample Participant Waiver...*137*

Chapter 9   **Event Ticketing** **141**

         Lessons Learned in Ticketing......................................*145*

         The AT&T National: Leveraging an Event Web Site for Ticket Sales *149*

Chapter 10   **Event Communications and External Relations** **163**

         Sixteen Rules for the Press Release.............................*170*

Chapter 11   **Event Safety and Security** **177**

         How Building Planning and Design Impact Safety and Security...*179*

         An Interview with Christine (Cusick) Moore *186*

         Sample Guest Code of Conduct *187*

SECTION III   **EVENT EXECUTION** **203**

Chapter 12   **Event Documents** **205**

         Sample Planning Timeline..*206*

         Sample Day of Event Timeline...................................*208*

         Sample Event Checklists *209*

         Sample Call Sign List *210*

         Sample Fast Facts *212*

         Sample Staffing Positions..*213*

         Sample Event Diagram...*215*

Chapter 13   **Event Staffing** **223**

         Jump Teams!...*229*

         Sample Call Time Meeting Agenda............................*236*

         How to Conduct Event Management Meetings *238*

Chapter 14   **Event Operations** **245**

         Organization Is Everything! *248*

         Creating and Managing Green Events........................*252*

         My Event Is Too Big..*257*

         Detailed List of Equipment.......................................*259*

         10 Event Operations Tips *270*

Chapter 15   **Event Settlement and Wrap Up** **275**

         An Interview with Lynda Reinhart and Renee Musson *278*

Chapter 16   **International Considerations for Events** **291**

         Cultural Awareness Tips *295*

         An Interview with Christine (Cusick) Moore *298*

References *305*

Appendix A   Event Management Professional Organizations and
             Related Resources 311
Appendix B   Event Resources (Examples) 315
Appendix C   Event Management Checklist: Multipurpose 319
Appendix D   Ratios 325
Appendix E   Glossary of Terms 329

PREFACE

For sport management students, often there is a gap between classroom instruction and on-the-job required tasks. The authors work to close that gap by providing current and future event managers with an event management template that can be used in the sports industry. Through use of this book, readers are challenged to create a sport event using a step-by-step process that breaks down tasks into manageable pieces, including the processes associated with conceptualizing and planning an event. The end result of the project is a set of realistic guidelines that encompasses much of what is needed to execute the proposed event. Although it may be difficult to actually execute the event while working through this book, the challenges are as realistic as possible and push students to determine the following:

- What type of event should be held?

- What is the purpose of the event?

- How can the theme and creative aspects enhance the core event?

- Why does this event have potential to be successful?

- Where will the event be held?

- What are the strengths and weaknesses of the event?

- What is the definition of success for the event?

- How will technology be used internally and externally in the management of the event?

- What is the budget?

- What contracts are important to consider?

- Which marketing strategies are the best fit for the event?

- What role will sponsorship play in the event?

- Is there a need for participant registration?

- Will tickets be sold? If so, how, when, and at what price?

- How will media be leveraged to ensure the event earns as much coverage as possible?

- How will the event manager ensure the event is safe and secure?

- What emergency planning is needed?

- What planning documents are needed?

- How will the event be staffed?

- How will staff be motivated to work hard?

- What is needed for the event day operations?

- What equipment is needed?

- How will the event flow?

- What happens when the event is over?

- Are there any international considerations for the event?

This book is written for advanced students and industry professionals and the authors assume that readers have basic knowledge of general management practices, sport management, sport marketing, sport sponsorship, sport finance, risk management, and sport facility management. The book builds on basic knowledge in these areas and delves into the details of each as they relate to the event. Practical application of these event management concepts are illustrated throughout the text. In so doing, topics are introduced and explained in ways that allow readers to understand the concepts and their application to an event.

College professors in sports administration/sports management will find this resource beneficial as it can be integrated into sport management, sport marketing, sport business, or event planning curriculums. Current and future sport managers and event managers will find this practical guide to event management very useful as many of the ideas and strategies provided are transferable to other types of events (i.e., fundraising, entertainment, festivals, exhibitions, concerts, family, and business); however, this book focuses on events where sport is the primary activity.

Although many aspects of event management occur simultaneously, three distinct phases *(conceptualization, development, and execution)* of event management have been identified and developed for this book to assist in the delivery of the content and organization of the chapters. For example, a topic such as facility management will be introduced early in the text and then expanded upon in following chapters as attention to the facility occurs at every stage of the event process.

The *event conceptualization* section of the book is covered in Chapters 1–4 and includes an overview of the various types of events, the role of the event manager, the event feasibility and bidding process, economic impact, information on contracts, and strategies for using technology in event management. These chapters also highlight additional information that is interesting and useful, such as interviews with industry experts, an outline of the Olympic Games bid process, and multiple sample contracts.

The section of the book on *event development* is covered in Chapters 5–11 and focuses on specific aspects of event development. Some of these areas tend to be overlooked by individuals involved with events because they may not fall under the specific purview of event managers. Savvy event managers, however, need to be knowledgeable about marketing, sponsorship, ticketing, communications, safety and security, and the budget. Many of these areas are revenue generators and thus will help event managers ensure that the event is financially viable. Beyond revenue generation, safety and security is of great importance to events of all sizes, and the budget is what guides many aspects of the event management process. In this section, readers will also find stories from industry professionals on lessons they learned in the industry, specific information on how to use Excel to set up an event budget, details on how to write a press release, and even research-based key drivers for event sponsorship.

Event execution is addressed in the third and final section of the book (Chapters 12–16). Event execution encompasses planning immediately prior to the event, the event day (or days), as well as event settlement and wrap-up. Operations are a key aspect of the management process and this section includes detailed information on necessary documents, how to staff the event, and the specifics of operations, settlement, and follow-up. The editors have also included a chapter on international considerations authored by experts who have been involved with major international events. This section also includes sample event checklists, information on going green in event management, an interview with the director of a major arena, and information on how to be culturally sensitive.

For purposes of demonstrating the scope of event management concepts, a variety of types and sizes of events are used as examples throughout the book. Regardless of whether the event is large or small (e.g., local youth basketball tournament, large marathon), event managers need to be educated and prepared. By highlighting a variety of events, the similarities and differences among various events will become apparent.

Authors from the sports industry and academia have contributed to the book and bring forth a variety of personal experiences and guidance that can be useful for new and experienced sport managers. The authors represent over 325 years of sport industry experience and over 60 years in academia teaching sport management. Having authors who have practical experience in areas in which they are writing about contributes to the practical focus of this book.

Throughout the text, core concepts are presented; however, in order to supplement the content, students are strongly advised to conduct external research appropriate for the event they choose. Space is provided following each chapter to assist students in organizing the various parts of their event. By tackling these issues for a specific event, readers will be able to visualize their event coming to life as they develop a deeper knowledge of event management. Upon completion of the series of challenges, the students' proposed events have the potential to become a reality for those choosing to implement their plan.

This book is undoubtedly written from a practitioner's viewpoint. Industry and academia have come together to make this book a reality because there was a need for a joining of forces to provide quality information to students and practitioners.

Regardless of whether the event is sport, recreation, fundraising, entertainment, family or business, all rely on individuals with specific skill-sets to ensure it runs smoothly. Although the skill-sets needed for success in planning events may be similar/transferable from event to event, there is no single road map available to event managers that is adequate in all event situations. The editors and authors recognize the need for event managers who understand the entire event experience. By learning more about event sponsorship, marketing, registration, checklists, timelines, and other areas covered in this book, students will be able to employ a variety of techniques to help them better manage any type of event. The editors and authors hope this book finds its way onto bookshelves of all types of sport managers and that they use it as a tool whenever an event is on the horizon.

FOREWORD

By Linda Logan

Sports events in America have become a ubiquitous part of our everyday lives. We routinely participate in youth and recreation leagues, attend the games of our favorite college and professional teams, and even travel to take part in such events as triathlons or road races. What is it, though, that distinguishes one event from another as a "successful" or "great" event? In my 30 years of working in the sports industry, and especially in my 12 years bidding on and managing hundreds of events for the Greater Columbus Sports Commission, the one factor that I've found to be key to success is planning. Being able to understand, plan, and then implement the various aspects of a sports event can lead to a rewarding career in an exciting industry.

In *Event Management Blueprint: Creating and Managing Successful Sports Events,* Heather Lawrence and Michelle Wells have effectively mapped out the process for planning first-class sports events. They bring to the book their own skills and knowledge from years of working in event management and are able to convey many event management concepts often left out of classroom instruction for sport managers. Additionally, the contributing authors represent an expert group from the sports and event management industry and together have over 325 years of work experience in sport. All of the authors are candid in their approach to sharing their real-world experiences (both good and bad) with aspiring event managers. This is the kind of knowledge that can only come from veterans who have worked through the many challenges that come with working in event management day in and day out. Overall, the book succeeds in capturing the process of planning sports events in a straightforward and to-the-point style that readers will appreciate.

If you are a young sports event manager or a student studying to become one, the best way to learn about events is by planning and working them. Reading *Event Management Blueprint* will give you a head start at learning this process.

Linda Shetina Logan has been executive director of the Greater Columbus Sports Commission since its inception in June 2002. Prior to the GCSC, she was the director of sports marketing for the Greater Columbus Convention & Visitors Bureau (GCCVB) for five years.

Before joining the GCCVB, Logan was the director of sales and services at the Greater Columbus Convention Center. An Ohio native, Logan spent the previous 10 years in Kansas City, Missouri, working for the Kansas City Convention Center, the Big Eight Conference, the Kemper Arena, and the Kansas City Comets of the Major Indoor Soccer League. She also worked for the Milwaukee Does of the Women's Basketball League and the Cleveland Nets of the World Team Tennis.

ACKNOWLEDGMENTS

I appreciate those in both my personal and professional life that have supported my efforts in working on this book. The project truly morphed and grew as we moved forward, resulting in a final product that I am very proud of. I would like to acknowledge and thank all of my colleagues in the Division of Sports Administration at Ohio University: Ming Li, Charles "Doc" Higgins, Misty Hutchison, Jim Kahler, Andy Kreutzer, Michael Pfahl, David Ridpath, Teresa Tedrow, Aaron Wright, and Athena Yiamouyiannis. This book never would have been finished without their daily support, contributions, and cheerleading. Graduate student, Navreet Gill, was my "go to" person for first round editing as well as ensuring that content was applicable to students. Student support was also provided by Evan Holmes and Janae Laverdiere throughout the process.

Thanks as well to my family and friends who provided extensive support and encouragement. In particular, Paul Benedict, my husband, was there to provide constructive criticism along the way. His input contributed to strengthening many areas of the book and for that—and so many other things—I am thankful to him. Finally, I want to express my gratitude to my co-editor, Michelle Wells. She was fantastic to work with, and I am looking forward to continuing our professional partnership in the future.

—Heather Lawrence

In the spring of 2007 while working at New York Road Runners, I developed an idea to try to write a sports event management book that covered practical topics and "how-to" areas. I am very grateful to my colleagues at NYRR at the time who repeatedly reviewed and gave feedback on the proposed topic list and the initial outline: Janae Laverdiere, Dale Shumanski, Kenneth Wong, Paul Ortolano, Shawn Mason, Alison Meyer, Peter Ciaccia, Jeff Decker, Arnold Sitruk, Michelle Doti Taylor, and Ann Crandall. They are all fabulous at what they do and were willing to share their insight with me. Thank you, also, to several of my students—Stefanie Rossman, Michael Drake, and Robert Spain—who gave us some very useful feedback once the chapters were initially written.

Thank you to Heather Lawrence who helped move this idea from concept to actuality. After one meeting with her, we were off and running with a lot of ideas toward a direction in which we wanted to go. As we progressed, the book changed in various ways from its original form, but always for the better. Heather kept me and the other authors on task throughout this project, and for that and many other things, she has my undying gratitude.

—Michelle Wells

ABOUT THE EDITORS/AUTHORS

CO-EDITORS:

Heather Lawrence, Ph.D., is an Assistant Professor of Sports Administration at Ohio University. Originally from Issaquah, Washington, she earned her Ph.D. in Higher Education Administration from the University of Florida, and her bachelor's and master's degrees in Sports Administration from Florida. She has authored 15 articles and presented both nationally and internationally in the areas of event and facility management, intercollegiate athletics, recruiting, and gender equity.

Prior to beginning her academic career, Dr. Lawrence worked in various administrative positions within intercollegiate athletics. At the University of Florida, she worked in NCAA compliance, was responsible for select facility renovation projects, provided administrative support to the swimming and diving teams, and assisted with football, baseball, and basketball game operations. The experiences at Florida allowed her to step into her next role at Southeastern Louisiana University as Associate Director of Athletics/Senior Woman Administrator. At Southeastern, Heather was instrumental in the launch of an NCAA FCS football team for the school. She was also responsible for 10 sport programs, event/facility operations for all sports, strength and conditioning, academic services, and CHAMPS/Lifeskills.

Michelle Wells has worked in the sports industry for nearly 15 years, starting as an undergraduate student employee at the Stephen C. O'Connell Center at the University of Florida. She received her bachelor's degree in business administration (marketing) from the University of Florida. In 1997 she received a master's in sports administration from Ohio University and currently serves as a member of the Alumni Advisory Board for the Ohio University Sports Administration Program.

Since graduate school, she has worked at various levels of event management for Disney's Wide World of Sports, Disney's Animal Kingdom, New York Road Runners (ING New York City Marathon), co-owned a sports event management company, and worked many other events. She has managed and/or worked over 200 sports and entertainment events throughout her career. Since the fall of 2008, she has been the program coordinator and assistant professor for the University of Charleston's (West Virginia) Sport Administration program.

CONTRIBUTING AUTHORS

Douglas L. Brown, AIA, NCARB, LEED®AP, has worked on and led the development of a diverse range of projects during the last 32 years and has been at Ellerbe Becket specializing in the design of sports venues since 1988. Mr. Brown has been in primary leadership positions providing project management and senior project architect responsibilities on arenas and stadiums for collegiate, professional, and civic clients. As an architectural director and a principal in the firm, he not only leads large high-profile projects at Ellerbe Becket, but also helps manage the Kansas City office. He earned his bachelor's and master's degrees in architecture from Iowa State University.

William D. Crockett, AIA, earned his master's in architecture at Tulane University and has more than 30 years of experience in the industry. He has led the successful completion of a wide range of technically complex and successful projects for government, private, and higher education clients as project manager and principal-in-charge during his 20 years with Ellerbe Becket. Mr. Crockett is Ellerbe Becket's National Director of Sports Architecture and serves on the firm's Management Committee and Board of Directors. He also leads the design of sports and entertainment projects in a hands-on manner while implementing firm-wide diversification and expansion strategies for health sciences and other strategic offerings.

Stephen J. Duethman, AIA, NCARB, is the Managing Principal of the Kansas City office of Ellerbe Becket. In his role as Project Manager over the past 17 years he has successfully and energetically directed the design of many large-scale professional, civic, and collegiate sports facilities for Ellerbe Becket. Some of his projects include John Paul Jones Arena at University of Virginia, McCarthey Athletic Center at Gonzaga University, and a major expansion and renovation to the Dunkin' Donuts Center in Providence, Rhode Island. Mr. Duethman earned his bachelor of environmental design at the University of Kansas.

Roy Edmondson has over 20 years experience in sports event management. He graduated from Florida State University and started the first official roller hockey club in the country while at FSU. He has worked for Disney Sports, the National Hockey League, owned and started Royal Sports International (a sports event management company), opened the Aviator Sports & Recreation Complex, and currently is overseeing Sports Tourism for the Myrtle Beach, South Carolina, area. Roy has managed registration for various types and sizes of events. While at Disney Sports, one of the events he managed was the 1999 National Senior Games where he managed the registration of over 12,400 athletes for the 18-sport mega event.

Paul E. Griesemer, AIA, NCARB, LEED®AP, is a nationally recognized leader in sports design with over 25 years of experience and has dedicated himself to pioneering the development of the highest-quality sports facilities with a particular passion on football stadia and training facilities. Mr. Griesemer has focused more than 20 years of architectural practice solely on providing leadership and groundbreaking design solutions to the most complex venue programs. In addition to stadia, his experience includes convention facilities, Olympic venues, and multipurpose facilities, including recreation and training. He has led the design efforts for 12 NFL franchises, many as repeat clients, as well as universities and stadium efforts in several countries. Mr. Griesemer attended Kansas State University where he earned a bachelor of architecture and graduated with honors.

James Kahler is the Executive Director of the Center of Sports Administration at Ohio University. Previously, he helped develop the MBA Sports Business Program at the W.P. Carey School of Business at Arizona State University and was the Senior Vice President of Sales and Marketing for the Cleveland Cavaliers (NBA) and Rockers (WNBA). Mr. Kahler has over 20 years of experience in sales and marketing in sport. He has also served on the NBA's Marketing Advisory Committee and is currently on the Advisory Board for a number of sports business organizations, including the National Sports Forum (San Diego, California), and In Stadium Advertising (Chicago, Illinois). He also sits on the Board of Directors for USA Table Tennis.

Ming Li, Ed.D., is the Director of the School of Recreation and Sport Sciences at Ohio University and a Professor in Sports Administration. He received his bachelor's in education from Guangzhou Sport University (PRC), his master's in education from Hangzhou University (PRC), and his doctor of education from the University of Kansas in Sport Administration. Dr. Li was the 2009 President of the North American Society for Sport Management (NASSM). He has served as a consultant to several institutions in academic program evaluation and development in sport management. Dr. Li has memberships on the editorial boards of several professional journals, including *Journal of Sport Management* and *Sport Marketing Quarterly*.

Dr. Li has published more than twenty-five articles in refereed journals, three books (i.e., *Economics of Sport, Badminton Everyone,* and *Research Methods in Sport Management*), and a number of book chapters. Presently, he is the lead editor for a book project, *International Sport Management*. In addition to publications, Dr. Li also made numerous refereed presentations at state, national, and international conferences. He has been appointed by five institutions in China as Guest Professor (i.e., Beijing Sport University, Central University of Finance and Economics, Guangzhou Sport University, Tianjin Sport University, and Sun Yat-sen University).

Colleen A. McGlone, Ph.D., is an Assistant Professor of Recreation and Sport Management at Coastal Carolina University. She earned her doctorate from the University of New Mexico in Sport Administration in 2005 with a minor in Exercise Science research. Dr. McGlone's research involves hazing in collegiate athletics, legal aspects of sport and recreation, institutional liability and organizational culture, as well as leadership in sport environments. She has worked with several sport organizations and has been involved in numerous event management endeavors, including founding and implementing nonprofit fun runs, organizing community events, managing sport operations for a nationally ranked NCAA baseball team, coordinating media relations for the NCAA regional tournament (men's and women's), as well as coordinating professional conferences. Additionally, she has managed both minor league baseball and minor league hockey events.

Packy Moran has eight years of industry experience in communications and event management at the community, collegiate, and professional levels. He has been involved with executing traveling events for a regional science center, organizing student employees for the opening of an on-campus assembly facility, and been responsible for managing the communications and marketing for a family-owned and operated arena and exhibition center. A native of Dayton, Ohio, he has served in several roles in event communications. Mr. Moran was on the sports desk for the *Columbus Dispatch,* was the Director of Communications and Marketing at Hara Arena and Exhibition Center, and served as the Director of Communications and Operations for the Columbus Stars of the United Hockey League and the Premier Development and W-League soccer organizations. Mr. Moran is currently completing his doctorate at Ohio University.

Jon D. Niemuth, AIA, NCARB, LEED®AP, is the Design Director at Ellerbe Becket for the Kansas City practice, responsible for the creative look and feel of the firm's collective work. In this role, he is responsible for the creative vision and work product for a diverse offering of project types from sports to healthcare. With a strong background in technology and design process, he has advanced the design and delivery process of the Kansas City office to a fully integrated Building Information Modeling (BIM) environment creating value for clients through elevated design quality and faster, better, higher-quality project delivery. Mr. Niemuth earned his bachelor of architectural studies, master of architecture, master of urban planning/urban design, and certificate of preservation studies at the University of Wisconsin at Milwaukee.

Jay Ogden has been at IMG since 1978 and is currently a Senior Vice President and Managing Director of the Events and Federations business unit. He has overall responsibility for Action Sports, Winter Sports, Olympic Clients, the International Skating Union (ISU), special projects, and new business development. During his 30 year career at IMG, he has represented many Olympic champions in a variety of sports and managed the sales and marketing of numerous world championships in skiing, gymnastics, and figure skating. He has also created a variety of sports and entertainment programming for network and cable T.V. Jay earned a bachelor of arts from St. Lawrence University and master of science from the University of Massachusetts. He is married and the father of three sons.

Michael Pfahl, Ph.D., is an Assistant Professor of Sport Administration at Ohio University. Previously, Dr. Pfahl was on the Management and Marketing faculties of Yonok College, Thailand, and the International College at Bangkok University in the same country. He has worked in various management and sales positions with the Cleveland Cavaliers and the Cleveland Lumberjacks during his career. Dr. Pfahl was also the cofounder and president of Players Management, Inc., a sport marketing and athletic representation firm. Current research interests include the convergence of media, technology and sport, environmentalism and sport, and human resource issues in sport organizations. Dr. Pfahl earned a master in business administration from the University of Toledo along with bachelor, master, and doctorate degrees from Ohio University.

B. David Ridpath, Ed.D., is an Assistant Professor of Sport Administration at Ohio University where he also earned his master's in sports administration. Prior to returning to Ohio University as a member of the faculty, Dr. Ridpath spent two years directing the graduate sports administration program at Mississippi State University. He also worked at Marshall University in Huntington, West Virginia, where he served as an Adjunct Professor of Sport Management and Marketing, Director of Judicial Programs, and Assistant Athletic Director for Compliance and Student Services. His research interests include intercollegiate athletics academic standards, reform, enforcement and infractions, and governance.

Mike Rielly is a 23-year veteran of the sports business, including 20 years with IMG, the world's premier sports marketing agency. At IMG, Mr. Rielly pioneered new markets and developed strategy, business platforms, and sales in the United States, Latin America, and Asia for many of the industry's iconic athletes, teams, leagues, and events. He received a bachelor of political science from Stanford University and recently completed his master's in sport administration at Ohio University. Mr. Rielly is currently a member of the Professional Faculty at UC Berkeley's Haas School of Business, where he teaches sports marketing. He is also Executive Director of the Mark H. McCormack Foundation and is responsible for a project that will provide students and scholars with access to Mark H. McCormack's extensive sports business archives, for the purpose of advancing education in the sports business field.

John P. Tafaro, J.D., received his master's in sports administration from Ohio University in 1977. He spent more than 20 years actively involved in the facility management industry, including close to 10 years as President and CEO of Cincinnati Riverfront Coliseum. He is a graduate of Salmon P. Chase College of Law at Northern Kentucky University, has practiced business law and consulted with or operated numerous business entities in various industries, including sports and entertainment facilities, teams, and attractions. He is the past Chair of the Cincinnati Bar Association Sports & Entertainment Law Committee. Mr. Tafaro has been an adjunct professor at several institutions of higher learning, and in May 2009 became President of Chatfield College in St. Martins, Ohio.

Robb Wade, Ph.D., attended undergraduate and played varsity hockey at Queen's University in Kingston, Ontario. Upon completion of that degree, he attended Ohio University where he earned a master's in sport administration as well as a Ph.D. While at Ohio University, he managed the ice arena, the golf course, and a facility that was used for academics during the week and during home games. He played hockey as a graduate student and then later coached and was the academic advisor for the Bobcat hockey team. Dr. Wade completed an internship with the Colorado Rangers professional hockey team and upon graduation from Ohio University worked as the ticket manager for the Ohio University Department of Athletics. He later moved to North Carolina State to become the Director of Ticket Operations for Wolfpack Athletics. During that time, he coached minor hockey in the Raleigh Youth Hockey Association. After six years in the ticket office, Dr. Wade moved into a teaching role at NC State in the Department of Parks, Recreation, and Tourism Management. He is currently the Director of the Professional Golf Management Program.

Athena Yiamouyiannis, Ed.D., is the former Executive Director of the National Association for Girls and Women in Sport (NAGWS). She joined Ohio University's Sports Administration faculty in fall of 2006 bringing 15 years of industry experience with her. Previously, she worked at the National Collegiate Athletics Association (NCAA) as the Director of Membership Services overseeing NCAA rules education operations and serving as liaison to the NCAA's Committee on Women's Athletics. Dr. Yiamouyiannis received a bachelor's in math and a master's in sports management from The Ohio State University, in addition to earning an Ed.D. in higher education administration from George Washington University.

SECTION I

EVENT CONCEPTUALIZATION

Frank Pergolizzi

The focus of the first section of this book (Chapters 1–4) is the conceptualization and determination of the feasibility of the event as well as the development of the critical infrastructure that supports and leads to successful events.

The opening chapter addresses event managers as well as the many different organizations that oversee events. The foundation for the remainder of the book is provided in this chapter so that readers can begin to understand the interaction between the event managers' role, those that own the rights to events, and the purposes of events. It includes helpful advice to event managers, a breakdown of the different types and purposes of events, and a sample job description for an event manager.

Chapter 2 discusses the important issues that help event managers determine the feasibility of pursuing, bidding for, and successfully landing an event. Extensive research and an understanding of the needs of the event is a critical step that can be overlooked in the initial excitement of the possibility of hosting an event. Without this background work, event managers may face unexpected barriers later in the planning process. Guidelines for the USA Diving Summer National Championships as well as a description of the bid process for the Olympics are included as valuable references for the reader.

The critical issue of contracts and agreements is introduced next. Readers will find useful and amusing the author's opening description of his first event management responsibility entitled "What I Wish I Had Known." Examples of typical contracts used in the planning of events are also provided as resources and help to illustrate the concepts discussed in the chapter.

Finally, a chapter on using technology in events provides an excellent outline for the integrations of technologies into the overall event management plan. There are a variety of opportunities that exist for event managers to leverage their knowledge of technology to make the event planning process more efficient and help in the promotion of the event. Overall, the Event Conceptualization section provides the framework for event managers to establish the guiding philosophies they will follow throughout the development and execution of the event.

CHAPTER 1

EVENT MANAGEMENT AND THE EVENT MANAGER

Heather Lawrence, Athena Yiamouyiannis, and Michelle Wells

This chapter focuses on the concept of event management, the role of event managers, the purview of sport-governing bodies associated with these events, and a discussion of the types of events. It also serves to set the stage for the remainder of the book by describing the characteristics of effective event managers and providing insight into the job market. Major concepts related to sport governance associated with sports event are introduced, along with discussions on the general types of sport events. An awareness of core concepts and the establishment of a solid foundation focusing on the purpose and goals of the event are necessary first steps in the planning process. They provide a framework for moving forward and contribute significantly to the development of a successful event.

EVENT MANAGEMENT

Sport event management has become a highly sought after career path for those with solid business skills, an interest in sports, and the ability to combine the two through the management of events. Event management is unique in the sport industry because it requires the managers to have a broad base of knowledge in many different areas of the sport industry. For example, the event managers for a minor league baseball team not only have to have an understanding of the principles of event management, but also must be educated in the areas of customer service, marketing, tickets, budgeting, grounds maintenance, risk management, and many other areas. The individual will also be working with all of the aforementioned departments to ensure each knows, understands, and executes its role toward the overall success of the event.

The process of event management can be broken down into three distinct phases, including conceptualization, development, and execution. Many processes begin in one phase and are revisited, rechecked, and reevaluated in other stages. For example, in the early stages of event conceptualizations, the event managers may begin discussions with a potential sponsor, then in event development that discussion may turn into a signed sponsorship contract, and finally in event execution the sponsorship will be activated and return on investment calculations made.

Event management is an exciting emerging industry. Based upon the complexity of some events and the economic impact to locales in which major events occur, it is also rapidly becoming known as a stand-alone industry. Author and event manager Julia Rutherford Silvers provides one of the best definitions of **event management** available:

> *Event management is the process by which an event is planned, prepared, and produced. As with any other form of management, it encompasses the assessment, definition, acquisition, allocation, direction, control, and analysis of time, finances, people, products, services, and other resources to achieve objectives (Silvers, 2003, ¶ 2).*

From this definition it is clear that the management of events encompasses a variety of business-related tasks; it is like managing a small business. These management functions often occur simultaneously, which creates challenges for all involved because change in one area may impact change in one or more other areas. For example, if the budget is reduced, the organization's ability to pay staff and provide services is also limited. As in any business, the overall objectives are reached through the leadership and work of the people involved. In the case of event management, the event managers are ultimately responsible.

THE EVENT MANAGER

Event managers are responsible for making the event "come to life." From conceptualization to execution, the event managers follow business functions in defining event management in a variety of specific areas that are part of the event. Additionally, there are certain personal characteristics that event managers must recognize as keys to success in the industry.

Beyond the business functions noted in Silvers' definition of event management, there are specific areas of knowledge in which event managers must be educated. According to Ammon and Stotlar (2003, p. 258), successful event management requires attention to the following content areas:

- Recruitment and Training of Personnel
- Planning Emergency Medical Services
- Risk Management
- Facility Rental and Venue Logistics
- Alcohol Management and Training
- Box Office Management and Ticketing
- Food Services Management and Catering
- Building Maintenance
- Marketing, Advertising, and Public Relations
- Hospitality and VIP Protocol
- Securing Proper Permits and Licenses
- Contract negotiations with promoters
- Merchandise, Concessions, and Novelty Sales
- Crowd Management
- Parking and Traffic Control
- Evaluating the Final Result

Event managers need to have a broader understanding of the sports organization than many of the other staff. For example, a box office manager must be an excellent salesperson, have customer service skills, be detail oriented, and have a comprehensive understanding of ticketing. But the event managers have to be jacks-of-all-trades. They also need to have the competencies associated with the box office manager (not quite to the level of a ticketing professional), and also excel in facility management, marketing, logistics, food service, building maintenance, and other areas.

Event managers find out quickly that their job responsibilities encompass a wide spectrum and that, as event managers, there is no "typical day." Job descriptions will vary substantially depending on the type of organization, objectives of the position, and level of employment. In order to be better prepared to handle the responsibilities and the variety of situations that may arise, it is important that event managers become better educated on the multitude of areas that are related to the event.

Personal Characteristics

As important as knowledge of the functional areas related to event management is, being able to lead, knowing how to effectively communicate, and consistently acting in an ethical manner are equally important attributes. High-achieving event managers must possess many of the same leadership characteristics that are valued in other aspects of life such as compassion, good listening skills, the ability to make decisions, and an understanding of the profession. Regardless of proficiency level, event managers can improve their leadership skills to become more effective and efficient in their position.

Based on candid responses of current event managers via the Event Manager Blog (2008), the top three qualities for successful event managers include flexibility, people skills, and organization. Event managers are faced with many tasks and responsibilities. Successful event managers must be flexible as things change around them. In many instances, event managers will have to handle multiple projects simultaneously. They need to be solution providers to problems that arise, because problems will arise during all phases of the event. Being a solution provider requires flexibility and resourcefulness, all the while maintaining a positive outlook. Addressing challenges and changes promptly is vital because that is an inevitable part of the event-management process. This will keep the event moving forward and on-track.

Communication skills, particularly the development of interpersonal skills and the ability to interact well with others, are contributors to success. Networking with vendors, being customer friendly, exuding a positive demeanor, demonstrating enthusiasm and passion for one's job, and creating positive interactions with others are examples through which event managers can serve as positive role models for their staff. These people skills will help to create new relationships and strengthen existing relationships with all of those involved in the event. Being able to communicate effectively is essential in the event managers' role of supervisor to other staff. As supervisor, the event managers are responsible for training staff, delegating work responsibilities, and evaluating/providing feedback to the staff. The event managers will also become responsible for conflict resolution and workforce motivation. Event managers who utilize good communication strategies will be more effective in getting event staff to work together as a team on projects and events.

Organizational skills are also essential. Event managers need to manage time effectively, be able to meet deadlines, and be committed to excellence. This requires the ability to think ahead, develop plans, pay attention to details, develop timelines, stick to deadlines, and execute events.

Event managers as leaders also make a habit of reflecting upon the ethical nature of their actions. One way sport professionals can evaluate themselves is through the use of the Six Pillars of Character as identified by the Josephson Institute Center for Sports Ethics (2009). The Six Pillars of Character include being trustworthy, respectful, responsible, fair, caring, and being good citizens. Conducting an honest self-evaluation in these areas and developing a personal plan for improvement can contribute to individuals becoming more effective and ethical event managers and leaders in the sports industry. As in other areas of life, ethical behavior is valued in event management. The sports industry continues to grow; it is a profession where everyone seems to know everyone. As a result, one unethical decision and/or action by event managers could follow them for a long time in the industry. By using the Six Pillars of Character as a guide to decision making, event managers are sure to act ethically when faced with tough decisions.

A solid knowledge base in a large number of content areas along with personal characteristics that are desirable to the industry is a good combination to have for anyone interested in working in event management. From a more macro perspective, event managers must understand the sport as an industry as well. Keeping abreast of sport stories, the current news, and recent scores and stats is important for event managers. But even more essential is a true understanding of how the sports industry functions as a whole. Central to this understanding is the idea of sport governance and the role of governing bodies in sport.

SPORT GOVERNANCE

It is important to realize that sporting events do not take place in a vacuum. They are usually part of a larger sport entity or sport governing body. Let's use the Mid-American Conference (MAC) Track and Field Championship as an example. The event itself is actually a subset of the MAC and the National Collegiate Athletic Association (NCAA). Therefore, sport event managers need to be aware of the organizational structures that govern their events. Events are not stand-alone operations. They are part of a larger industry. Whether the event is related to college athletics, professional sports, or a community sports organization, understanding sport governance, including organizational structures within sport organizations, is important for event managers.

Hums and McLean (2008, p. 4) defined **sport governance** as "the exercise of power and authority in sport organizations, including policy making, to determine organizational mission, membership, eligibility, and regulatory power, with the organization's appropriate local, national or international scope." How the governing organization operates, the staff reporting lines, and where the power lies within that organization are key pieces of information event managers must learn to discern to be successful. Additionally, an understanding of the policies and procedures of the governing body is required. Knowing who has final authority in the decision-making process and establishing good relationships with these key individuals will benefit event managers, particularly if problems arise.

Governing Bodies

Governing bodies are organizations charged with setting the rules for the sports they oversee. Adopting playing rules, selecting championship sites, certifying officials, and sanctioning events are all under their purview. They exist at many different levels, from local youth sports to elite international competition.

Youth Sport

There are too many youth sport governing bodies to mention here, but some of the most recognizable national organizations include the Amateur Athletic Union, Inc. (AAU), the United States Specialty Sports Association (USSSA), Little League Baseball, and Little League Softball. These governing bodies provide support to their regional, district, state, or local office through leadership, organization, and the creation of competitive sport opportunities. There are some youth sport governing bodies that extend beyond the borders of the United States such as Little League, which has more than 7,400 programs operating in over 100 countries (Little League, n.d., ¶ 2). At the local levels, additional governing bodies develop as a result of a need in the community for organized sports participation and competition opportunities. These governing bodies are not nearly as sophisticated as those at the national level, but they still provide structure and guidance for youth sport in their locale. Often times, these organizations take the form of leagues run from the city or community recreation center.

Interscholastic Sport

The National Federation of State High School Associations provides oversight to 50 state associations (plus the District of Columbia) for athletics and other activities, and it also publishes playing rules for all 16 of their sports (National Federation of State High School Associations, n.d.). In addition, in North America, individual states and provinces have direct authority over public high school sports. Private schools, religiously affiliated or not, have many choices in selecting athletic governing bodies.

Intercollegiate Athletics

For intercollegiate athletics competition, the NCAA is the largest and most powerful governing body with 1,051 institutional members (NCAA, n.d.a.). However, there are other entities that govern intercollegiate athletics. The National Junior College Athletic Association (NJCAA) and the National Association of Intercollegiate Athletics (NAIA) both govern their member institutions' athletic competitions. All of these organizations offer structure to the intercollegiate athletic operations of their member institutions.

Professional Sport

In professional sports in the United States, sport-specific leagues (e.g., National Basketball Association and Major League Baseball) are generally responsible for all aspects of the sport, including rules related to trading and payment of players. There is not one national governing body for all professional sports in the United States, and this is similar to how most other countries organize their professional sports.

National and International Governing Bodies

Most amateur sports in the United States have a **national governing body (NGB)** (e.g., USA Volleyball, USA Swimming, and USA Table Tennis) recognized by the United States Olympic Committee (USOC) to oversee that particular sport. What separates an NGB from other governing bodies previously discussed that oversee aspects of amateur sport is that the NGB has a formal relationship with the USOC and thus the International Olympic Committee (IOC). However, the NCAA and many of the governing bodies work together closely with NGBs on competition schedules, sport competition and eligibility rules, and policies that impact athletes.

Many times, a member of the United States National Team is also a student-athlete at an NCAA institution and thus, care must be taken for NCAA rules not to conflict with NGB's rules.

NGBs also have international counterparts (e.g., Fédération Internationale de Natation [FINA] for many aquatic sports, and International Federation of Associated Wrestling Styles [IFAWS] for wrestling) that are responsible for international and Olympic competitions in specific sports. The IOC is the international umbrella organization for all the sports specific to the various international federations. In addition, the IOC is responsible for the bid process and site selection for the Olympic Games.

Rights Holders

Rights holders are organizations or businesses that control and own the rights to an event. In many cases, the rights holder is also the NGB or governing body, but in other cases, the rights holder is a corporation or business. For example, ESPN owns the X Games and controls everything associated with the event. If another organization wanted to use the X Games name, logo, or brand, permission from ESPN would first be required. Because ESPN does not govern the sports that are contested as part of the X Games, it is not a governing body, but its ownership of the event makes it the rights holder.

Although governance structures vary between various segments in the industry, it is clear that some form of governance structure is needed to establish policies and procedures as well as competition rules. To ensure that competitions are conducted in keeping with expectations of the rights holder and within established sport rules, event sanctions are required for many sporting events. In this case, a "sanction" is not a "punishment," but rather the official recognition by the rights holder.

Event Sanctions

Event sanctions ensure consistency between sports events and provide standards related to competition. Any event that seeks to be associated with an NGB, international governing body, or collegiate governing body will be required to acquire a sanction. **Event sanctions** are considered an official approval for the event and are granted by the governing body associated with the sport (Solomon, 2002). "The sanctioning process allows the governing body to control the game. . . . so that it is played under authorized rules with approved equipment" (p. 9). There is usually a fee associated with obtaining the sanction, but in return the host organization has proof it has met the standards of the governing body.

Sanctions are also important because they help to ensure fairness, safety, and consistency among competitions held under the auspices of the governing body. It would be unfair for a swimmer to set a national record in a pool that was a few inches shorter than it should be. The sanction will provide for course certifications for swimming, running, and biking events to ensure consistency across venues. Sometimes sanctions also often require a certain amount of medical personnel to be available as well as the provision of insurance coverage for the event operators and the participants.

USA Triathlon (USAT) is one example of an NGB that sanctions events. USAT annually sanctions over 1,000 events (e.g., triathlons, duathlons, and aquathlons). When USAT (2008) sanctions an event, it means they are confirming that certain conditions have been met. A USAT-sanctioned event means the event has been reviewed by the USAT staff, is considered to be well planned and free of preventable dangers, and that event planners have proper insurance in place. The benefits to being a USAT-sanctioned event include insurance coverage for event staff, volunteers, and participants; inclusion in the USA Triathlon National Ranking System for participants; access to USA Triathlon officials; access to the USA Triathlon membership mailing list; and access to sponsor programs and benefits.

The type of event will impact whether a sanction is needed, and not all competitions need to be sanctioned. Event planners interested in starting a new event should contact the appropriate NGB to determine whether sanctioning is needed, the benefits to getting an event sanctioned, and information on the application process. The variety of sport related events that can be created and executed is endless. But, most events can be categorized into one of four main types of events which helps in making event related decisions (such as whether or not a sanction is needed) moving forward in the event management process.

The Harlem Globetrotters

Brian Brantley

The Harlem Globetrotters have been around for 82 years and are still going strong. What started as a small basketball team in Chicago has turned into one of the longest running entertainment events in the world. Because of the ever-changing nature of the sports and entertainment industry, managing the events of the Globetrotters and other traveling shows has become more complicated.

When putting on a family show that travels across the country, finding a suitable site for the event comes first. The great thing about the Harlem Globetrotters is the fact that they will play, and have played, in all types of facilities. They have played in recreation halls, high school gymnasiums, small arenas, mid-size arenas, large arenas, and even on the deck of an aircraft carrier. To play a broad spectrum of venues, there has to be a lot of coordination between individuals responsible for scheduling, marketing, community involvement, public relations, media, operations, ticketing, and facility management.

Because of the variety of locales the Globetrotters play in, the goals of each show vary somewhat. If the Globetrotters are exploring a new, small market, the goal of the event might be exposure and brand awareness in that area. However, in a major market, goals tend to be more directly tied to revenue generation. But whatever the goals of the organization are for a specific show, the underlying theme is one of community fun. If the event is entertaining and the fans enjoy it, then the secondary goals are sure to be accomplished.

For example, let's examine the Harlem Globetrotters playing in Athens, Ohio. First, it must be clear who is hosting the event. Is it the building that would like to bring the Globetrotters to the arena (Convocation Center), or is it the Globetrotters that would like to play the Convocation Center? Sometimes, it may be an outside group that would like to host an event and bring a family show like the Globetrotters to their community. In this scenario, suppose it is the Convocation Center that would like to bring the Globetrotters to Athens. The building probably has open dates (days/nights without events) and wants to fill its event schedule. Timing, of course, is key here. Many scheduling conflicts such as other athletic events, other traveling family shows, university events, and community events can potentially arise and make scheduling an event a challenge. In a small college town like Athens where the Globetrotters have played before, the primary goal of all involved might be to provide entertainment to the community while generating revenue for the venue and the Globetrotters. Achieving these goals would ensure that the show would return to Athens in the future.

Marketing of such family shows also evolves with each show and city. No matter who is putting on the show, all parties want a show that reaches as many people as possible and brings a positive experience to the community. Marketing can take many forms, including TV, radio, print advertisements, and local and national sponsorships. Because the show is usually in town for only one night before heading to a new area, the marketing is done way in advance of the show. This ensures that the maximum number of people have been reached. Creativity in marketing is extremely important. An example of a promotion related to our previous example would be having a local grocery store sell discounted tickets to shoppers. The store would then be mentioned in other publicity events about the show such as print, TV, and radio advertising.

When all of these elements are put together, the result is a show that is unforgettable and will have people ready to come back for more the next time the show is in town. For event managers and marketing professionals, the Harlem Globetrotters family show brings many different elements to the forefront. From a public relations standpoint, there is the famous song "Sweet Georgia Brown" and memorable former players such as Meadowlark Lemon, Curly Neal, and Sweet Lou Dunbar. From an event management perspective, the unique elements of the Harlem Globetrotters show are merely opportunities to enhance the event experience for all. Event managers who are able to set realistic goals, use creativity throughout the planning process, and create a memorable experience for fans will, like the Globetrotters, find success in the sports and entertainment industry.

TYPES OF EVENTS

It would be great if sports events all fit neatly into a certain category and the management of each event within a category was standard. But, if that were the case, there would be no need for an entire book on event management, nor would competent event managers be in such high demand. It is the diversity of sporting events that makes the field an exciting and challenging place to work.

That being noted, there are four broad categories in which most events will find a "best fit" and will aid in the discussion of event management throughout this book. The four categories include the following:

- Recurring Events
- Traveling Events
- Mega Events
- Ancillary Events

Determining which category is most like a specific event includes careful consideration of the event goals and objectives, the event frequency, the perceived importance of the event, the number of participants and spectators, media presence, and the extent of involvement by a sport governing body or the rights holder.

Recurring Events

The most common event for sport managers is the recurring event. A **recurring event** is one that happens on a regular basis (e.g., university basketball game or youth soccer game). Although these events may vary in the number of participants and spectators, many of the operating characteristics are consistent each time the event takes place. Most recurring events appeal to local or regional spectators, but there are recurring events of national magnitude (e.g., college football rivalry games). Recurring events are very common in community organizations, universities, and in professional sports.

A community organization may provide opportunities for local youth to participate in a soccer league, offering the kids multiple games throughout the season. A local community might also host a 5K run each year to promote fitness within the locale. Both of these types of events are grassroots efforts where local event managers organize and operate the recurring events.

Within a university setting, a sport event manager will likely supervise upwards of 6 football games, 10 soccer games, 10 volleyball games, 30 basketball games (men's and women's), 10 swimming and diving meets, 15 softball games, 20 baseball games, 15 ice hockey games, and many other sports depending on what their schedule requires. It is common for intercollegiate athletics event managers to average four to five events per week during the academic year at institutions that sponsor a full complement of competitive teams. The University of Florida reported that over 1.1 million fans attended 169 home events in the 2007–2008 season (University of Florida Athletic Association, 2008). A small event such as a cross country meet may have mostly friends and families of the student-athletes in attendance with only a few personnel working the event. A much larger event such as an NCAA division I football game may have a championship title at stake, millions of dollars in potential revenue, and over 100,000 fans in attendance. But each cross country meet is managed in a similar manner to a football game.

In professional sports the events are usually larger in scope than most sports events in colleges and universities. However, in professional sports the event managers are commonly only dealing with one specific sport. This allows for consistency in operations from one event to the next. There will always be some variation in planning, depending on the opponent, importance of the game, marketing and promotions activities, and other variables. But just as in the university sector, each college game begins with a similar plan and structure for its operations.

Generally, recurring events share the following characteristics: (a) a set schedule; (b) a known facility; (c) employees and participants familiar to the event managers; and (d) an existing event management template to work from. The common theme throughout recurring events is that the basic planning and processes are similar each time the event occurs. Whether it is the first or twentieth Major League Baseball game of the season, the planning template is similar.

Traveling Events

A **traveling event** is one that does not occur on a regular basis at a consistent location, but a traveling event may either occur on a regular basis or at a set location. For example, the NCAA Women's Basketball Final Four occurs every year but not in the same location, thus making it a traveling event. Conversely, the Harlem Globetrotters (see the box on page 8) visit some venues more than once in a multi-year period, but not on a regular basis, thus making their visit a traveling event. Traveling events require more up-front planning than recurring events because event managers do not have the benefit of hosting the event on a consistent basis in the venue. Many of these types of events use a bid process to secure locations or a booking agency to handle scheduling.

Traveling events can vary substantially from one another and coming up with a list of similarities is impossible. Goals for traveling events can range from providing an opportunity for athletes to qualify for the Olympic Games to providing an opportunity for youth to experience competition in a fun environment. Most traveling events have an owner or governing body that requires specific aspects of the event to occur within its established framework. So event managers are required to ensure that the needs of the event can be met in the available facility and that appropriate financial and personnel resources are available. For example, for NCAA Championships, the NCAA provides sponsor banners that must be displayed throughout the venue. In most cases, existing sponsor signage must be covered up to ensure there are no conflicts between NCAA sponsors and existing venue sponsors. Event managers who have not given careful consideration to NCAA requirements may have to scramble unnecessarily at the last minute.

Mega Events

Mega events are the most complex category as they often take years of planning prior to the event taking place. Often, mega events are international in nature (whether through media exposure, participation, or location) and are easily identifiable to sports consumers because the event is a brand in itself. Budgets can be in the multi-millions of dollars, as can the economic impact on the location. These events become stand-alone business ventures because many of them have organizing committees composed of full- and part-time personnel dedicated solely to the execution of the event. Although the Olympic Games is the ultimate example of a mega event, there are many others such as world championships in a variety of sports, major international marathons and bicycle races, World Cup Soccer, the Asian Games, and the Commonwealth Games.

The bid process for hosting these types of events is complex, lengthy, expensive, and has multiple phases. Hosting a mega event is a huge undertaking that requires the cooperation of many entities (i.e., governments, organizing committees, national governing bodies, international governing bodies, military and police). National and international sports governing bodies are heavily involved in the planning and execution of mega events because the integrity of the sport is on display for an international audience during the competitions. Additionally, many of these events encompass multiple competition days, venues, and sports, resulting in many special events within the mega event. Another common feature of mega events is the presence of ancillary events (e.g., opening ceremonies, concerts, fan experience exhibits) that enhance and support the core sports event.

Ancillary Events

Ancillary events have become an increasingly common aspect of sports event planning and management. They commonly supplement and surround the predefined core sports events and can range from a spaghetti dinner the night before a 5K road race to a tailgate party before the Super Bowl. Ancillary events provide event managers the opportunity to generate additional revenue through sponsorships, ticket sales, media contracts, and merchandise. Plus, ancillary events promote brand awareness of the event, create excitement, and increase economic impact of the event by organizing the events in a way that makes spectators spend more time in the host area.

Some sport events fit neatly into one of the four categories mentioned above, and others have characteristics that cross categories. In either case, event managers are charged with ensuring that all of the stakeholders (i.e., participants, spectators, sponsors, and media) experience the best event possible, given the objectives and parameters of the event. The goals and limitations of an event are often the result of the actions of various governing bodies associated with the event.

GOALS OF EVENTS

Sports events take place for a multitude of reasons. As event managers begin to plan, understanding the overall goals for the event will assist them as they move forward. One obvious reason to hold an event is to make money for an organization or municipality. A city may want to create an event that will help establish itself as a travel destination. Some events are used to drive economic impact for a city. The locations of summer youth championship tournaments often turn into locations where families spend summer vacations. Sports commissions know that hosting these tournaments can draw in hundreds or thousands of people, all of whom will spend money at local hotels, restaurants, and shops. On the other hand, some events are driven by charity or by the goal to create awareness about a topic. The Susan G. Komen Race for the Cure is held to raise awareness about breast cancer and to fund research. Other events may be community "give-backs" for an organization. When companies receive support from local governmental agencies, they often act as good corporate citizens and return the support by assisting in the management of agency events. Some events are even created to further establish brand awareness. A multisports complex may target youth sports as its key demographic, yet may hold several pro sports events to get its brand in the market. The cost of the event in exchange for the awareness created by broadcast exposure may be seen as a fair tradeoff.

Event Purpose/Mission

The **purpose statement** is a short, to-the-point acknowledgment of the overall motivation for holding the event. For a high-level adult triathlon, the purpose statement might read, "To host an elite level competitive triathlon that is operated under a recognized sanction with national rankings implication for the participants." Another event may target local recreational cycling athletes where socializing with other participants is an important part of the event. The purpose statement for the cycling event might be, "To provide a fun community bike ride while providing opportunities for personal connections." Whatever the purpose statement is, it should be the driving force behind the goal-setting process.

Event Goals

Establishing the goals of the event first will ensure that everyone in the organization is on the same page. It is important to make the goals specific. The purpose statement and goals should be the focus throughout the planning process as decisions are made for each aspect of the event. For example, the goals of the above-mentioned triathlon might be threefold: (1) to bring in hard-core participants in a sport that requires high discretionary income; (2) to expose participants to the great training facilities in the area; and (3) to generate interest in the area so that participants might return for vacations and/or to buy a second home (because they know that they can continue with their sports in the area). The community cycling event, on the other hand, might have entirely different goals that might include the following: (1) to provide a safe bike route where cyclists of all levels can participate; (2) to create a reasonable schedule, with participant socializing being a priority; (3) to provide a physical setting that encourages socializing.

The way these two events would be set up would be very different based first on the purpose statement and then on the goals. The schedule for the community cycling event would include plenty of down time and a social setting nearby (e.g., a beer garden) where participants could sit and talk. The triathlon registration packets may include literature on local trails that participants can seek out on their own. A lot of bells and whistles can be added to events that will impress people—opening ceremonies, free meals, clinics—but if the money spent is unrelated to achieving the goals, it is not money well spent.

CREATIVITY IN EVENT MANAGEMENT

The word *creative* is not one that immediately comes to mind with sports event management. However, when working on three of the four types of sports events addressed in this book— traveling events, mega events, and ancillary events—creativity becomes particularly important. The opportunity to be creative in the planning of sports events is also one of the fun parts of working on them. It allows event managers to have a blank slate to ask the limitless question—what if . . . ?—that can lead to new types of events that could be major money earners for an organization. Creativity in developing events can reveal itself in several ways. It can involve coming up with a new theme for a preexisting event format (Rock 'n' Roll Marathon created in the 1990s), or developing an entire bid package and theme for a multisport event (National Senior Games or Asian Games), or generating ancillary events that tie in well with existing ones (a music concert or barbecue held the night before a big rivalry game).

Ancillary events particularly allow creativity to come into play. Event managers often work on sporting events that have been in existence for many years. Creating new ancillary events can add both a novel perspective and a new revenue stream. These are the types of events where event managers can use their creativity to explore new events. It may not be feasible for an organization to take on the financial risk for a new large-scale event. It is often easier to add on to existing events and expand their reach. Ancillary events may be created to complement a present theme or to add another related theme. They can help expand the overall brand of the event and create a longer timeframe. For the ING New York City Marathon, marathon week begins the Sunday before the actual event with the six-mile Poland Spring Marathon Kickoff race in Central Park. During the week, there are press conferences, fireworks, photo exhibits, pasta dinners, and other races that lead up to marathon day. For the NBA All-Star Game, the NBA puts on events such as the All-Star Jam Session, the Slam Dunk Contest, and many others. Sometimes ancillary events are creatively designed to alleviate traffic pressure by trying to entice spectators to delay their departure from the event. A free concert after an MLB baseball game is one example. Developing events that are fun and innovative helps ensure that they will be successful. These types of events allow event managers to use their full range of creativity and expand the organization's brand identity.

Event Themes

Take a look at any major sports event—Super Bowl, NCAA Final Four, Olympic Games—and it is noticeable that each has a consistent theme running throughout it. The **event theme** helps establish an identity that people will associate with it and should be a part of every aspect of the event. Much of the discussion of themes has to do with branding the event. Take, for example, the 2008 NBA Playoffs. The event name has been consistent for years—The Finals—but the theme is changed from year to year. For 2008, the added tagline was "There Can Only Be One." It was in every commercial, promotion, and ad for the 40+ days of the NBA playoffs. This branding was one thing that differentiated it from other sports events and other years of the NBA playoffs. This message should not deviate and it should be nearly omnipresent for the event—on letterhead, in PA announcements, in commercials, on promotional give-aways, on invitations, on signage, on T-shirts, and so on. All of the areas should complement each other to create the theme and brand image for the entire event. The event stays the same each year, but the application of the theme can change and distinguish one year's event from another.

BREAKING INTO EVENT MANAGEMENT

Even students that have event management experience understand the various responsibilities of event management, and have a strong desire to work in the industry that is sometimes difficult to break into. This is not

An Interview with Paul Ortolano

Director, Event Management and Logistics, New York Road Runners

The following interview was conducted with Paul Ortolano, Director, Event Development and Production, New York Road Runners. Celebrating its 50th anniversary in 2008, the New York Road Runners (www.nyrr.org) continues to promote the sport of distance running, enhancing health and fitness for all, and responding to community needs. Their road races and other fitness programs draw upwards of 300,000 runners annually, and together with their magazine and Web site support and promote professional and recreational running. Annually, Mr. Ortolano, in his capacity as the leader of the department that manages over 55 road races per year, such as the ING New York City Marathon, reviews hundreds of resumes of aspiring event managers. Paul provided some insight on the attributes he looks for in event managers.

What qualities do you look for in event managers?

I think communication skills are *the* most important thing in event management, absolutely the number one thing. The reason communication skills are number one is because a significant part of this type of work revolves around the ability to communicate well. The relationships with my agency partners, the relationships with my team members (other New York Road Runners employees), the relationships with vendors, and the relationships with facilities are critical to success in managing road races.

Looking at a resume, how do you determine if a person has good communication skills?

I look at how well the resume is written and ask myself two questions: (1) How articulate are they? and (2) Are they specific in expressing what they have done professionally? What I mean by being specific is not just listing activities, but being specific about revenue generation, size of budgets, and how they impacted the organization or event.

What other areas are you assessing in potential event managers?

Other things that are also extremely important include how they have utilized the experiences they have had. Just because an undergraduate student recently graduates does not mean they have not had valuable experiences. There could be things they did while in school (i.e., internships, working events, or volunteering) that gave them a feel for event management and an understanding of what it takes to succeed. If job candidates have no experience and want to work in sports event management, how do they really know it is the right career for them? If a person is changing careers to come into sports event management, I prefer they have at least a little experience in planning projects. My background is in project management and I was always planning things. I developed very long-term information systems and that is how I got into sports event management because I was utilizing my project management skills from a prior career. Again, it is all about how they have used their time so far in their career.

Are there different things you look for, depending on the level of the job?

Communication skills are going to cover all levels of jobs. At the coordinator level, I am looking for eagerness, someone who really is passionate and wants it. But, it is not just about wanting the job; it is also about having a joy for doing the job. In the case of the New York Road Runners, candidates do not have to be runners; it can be the idea of "I've always loved sporting events and the reason that running is compelling to me is . . ." and then they go into that. I am looking for the passion in reference to that at the lower level because typically when coming straight from undergraduate work, or even straight from graduate school, it should be all about eagerness to learn and wanting to be mentored and developed. They should want to be a sponge and absorb everything. That is what I look for at entry-level positions.

When I get up to a manager level, I am looking for two to four years of experience. They have been out there in the industry, even if it is just working a small component of an event, maybe as a support person for a production company working on the production of a major event. Or maybe they were the administrative assistant for an executive at a sports league or something similar. I am usually looking for something related to sports and event planning and their core components.

At the senior management level, I am looking for people with four to seven years of experience who have gone through the full event life cycle multiple times. They should have planned on-going events and maybe even created new events. In creating new events it demonstrates that they had this idea and then they created it, they developed it, they executed it, and they can discuss the outcome. Sometimes the event is not successful, but it shows their eagerness and that they have tried to take a concept and bring it to life. Maybe it did not work, but they learned something from it. At the senior level, I'm concerned with, What did they learn and how did it make the next thing they did better?

Once you hire a person with the ideal characteristics and they are out there managing events, what do you think are some of the most important traits to have as an event manager?

What I look for and what I try to teach is to go out and do it. Do not just be a pencil pusher and stand on the sidelines with a clipboard and tell people what to do. They should go out there and show the people that they are working with that they will do everything that they ask their event staff to do. This is one of the things that is really important—to get their hands dirty and be hands on. Show the people that they are working with that no one is better than anyone else. Everyone is trying to get to the same goal, and doing whatever it takes to achieve the best event is how to get there.

The other thing is to have a plan in place. The worst thing an event manager can do is go out on an event day without a plan. If they do not have a plan, things are going to fall through the cracks. Have a plan early and review the plan over and over, especially with the people who are working the plan. This will ensure that when the event manager gets to the event day and surprises come up, the basic event plan remains without major adjustments as the surprise is handled. Along with event plans, a contingency plan should also be developed. Always having the brain in the background asking the questions such as, What if a lightning storm comes through?, or What if new construction is in the way of one of the road race courses?, or What if we mistakenly oversold the bleacher seats at a particular event? will help them plan ahead for the surprises that are inevitable in this profession.

What do you think are some of the biggest misconceptions that people have about being a sports event manager?

I think the biggest misconception is that it is all about the glitz and glamour of putting on sports events. I would say that 99.9% of the events and 99.9% of the time we are planning events for someone other than professional caliber athletes. It is only that small amount that is the glitz and glamour, but what we have to do is to always focus on the target audience, and that target audience is the 10 minute milers or 15 minute milers or weekend warriors who are out there and supporting the events. This is really who we most often plan events for and people should not expect the glitz and glamour.

an industry where people can wait for the jobs to come to them. Conversely, those interested in event management must understand the market, develop their professional network, and actively seek out positions.

Trying to get a first job in sports is a difficult and frustrating time for many people attempting to break into the industry. With 330 academic programs in sport management in the United States, there are plenty of applicants and not enough jobs (North American Society for Sport Management, n.d.). For example, the Red Sox annually hire fewer than 10 new employees, but receive 2,500 resumes for those 10 positions (Kladko, 2008). However, for those individuals who put extra effort into preparing themselves for their career and take time to understand the needs of employers and what they are looking for, a job in sports and event management is sure to become a reality.

Other realities of the sport industry are low starting pay and long hours. Entry-level jobs in sports generally do not pay as well as job seekers anticipate (starting salaries range between $20,000 and $40,000) and sometimes multiple internships are required before one can obtain a full-time job. The hours are also long because sports managers (especially event managers) are working when everyone else is playing. For example, a local 10K road race would never happen on a Tuesday afternoon around 2 pm because that is when most people are at work. Event managers are at work all week planning the race and then back at work Saturday morning to execute the race. Then the teardown and cleanup occur after the race and could last well into Saturday afternoon. So it is likely that the race manager will work in excess of 50 hours per week during the events. But for those who are truly passionate about sports, business, and entertainment, the job will be enjoyable and will not feel like work. By working hard, gaining experience, and working toward having the content knowledge and personal characteristics explored in this chapter, event managers will quickly work their way up the organizational hierarchy. An example of a mid-level event manager position for a university is provided in the box on page 16 to demonstrate the responsibilities one might find while moving up in the industry.

Given the current ultracompetitive landscape in the sports industry, job seekers must strategically separate themselves from the competition. Recently, some sports management degree programs have been criticized for not providing a diversity of skill sets to students (Kladko, 2008). This is pointed out not to be negative, but to make readers aware of the reality of the needs of sports employers. Students seeking a job in the sports industry must take it upon themselves to go above and beyond the work in the classroom and gain real-life experiences in sport. The goal of obtaining these extra experiences should be to develop all of the competencies identified throughout this chapter. As demonstrated in the interview with Paul Ortolano, Director, Event Development and Production, New York Road Runners (see the box on page 13), individuals who make good use of their time are more likely to be hired than those who have simply completed their academic requirements. The interview with Mr. Ortolano provides detailed information of what a sports employer looks for when hiring event managers, and it provides an excellent starting point for students looking to make themselves more marketable to employers.

Another way to become more marketable is to know more people. If people in the industry are aware of a talented person, it is likely that when a job does become available, those "in the loop" will be contacted first. Professional organizations are a good way for new event managers to get involved and begin to create their own professional network.

PROFESSIONAL ORGANIZATIONS

In the world of sports, building a professional networking system is essential to functioning and excelling in the industry. Whether looking for a new job, seeking information on a specific challenge being faced, or taking advantage of professional development opportunities, professional organizations are a good place to start. For sports event managers, there are multiple organizations that relate to specific types of event management. Recently, the National Association of Collegiate Directors of Athletics (NACDA) formed a subdivision for event managers in college athletics called the Collegiate Event and Facility Management Association (CEFMA) (http://nacda.cstv.com/cefma/nacda-cefma.html). For those interested in event or facility management within college athletics, membership in this organization provides access to current information, top professionals in the industry, and networking opportunities.

The International Association of Assembly Managers (IAAM) (www.iaam.org) is another well-known industry organization. IAAM provides opportunities for public assembly facility managers of all types. Often, industry segments are grouped together in professional organizations and IAAM is one example of that. IAAM is broad in scope and targets those individuals involved in managing facilities such as sports stadiums, sports arenas, performing arts centers, convention centers, exhibit halls, and amphitheaters. The organization is also dedicated to providing opportunities for students through volunteer opportunities at their annual conference and professional development programming through their institutes and certification programs.

The Stadium Managers Association (SMA) (www.stadiummanagers.org) includes members who are involved with administration and operations of sports stadiums. SMA holds annual meetings where information is shared between vendors and stadium managers. SMA was formed in 1974 and its purpose and membership groups are as follows:

> *SMA promotes the professional, efficient, and state-of-the-art management of stadiums around the world. Our members are administrators, operators, and marketing personnel from teams, government entities, colleges and universities, and suppliers to the industry (n.d., ¶ 2).*

SMA is a niche organization focusing on specific issues related to sports stadium managers. As such, future event managers interested in this segment of the industry should consider membership in this organization.

These are just a few examples of organizations related to event and facility management in sport. There are hundreds of others associated with job function (e.g., Sport Marketing Association), type of sport (e.g., Road Runners Club of America), or a combination of characteristics (e.g., National Association of Collegiate Women Athletic Administrators). The authors have compiled a list of professional organizations (see Appendix A) as a starting point for those looking to affiliate with one. The organizations highlighted are related to aspects of event management and readers are encouraged to explore them by evaluating the objectives, professional development opportunities, information sharing opportunities, annual conference content, and the cost of membership compared with anticipated benefits.

Sample Job Description for a University Event Management Position

Function

The event manager will report to the Senior Associate Director of Athletics and provide support in the areas of event management, facility operations, new construction and renovations, special events, and general administration.

Duties

1. Responsible for all athletic events.

2. Effectively and efficiently direct all event staff.

3. Responsible for assisting in the design, bidding, and construction of new softball stadium and new basketball practice facility.

4. Responsible for all athletic department special events (i.e. student-athlete banquet, alumni BBQ, and football booster auction).

5. Additional duties as assigned by the Senior Associate Director of Athletics and Director of Athletics.

Knowledge and Abilities

1. Knowledge of principles of athletic management (i.e. customer service, budgeting, contracts, sponsorship, marketing, and risk management).

2. Understanding of turf management, athletic surfaces, facility maintenance, custodial considerations, and construction processes.

3. Knowledge of NCAA rules and regulations.

Qualifications

1 Bachelor's degree in Sport Administration required (Masters Degree preferred), Management, Communications or related field.

2. Previous experience in a facility management or collegiate athletic department.

3. Excellent communication skills, work ethic, and a record of dependability and reliability required.

4. Proven ability to interact with coaches and staff in a positive manner.

5. Ability to work nights and weekends.

Salary

1. Commensurate with experience and education.

SUMMARY

The main purposes of this chapter were to discuss what event management is, the role of event managers, and to establish the competencies needed to be a successful event manager. Information was also provided on breaking into the event management industry as well as the realities of the occupation. As discussed, the challenges that event managers face (i.e., tasks changing daily, a solid base of knowledge in many areas) are the same things that make the job fun and exciting. Those interested in getting started in event management need to educate themselves on all aspects of event management, assess their own abilities, acquire an understanding of what employers are looking for in the field, and be ready for the competiveness of the job search.

Another purpose of this chapter was to provide an overview of some of the core event management concepts that come into play during the event planning and management process. From defining the event purpose and goals to understanding how governing bodies are involved, event managers must be well versed in a variety of areas internal and external to their event. Those event managers that understand the creative aspects of event management and how to leverage them to generate revenue will certainly be successful. It is not enough to simply put on an event in the current sports culture; participants, spectators, media, and sponsors all expect something more than the core sports product. It is the ability to conceptualize and execute this "something more" idea that will separate the good event managers from the great ones.

Student Challenge

NAME _____ DATE _____

STUDENT CHALLENGE #1

In Challenge #1, explore the job market in event management, self-reflect about individual strengths and weaknesses related to skills needed to manage events effectively, and brainstorm possible event ideas.

QUESTION 1-1

Explore two current job postings in the field of event management and respond to the questions about each position. Websites such as IAAM.org, NCAA.org (event management is listed under facilities), and TeamWorkonline.com often have event management jobs posted.

Job #1 Title:

- Responsibilities:

- Education Required:

- Other knowledge/skills required:

Student Challenge

Job #2 Title:

- Responsibilities:

- Education Required:

- Other knowledge/skills required:

Evaluation:

- What similarities did you find between the two jobs?

- What differences did you find between the two jobs?

Student Challenge

QUESTION 1-2

Conduct research on five events and determine the type of event (e.g., recurring, traveling, mega, or ancillary) each most closely resembles. Each category must be represented at least once. Use the event Web sites to determine what the event theme is and how creativity was integrated into the event.

Event #1:

- Type of Event:
- Theme:
- Creativity:

Event #2:

- Type of Event:
- Theme:
- Creativity:

Event #3:

- Type of Event:
- Theme:
- Creativity:

Event #4:

- Type of Event:
- Theme:
- Creativity:

Event #5:

- Type of Event:
- Theme:
- Creativity:

Student Challenge

QUESTION 1-3

Brainstorm for 5 minutes focusing on generating ideas for events to explore throughout the remainder of this book. During the 5 minutes, write down as many ideas as possible. At the end of the brainstorming session, choose the best three event ideas to keep on the list as options moving forward. Use the space below to write.

CHAPTER 2

EVENT FEASIBILITY

Heather Lawrence

When evaluating the **feasibility** of an event, the event managers are figuring out whether or not the event can be produced successfully. The potential success of the event should be defined by the purpose/mission and goals that have been determined previously. To decide if the event should be held, an honest assessment of many aspects of the event is conducted. To begin, event managers should research the following areas of the event:

- Does hosting this event require a bid submission?
- Is an event sanction needed? If so, can it be obtained and at what cost?
- Where will the primary event be held?
- Is the facility available and adequate?
- Are ancillary facilities needed?
- What competing events are taking place (sport and non-sport)?
- Are permits required?
- Is lodging available?
- What type of transportation exists for participants, spectators, officials, and volunteers?
- What is the media interest?
- Are there potential sponsors?
- What are the security needs?
- What are the staffing needs?
- What are the rough costs?

These questions will guide the decision making process as to whether the event managers should move forward with the event or not. Many of these topics are discussed in detail later in this text, but an introduction to some of them is presented here to assist event managers in their initial assessment of an event.

EVENT BIDDING

Bidding on an event involves competing with other potential host sites for the right to host an event. The process can range in scope from filling out a one page document to a multi-year, multimillion dollar endeavor. Bidding is used by rights holders to solicit potential host sites for events. Rights holders encompass any entity, including national governing bodies (NGBs), which control an event through ownership. The bid process allows rights holders to screen sites and organizers to ensure that the parameters set for the event can be met successfully by the host site. For those events that are attractive to many locations, the bid process is also used to generate the most revenue possible through guarantees and sponsorships offered by the potential host.

Not all events require a bid, but early in the feasibility evaluation process the event organizers should determine if the event they are interested in hosting does require one. For most recurring events, there is no bid process. Traveling and mega events will most likely have some sort of bid process and require that an organizing committee be established. In some cases, a venue may choose to bid on an event independently and thus function the same way an organizing committee would.

Depending on the sport and the rights holder, different criteria exist for selecting a host site. In some cases the rights holder might be looking to attract new participants to the sport, while in other cases the goal is purely revenue generation. Still other sports may be focused only on providing a good experience for the participating athletes. Understanding the objectives of the rights holder is critical to a successful bid submission. One of the best ways to prepare for the bid process is to attend the event the year or two prior to bidding. If that is not possible, bidders should at least contact previous hosts of the event. Through attendance at the event and discussions with former hosts, information on bid expectations, event goals and objectives, event attendance, event setup, and the ease of working with the rights holder can be gathered.

If the event organizers are creating a new event from scratch, then there will not be a bid process, but the organizers will often need the approval of the sport NGB through an event sanction to create the event. The event sanction is often tied to the bid process. A host that is awarded an event by a rights holder is generally required to also complete the paperwork and pay the fees associated with the NGB event sanction. As discussed in Chapter 1, the event sanction is considered an official approval for the event and is granted by the governing body associated with the sport (Solomon, 2002). There are few competitive sports events today that are exempt from sanctions.

The Role of Organizing Committees

Organizing committees play a large role in the bidding, obtaining, and hosting of some events as the local group that hosts the event. Organizing committees can be composed of a variety of individuals. Many cities have **convention and visitors bureaus (CVBs)** which assist in attracting various events, tourism, and business to the local area. In some communities, a **sports commission** exists specifically to attract sports events to the area and assist in hosting. In conjunction with the CVB and/or sports commission, there might also be a sport specific group that has a vested interest in attracting an event. For example, a local track club might be interested in bidding on the Junior National Track and Field Championships to generate revenue, increase the profile of their club, and give their athletes a home track advantage. Any combination of these organizations may be involved in the bid process.

Representatives from these groups along with other influential individuals in the community will make up the organizing committee. Local politicians, community leaders, members of the media, business leaders, representatives of special interest groups, and prominent sports figures should be considered for membership on the organizing committee. Conducting research and building relationships with successful sports coaches, teams, and individual athletes can have a positive impact on the success of a bid. If an Olympic gold medal winner now coaches in the community, it would behoove the organizers to recruit this person to the organizing committee and emphasize his or her accomplishments and role on the organizing committee during the bid process. Having a diverse and interested group of people serve on the organizing committee will help in submitting a strong and informed bid, as well as helping to generate community excitement if the bid is won.

Economic Impact Through Events

CVBs and sports commissions exist to generate economic impact. Many times, these groups are the driving force in a locale seeking events on which to bid. A detailed explanation of economic impact is beyond the scope of this book, but event managers should be aware of and understand the importance of economic impact when analyzing the feasibility of an event. **Economic impact** in sports refers to new money entering a region resulting in a change in regional output, earnings, and employment (Humphreys & Plummer, 1995). When an event is hosted in a city, the result is an infusion of money during the time of the event, as well as a lingering impact on the location as the new money is re-circulated within the community. For example, an out-of-town visitor will attend an event at a stadium and spend money on tickets, concessions, and parking. A stadium worker will earn wages for working the event and be paid by the stadium owners using the money spent by the out-of-town spectator. The stadium worker then will have money to spend on other items in the community (e.g., groceries, entertainment) and the cycle of spending may repeat again in the same locale, creating an impact well beyond the actual event.

Economic impact is measured for single day events and multiple day events. Calculation methods for economic impact vary by organizations performing the measurement and are beyond the scope of this textbook. Some events, such as the ING New York City Marathon, only occur on one day while others, such as the Olympic Games or Commonwealth Games, occur over many days. The economic impact for the 2008 ING New York City Marathon was estimated at $220 million by the New York City Sports Commission. In America's largest city, with many sizeable sports events, this is the largest economic impact for any one day sports event in New York City (The New York City Sports Commission, 2008). Many high profile events that may have only one day of focused activity have built up an entire week of related or ancillary events. In a press release from New York City Mayor Michael Bloomberg's office on January 31, 2007, the city announced that the 2008 MLB All-Star Game at Yankee Stadium and its activities for the week were estimated to generate $148 million for New York City (NYC.gov, 2007).

The event does not have to be something that attracts a large national television audience to impact the community. In 2007, Ohio University hosted the first round of the NCAA Women's Volleyball tournament. The University found out it was hosting just three days prior to the participating teams (Ohio University, Xavier University, Purdue, and Cal Poly) arriving for their matches (Corriher, 2007). Overall, the Visitor's Bureau estimated that the tournament resulted in $283,318 of economic impact to the area through money spent on lodging, meals, entertainment, and shopping (Corriher, 2007). Events in larger cities and those that attract thousands of tourists to a location generate huge economic impact. The average economic impact of the Super Bowl is $300–$400 million for the host city (Official Site of the 2008 Super Bowl, n.d.).

Often it is the economic impact of events that makes hosting sports events appealing to communities. It is also why there is a competitive bid process for so many events. However, event managers should be wary of the numbers seen in many calculations of economic impact because of the variety of methodologies used by economists. Event organizers that are asked to provide estimated economic impact figures should remember the rule, "under promise and over deliver." With great possible economic impact at stake for the host site, the bid process allows for a comparative look at all the possible sites by the rights holder so that the best fit can be selected.

Economic impact numbers generally look great to event organizers and especially to cities, but they should be evaluated with caution. Saying that economic impact will occur is easy, but showing hard numbers to prove it may be more challenging. For example, some research of the economic impact of the Super Bowl by economist Philip Porter from the University of South Florida has shown that the average sales tax revenue in a city that hosts the game is not significantly different from the year before or the year after the city hosts the Super Bowl (Deeson, n.d.). Cities may still want to host events such as the Super Bowl for the prestige or for other reasons, but if economic impact is one of the major determining factors, it should be assessed with care.

The Bid Submission

Bidding for an event requires extensive knowledge of the community, venue, hotels, transportation, and the availability of financial resources. A list of possible bid components has been provided within this chapter. Generally, the rights holder will require answers to questions related to the facility location, availability, size, and amenities to ensure it meets the needs of the event. Oftentimes the venue must be available days prior to the event for setup and practices. Spaces for hospitality, locker rooms, and storage may also be required. Information on media accommodations is critical for those events that will attract a media presence. Modern media amenities such as broadcast compounds, adequate internet connections, and workspaces are expected for major events. Additionally, it is customary to provide meals to members of the media, volunteers, and sometimes participants. The ability or inability to provide meals could impact the strength of the bid. External to the facility, the availability, quality, and price of hotels close to the venue will be important to the organizing committee so they know that all parties involved in the event will have access to adequate accommodations.

Having qualified, competent, and dedicated people on the organizing committee will also help to inspire confidence in the bid submission. The rights holder will have to trust that the event organizers can execute the event as described in the bid submission. Thus, having organizing committee members with a background in the sport and in executing similar events is an asset to the submission. If allowed by the rights holder, ancillary events can be used to enhance a bid package. Ancillary events provide additional excitement about the event and can also generate revenue. Other areas where a bidder might enhance the offerings to the rights holder are in free hotel rooms and workspace to the governing body, hosting a participant banquet as part of the event, securing potential sponsors prior to bid submission, guarantees of media presence, and offering creative cross-promotions with other businesses.

Even though the bid process is a competition between potential sites, it is important that the bid focuses on the abilities and dedication of the bid location, and is not critical of competitors. Most rights holders are experts in evaluating potential host sites and anything that varies from concise, accurate, and professional presentation will not be well received.

Events Without Bidding

For those events without a formal bid process, event managers must still evaluate event feasibility by answering many of the common questions that would be posed in the bid for themselves. With no set formula to evaluate the potential success of the event, this is an often overlooked step in successful event management. To find answers to these questions, event managers must get out of their offices and meet the people who would be impacted by the event, whether they are participants, potential sponsors, or local government officials. It can be beneficial to attend similar events and talk to event managers to gather as much information as possible.

Existing events are also a concern when considering new events. Longstanding relationships deserve attention, and the economic impact provided by repeat business should not be taken for granted. Any time a new event enters the marketplace, the business space becomes more cluttered when attracting spectators, sponsors, and media. Integrating a new event into an area that already hosts successful, well-recognized events should be approached carefully because it could negatively impact existing relationships. With either the bid process or an independent evaluation of an event, there must be a positive working relationship with all of the stakeholders.

The following list illustrates the type of content required for a bid submission. This example includes the type of possible questions a governing body might ask on a bid document for a traveling event to be held in a stadium. Even with these specific questions being asked, there is usually an opportunity for the bidders to also create a unique selling proposition for why they are the best host for the event.

I. General Stadium Information
  A. Owner/address
  B. Management
  C. Year opened
  D. Renovation information
II. Stadium Specifics
  A. Size of main stadium floor
  B. Storage space for equipment
  C. Field surface
  D. Field lighting
    i. Foot candles
    ii. Warm-up time of lights
    iii. Shutters availability
    iv. In-stand spotlight locations
  E. Number of Seats
    i. Permanent seating in main seating bowl (non-premium)
    ii. Permanent club seats
    iii. Suites (number and seats in each)
    iv. Ability to add temporary suites/club seats

v. ADA seats available and location in stadium
    F. Stadium availability for practice
    G. Description of union contracts
III. Media
    A. Number of working media seats in press box
        i. Type of work setup (internet access, telephone, power)
    B. Number and location of working media seating
        i. Type of work setup (internet access, telephone, power)
    C. Size and location of post-event press conference room
    D. Size and location of post-event media work room
        i. Type of work setup (internet access, telephone, power)
    E. Media lunch/dinner location
IV. Television/Radio
    A. Domestic broadcast abilities/compound
    B. Network broadcast abilities/compound
    C. Interview areas
    D. Photographers areas
V. Sound/Scoreboards/Signage
    A. Press box sound system
    B. Stadium scoreboard screens (number, location, and size)
    C. In-stadium electronic message boards (number, location, and size)
    D. Exterior stadium electronic message boards (number, location, and size)
    E. Nature of all existing advertising contracts (including naming rights)
VI. Hotels
    A. Number of available rooms in vicinity
    B. Anti-gouging agreements
    C. Headquarters hotel for rights holders
    D. Headquarters hotel for media
    E. Headquarters hotel for participants
VII. Ancillaries
    A. Club/restaurants in stadium
    B. Existing stadium stores
    C. Novelty vending
    D. Concessionaire
        i. Name and contact
        ii. Terms of agreement
        iii. Other relevant information
        iv. Any differences with suite catering
    E. Security
        i. Name and contact
        ii. Terms of agreement
        iii. Other relevant information
    F. Relevant alcohol laws
    G. Parking
        i. Stadium owned/controlled spaces (number and location)
        ii. Regular prices charged
        iii. Availability of disabled parking spaces
    H. Sponsor tent location
VIII. Host committee description
    A. Members
    B. Mission

LOCATION AND VENUE

Choosing the right location and venue might be the most important aspect of event planning. The city or locale of the event is the first decision that must be made in the conceptualization process. If the event organizers represent a community, then it is only logical that the event be held within the community. If the event is a recurring event with spectators used to a certain location it also may not make sense to explore new locations. However, there could be some circumstances where moving a recurring event to a different location might be a great idea. For example, colleges and universities occasionally schedule basketball games at neutral locations to expose a different fan base to the team and create excitement in a neighboring community. If the event organizers represent a state association or are a private entity, or if a traveling or mega event is being considered, then the location might be more difficult to choose.

Considerations for choosing a location vary by the type of event. Event managers should rely on their established goals and objectives for their event when examining location and venue options. For many events, demographic and psychographic research should also be conducted to ensure that the locale is a good fit with the event. United States Census data is available online (http://factfinder.census.gov) and can help event managers analyze demographics such as population size, population centers, age, sex, educational level, and income.

Understanding the community is important during the feasibility analysis process and also later when marketing for the event begins. Many of the non-traditional sports such as skateboarding are popular with younger age groups. If a skateboarding event is being planned, it makes sense to examine the types of individuals interested in skateboarding (i.e. age, gender, income level) and then look for a community which mirrors those characteristics. There are a plethora of market research reports in sports available for purchase that examine market segments of specific sports, and many libraries have this information available at no charge.

The appropriateness and quality of the venue should also be of paramount concern. For participant-driven events, the location and facility should accommodate participant needs and provide a chance for all to perform at their best. A beginner's triathlon that is held in a location with unsuitable weather (e.g., average winter temperature of 20°F) for the strenuous event or that does not provide adequate transition and water stations will not be a good experience for participants. For spectator-driven events, the participant needs must be met, but spectator accommodations enter the equation. An NBA All-Star Game must not only be able to accommodate a large number of in-person spectators for the game, but also be able to attract visitors to the city for the entire weekend of ancillary events associated with the event. Television is also a key factor for an event such as the NBA All-Star Game, although regardless of the host site the television audience will be attracted to this event.

Convenient parking is vital to spectators and participants starting their event experience on a positive note. For many, it is the first thing they associate with the event upon arrival. The availability of parking at some locations may vary by day and time, so the normal patterns around the venue should be investigated to ensure that the parking lot that is empty on Sundays will also be available whenever the event is scheduled. If parking is part of the venue rental agreement, it should be clearly communicated and understood during the feasibility assessment process whether or not there is a fee to park, which entity retains that revenue, and who is responsible for staffing the parking areas.

Accessibility and ease of use for all should also be part of any discussion on venue choice. The concept of universal design is one that will help event managers evaluate venues for ease of use for all. **Universal design** refers to "The design of products and environments to be usable by all people, to the greatest extent possible, without the need for adaptation or specialized design" (The Center for Universal Design, 1997, ¶ 1). This concept goes beyond only focusing on making events and facilities accessible for those with disabilities, but takes into account other characteristics that may also impede full enjoyment of the experience (details are outlined in "The Principles of Universal Design"). For example, visually impaired spectators new to the event will rely on the information provided by the event manager to find their way around. Large, well-lit signage and even Braille signage can help accommodate the visually impaired. It is easy to overlook the needs of those that are dissimilar to the majority. So, these principles can be applied during all aspects of the event to ensure the experience of everyone involved is as positive as possible.

If ancillary events are associated with the primary event, there are additional considerations for the location. Tailgating parties, interactive sponsor tents, and concerts all need their own space if they are planned as part of the event. Since event managers may not be sure of ancillary event needs at this point in the conceptualization process, every effort should be made to secure a venue with extra space in case a need arises.

Once the location and venue options have been narrowed to a few, inquiry into available open dates for the venue begins. Sometimes the event manager has control of the event date and other times it is set by the rights holder with no flexibility. In addition to competition dates, the venue must also be available for practice times, warm-up, equipment setup, and equipment teardown. In the case of outdoor events, weather can significantly impact attendance at the event and thus impact revenue. Event managers should research weather patterns on that date for past years to help in predicting good weather on the event day.

The Principles of Universal Design

Universal design refers to the design of products and environments to be usable by all people, to the greatest extent possible, without the need for adaptation or specialized design. The Principles of Universal Design were conceived and developed by The Center for Universal Design at North Carolina State University. The following principles are intended to provide an overview (detailed information is available at http://www.design.ncsu.edu/cud/index.htm) for event managers to become familiar with the concept.

PRINCIPLE ONE: Equitable Use

The design is useful and marketable to people with diverse abilities.

PRINCIPLE TWO: Flexibility in Use

The design accommodates a wide range of individual preferences and abilities.

PRINCIPLE THREE: Simple and Intuitive Use

Use of the design is easy to understand, regardless of the user's experience, knowledge, language skills, or current concentration level.

PRINCIPLE FOUR: Perceptible Information

The design communicates necessary information effectively to the user, regardless of ambient conditions or the user's sensory abilities.

PRINCIPLE FIVE: Tolerance for Error

The design minimizes hazards and the adverse consequences of accidental or unintended actions.

PRINCIPLE SIX: Low Physical Effort

The design can be used efficiently and comfortably and with a minimum of fatigue.

PRINCIPLE SEVEN: Size and Space for Approach and Use

Appropriate size and space is provided for approach, reach, manipulation, and use regardless of user's body size, posture, or mobility.

Copyright 1997 NC State University, The Center for Universal Design

DATE AND TIME

The idea of choosing a date for an event might seem simple at first, but much more goes into choosing a date than simply venue availability. No similar events should be going on in the region on the same day, other entertainment events on the day should be considered, and the time should align with spectator and participant availability. In some instances, the governing body might have established dates and event timelines that cannot be altered. Dates that are dictated by a governing body have been established because they make sense for the sport and the competition season. Generally the national championship in a particular sport follows the regular season competition season and precedes important international events.

Flexible Dates and Times

The first consideration when choosing a date for an event without an established date is participant availability. The date chosen should coincide with participant interest. Not only does this premise hold true for the time of the year chosen, but also the day of the week. Many youth sports have their heaviest travel competition season during the summer because that is when parents are able to transports kids to competitions without them missing school. When dealing with a participant-driven event, weekend dates are essential to participation. Organizers should also consider if traditionally slow travel times such as Easter and Thanksgiving (often termed *opportunity scheduling*) are a possibility for the event. These dates can allow organizers to receive deep discounts on hotel and venue rates. A youth soccer tournament that is scheduled for Tuesday through Thursday in October is not a good fit with participant needs because many adults cannot take time off from work to take their kids to a midweek event. Additionally, the kids would miss a full week of school with travel.

If the event is spectator driven, times outside of normal working and school hours, Friday and Saturday evenings, and Sunday afternoons tend to be good times. A recent phenomenon is that more and more event dates and times are dictated by live television scheduling. In some circumstances, the availability of television revenue and the exposure provided by television will supersede the value of scheduling to maximize spectator attendance. This has become especially apparent in college football, where revenue is of paramount importance. The challenges of midweek games on college campuses are many and they come from all constituent groups. Robert Zullo (2005) discusses the struggle of athletic directors related to scheduling of football games.

> *Faculty sometimes complain that a mid-week game hurts the academic progress of both student-athletes and student fans, and it sends the message that athletics takes precedence over academics on campus. Students lose focus in the classroom the day of the game, then often neglect their classes the day after (¶ 15).*

Zullo (2005) goes on to discuss the impact on other areas of the campus such as parking, security, and night classes that may have to be cancelled, rescheduled, or are disrupted. There are operational as well as public perception issues with midweek college football games. These are the types of issues that event managers must consider before choosing a date and time for their event.

Competing events in the area are another scheduling consideration. A small community that is already hosting a road race on a particular Saturday does not need one the following weekend. If high school football is a big community event on Friday nights in the fall, then another sports event in the area will not be as successful on a fall Friday night as on another day. Non-sports events should also be considered here. Even in urban locations, it is difficult to support more than one major event on a given day. To schedule a monster truck event the same evening as a professional hockey team is playing in the same city could force some people to choose one event over the other. If the monster truck show was scheduled on a week when the hockey team was playing on the road, there would be less competition for spectators.

Established Dates and Times

For events with more guidance provided by the rights holder, it is the responsibility of the event managers to ensure that they can execute the event within the timeline. For example, along with many facility requirements, United States Diving has an established schedule of events for their National Championships that includes exactly when warm-up and competition times are for each event as well as stipulations for needed schedule changes in the event of inclement weather (USA Diving, 2007). The specifics listed by the rights holder are important for event managers to know early in the event feasibility evaluation process. If an aquatics venue is unable to meet the extensive requirements for these national championships for diving, it is better to know early in the process as opposed to after planning has begun and a financial investment has been made. Overall, the selection of the date and time of an event is critical to its success.

PERMITS

Events that are held outside of a traditional venue will most likely need a permit from the city or county to allow the event to occur. **Permits** are generally required for road races, bike races, open water swims, and ancillary events in parks or on roadways. When a permit is required, it should be investigated and obtained early so that organizers have the date held and meet any requirements for submission dates that might be in place. Generally, the information is located on the city Web site and is called a special event, public assembly, parade, parks, road race, or bicycle race permit. Vending, food and beverage, and sound permits may also be required, depending on the scope of the event. It is not uncommon for municipalities to require 90 days or more lead time for permit applications. There also may be other stipulations in the permit such as paying for overtime police officers, participant limits, escort vehicle requirements, signage parameters, or allowable roads for races.

LODGING AND TRANSPORTATION

Depending on the purpose of the event, the lodging and transportation needs will vary substantially. For single day events featuring local participants and spectators, lodging and transportation may not even factor into the decision-making process (except for parking). However, for mega events such as the Super Bowl, requirements in these areas are extensive. The NFL requires that the Super Bowl host site provide 750 buses, 500 limousines, 1,000 taxis, and 10,000 rental cars. In addition to spectator hotels, the NFL also requires a minimum of 19,000 high quality hotel rooms for their use. These parameters are common among mega events, and transportation and hotel requirements alone exclude many locations from hosting events such as the Super Bowl.

When calculating the number of hotel rooms needed for an event, research can be conducted to assist in planning. Event organizers can contact hosts of past events, or oftentimes CVBs and sports commissions have access to national databases with information on past event hotel usage rates. For new events, it is important that organizers do not underestimate the number of rooms needed. It is better to have too many rooms than too few in the locale of an event.

In addition to ensuring that there are enough hotels in the area to accommodate the event, it is important that they meet the specific needs of the event. This will include accommodating any participants or spectators with special needs (e.g., wheelchair access). Organizers should leverage their event to negotiate special prices for participants and spectators and even free rooms for event officials. It is common that one hotel room is provided free for every fifty rooms booked and some hotels will provide as many as one free room for every ten or twenty booked. Event managers have significant power when they can guarantee that the hotel will be touted the "official host hotel" and that they will drive business to the property. Beyond room rates, event managers can ask hotels for perks such as free breakfast for participants or transportation to and from the competition venue. Many hotels already own vans or small buses for airport transportation. These vehicles are perfect for transporting participants and spectators to and from the competition venue and will enhance the event experience for both participants and spectators. Consideration should also be given to ensuring the transportation can accommodate those with disabilities so as to not exclude some spectators or participants from using the provided services. Additionally, this is a nice perk to include in the bid. For events requiring bids, rates and perks should be negotiated and a tentative hold put on blocks of rooms early in the bidding process. This will ensure that the rooms are available if the bid is awarded.

Event organizers may or may not choose to get involved with transportation for their event. For many events it is not necessary, but for those located far from an airport or for team events, transportation may become an issue. As with hotels, negotiating rates and benefits for rental cars is part of organizing a successful event. Events that feature teams often need 15-passenger vans or buses. In some locales these types of vehicles are scarce, so event organizers may need to work with rental car agencies to have additional 15-passenger vans available, or with bus companies to make sure an adequate number of buses are available during the event dates. Event mangers should also consider that for some events, athletes need to transport large pieces of equipment, may need to move wheelchairs, may not speak English, or may need other special accommodations. Each of these situations requires a different type of research to be conducted on available transportation in the area.

High profile athletes will expect transportation to be provided for them. For some events, cars are borrowed or rented and event staff is assigned to airport runs to pick up and drop off athletes as they come and go. Golf and tennis events regularly work with car dealers and manufacturers as part of their sponsorships to provide cars for athletes to use while they are in town at the event, or for organizers to use to transport the athletes.

While researching lodging and transportation, event organizers may find that other events (e.g., conventions, conferences, or entertainment events) are planned for the same time period. This could be a deal breaker for the event. Major conferences and conventions can take over small and mid-size cities and make it difficult to hold a sports event, even if it is not a direct competitor. It is better to know about problems such as a lack of hotel rooms or other events early in the process, prior to event organizers signing contracts.

The Olympic Bid Process

The magnitude of the Olympic bid process is difficult to explain, but the timeline should provide an idea of what a massive undertaking bidding on the Olympics is. It is a multi-phased process beginning at the National Olympic Committee (NOC) level and then moving to the International Olympic Committee (IOC). The 2016 Olympic bid process began with countries interested in bidding putting forward a city as a potential host by September 2007. In the United States, Chicago was chosen to move forward by the United States Olympic Committee (USOC) (IOC, 2007a). Other candidates submitting bids to the IOC included Baku (Azerbaijan), Doha (Qatar), Madrid (Spain), Prague (Czech Republic), Rio de Janeiro (Brazil), and Tokyo (Japan).

There is then a two-phase process during which the IOC reviews the bid, visits the potential host sites, and evaluates each city's potential to successfully organize the Olympic Games (IOC, 2007b). Phase I (candidature acceptance procedure) involves about a year of evaluation of the potential host city by the IOC (IOC, 2007b). If a city advances through phase I, it then moves into phase II (candidature procedure), which takes another year. Phase II involves submission of an in-depth report on the city's Olympic project, a visit from city representatives to observe the current Olympic Games (8 years prior), a visit to the potential host city by the IOC Evaluation Commission, and a full report published by the IOC Evaluation Commission prior to final bid award (IOC, 2007b). Finally, the IOC selects a host and announces a winner. The entire process takes approximately two years at the IOC level, but many Olympic Bid Organizing Committees work years in advance just to be the city representing its country in the Olympic Bid process.

The Road to the 2016 Summer Olympic Games Selection:

Phase I

  NOCs to inform the IOC of the name of an Applicant City (September 13, 2007)

  Signature of the Candidature Acceptance Procedure (October 1, 2007)

  Payment of the Candidature Acceptance Fee ($150,000) (October 1, 2007)

  Creation of a logo to represent the application (no date)

  IOC information seminar for 2016 Applicant Cities (week commencing October 15, 2007)

  Submission of the Application File and guarantee letters to the IOC (January 14, 2008)

  Examination of replies by the IOC and experts (January – June 2008)

Phase II

  IOC Executive Board meeting to accept Candidate Cities for the Games of the XXXI Olympiad in 2016 (June 2008)

  Payment of the Candidature Fee ($500,000) (no date)

  Creation of an emblem to represent the candidature (no date)

  Olympic Games Observer Programme—Beijing 2008 (August 8–24, 2008)

MEDIA AND SPONSORSHIPS

Many marketing details can be left until after it is decided whether to host the event or not, but it is beneficial to get the measure of the media and sponsorship climate prior to making the decision to host an event. Having a member of the local media on the organizing committee can help gauge whether or not the event would be of interest to media outlets. For local and youth events, media interest may not matter when assessing event feasibility. However, when considering hosting a major event, television revenue can be critical to a financially successful event. Most rights holders retain the television rights and revenue associated with their major events, but for new events securing a television deal could mean the difference between success and failure.

It is likely that organizers will be actively seeking potential sponsors very early in the event planning process. For all sizes of events, sponsors can impact the viability of the event. The challenge is finding the "right" sponsors that match the needs of the event with the needs of the company. When dealing with community or high school events there might be businesses willing to sponsor the event just to help a local group. For larger events, the sponsorship prospecting and acquisition process is much more complex. Securing sponsors and creating partnerships with companies can be a fantastic win-win situation for both the event organizers and the sponsor.

The specifics of sponsorship are discussed in Chapter 7, but potential sponsors should be approached prior to deciding to host the event if they are needed to make the event a success. For example, a community examining the feasibility of hosting a 10K charity road race might need to secure a corporate title sponsor to offset the costs of the event and ensure that as much money as possible goes to the specified charity. It would not make sense to plan the race, advertise, and register participants without first knowing if a sponsor was willing to be involved. In this scenario, without the sponsor, the event does not meet its purpose of raising money for a charity. If the purpose cannot be met, then the event should not take place. If the event organizers discuss the race with potential sponsors early in the process, the sponsor can then be an integral part of the planning and execution of the event, resulting in a better event and more benefit to the sponsor.

STAFFING AND SECURITY

Staffing and security needs are dependent upon the type and size of event being considered. Whether or not the event is ticketed, the type of crowd expected, and the history of the event should all be considered when evaluating staffing and security. Organizers should decide whether or not staffing and/or security needs are a big enough job to outsource to a professional staffing company, or if those needs can be met by the organizing committee using part-time employees and volunteers. If the event is in a traditional sports venue, the facility may provide these services as part of the rental agreement. For events that are being held in parks, on roadways, or on waterways, the permitting process may require a certain level of police and security presence. Organizers should also assess any uniqueness to the event that may require additional security or staffing. The exact numbers of staff needed are not required at this point in planning, but the availability of people (through part-time employees and volunteers or through outsourcing) should be evaluated.

EQUIPMENT

Common equipment for sports events is usually either owned by sports facilities or can be rented fairly easily. If there are unusual needs that the proposed event has, it is critical to ensure the equipment can be obtained prior to making the final decision to hold the event. For example, it may sound like a great idea to have an indoor skateboarding competition. However, the ramps needed for the athletes may not be available for the date/time of the event or even in the local area. To schedule the event without 100% certainty that the ramps are available would be embarrassing for the organizers when they are forced to cancel the event or pay large sums of money to build ramps due to poor planning.

FINANCES

Understanding the budget can make or break the event. There are costs associated with almost everything related to hosting an event. The venue, officials, staff, security, medical personnel, marketing, equipment, sponsor activation, hospitality, ticket stock, insurance, awards, and office supplies are a partial list of what will be part of the overall event budget. Some of these expenses will require payment or partial payment prior to the event. If organizers are relying on ticket revenue to pay expenses, it could result in cash flow problems because much of the ticket revenue will not be available until after the event concludes. Marketing and sponsor activation are just two of the areas that will cost money prior to and during the event. During the feasibility assessment stage, organizers should begin to get a handle on the major costs associated as well as potential revenues. Seeking out information on past event budgets from other hosts and conducting research into the costs associated with the major operational areas of the event will begin to bring the overall budget into focus. A detailed explanation of how to create and manage an event budget is provided in Chapter 5.

MORE IS NOT ALWAYS BETTER

Some event managers fall into the "more is better" trap of hosting events. However, more is only better if each and every aspect of the event is feasible, has a purpose, and has the potential for success. Sticking to the stated mission and objectives of the event is important when beginning to explore the feasibility of the event. For example, if a youth fun walk is the event and the goal is to get kids moving and fit, it would not make much sense to have a breakfast station setup being sponsored by a donut company. So, in this case the sponsor might be attractive because it can provide cash to help run the event, but it does not fit within the mission of the event and therefore should be avoided. All decisions must keep the purpose/mission of the event in mind.

Over-committing is another common pitfall in the planning process. It is easy to get caught up in the excitement of all of the possibilities surrounding an event during discussions. But when it comes down to executing all aspects of the event, everything takes time and energy, and probably more time and energy than anticipated. If the event management team consists of three volunteers, the team needs to be realistic in what can be accomplished. Planning to set up an entire race course and manage it with three people is not going to work out well for anyone. The feasibility analysis stage of event conceptualization is the time to examine and gain an understanding of the limitations related to human, financial, and facility resources.

SUMMARY

The feasibility analysis process varies in depth based upon the type of event being considered. A potential Olympic Games bid might involve a multi-year feasibility study, while a high school track and field meet might only require a few hours or days to think through all the areas discussed. A comprehensive evaluation of the event will help organizers decide whether or not accomplishing the event goals is feasible. For events with a bid process, organizers will work to position their location as the best host for the event. CVBs and sports commissions often take the lead in seeking out possible events that will result in economic impact to an area. By establishing a qualified organizing committee and submitting a well thought out bid package, the host location is able to highlight what they have to offer to ensure a great event. Whether through a bid process or independently, event organizers should evaluate the location, venue, date and time, lodging, transportation, permits, media, sponsorships, staffing, security, equipment, finances, and any other unique aspects of the event when deciding whether or not to proceed. Results of this research will provide information not readily apparent, but nonetheless critical, to gauge the potential success of the event.

Student Challenge

STUDENT CHALLENGE #2

In Challenge #2, examine existing real events to identify event type, themes, and creative aspects of the event. Additionally, the three events identified in Challenge #1 will be further explored. Develop the purpose for each event, set goals, and examine the governing bodies and/or rights holders that may influence the overall execution of each event.

QUESTION 2-1

Using the three possible events from Challenge #1, identify the type of event, research associated governing bodies and/or rights holders, develop a purpose statement, and list three event goals. The goals must directly relate to the purpose statement.

Event #1:

- Rights Holder:
- Purpose Statement:

- Goal #1

- Goal #2

- Goal #3

Event #2:

- Rights Holder:
- Purpose Statement:

- Goal #1

- Goal #2

- Goal #3

Event #3:

- Rights Holder:

- Purpose Statement:

- Goal #1

- Goal #2

- Goal #3

QUESTION 2-2

Choose two of the three events from Question 2-1. Conduct research into each area listed for the event to establish whether or not the event is feasible.

Event #1:

a. Is there a bid process?
b. Identify the rights holder.
c. List potential organizing committee members.

d. What are the facility needs?

e. Is a facility available in the locale that meets the event needs? If so, which one?
f. When will the event be held? Why was that date/time selected?

g. Are permits required?
h. How many hotel rooms are needed? Are there enough in the area?
i. What are the transportation needs?
j. What type of media will the event attract?
k. List potential sponsors.

l. Can staffing and security be done in-house or will it be outsourced?
m. Are there any special equipment needs?
n. List the major cost categories associated with the event.

Event #2:

a. Is there a bid process?
b. Identify the rights holder.
c. List potential organizing committee members.

d. What are the facility needs?

e. Is a facility available in the locale that meets the event needs? If so, which one?
f. When will the event be held? Why was that date/time selected?

g. Are permits required?
h. How many hotel rooms are needed? Are there enough in the area?
i. What are the transportation needs?
j. What type of media will the event attract?
k. List potential sponsors.

l. Can staffing and security be done in-house or will it be outsourced?
m. Are there any special equipment needs?
n. List the major cost categories associated with the event.

QUESTION 2-3

Using the purpose statement and goals from Question 2-1 along with the results of the feasibility study from Question 2-2, choose one event to move forward with for the remainder of the Challenges. Also, provide an explanation on why the event was chosen as well as the locale in which it will be held.

Note: From this point forward, all Challenges (unless otherwise noted) are specific to this event.

Event to Move Forward With:

Established Purpose Statement and Goals:

Location:

Why was this event chosen?

CHAPTER 3

EVENT AND FACILITY CONTRACTS

B. David Ridpath

This chapter introduces some of the major concepts related to contracts, contractual agreements, and other legal considerations related to event management. Contracts and contractual arrangements are a necessary part of life. Individuals enter into some form of contract each day during the course of their lives. It might be something as simple as saying, "I promise to pay for this," or something a bit more serious and official like a marriage license, the purchase of a car, a house, or entering into an employment agreement that covers salary, benefits, and associated items. While stating a payment will be made for something may not be an enforceable contract per se, it is important to simplify exactly what a contract is.

A contract is an agreement between two (or more) parties. Now, whether an agreement is legally binding or not is another story. Understanding and having knowledge of contracts and contract law is important for all event managers. In this chapter, the following questions will be addressed: (a) What is a contract? (b) What are the components of a valid contract? (c) Why should contracts be used in event management? and (d) What types of contracts are common in event management?

What I Wish I Had Known

Much of what I know about event contracts, I learned the hard way. In the mid-1990s, I was a young athletic administrator at Weber State University in Ogden, Utah, hoping to prove myself and move up in the ranks of college athletics administration. I had just finished a one year internship and then spent a short time as the Assistant Director of Marketing/Director of Compliance when the Associate Athletic Director left Weber for a new job. I was immediately asked to step in and take on responsibilities in event management to fill in for the newly vacated duties. Of course I agreed and was thrust into action.

The first event I managed was a football game and it was one I will always remember for many reasons. Prior to entering my career in college athletics administration, I had been in the Army and was responsible for hundreds of troops and million dollar budgets. I thought my Army experience would make managing a football game a breeze, but I was wrong. What I quickly learned is that there is a variety of competing constituency groups involved in presenting a successful football event and my "militarism" was not going to work to get things done.

All of the different groups had different understandings of what needed to be done and what they got in return for providing a service. As with most sports events, a major challenge is organizing and motivating volunteers and part-time employees. From the sideline chain gang and ball boys to the referees and press box personnel, all had different understandings of what the expectations were and what they received for doing their job. The week prior to the game, I had sent out a memo to all personnel, followed by phone calls and emails informing all personnel to be "on station" at least one hour prior to kickoff. But it seemed to fall on deaf ears. For example, the chain gang showed up so late that I was not even sure they were going to make it for kickoff. By the time they arrived, I was upset and nervous. I immediately went to the head of the chain gang crew and asked why they were so late. His response was that they never had to show up at a specific time.

He then added, "Where's our pizza and Coke?" To which I simply replied, "What?" He then went on to inform me that chain gang was always provided with pizza and Coke, as were the ushers and others. Well, this was the first I had heard of it and I was not sure if I could or would provide the snacks.

As the game progressed, more challenges began to crop up and other groups were asking for things they "always got" from the previous game manager. The band also threatened to head home because I had not given them any food. Thankfully, I was able to quickly get some free hotdog coupons to prevent an uprising, but things were spiraling out of control and it became my goal to merely survive the game.

Even after the game ended, I was still being surprised by things. The stadium maintenance workers informed me that union rules had them waiting until Monday morning to begin trash cleanup. Between Saturday night and Monday morning there was plenty of time for trash to blow all over campus and create a bigger mess than there needed to be. The concessionaire had generated thousands of pounds of trash, and I figured they would clean up after themselves. But I was wrong. The concessionaire supervisor let me know that it was not in their contract to pick up trash and it was the stadium staff's responsibility. It was then that I nearly quit my job!

While quitting was only a passing thought, I was determined to improve the event management system and begin to hold staff accountable for their jobs to make the event a better experience for participants, spectators, and employees. The next week, I began to prepare an operations manual, and I created a specific employment contract for each and every person that worked at the game. I had decided that having a group supervisor would be my first step in organizing my staff. The group supervisor would be responsible for carrying out the duties outlined in the game management manual. The manual was reinforced by a contract outlining his or her specific areas of responsibility. I was determined to get rid of the handshake agreements of the past and set clear expectations for all event staff. I also needed to clarify what people received for their service (i.e., payment, snacks, game tickets). The use of contracts made my job much easier and provided a template for what needed to be done, by whom, and when.

While the responsibility of facility and event manager was probably the most enjoyable part of all my jobs during my intercollegiate athletic administrative career, it was also extremely challenging. I learned a lot through my experiences at Weber State, and specifically learned the value of well-written contracts. I was able to prove that with a written policy and procedure manual in place, backed up by comprehensive and specific contractual agreements, an event can be run efficiently and professionally.

CONTRACT BASICS

It is important when discussing contracts specific to event management, or any contracts in general, to define what a contract is and how it is used. By simple definition, a **contract** is a legally binding agreement or a way to enforce a promise made as a bargained exchange (Epstien, 2003; Schaber & Rohwer, 1984). Sport administrators must have a working knowledge of contracts and how they fit into the overall scheme of managing a sport or entertainment event. In addition, penalties associated with non-completion of the terms of a contract should be understood. The failure of any party (e.g., event manager, vendor, auxiliary entity) to meet the terms of the contract can have a major impact on the execution of an event as well as the possibility of causing financial hardship to all involved.

The principles of contracts and the process of entering into a contract in sports and events are similar to those of other contracts. Typically, negotiations between parties occur and revisions are made prior to a contract being finalized. The goal of any contract negotiation is to protect all involved through ensuring all parties involved will get what they expect, within the timeframe needed, at the anticipated cost.

Regardless of what one might personally think, it is highly recommended that a lawyer is consulted when a contract is involved. During the process of drafting the contract, negotiating the terms, understanding ramifications of penalties, and final signature of the contract, a lawyer is essential.

Most organizations, teams, and facilities have legal representation on retainer, meaning that, if needed, a lawyer is available to them 24/7. **Legal representation** could be in the form of an internal General Counsel or an outside legal firm that represents their interests. While there are no laws that that require a contract be reviewed by a lawyer to be valid, it is recommended that event managers do so.

COMPONENTS OF A VALID CONTRACT

Many aspects of contracts are consistent across all types of business, sports included. Although there is room for creativity with respect to areas of performance indicated in the contract, there is less room for creativity when dealing with the contract components and structure. Specifically, all contracts are subject to the "Big Four" standard elements that ensure validity of a contact. The four elements are:

- Offer
- Acceptance
- Consideration
- Capacity

All four of these must be present for a legally binding contractual arrangement to exist (Epstien, 2003). If one of these facets is missing, then there is not a legally binding contract that will hold up against the scrutiny of the legal system. The following section provides detailed definitions of each of the Big Four related to a valid contract.

Offer

The **offer** is the proposal that forms the contract. In layman's terms, it is a promise to do something or refrain from doing something. Examine the "What I Wish I Had Known" example in this chapter. As described in "What I Wish I Had Known," the concessionaire refused to pick up the trash after the football game and they certainly did not promise to do it. So, by contract, they did not have to.

As another example, a local running organization may put forth an offer to a city to put on a marathon. Event managers may solicit arenas, communities, or sports commissions to hold events. Conversely, a city, municipality, or other organization may approach event managers asking them to host an event or putting forth the offer. In many cases, a formal bid process would follow. Regardless of which entity initiates the discussion about hosting an event, to start the contractual process an offer to host must be made.

Acceptance

No contract is official until the offeree accepts the offer from the offeror. **Acceptance** means exactly what it implies. It is consenting to receive the terms of the offer for the purposes of fulfilling the contract. Only the person being offered the contract (or his or her legal designee) can agree to the terms of the offer. Of course negotiation and counter offers can precede the actual acceptance of the offer.

Using the marathon example, the city decides to allow the marathon to happen, thereby accepting the offer. With the thousands of sporting events happening worldwide, there are many offers and acceptances. Some events like the Boston and New York City Marathons are static and remain in the same area, while others, such as the Olympic Trials in most sports, are held in different locations and use an extensive bid process to determine the host site. Either way, several types of contracts are involved, beginning with a simple offer and acceptance.

Consideration

Consideration is the formal way of saying "the devil is in the details." **Consideration**, or the details of the contract, is necessary for the formation and validity of the contract. There must be an exchange of value between the parties involved in the contract. This means one party involved in the contract does or gives up something in exchange for the other party doing the same. This is where the contract can become detailed and filled with complex legal language. At this point, the contract is no longer a simple offer and acceptance; it is now what is known as the exact offer and exact acceptance.

Details such as when the marathon will be run, where the route will be, which city offices will be involved, and how much cost will be associated with each area enter the contract at this stage. For large events such as a major marathon, hotel space, ancillary events, ticketing, required permits, hospitality, and security all might be addressed in the contract. There can be as many or as few details as all parties want. Basically, this is the meat of the contract.

Capacity/Legality

Capacity/legality means that the parties involved in the contract must have the legal right to enter into that contract. Capacity also means that the person signing the contract is authorized to represent the organization in the execution of the contract, is of legal age (18 years old or older) to enter into the contract, is mentally competent, and is not under the influence of drugs or alcohol. In event management, there are only certain people, such as facility managers, athletic directors, and so on, that are designated as signing authorities. Sport managers must make sure that the person signing the contract is authorized to do so.

Using the marathon example, both parties must have the capacity to enter into the contract. It must be confirmed that the individual signing on behalf of the city is allowed to enter into agreements on behalf of the city, and the representative of the marathon must also be someone designated to enter into such agreements.

Written vs. Verbal Contracts

Not all legally binding contracts have to be in writing, but it is a good business practice and highly recommended to do so. Handshake agreements are part of the past in the United States and are not recommended in event management. In fact, there are some contracts that must be in writing to be valid, in addition to possessing the four elements listed above (Epstein, 2003; Sharp, 2003). Contracts associated with the sale of land or interest in land, the sale of items worth more than $500, and contracts for items that cannot be produced within one year must all be in writing. These categories must be in writing, and contracts related to event management commonly fall into one or more of these three categories.

Sale of Land or Interest in Land

The sale of land or interest in land is self explanatory in that land is a valuable commodity. Individuals who have bought or sold a house are intimately familiar with the detail and potential length of a contract in this scenario. Certainly this might be an area that event managers find themselves involved in, such as renting, leasing, or possibly purchasing land or facilities for certain events such as fairs or trade shows.

Sales of Goods in Value of More Than $500

It is common in today's society to get a receipt for everything, even a stick of gum. While not much thought is given to receipts for small purchases, most people pay close attention to a receipt for something that costs $500 or more. In fact, under contract law it is required that a receipt is provided for purchases over $500 (Epstien, 2003; Sharp, 2003). Sometimes there may be more than a receipt or bill of sale needed, but for expensive purchases there must be a contract including information related to whether items can be returned or not. With respect to event management, this guideline applies directly to many purchases of equipment and facility rentals.

Contracts That Cannot be Completed within One Year

There is a variety of circumstances where an event contract would not be able to be completed within one year. Most major intercollegiate athletic game contracts would fall into this category. Generally, these events are scheduled years in advance. In cases such as a college football game scheduled five years in advance, a written contract would be required. Many other traveling, mega, and ancillary events are also scheduled more than a year in advance. In these instances, contracts related to the venue for the event, execution of the event, television agreements, or sponsorship of the event would need to be in writing.

These categories provide event managers some guidance as to when a contract must be in writing, but it cannot be emphasized enough that it is highly recommended that all contracts related to event management be written.

Basic Provisions

The **basic provisions** section of a contract lists the fundamental areas for which each party will be responsible. The basic provisions usually begin on the first page of a contract and differ from event to event. The opening paragraph will simply identify the parties and the contact information of each. The remainder of the information is broken down into small sections of bulleted lists. Following is a simple example of a basic provisions section using fictitious organizations:

This letter confirms the terms of the agreement in connection with XYZ Tournament between **ABC DOME AT THE ORANGE REGIONAL SPORTS COMPLEX ("Complex")** authorized to do business in the state of Ohio, whose mailing address is 1010 Championship Way, Anytown, OH 99999 and **XYZ SPORTS, INC., ("Licensee")** a Delaware corporation whose mailing address is 890 Regents Blvd, Anytown, FL, 99991.

The terms of our agreement, consisting of the BASIC PROVISIONS and GENERAL TERMS AND CONDITIONS, are as follows:

I.   EVENT

XYZ Tournament in 2009 and 2010

II. EVENT VENUE

ABC Dome at the Orange Regional Sports Complex

III. EVENT SCHEDULE

June 1 – 7, 2009; Dates for 2010 to be mutually determined. These dates include load in, competition, and load out.

IV. TERM

Subject to paragraph 20 in the General Terms and Conditions, the term of this agreement will be for a period of two (2) years, commencing as of the date of this Agreement and terminating on the last day of the Event in 2010, or such later date as required in order for both parties to comply with the obligations of this Agreement.

V.   LICENSEE RESPONSIBILITIES

Licensee shall provide, at its sole expense, the following:

a. All event participants, staff, and equipment necessary to conduct the Event, except as otherwise set forth in this Agreement.

b. All officials and judges necessary to conduct the Event.

c. Selection and management of volunteers.

d. Assistance to Complex with field of play security.

e. Promotion of the Event through newsletters, mailings, email, and the Internet to possible event participants.

VI. COMPLEX RESPONSIBILITIES

Complex shall provide:

a. Field markings and equipment; tables for awards; water cooler and cups for participants; seating at each field of play.

b. Awards for each age division, number and type to be mutually agreed upon.

c. On-site emergency medical and first aid services.

d. Audio equipment and announcers for the Event.

e. Assistance to Licensee with field of play security.

VII. LICENSEE'S CURRENT CONTRACTUAL EVENT SPONSORS

Licensee shall present potential Event sponsors to Complex for approval no less than ninety (90) days prior to the Event. Event sponsors will be mutually agreed upon in advance, subject to any conflicts with existing Complex corporate sponsors.

VIII. LICENSEE CONTACT

Jane Smith

President

XYZ Sports, Inc.

890 Regents Blvd

Anytown, FL 99991

IX. COMPLEX CONTACT

David Brown

Vice President, Business Development

Orange Regional Sports Complex

1010 Championship Way

Anytown, OH 99999

The basic provisions set the stage for those items that are specific to the event being contracted. As with any contract, additional areas can be written into the contract depending on the needs of both parties.

General Terms and Conditions

In addition to the basic provisions, most event contracts will have the general terms and conditions as another section. **Terms and Conditions** can be defined as the consideration and remaining details of the contract. This can include almost anything else not mentioned in the basic provisions and further expansion on the basic provisions. It can be as much or as little as needed. Some things commonly mentioned in terms and conditions sections include items like approval clauses for co-sponsors, cancellation clauses, indemnification agreements, fees and expenses, performance incentives, and buy-out provisions, among a litany of other possibilities. Because of the detail involved in this section, it is common for organizations to put the general terms and conditions of their agreements in a boilerplate. With regard to contracts, a **boilerplate** is the detailed standard wording of the consideration of the contract (e.g., insurance, warranty, rules, and regulations). This section of the contract will remain the same for all clients unless all parties agree to specific changes. Having a boilerplate can make the writing and execution of a contract more efficient and provide a basic organizational structure for the various sections. Having a clear and consistent structure helps both parties understand the terms and ensure that the content order makes logical sense to the reader.

Specific to event management are terms related to event administration, merchandise, food and beverage, promotional rights, and insurance. General business contracts will not have the same types of terms as an event contract, and event managers should be cautious to choose legal counsel with expertise in sports and entertainment. Following are some of the sections that a sport organization may include in the general terms and conditions boilerplate. As with any aspect of contracts, legal counsel should be sought in the generation of a specific contract as well as for contract review.

1. Definition of Terms: Lists and describes certain words that are routinely used in the rest of the contract.

2. License: General statement allowing event organizers access to the facility for the purposes of executing the contract. Some contracts will be more specific than others in this area.

3. Event Administration: Defines which party is responsible for which event management functions.

4. Organization Standard: A statement noting that because of the organization's current positive reputation, a certain standard will be expected for the event, and the party signing the contract agrees to adhere to that standard.

5. Exclusivity: Prohibits those involved in the event from copying the theme and other attributes of the event.

6. Merchandise: Artwork, event logo, and event merchandise development, approval, sales, and revenue sharing process.

7. Food and Beverage: Catering and concessions rights, sales, and revenue sharing agreement.

8. Promotional Rights and Responsibilities: Which party will be responsible for developing and implementing specific promotional aspects, and which party is responsible for paying for them.

9. Reserved Rights: Outlines which party will retain the rights to filming, videotaping, audio recording, photographing, or any other manner of recording, and which party has the right to exploit the material. Both parties may mutually retain these rights rather than just one party retaining them.

10. Sponsorship: Specifies what rights existing sponsors of both parties have, if any. Also specifies what sponsorship sales rights each party has and the revenue sharing of those sales.

11. Right to Photograph: A party's right to take and use photographs of the event for commercial or other purposes, during the contract period and beyond, without paying compensation to the event.

12. Waivers/Consents: Requirements related to whether or not participant waivers are required.

13. Insurance: General liability required limits for the venue user (minimum of $1 million is standard). Workers compensation insurance is also often mentioned here.

14. Indemnification: Prohibits lawsuits between parties involved in the contract and explains legal defense relationships between parties if sued by anyone. Essentially an indemnification agreement is one when a party agrees to indemnify or reimburse another if an anticipated loss occurs.

15. Warranties: Promises made by a seller who may be liable if promises are broken.

16. Force Majeure: Specifies that certain conditions may allow for non-performance of the contract. Conditions generally include those deemed an "act of God" or other conditions out of the control of those involved in the event.

17. Alterations: Notes allowable changes to the venue (e.g., drilling, hanging posters).

18. Risk of Loss: Defines which party is responsible for loss or damage of equipment/personal belongings during the event.

19. Rules and Regulations: States which party has authority to create venue rules.

20. Termination: Describes under what circumstances the event could be cancelled.

21. Joint Venture/Partnership Disclaimer: Disclaimer that the parties entering into the contract do not wish to form a legal formal relationship.

22. Signatory's Warranty: States that the person signing the contract has the authority to do so.

23. Confidentiality: Explains what is confidential and to whom.

24. Governing Law and Waiver of Jury Trial: Specifies which State has jurisdiction over legal proceedings.

25. Entire Agreement: Waiver/Modification: Confirms that the contract replaces any previous agreements and outlines the conditions under which aspects of the contract could be changed.

26. No Offer: Specifies what constitutes the offer (a general discussion between the parties does not constitute an offer).

27. Notice: Provides for the specifics of mail communication (i.e., address on front of contract will be used for mail).

It is apparent from the above list that the general terms and conditions section of a contract covers many aspects of the event. Issues such as merchandising, sponsorship, rules and regulations of the facility, insurance requirements, and confidentiality are all discussed in the boilerplate. Remember, aspects of the basic terms and general terms and conditions can be changed with the consent of both parties. The boilerplate merely provides a structured guide to writing a contract. Signature and date lines will be the last portion of the contract, and oftentimes the signatures must be witnessed by another person or even by a notary public to ensure the signature is valid.

Breach of Contract

Sometimes, intentional or not, certain aspects of the contract are not completed. When this occurs, it is termed **breach of contract**. In the case of unintentional non-completion of a task or term of the contract, the error can be corrected and there is no harm done (Sharp, 2003). However, at other times the breach may cause financial harm, negative publicity, or prevent the full execution of other aspects of the contract. When one party involved in the contract fails to meet the obligations in the contract, one side might be able to claim breach of contract. A legal claim of breach of contract would be made if one party sought to recoup losses and damages via the legal system.

WHY CONTRACTS ARE USED IN EVENT MANAGEMENT

The reason contracts are used in event management is to protect all of those involved. For any sporting or entertainment event, there will be a multitude of groups and individuals that need to be under contract with the host organization or venue (McMillen, 2003). Misunderstandings and miscommunications are avoided though the use of a well-drafted, legally binding contract. Sport events can involve large sums of money, thousands of people, safety concerns, and have many potential pitfalls. Thus, protection through various types of contracts is important. Think about it: If event managers are in charge of an event bringing in thousands of people, they have needs in the area of customer service, security, food and beverage service, logistics, parking, sponsorship, and merchandise. The massive list of what needs to be done, which people need to do it, how it needs to be done, and when it needs to be done can be daunting for new event managers. The use of contracts is one way to ensure that all involved understand their roles and responsibilities.

Besides the who, what, when, and where aspects of contracts related to events, contracts also commonly contain language that provides for legal liability protection for individuals and groups working the event (McMillen, 2003). So, individuals working events should also demand that they receive a contract in writing specifying their formal working relationship with the sport organization and the expectations of the organization. In rare circumstances, breach of contract may occur and the contract will be the primary documentation used by the legal system to determine if there was non-fulfillment of any aspect of the contract and what the remedy will be.

COMMON EVENT MANAGEMENT CONTRACTS

Organizations that enter into contracts for sporting events include vendors, concessionaires, game officials, sponsors, insurance agents, mascots, entertainment, promotional activities, essential personnel, and media (specifically television and radio). There are four main types of contracts that event managers should be familiar with. The type of contract will determine the specific consideration of the contract. These types of contracts are:

- Game Contracts
- Event Contracts
- Venue and Facility Contracts
- Sponsorship Contracts

Game Contracts

A **game contract** (Figure 3-1) is a contractual agreement that arranges a contest or contests between two organizations. The focus of a game contract is on time and place for the game as well as financial considerations. If a **game guarantee** (payment for one team to play another team) is part of the agreement, it will be specified in the contract. Travel (which may include payment for a team to travel to a certain location), housing (which may include some complimentary hotel rooms), officials and officials' pay scales, concessionaires, television and radio broadcast rights, sponsorship exclusivity, potential escape clauses, and breach of contract provisions also will be addressed in a game contract.

For example, it is customary in college athletics to schedule games many years in advance in football, men's basketball, and women's basketball. Rarely does a year go by when institutions are not jockeying for better games with better guarantee payouts, or trying to get out of a game that looked better several years ago when the game contract was agreed upon. Typically, these game contracts have escape clauses or predetermined buyout clauses. Many times the agreement can be terminated by both parties through a mutual release. As always, the devil is in the details. See Figure 3-1 for an example of a game contract.

Event Contracts

Event contracts (Figure 3-2) are very similar to game contracts in that the time and place is paramount. Many times, an event contract will also address an athletic contest between two parties. The key term is the word "event." An event, in a sporting context, can include a contest, a single special event like the Super Bowl, or multiple events like the Olympics or AAU, Inc. Junior Olympics. Event contracts differ from game contracts in that they often include ancillary event stipulations. Ancillary events might include athlete banquets, a related sponsor tailgate, or a concert associated with the main sporting event.

Any special event would apply here. From a local 5K run to a major event, this is where an event contract or several event contracts would apply. Figure 3-2 provides an example of a traveling family show (The Harlem Globetrotters) contract. Not only does the contract address the main event (Harlem Globetrotters), but specific ancillary items are also addressed including an autograph session, and stipulations regarding load in/load out, merchandise, ticketing, marketing, advertising, sponsorships, and insurance.

Venue/Facility Contracts

A **venue or facility contract** (Figure 3-3) is essentially a rental agreement for use of a venue/facility and must be in writing. This would be the same for an apartment or car lease, and the agreement should include the specific terms of the lease including time, length of event, how much rent is to be paid, maintenance, custodial, grounds, security, medical support, and so on. In addition, individuals or groups renting and using a venue for an event usually must present evidence of a certificate of insurance with minimum policy limits (typically a minimum of $1 million of coverage). Even though venue/facility contracts can be specific to the event, many venues use a basic boilerplate contract for almost every group coming into their venue.

The Ohio University Facility Rental Agreement (Figure 3-3), covers all of the above items and is a good example of a standard venue or facility contract. While many venue contracts may have more terms and consideration, this example is sufficient for most any venue or facility rental. Also, the Globetrotter contract (Figure 3-2) example contains some facility contract information within an event contract, and many times these two types of contracts are combined.

Sponsorship Contracts (May Also Include Trade and/or Gift-in-Kind in Lieu of Cash)

A **sponsorship contract** (Figure 3-4) is a legal agreement that binds two or more parties to agreed-upon obligations. This is very similar to the basic definition of a contract. However, the purpose of a sponsorship is one of quid pro quo. **Quid pro quo** means the sponsor will give money, product, and/or services, but expects something in return to benefit the company and provide an effective ROI (Return on Investment) (McMillen, 2003).

Sponsorship contracts can be relatively simple, covering signage, media advertising, and public address announcements. Alternately, they can be extensive and require substantial consideration of both of the parties. A sponsorship contract is not a one-sided relationship. It should be a mutually beneficial partnership in which each organization is helping to activate the sponsorship and work with the other to fulfill its goals. For example, a high-profile naming rights deal like Nationwide Arena in Columbus, Ohio, also includes much more than the name on the arena. Since Nationwide is an insurance company and spent millions of dollars on the rights to have its name on the outside of the arena, it needs to be able to leverage that sponsorship into new business. Most sponsors need leads and sales contacts to generate business and stay ahead of their competitors. The benefits and activation plans agreed to by both parties are geared toward helping the sponsor achieve its goals. See Figure 3-4 for an example of a sponsorship contract.

SUMMARY

The purpose of this chapter was to provide an overview of contracts and contract law specifically applied to the event management industry. Basic contract knowledge is essential in that contracts are a set of promises made in some type of a bargained exchange. A basic contract has four parts: the offer, acceptance, consideration, and capacity. These basic tenets of a contract are also applied in event management through game, event, venue, and sponsorship contracts. These four types of contracts are the primary types used in event management and examples of each type are included following this summary. The sample contracts provided should assist event managers in preparing contracts for future events. Of course, in all contract dealings it is recommended to use legal counsel to make sure the contract passes legal standards and provides for adequate insurance coverage in the event of unforeseen circumstances. As discussed through real-life examples throughout the chapter, well-written contracts are essential to successful event planning and management.

Acknowledgments

Special thanks to the Ohio University Athletic Department, Jason Farmer, Director of Facilities and Operations, Athletic Director Jim Schaus, and Senior Woman Administrator, Amy Dean.

Figure 3-1. Example of a Game Contract

Ohio University
Department of Intercollegiate Athletics
Athens, Ohio 45701
Phone (740) 593-0982 Fax (740) 597-0798

Ohio Athletic Participation Agreement with Visiting Team

This agreement made and entered into this <Insert Date> day of <Insert Date>, <Insert Date> by and between <Insert College/University> ("Visitors") and Ohio University ("Ohio"), by their duly authorized agents:

1) That the teams representing the above named institutions agree to meet in the sport of <Insert Sport>.

2) That each party shall agree in principle to adhere to the rules of the sport of <Insert Sport> in accordance with the terms of this agreement. The game(s) shall be held as set forth below:

   Date (s):   <Insert Game Date>

   Site (s):   <Insert Location/Venue>

   Time (s)   to be determined by host institution

3) That the contest shall be played under eligibility rules of the NCAA.

4) The officials are to be secured by the host institution and the expenses are to be borne by the host institution, unless otherwise stipulated. The Mid-American Conference Office will assign MAC officials for the game scheduled in Athens, OH.

5) That in consideration of playing the above named contest, the host institution shall pay the Visitors in the sum of <Insert Dollar Amount>. The payment of <Insert Dollar Amount> should be paid no later than <Insert Payment Date> .

6) The host institution shall provide <Insert Number of Tickets> complimentary tickets to the Visitors.

   a. The host institution shall extend <Insert Number of Tickets> reserved tickets for the Visitors to purchase on consignment. All unsold tickets must be returned to the host institution no later than fifteen (15) days before the contest. All unsold tickets not returned will result in payment by the Visitors to the host institution.

7) The host institution shall have the exclusive right to sell game programs and operate concessions and parking. All income from game program sales, concessions, and parking shall be the sole property of the host institution.

8) The host institution shall provide a medical doctor and an emergency ambulance to the game site throughout the entirety of the game.

9) The Visitors shall present themselves at the site of the game in condition to play at least sixty (60) minutes before the time set as the starting time of the game.

10) Each party shall have the right to its own radio broadcast of the contest and shall retain all revenue from these broadcasts. Accommodations include press row space for three persons.

11) The host institution shall control all television broadcast rights to the game according to the following, including MAC operations.

   a. If the game is not televised by a national network, the host institution may cause the game to be cablecast on a national/regional cable television network or to be broadcast on an over-the-air television station, and the host institution shall be entitled to retain the negotiated rights fee.

   b. The host school shall retain all television and new media rights for each contest.

   c. Each party shall have the right to produce films and/or video tapes of the game for use in a coach's show or locally originated delayed television broadcast of the game subject to compliance with the rules governing delayed television broadcast by the NCAA or other agencies of which either or both institutions are members. Each party may retain all income received from such commercial opportunities.

   d. The host institution agrees to provide reasonable facilities and production accommodations for the origination of programs herein. The Visitors shall reimburse the host institution for costs associated with and incurred on the Visitors' behalf, or the Visitors will be responsible for such services individually contracted.

   e. Each party shall be solely responsible for payment of any assessments due its own conference or other governing body.

   f. Any discussion regarding the conditions of MAC television products should be directed to the MAC offices.

12) It is recognized that neither party can foresee the exigencies, which may hereafter arise by reason of emergency, catastrophe or epidemic making it necessary or desirable, in sole judgment of the host institution, to cancel this Agreement.

13) If either party, for any reason other than those stated in paragraph 12 above, breaches the Agreement by failing to appear at the time and place scheduled herein for the game, they shall pay liquidated damages in the amount of <Insert Dollar Amount>, unless otherwise agreed upon.

14) This Agreement shall be governed, construed and enforced in accordance with the laws of the state of Ohio, regardless of its place of execution. Any legal action arising under this Agreement shall be brought in a Court of Claims in the State of Ohio.

15) This Agreement is the whole agreement between the two parties with respect to the subject matter hereof and supersedes in all respects all other agreements either written or oral. Any additions or modifications must be in writing and must be signed by both parties.

16) Ohio has a pre-existing agreement that contractually binds Ohio to place and utilize Gatorade-identified cups, coolers, ice chests, squeeze bottles, towels and product ("Branded Items") exclusively within the players' bench area during the event. The Visitor hereby acknowledges Ohio's obligation to exclusively place Branded Items in the Visitors' bench area and agrees that Ohio shall have the right to place such Branded Items at the Visitor's game activities.

The parties hereto by their respective offices duly authorized, have caused this Agreement to be executed as of the day, month, and year first written above.

Ohio University   **College XYZ**

By: _____   **By:** _____

Name: Jim Schaus   **Name:** _____

Title: Director of Athletics   **Title:** _____

Date: _____   **Date:** _____

Please sign both copies and return one to:
Jim Schaus
Director of Athletics
Ohio Athletics
S130 Convocation Center
Athens, Ohio 45701

Figure 3-2. Example of an Event Contract

HARLEM GLOBETROTTERS STANDARD CO-PROMOTION AGREEMENT

This AGREEMENT dated August 6, 2007 by and between **HARLEM GLOBETROTTERS INTERNATIONAL, INC.**, a Nevada corporation, One Arizona, 400 E. Van Buren Street, Suite 300, Phoenix, Arizona, 85004 **("Producer")** and **OHIO UNIVERSITY, ATHENS OHIO 45701 ("Operator")**.

Operator hereby agrees to furnish facilities (the "Arena") for the presentation of a Harlem Globetrotters Basketball Show (the "Performance"), and to make said facilities available to the Producer from 6:00 A.M. until 11:00 P.M. on the Performance date listed below, and Producer hereby agrees to use the Arena, upon and subject to all of the provisions set forth below and attached hereto.

ARENA NAME AND LOCATION: **CONVOCATION CENTER**

**OHIO UNIVERSITY
ATHENS, OHIO 45701
740-593-4666**

PERFORMANCE: **DATE: WEDNESDAY, JANUARY 16, 2008 at 7PM**

NUMBER OF SEATS   Operator certifies that capacity for this performance is **13,000.** If such capacity is reduced following the full execution of this contract, Operator shall reimburse the Producer for the number of the reduced seats at the average ticket price.

TIME LINE:

- **Move In:** Approximately four (4) hours prior to Performance, unless otherwise notified.

- **Globetrotter University:** Operator agrees to open one single entrance, mutually agreeable to both parties, for Globetrotter University will begin approximately thirty (30) minutes prior to doors opening to the general public and last approximately fifteen–twenty (15–20) minutes.

- **Doors Open to General Public: 6pm**; approximately one (1) hour prior to start of Performance.

- **Start of Performance: 7pm**

- **Length of Performance:** Approximately two (2) hours. The performance has four (4) ten (10) minute quarters with a half-time intermission; (occasionally, a running clock may be used during game time).

- Autograph Session: Immediately following game. There shall be an autograph session lasting no more than thirty (30) minutes.

- **Move Out:** Approximately three (3) hours after scheduled start of Performance.

CREDIT CARD FEES: All fees to be paid by operator.

HARLEM GLOBETROTTER SURCHARGE: It is agreed that a **$1.00** surcharge shall be added to the Producer's established ticket price, and added to the gross ticket sales amount. After deduction of all applicable admission taxes, if any, Producer shall receive the remainder. The surcharge is as stated above for each performance and is not subject to change without the prior written consent of Producer. A Surcharge shall not be added on complimentary tickets.

GROUP SALES COMMISSION: All commissions paid for Group Sales must be approved by Producer's Marketing Department and said commissions shall be paid after applicable facility fees and taxes.

ADMISSIONS TAX:

It is agreed by both parties that the following taxes shall be assessed on Gross Ticket Sales only, and deducted from Gross Sales before any and all divisions of Proceeds (as defined below): State- N/A   City-N/A   Other-N/A

Operator shall be responsible for collection and submitting payment for all admission taxes (and other such taxes) and for the filing of any reports and returns with respect thereto. Operator shall hereby indemnify and hold Producer harmless from any and all cost and liability with respect thereto. Operator agrees to furnish to Producer receipts for the payment of all such taxes.

FACILITY FEE: **NONE**

I. DIVISION OF PROCEEDS:

The "Adjusted Gross Admission Proceeds" defined as all proceeds derived from the sale of all tickets, including but not limited to Main Concourse seating, Club Level seating and Mezzanine seating, Sponsorship revenue(as defined in Section VIII), etc., less:

1. Any applicable admission taxes;

2. $1.00 HGI Surcharge as defined above;

3. The advertising, publicity and Group Sales commission and materials expense billed at Net as defined in Section VII;

Shall be divided in accordance with the percentages as set forth below:

Share to Producer	Share to Operator
80%	**20%**

II. MERCHANDISE:

Producer and/or designee, ("Merchandiser"), shall have the exclusive right to furnish and distribute all programs, novelties, and souvenirs, ("Merchandise"), in connection with the Harlem Globetrotters or the Performance(s). Such Merchandise, the nature of which shall be determined at the sole discretion of Producer, shall be the only Merchandise items sold and displayed before, during and after the Performance(s).

1. All Gross proceeds received from the sale of Merchandise, less the payment of sales taxes and credit card fees, shall be called Net Merchandising Proceeds. **Producer** shall retain 100% of the proceeds from said Merchandise

PRODUCER SHALL SELL PRODUCER'S MERCHANDISE

2. Operator shall provide prominent and adequate space for Merchandiser or Concessionaire to vend such Merchandise and Operator agrees that Merchandiser shall, as it may require, have reasonable access to appropriate hall facilities and areas adjacent to the venue.

3. It is understood that the term "Merchandise" as used herein shall not include food, such as hot dogs, burgers or nachos, refreshments, parking or checkroom services.

4. Operator shall retain all proceeds from the sale of food concessions.

III. THE ARENA

A. Operator shall, at its sole expense, furnish the Arena to include the following:

1. Audience seats of a number no less than as specified on the cover page;

2. Facilities, supplies, equipment (including, but not limited to, general house lighting, two (2) spotlights, Jumbotron/video board and Clearcom communication), team dressing room requirements (including, but not limited to, locker room refreshments as specified in the Harlem Globetrotters Technical Rider, and staffing/stagehands (including, but not limited to, a scoreboard operator, a house person to turn house lights off and on, Jumbotron/video operator and two (2) spotlight operators) as specified in the Harlem Globetrotter Technical Rider attached hereto and made part of this Agreement as required for the professional presentation of Producer;

   a. Any items, equipment or staffing/stagehands which Operator cannot supply shall be mutually agreed upon by both parties.

3. 10' X 10' space, in high traffic area, for each of the Producer's sponsors. Producer's sponsors shall not conflict with Operator's sponsors. There shall be no fees or commissions paid to Operator for said space;

4. Storage space in the Arena sufficient for the equipment required for the Performance(s);

5. The Arena and all other facilities included therein, in good, clean and safe condition;

6. Parking for two (2) 40-foot Globetrotters coach-style tour buses, one (1) 25-foot Ryder truck for merchandise and one (1) 25-foot Ryder truck for equipment, as close to artist entrance as possible;

7. A clean professional or collegiate basketball floor, with a 3-point line and professional breakaway rims, permanent and temporary seating, and ample lighting for the presentation of the Performance, installed in a safe and professional manner by Operator, and according to all current industry standards;

8. Full compliance with all applicable governmental statues, regulations, ordinances and codes relating to health, safety, maintenance, fire or otherwise, with respect to the Arena building and any part thereof, any equipment or facility contained therein and any activity carried on therein, whether by Operator or others;

9. Heated and ventilated dressing rooms, audience seating areas, and such other parts of the Arena as may be necessary for the proper comfort of the audience and the performers;

10. All licensed required under any applicable governmental statues, regulations, ordinances or codes with respect to the operation of the Arena and the hosting of the Performance; (excluding rights of music for the Performance)

11. Discharge all obligations imposed on Operator by any federal, state or local law, regulation, ordinance, code or order now or hereafter in force with respect to employees, including, but not limited to, taxes, unemployment compensation or insurance, disability insurance, social security and workers' compensation, and Operator shall

file all returns and reports and pay all assessments, taxes, contributions and other sums required in connection therewith;

12. All personnel, equipment and facilities necessary to adequately safeguard Producer and its employees from thefts of personal property, and any other damage or injury to their person or property;

13. Ushers, door keepers, electricians, ticker sellers, telephone operators, cleaners, watchmen, security guards, firemen, and all other personnel to operate the Arena and to carry out the obligations of Operator under this Agreement;

14. Conform to, comply with and abide by all applicable labor or collective bargaining agreements to which Producer and/or Operator are or may become a party, as the same now exist or may be amended; and

15. Reimburse Producer for fees and expenses which may be incurred by Producer as a result of Operator's default or failure to provide any of the foregoing.

B. Operator shall not permit the use of the Arena, or any part thereof, for the presentation of any basketball exhibition for a period of eight weeks prior to the Performance and six weeks subsequent to the Performance and warrants and represents that no such presentation will be made. A professional league, collegiate, high school or local amateur basketball game shall not be considered a basketball exhibition.

IV. HARLEM GLOBETROTTERS INTERNATIONAL, INC.

A. As between Producer and Operator, Producer retains sole and exclusive ownership and control of all of the properties, materials and rights of Harlem Globetrotters International, Inc. and any other third party marks used by the Harlem Globetrotters in connection with its basketball exhibitions, including certain service marks, trademark registrations and attendant goodwill relating to, inter alia, the unique entertainment services in the nature of basketball exhibitions performed in the United States and the world(such marks including, but not limited to the following registered trademarks: "Harlem Globetrotters," "Globetrotters," "Magicians of Basketball," "Magic Circle," and "Globie") and certain designs, characters, symbols, logos, musical renditions, likenesses and visual representations heretofore used in connection with said marks. Operator is licensed to use the aforesaid marks and the names and likenesses of the performers only during the period beginning with the group sales and/or advertising campaign through **January 16, 2008** and to the event expressly authorized by Producer.

B. The Arena shall insure that the Performance(s) shall not, in whole or in part, be recorded or carried by any mean outside the Arena, without the prior, written consent of Producer, except for bona fide news coverage.

C. If Producer authorizes broadcast coverage, phonograph or tape recordings, motion pictures or other commercial tie-ups of the Performance(s) hereunder, any and all proceeds therefrom shall belong to Producer.

D. The "Magic Circle" shall not be video taped, filmed or broadcast by anyone other than Producer. There shall be no exceptions.

E. The rights to any and all audio and/or visual transmission, reproduction or recording of the Performance in the Arena, or any part thereof, shall be the sole and exclusive property of the Producer, whether the same be for simultaneous, in-house or subsequent use, except for bona fide news coverage by local media as set forth in Section III.B. above.

VI. SALE OF TICKETS

A. **Printing.** Operator shall, prior to the commencement of the advanced sale of tickets, and subsequent to mutual determination by Operator and Producer of ticket prices and locations:

1. Cause to be printed tickets for all audience seats in the Arena or arrange for sale of tickets through a computers ticket service, and

2. Furnish to Producer a certified printer's manifest or a certified computer program manifest of all tickets, together with a summary showing the number of seats at each price for each Performance.

B. **Sale.**

1. Prior to the Performance:

   a. Producer shall solely determine a date to place tickets for the Performance(s) on sale and Operator shall from that time until the end of the Performance furnish the facilities and personnel (including box offices, ticket sellers, telephone lines and operators) required for the proper sale of tickets at the Arena and at such other places as may customarily be utilized by the Operator for such purposes.

   b. The box office at the Arena shall remain open at least six(6) hours per day during normal box office hours, including the last seven (7) days leading up to the day of the Performance, and must be open for business from 10:00 AM through halftime of the Performance. **Normal box office hours shall be: Day(s) Time.**

   c. On weekends and holidays, Operator shall designate hours of operation at the box office for those days and make tickets available to the public during those times. If Operator is unable to perform this function, they must notify Producer in writing at signing of Agreement.

   d. Operator will insure that ticket information will be readily available to the public by supplying adequate telephone lines and operators during the time the box office is open.

   e. Operator shall provide sufficient ticket sellers in a sufficient number to properly service the public two (2) hours prior and throughout each Performance.

2. Operator shall furnish Producer with complete daily reports of tickets sold and other ticket sales information beginning the say after Performance tickets have gone on sale. Ticket sales information shall include such information as ticket outlet, telephone/credit card, discount and cumulative ticket sales.

3. Immediately after each Performance, Operator shall furnish Producer with a complete report showing the number of tickets sold and unsold, complimentary tickets issued for said Performance, and all other information relevant to the proceeds from the sale of tickets for said Performance, including a box count of all tickets collected for said Performance, and shall at such time have all unsold tickets available for inspection by Producer. Operator shall grant Producer approval to directly access TicketMaster for all ticket sales pertaining to Harlem Globetrotters International.

4. All ticket sales and/or box office reports are **public records under Ohio law.**

C. **Gross Admission Proceeds.** Gross Admission Proceeds as used herein is defined as all proceeds derived from the sale of tickets and local sponsorship revenue (as defined in Section VIII(B)), including applicable taxes and excluding any facility fees, parking, concessions, and merchandise, etc. shall not be included in the Gross Admission Proceeds. Operator shall be responsible for the collection of all monies and proceeds of sale of tickets, including Main Concourse seating, Club Level seating and Mezzanine seating and shall, at its own expense:

1. Bond all ticket sellers and other persons handling such monies and proceeds of an amount sufficient to cover the value of the monies and proceeds handled by them, and

2. Insure such monies and proceeds against all other risks which might result in a loss thereof. The Gross Admission Proceeds shall be a confidential matter between Producer and Operator and this information shall not be disclosed to any unauthorized individual(s) without the written consent of the other part.

3. In addition to above, Gross Admission Proceeds does/does not include all Suite sales which represents a total of n/a ticket and a total of Suites.

D. **Complimentary Tickets.**

1. Operator shall set aside for the exclusive use of Producer's Team Tour Manager sixty (60) complementary seats for each Performance at the highest prices **(shall not be MAGIC CIRCLE COURTSIDE seats)** located behind the Harlem Globetrotters player's bench. The specific location of these seats must be approved by Producer.

2. Operator shall set aside for the exclusive use of Harlem Globetrotters Corporate Office sixty (60) complimentary seats for each Performance at the highest prices **(shall not be MAGIC CIRCLE COURTSIDE seats)** located in the Center Section. The specific location of these seats must be approved by Producer.

3. Operator shall honor all written requests for complimentary tickets by Producer. In addition Operator shall honor all official complimentary ticket coupons used in Producer's advertising, promotional campaign, and sponsorship ticket requirement.

4. **MAGIC CIRCLE COURSIDE and VIP tickets shall not be issued or used as complimentary, discounted or Group Sales tickets without the express written consent of the Producer.** MAGIC CIRCLE COURTSIDE ad VIP tickets issued without the express written consent of the Producer shall be deemed paid admissions valued at the manifested ticket price per ticket for the purpose of computing the Gross Admissions Proceeds to the Performance hereunder.

5. Trade tickets used in the Advertising, Publicity & Group Sales campaign must be approved by Producer's Marketing Department prior to distribution.

6. Operator will be entitled to the following number of complimentary tickets: <u>One percent (1%) of manifested seating capacity.</u> Such complimentary tickets **shall not include Magic Circle or VIP tickets** without written approval of Producer. Accurate records and accounting of these complimentary tickets shall be provided by Operator to Producer at the time of settlement.

E. **Records and Inspection.** Operator shall maintain full and complete accounting and other records with respect to the sale of tickets and the proceeds thereof and Producer and accountants of Producer shall have the right at all reasonable times to examine all such records or to verify the program of the computer ticket service. Throughout the duration of this Agreement and for a period not exceeding six (6) months following the completion of the Performance Producer or it's authorized representatives shall have the right to audit any and all accounting and other records relating to this Agreement including, but not limited to, box office and admission proceeds, unsold tickets, the drop count, any and all other ticket proceeds, advertising expenses and agreements, and admission taxes. Such right to audit may be exercised upon reasonable notice to the Operator.

VII. ADVERTISING, PUBLICITY & GROUP SALES

A. The advertising, publicity and Group Sales budget shall be mutually agreed upon at Net by the Producer and the Operator. "Net" is hereby defined as the gross advertising, publicity and Group Sales material expense, less any media commission, Group Sales commission and any marketing company's fee or commission,. The budget shall itemize advertising expense, publicity/advance ambassador expenses, and Group Sales material expenses. Any media commission, group sales commission, any marketing company's fee or any other commission shall not be included in the budget and shall be at the sole expense of the Operator.

B. With respect to the billing of advertising, publicity and Group Sales material expense, all advertising, publicity and Group Sales material expense shall be billed at Net. All such billing shall be completed at the offices of the Operator (or Arena) and Operator (or Arena) shall draw and issue checks for all such media expenses without any commission resulting there from being billed to Producer.

C. Operator shall, at its sole cost and expense, unless specified in Division of Proceeds on Page 3, provide for an advertising, publicity, and Group Sales campaign billed at Net for the Performance(s) under the supervision of Producer and shall, in connection with said campaign, expend no more or no less than the amount mutually agreed upon, between Producer and Operator, without the prior written consent of Producer. Twelve weeks prior to the Performance, Operator shall furnish Producer with proposed budget allocations of advertising, publicity, and Group Sales expenses. Detailed schedules of newspaper advertisements, radio and television commercials shall be furnished to Producer not less than eight weeks in advance of the first Performance. The campaign shall commence at least four weeks prior to the first Performance at the Arena and shall continue through the date of the last Performance.

D. The objective of the campaign shall be to attain the greatest possible amount of ticker sales for the Performance(s) at the Arena using various forms of advertising media, including radio and television broadcasting, outdoor and transit advertising, and newspapers of general circulation. Operator shall utilize the advertising and promotional materials, designs and forms designated by Producer without modification and shall use no other advertising or promotional materials, designs and forms without the prior written consent of Producer. Production costs incurred by Operator for radio, television newspaper or other advertising materials shall not be included in the advertising or publicity expenses unless otherwise agreed by Producer. The campaign shall feature the name "Harlem Globetrotters." Producer shall furnish Operator with advertising ad promotional materials prior to the Performance. Such materials shall include a press kit and one set of photographs of performers.

E. Any promotional materials or merchandise that Producer and Operator deem appropriate to the campaign shall be paid for according to the Producer's price schedule. Operator shall not utilize the advertising and promotional materials, designs and forms designated by Producer subsequent to the advertising campaign without the prior written consent of Producer.

F. With respect to Magic Circle Courtside seating in the Arena for the event hereunder there shall be no promotional item ("Premium") with the purchase of a Magic Circle Courtside admission ticket.

VIII. SPONSORSHIP(S)

A. All sponsorship revenue derived from any designated local sponsor(s) secured by operator and or producer shall be shared by adding said sponsorship revenue to the gross admission proceeds prior to its division.

B. If operator obtains sponsorship revenue from a single local sponsor, operator shall be entitled to receive a commission of 20% of said sponsorship revenue. The remainder of the sponsorship funds shall be added to Gross Admission Proceeds prior to division. In no other instance shall the Operator or Producer be entitled to any other fee or commission with respect to sponsorship revenue.

C. Any expense associated with sponsorship agreements such as, but not limited to, banners, floor decals, pre/post game parties shall be included in advertising, publicity and Group Sales materials expense budget and deducted from the Gross Admission Proceeds.

D. Producer shall retain one hundred percent (100%) of any sponsorship revenue derived from any regional, national, and international, corporate sponsor(s) secured solely by Producer.

E. Producer shall be allowed to display any of the Producer's regional, national, and international sponsors' banners, and/or signage in the Arena during the performance, at Producer's press conferences, and at events promoting performance(s). Also, Operator shall supply, upon request, a 10' x 10' space, in a high traffic area, for each of the Producers' sponsors. Producer's sponsors shall not conflict with Operator's sponsors. There shall be no fees or commissions paid to Operator for said space.

F. Producer must approve in writing all local sponsors secured by Operator. In addition Producer must approve in writing the use and placement of all logos and the copy of local sponsors in all advertising for the Performance.

IX. ADA

Operator ids responsible for the compliance with Title II of the Americans with Disabilities Act of 1990 or as amended and all regulations thereunder as they shall or may relate to permanent Arena access accommodations such as, but not limited to, wheelchair ramps, elevator standards, door width standards, and restroom accessibility. In addition, Operator should be prepared to respond to reasonable request for auxiliary aids from patrons with disabilities and shall bear the financial cost of providing auxiliary aids such as assistive listening device rental, readers, and interpreters.

X. INSURANCE AND INDEMNIFICATION

Thirty (30) days prior to the Performance, Operator shall provide Producer with certificate(s) of insurance evidencing that insurance policies covered by this paragraph are with an insurance company recognized as an authorized carrier in the state where the Arena is located, and acceptable to Producer.

Said certificate(s) and policy shall be in a form and content satisfactory to Producer, which shall:

1. Provide Commercial General Liability having a combined single limit (bodily injury, property damage and personal injury) of at least $1,000,000.00 per occurrence ($2,000,000.00 aggregate);

2. Provide Workers' Compensation insurance coverage and Employer's Liability for Operator's employees;

3. Specify as additional insureds; **Harlem Globetrotters International, Inc.**;

4. Indemnify and hold Producer harmless **in accordance with Ohio law if possible** during the term of this Agreement from any and all claims, demands, judgments, losses and expenses, including reasonable attorney's fees, which may be made against Producer and which is in an y way related to the Arena or to the Performance in the Arena, except those claims which may arise through the negligence of the Producer or its employees;

5. To the extent not covered by insurance, Operator shall and does hereby indemnify and hold Producer harmless **in accordance with Ohio law** from and against any loss, damage, cost or expense arising out of or in any way related to Producer's occupancy of the premises or use of the Arena (except in any case where such loss, damage, cost or expense is caused by the negligence of the Producer or its employees);

6. When timely requested, Producer shall furnish to the Operator or facility a certificate of insurance evidencing a policy of comprehensive general liability insurance having limits not to exceed a combined single limit of $1,000,00.00 per occurrence, ($2,000,000.00 aggregate) which will name Operator as additional insured thereunder, but only or liability arising out of the negligence of the Producer its agents, servants, licensees or employees with respect to the operations of Producer in the Arena.

7. It is agreed that neither of the parties shall be deemed to have accepted the obligation of the other, whether by reason of loss hereunder or otherwise. Producer and Operator agree to assume responsibility for its own negligence in situations involving joint negligence. It is not intended that Producer assumer protection for sole negligence on the part of the Operator or vice-versa.

XI. GENERAL

A. Operator and Producer each represent and warrant to the other that they have full right and power to enter into and perform this Agreement according to its terms.

B. Neither party to this Agreement shall be liable to the other for nay failure to perform any of the terms or conditions of this Agreement which is attributable to war, an act of God, a strike, a lockout, or any other cause beyond the control of such party.

C. This Agreement shall remain binding and in full force and effect and constitutes the entire understanding between the parties and supersedes all prior and contemporaneous written or oral agreements pertaining thereto and can only be modified by a writing signed on behalf of both parties hereto. This Agreement shall be governed by and construed in accordance with the laws of the state of **Ohio** applicable to contracts entered into and fully performed therein. In the event of any breach, termination or cancellation of this Agreement by Producer, Operator's sole and exclusive remedy shall be an action at law for damages. Operator hereby waives any right to seek and/or obtain rescission and/or equitable and/or injunctive relief.

D. Neither this Agreement nor nay of the duties, obligations or rights hereunder may be assigned by either of the parties hereto without the express written consent of the other, provided that Producer may at any time this Agreement, and all or any part of its rights hereunder, to any person, firm, or corporation controlling, controlled by or under a common control with Producer or with which Producer may be merged or consolidated.

E. The delay or failure of either party to asset or exercise any right, remedy or privilege hereunder, with actual or constructive notice or knowledge of the breach of any representation, warranty or provision herein, shall not constitute a waiver of any such right, remedy, privilege or breach. No waiver shall in any even be effective unless in writing, and then it shall be effective only in the specific instance for which given.

F. This Agreement shall inure to the benefit of and be binding upon Producer and Operator and their respective successors and assigns.

G. The Arena and facilities being furnished by Operator to Producer pursuant to this Agreement are of a special, unique and extraordinary character and accordingly in the event of a default, threatened default or cancellation by Operator under this Agreement, Producer shall be entitled, in addition to any other remedies it may have, to equitable relief by way of injunction, specific performance or otherwise.

H. Nothing herein contained shall constitute a partnership between or joint venture by the parties hereto, or constitute either party the agent of the other. Neither party shall hold itself out contrary to the terms of this paragraph, and neither party shall become liable of the representation, act or omission of the other contrary to the provisions hereof. This Agreement is not for the benefit of any third party and shall not be deemed to give any right or remedy to any third party, whether referred to herein or not.

I. This instrument shall be and become a binding Agreement when executed by authorized officials of Producer and Operator and until then shall have no force or effect.

J. If language in this agreement conflicts with any agreement provided by the Operator, the language in Harlem Globetrotters Standard Co-Promotion Agreement shall govern.

SPECIAL CONDITIONS:

1. **Operator pays all other direct game related expenses.**

2. **HARLEM GLOBETROTTERS TECHNICAL RIDER shall be attached to, or otherwise made a part of, the Harlem Globetrotters Standard Co-Promotion Agreement.**

ACCEPTED AND AGREED:

OPERATOR:
CONVOCATION CENTER GLOBTROTTERS
OHIO UNIVERISTY:

By: _____

PRODUCER:
HARLEM
INTERNATIONAL, INC.:

By: _____

Figure 3-3. Example of a Venue Contract

FACILITY RENTAL AGREEMENT

This facility rental agreement is entered into between Ohio University Department of Intercollegiate Athletics (hereinafter, Ohio) and

(hereinafter, Lessee) under the following terms and conditions:

1. Beginning Date: _____   Concluding Date: _____
   Purpose of Activity: _____

2. Person in Charge: _____
   Phone: _____   Email: _____

Ohio agrees that Lessee shall have use of the during the time and for the purpose listed above. No alcohol may be sold, given away, or consumed on Ohio property during the Lessee's use of said facility.

Ohio agrees to make the following arrangements on behalf of Lessee:

Special Arrangements: _____

_____

_____

_____

The Ohio athletic department reserves the right to charge for parking. If this process is instituted for the event, the Ohio athletic department will make all arrangements and benefit from the proceeds.

In consideration for said use of Ohio's facilities, the Lessee agrees to pay Ohio the following charges:

$ _____ Rental
$ _____ Maintenance Support
$ _____ Custodial Support
$ _____ Grounds Support
$ _____ Video Board Rental/Production
$ _____ Event Manager (from Ohio staff)

Lessee agrees to provide upon request of Ohio a public liability insurance policy, in which, Ohio University, its trustee directors, officers, employees, agents, and contractors are named as insurers, and an acceptable Certificate of Insurance, with minimum policy limits of:

- $1,000,000 for injuries, including death, sustained by one person.
- $2,000,000 for injuries, including death, sustained by two or more persons from a single occurrence.
- $500,000 for property damage.

Lessee indemnifies and holds harmless Ohio from any and all claims, demands, actions, liabilities, and attorney fees arising out of, claimed on account of, or in death of, and all persons whatsoever, in any manner caused or contributed to by the Lessee while in, upon, or about the property and/or facility, or while going to or departing from the same.

Any property of Ohio damaged or destroyed by the Lessee incident to the exercise of privileges herein granted shall be promptly prepared or replaced by the Lessee to the satisfaction of Ohio, or in lieu of such repair or replacement, the Lessee shall, if so required, pay to Ohio money in the amount sufficient to compensate for the loss sustained by Ohio.

In occupying the building, property, and/or grounds at the site/facility, the Lessee understands that Ohio does not relinquish the right to control the management thereof, and to enforce all necessary laws, rules, and regulations.

All labor, administrative fees, maintenance, and services not specifically mentioned, but required for the execution of the Lessees' event shall be secured by Ohio and be considered reimbursable costs payable to Ohio by Lessee. Make check payable to the Ohio Athletics Department.

Lessee shall not discriminate in any manner whatsoever on the basis of race, sex, creed, national origin, age, handicap, or sexual preference and shall only use the stated facility for lawful purposes.

This Facility Rental Agreement is neither assignable nor transferable by the Lessee. Ohio reserves the right to determine facility and/or property usage and playability.

In witness whereof, the parties hereto have executed this Facility Rental Agreement on this _____ day of _____, 2008.

_____

Director of Athletics

Lessee:

By _____

_____
Signed By

Figure 3-4. Sample Sponsorship Contract

Offer to the sponsor (Sponsor Redacted)

Video Board Feature $7,000

Entitlement of one (1) exclusive video board feature per game.

Opportunity beings with 2009 season.

Game Day Promotion at Home Football Stadium $2,000

Opportunity to sponsor Exclusive Day at Home Football Games
<INSERT DATES>

Promotion includes table in the North end zone, ability to distribute materials, exit couponing for upcoming events, and ability to showcase products.
Includes opportunity for Company Trivia at game in which we would take one fan and ask them a multiple choice question about your business animal OR PA announcer could read a Company Trivia Question to all fans and encourage them to submit their answer to the Company table in the endzone.
Successful fan would win a gift from the Company
Also includes two (2) PA announcements during the game

Game Day Promotion at Home Basketball Arena $2,750

Opportunity to sponsor Company Day at Home Basketball Games

Promotion includes table in the concourse, ability to distribute materials, exit couponing for upcoming events and ability to showcase Product.

Includes opportunity for Company Trivia at game in which we would take one fan and ask them a multiple choice question about Company animal OR PA announcer could read a Company Trivia Question to all fans and encourage them to submit their answer to the Company table in the endzone. Successful fan would win a gift from the Company.

Also includes two (2) PA announcements during the game

Video Board Feature $3,000

Entitlement of one (1) exclusive video board feature per game – Company Trivia

Coupon Book $1,000

One (1) ad in 20,000 coupon books to be distributed in at <INSERT DATE> football game and distributed in all football season tickets. Artwork deadline <INSERT DATE>.

Football Game Program $1,500

One (1) half page, black and white program ad
Circulation of 1,000 at each game

Basketball Season Yearbook   **$1,000**

One (1) half page, black and white program ad

Circulation of 2,000 per season

TERMS AND CONDITIONS

1. This proposal is effective through <INSERT DATE>, or until described inventory is sold.

2. The term of this agreement shall be from <INSERT DATES>. Neither party shall have rights defined in this agreement after contract expiration.

3. Payment terms

   CASH:

   BILLING TERMS: Net due upon receipt of invoice. Late payment(s) are subject to interest charges of 1.5% per month (18% APR).

4. In the event that the Company produces a football bowl guide, sponsor would have the choice to participate in the publication at the rate of $1,000 for a full-page ad each year of this agreement. Sponsor will have the opportunity to change the artwork for the football bowl program ad.

5. As used herein, Sponsor includes any successor in interest thereto. This contract is non-cancelable.

6. This agreement is governed by the laws of the state of Ohio.

ACCEPTED AND AGREED:

Sponsor
Anytown University

Phone:
Fax:
By: _____
        Jane Doe
        Vice President

Date: _____
        Company
        107 Main Street
        Anytown, USA

Phone:

By: _____
        John Doe
        General Sales Manager

Date: _____

Phone:
Fax:

Payment Remittance Address:
University Sponsorship Inc.
PO Box 1000
Anytown, USA

Student Challenge

STUDENT CHALLENGE #3

In Challenge #3, prepare an event contract and examine the other contract needs of the event.

QUESTION 3-1

Prepare the Basic Provisions section of an event contract for the event. As discussed in Chapter 3, contracts are an essential piece of planning an event. Begin by re-examining the Basic Provisions described in the chapter; use the responses to Challenge #1 and Challenge #2 to determine specifics of the event contract. Use the space provided to brainstorm and take notes on the contract necessities and then type up the contract using one of the formats provided as an example in this chapter.

Basic Provisions:

Student Challenge

QUESTION 3-2

What other contracts will have to be executed for the event to be successful? First, identify the types of contracts needed and then explain why each contract is needed. Finally, note any important areas that should be addressed in the contract.

* Note: Specifics related to media, marketing, sponsorships, participant waivers, and equipment will be discussed later in this book, but consider these areas when completing this challenge.

Contract Type #1:
  Why:

  Special Notes:

Contract Type #2:
  Why:

  Special Notes:

Contract Type #3:
  Why:

  Special Notes:

Contract Type #4:
  Why:

  Special Notes:

Contract Type #5:
  Why:

  Special Notes:

CHAPTER 4

TECHNOLOGY AND EVENT PLANNING

Michael Pfahl

Technology can serve the event-planning process in many different ways. The purpose of this chapter is to provide a set of thought-provoking issues related to a variety of technologies and the process of planning an event. As discussed in Chapter 1, an event can be recurring, traveling, mega, or ancillary; and the types of events that fall within each of these areas vary by size, scope, and purpose. To address this variation, a set of key conceptual areas are introduced that cover technology issues that should be addressed regardless of the size, duration, or purpose of an event. In other words, if event planners examine their event in light of these technology issues, they will be able to select and implement appropriate technologies for their needs. To borrow an old motorsport term, the event planners will use the right *horses for courses*.

The individuals who participate in events are as varied as the events themselves. Thus, it is also important for event planners to remember that the technologies and ideas discussed in this chapter are subject to a person's ability to use the technologies in meaningful ways. As discussed in Chapter 2, universal design, as it relates to technology and event planning, goes beyond making user interfaces simpler for individuals and takes into account the multiple ways individuals experience an event or event Web site (e.g., visual, audio) in order to be as inclusive as possible for people of different abilities and cultures. The event itself can provide alternative means of delivering information (e.g., materials on CD). Technology, then, is not a solution in and of itself, but requires thoughtful planning to achieve desired goals and objectives.

This chapter presents four key areas that apply to technology usage in event planning: information dissemination (external), information management (internal), monetization/promotion, and entertainment/education. Each of these sections will be examined in detail, and examples will be used to illustrate how certain technologies can be utilized across a variety of different events.

INFORMATION DISSEMINATION (EXTERNAL)

Creating, disseminating, and evaluating messages about an event is a critical component in any marketing plan. **Information dissemination** reflects the ways in which different technologies can help to promote an event and its message (e.g., marketing plan), in addition to sponsors, partners, and just about anything else the planners want to have people know about their event. This section will examine several important areas to consider when deciding upon technological means to disseminate information about an event: Web sites, text messaging, media centers/media interactions, question and answer availability, and registration.

Web Sites

One of the most common information sources in the world today is the Web site. A **Web site** is a portal of information, multimedia, and interaction that allows users accessibility to its contents around the clock and around the world. This may be the first interaction a potential participant or spectator has with the event and will leave a lasting impression. Preparing a Web site requires as much preparation regarding message and marketing issues as it does technical issues. Please see Table 4-1 for foundational issues in Web site development.

Table 4-1. Issues in Web Site Development

Issues	Examples
Event information	History, sponsors/partners/charities, previous year or event information, electronic newsletters.
Attendance information	Registration, admissions, and ticketing information including rules and regulations.
Calendar of events	Relevant days and times of the event program.
Media interactions	Information area for media members.
Multimedia	Interactive points including video, photographs, and others.
Travel and destination information	Travel and direction information including event maps.
Sponsors and/or partners	Sponsors and partners (if charitable event, list partner charities).
Merchandise	Merchandise (if applicable).
Safety and security issues	All relevant safety and security information, forms, etc.
Multicultural awareness	Sensitivity to language and images used at the site.
Contact information	Contact information for key event personnel.
Technical issues	Server location, capacity, and performance
	Technical support types, levels, and contact information.

Exactly how these elements are utilized will vary by event. However, including each provides a well-rounded Web site that is informational and educational for interested parties as well as participants.

In addition to these event-based points, it is important to remember to give the design and layout of the Web site proper consideration. These **design issues** are the areas of the Web site evaluated for ease of use and usefulness to visitors. To the greatest extent possible, universal design issues must be addressed when designing a Web site. User interaction with the Web site should encourage exploration while informing and entertaining visitors. As with the foundational Web site elements described earlier, Table 4-2 shows the key points regarding a user's experience to remember during the Web site design process.

Table 4-2. User Experience Issues in Web Site Design

Issues	Examples
Aesthetics	Color schemes (e.g., complimentary, contrasting), font sizes (small versus large), images (e.g., photographs, advertisements).
Data collection points	Registration for contests, the event, or information (e.g., text message alerts). Manage this carefully, because too much will distract a visitor and too little will leave the event organizers with a lack of participant and/or visitor information.
Multimedia	Presentation and issues related to opening and viewing the files, such as time for a file to load (from click to play).
	Information load time for files (e.g., PDF), downloads (e.g., wallpapers), and HTML documents.
Sponsors and/or partners	Placement and utilization of sponsor and partner advertising or images (e.g., top, bottom, left side, right side, skyscrapers, banner ads, above or below the *fold* of the page).
Languages	Making the Web site available in different languages to reach the broadest possible audience.
User accessibility	Allowing most or the entire Web site to be read aloud by computer software.
Evaluative criteria	Analytical instrument to assess the success of these and other factors included on the Web site.

Table 4-3. Sample Evaluative Criteria Scale

Site layout	Poor	1	2	3	4	5	Excellent
Ease of use	Difficult	1	2	3	4	5	Easy
Experience	Poor	1	2	3	4	5	Excellent
Return to site in future?	Unlikely	1	2	3	4	5	Likely
Usefulness to fans	Not useful	1	2	3	4	5	Useful
Usefulness to media	Not useful	1	2	3	4	5	Useful

As shown in Table 4-2, an important aspect of design is evaluative criteria to determine the usability of a Web site, its interactivity levels, or any other relevant criteria. The evaluative criteria scale is a self-check instrument used by designers (and non-designers if desired) to establish points of success, failure, strength, and areas for improvement. An example of an evaluative criteria scale used to assess the Web site is shown in Table 4-3.

By taking a multileveled approach to Web site design, event planners can maximize the impact of their event and event messages by making a site user friendly and useful. A well-designed Web site will address visitor and participant concerns in a proactive manner, which should lead to a more pleasant event experience for the participants and more organized planning and implementation process for the planners.

Text Messaging

The ubiquitous cell phone can also be used to keep interested parties and participants up-to-date with current information. A potential sponsorship or partnership opportunity exists as a cell phone provider can work with event planning staff to configure a network text messaging service that will send updated information to registered users. Interested individuals can text a pre-arranged number, code, or word(s) to a phone number or register at an event's Web site. Once the network has been configured and parties registered, the event planners can send mass text messages at little cost and effort. One benefit of such a strategy is the valuable information (e.g., telephone numbers, names) gained from the registration process, which can be used for other purposes, including any future event marketing campaigns, for example.

Key to the success of this activity is that it remains easy to subscribe and is offered at no cost to the subscribers. If desired, the event planners or subscribers can set a fixed number of text messages that can be sent/received per day, week, or month. Fully disclosed terms and conditions should be included as part of the registration process. Finally, information to subscribers should have a clear description of how a person can cancel the subscription at any time. Bombarding individuals with messages should not be the goal of a text message information opportunity. Rather, the event planners can utilize this technology as a way to enhance the individual's event experience.

As stated earlier, such an activity lends itself to a strong sponsorship or partnership opportunity. While the process of obtaining a sponsor is explained in Chapter 7, a later section in this chapter will highlight the importance of such relationships to an event and the planners' ability to maximize technology-based opportunities.

Media Centers/Media Interactions

The members of the media should receive special attention from event planners, especially in relation to developing Web-based information areas. A **media center** is a special section on the Web site and a centrally located physical site at an event that seeks to provide maximum information to all members of the media. The more information the media has about an event's story, the easier it will be for them to cover it.

On the event's Web site, there are several potential strategies that can be used to interact with the media. Some organizations simply provide information (e.g., game notes, media releases) as PDF downloads or HTML text. In these cases, there is not a specific *media* section, but the entire Web site serves to inform.

Another strategy is to have a separate section for media members. The Phoenix Suns of the National Basketball Association (www.nba.com/suns) group all of their media and public relations communication information in one media center location. Included here are PDF files and HTML text of public relations, basketball communications, media guide, and media release information (Phoenix, 2009). Also included are the names, telephone numbers, and email addresses for public relations staff, including the director.

However, some organizations take their relationship with the media to another level. Vodafone McLaren Mercedes (www.mclaren.co.uk), a team competing in Formula One, has a special section for the media requiring registration in order to gain additional access to the team and its members. The team utilizes electronic forms for both print media and Web media (McLaren, 2009) and, once registered, a login and password are required for access.

The online media center should receive the same attention to structural development and design issues as the overall Web site. A well-designed media campaign will fail if the media have difficulty accessing information regarding an event. An important issue that can sometimes be overlooked is to have contact information for relevant event staff available for the media members. With some teams and events utilizing a Web site as a media offering, they neglect to post information for public relations staff or other parties who would be of interest to the media. While it is understood that these individuals should not have to be in constant contact with anyone that has a question about the team, the media members will need this information. In the McLaren example, this information can only be accessed by registered members of the media. Events that do not wish to include a dedicated media section must provide for some method of contact with the media.

At the event itself, it is important to have a designated area for media members. At high profile events such as collegiate and professional sporting events, media areas are clearly defined. In some instances, full broadcast studios have been constructed in arenas and stadiums in recent years. Conversely, in non-traditional venues (or traditional venues without full studios), broadcast equipment is brought in by truck or created on site (e.g., live reports). Events of smaller size and/or local scope also need to take a similar approach to media member management, just on a smaller scale. The size of the event will have a significant impact on the technology needed at a site. The technology expectations for a media area include a power supply (and backup), Internet access (as available) via T1 lines or wireless access, security, and a support presence in the form of an event staff member or outside organization members who can address technical difficulties that might arise.

Question and Answer Availability

Participants of an event or curious visitors should be able to access information relating to the event in a number of different ways. Sometimes merely providing information on a Web site, even a regularly updated one, is not enough. **Question and answer availability** speaks to the different ways in which questions and concerns can be directed to event planning staff. Addressing the questions or concerns in a timely and accurate manner helps to build goodwill. However, event planners should only employ such a system if they believe they can afford it and manage it properly (e.g., reply to questions in an accurate and timely manner). The Web site can be an effective means of gathering and addressing questions, but there are also other methods of interacting with the public, including instant messaging, text messaging, and Twitter.

Web sites

Many Web sites provide information regarding **frequently asked questions (FAQs)**. Here, common questions are listed in a section of the Web site along with answers to those questions. By providing information in this manner, event planners are able to minimize the number of repetitive inquiries and focus their attention on questions that are individualized or might take greater time to answer. In addition, all forms required for the event can be listed in one section. The forms can be organized by type to help visitors quickly identify and utilize relevant information, especially related to health, legal, and religious needs. These forms can be hyperlinked, placed in downloadable PDF files, or both.

Web sites can also include form templates that allow visitors to enter questions and provide different types of contact information. A standard form would include space for name, email, telephone number, mailing address, and a section to enter the question or comment. Many professional team Web sites have posted guidelines as to how to use their feedback forms (usually found under a *Contact Us* link) and assistance in determining to which department the information should be directed.

Q&A with the Montreal Canadiens

The Montreal Canadiens of the National Hockey League inform visitors who wish to contact them to "Help us help you! Please take a moment to review the 'Guidelines' section below so your request is treated in a prompt manner. Failure to direct your inquiry to the proper department may cause needless delays in your obtaining a response" (Montreal Canadiens, 2009 ¶ 2). In addition to mailing address information, telephone directories, and their Web form, the team also includes detailed accounts of which departments handle which inquiries. An example of this is the department that handles booking the ice for private events; "Ice rentals— *Help with booking the Bell Centre ice for such programs as 'Habs for a Day', 'Young Canadiens', 'The All-Star Game Experience', and 'The Corporate Canadiens Hockey Experience'*" (italics in original; Montreal Canadiens, 2009, ¶ 8). Not only does the team help visitors better direct their questions or comments so that they can be acted upon more quickly, but they also provide an additional marketing message for this special opportunity and the types of events offered.

Instant messaging

Instant messaging (IM) is a near-real-time information exchange. IM is offered by a number of different organizations including Microsoft, Google (Gmail), Skype, and Yahoo. Organizations can create an IM interface on their Web sites and have staff monitor it. This type of interface was utilized by some teams during the 2008–2009 season of the National Basketball Association (NBA). For example, the Detroit Pistons and Cleveland Cavaliers both utilized this customer service platform on their respective ticket sales pages. One click on a banner graphic produced a small pop-up screen that allowed visitors to ask questions of ticket sales personnel. The box was 85 mm x 25 mm in three colors (wine, gold, white) with a smiling female attendant wearing a headset. The graphic included the text "CAVS LIVE IS AVAILABLE," "To Chat with a Cavaliers ticketing representative CLICK HERE NOW!" and included the team's sales telephone number (Tickets, 2009, ¶ 4).

While IM chat provides an immediate link to the organization, it does still require staff members to serve customers. Taking event staff away from other duties to monitor an IM service must be carefully planned and included in any strategic decision process.

Email

In addition to corresponding with visitors or participants about event issues, providing a dedicated email address for visitor questions is a simple way for inquiries to be submitted to event staff. The email address can also promote the event and for a 5K fun run in Austin, TX, the email address might be Austin5k@yahoo.com or similar. As with the IM chat service, email requires a dedicated person or team of people to monitor and respond to all inquiries. Delays due to volume or inattention can produce negative visitor or participant experiences. Again, including email monitoring as part of overall strategic planning is an important part of the event planning process.

Other Technological Possibilities

Two more recent developments in information dissemination include RSS feeds and Twitter. With the emergence of Web 2.0, **RSS feeds** allow people to create links to information sources (e.g., other Web sites) on their Web browser or computer desktop. Whenever an organization or individual adds new content pertaining to that link to a Web site, a hyperlink is created at the individual's browser or desktop indicating new information has arrived. RSS feeds can be utilized to proactively distribute information to individuals rather than wait for them to visit a Web site. Placing the RSS symbol on the information section encourages individuals to connect to the event and allows event staff to keep interested parties up-to-date with the latest information pertaining to a topic (e.g., registration, traffic information).

Twitter is a text-based application for cell phones and computers. Twitter accounts allow individuals to send mass text messages or emails to all individuals registered to receive, or *follow,* them. This technology has been utilized by celebrities and athletes as a way to communicate *inside information* to fans or media members. As with RSS, encouraging visitors or participants to register to follow the event Tweets (individual messages through Twitter) allows event staff to take a more proactive approach to information dissemination. The case below illustrates one way in which Twitter technology can be utilized to provide constant information to individuals.

The Power of Twitter

Shaquille O'Neal of the National Basketball Association's Phoenix Suns has been an avid user of Twitter, a text-based social networking platform (www.twitter.com) since an imposter began sending messages on his behalf. Prompted to set things straight, Shaq began what has become a Twitter phenomenon. Only a few thousand users subscribed to his feed when he began, but as of March 2009, he had more than 450,000 followers (The Real Shaq, 2009). In one sense, O'Neal has bypassed traditional media routes to his audience(s) and now sends information directly to them. He "is tweeting with the unbridled zeal of a 12-year-old. He posted 17 times . . . making references to Oprah, yoga, Kobe and fettuccine" (Beck, 2008, ¶ 20). Of course, media members can be included in a Twitter list. However, the technology provides a great way for individuals to communicate a message to a large number of people in a quick and popular manner (i.e., text messaging).

Services such as email and Twitter can be utilized to send information out quickly should a question be raised that affects a significant number of people, for example, a change in event starting time or location. Taking advantage of a number of information dissemination outlets allows event managers to inform people of changes that might occur with the event. However, as with email or IM, these applications require monitoring. It is recommended that strategic plans include a multi-leveled information dissemination plan utilizing the above technology aids, especially for addressing questions and comments about an event.

Participant Registration

While registration appears to be an information-receiving function, creating an easy-to-use and interactive registration process enables event planners to control the flow of critical event information and minimize misunderstandings or concerns by participants. **Participant registration** is the act of providing information and/or payment to an event with the expectation of participation and access to all of the rights and benefits associated with event participation. Thus, effective and efficient participant registration procedures are crucial and require special attention to detail. While participant registration is specifically discussed in Chapter 8, this section will examine technology-related issues to registering event participants.

Event planners will have to decide whether they wish to create Web sites and accompanying aspects of the sites (e.g., registration database construction and management) themselves or outsource the work. In either case, technology can help to alleviate many difficulties inherent in a registration process including lost or incomplete applications, lack of payment, printing and delivering tickets, or keeping track of a never-ending paper trail. A simple computer interface can be constructed on the Web site to gather all relevant data and information for a particular event. As a data acquisition point, registration information can be sent directly to a database for use in any number of ways including future event mailing lists, post-event customer service surveys, and demographic reports to solicit sponsors or partners. Within the registration process, event planners can include RSS feed links, IM chat help, and any of the other technology applications discussed earlier in this chapter.

Further, payments can be made by credit or debit card through the site or from a third-party payment source such as PayPal. After the registration is complete, the individual (and event managers) receive confirmation of the registration and a unique identification number or code that can be used to trace accounts in case of problem or other error. Tickets or event materials can be generated online and printed (an *e-ticket*) by the individual, reducing the cost for the event staff. Other technologies allow for no tickets at all (see Tickets and Technology insert).

Finally, the use of online registration has an environmental impact as well. Participants who register online and obtain information and confirmation online (as well as the event planners) reduce the need to use paper and other resources. Many pounds of paper can be wasted in sending out receipts, envelopes, and application materials. When the registration process is computerized, all parties play a part in reducing unnecessary environmental waste.

INFORMATION MANAGEMENT

The same care and attention given to the creation and dissemination of messages to external audiences should be given to the use of behind-the-scenes information management. However, it is important to remember that all technological choices are dependent on an event's budget. **Information management** describes all of the back-end technology employed to plan an event. Examples include the internal work applications, event management software, database structure to handle the information gathered from the event registration section, questions and comments submitted to the staff, and the server that holds the Web site and other event-based information and the benefits of a near paperless planning process.

Internal Work and Communication Applications

Creating a framework for internal communication helps to ensure that ideas, information, and work that must cross offices or countries is done in the most efficient and effective manner possible. Software applications exist that facilitate information flow in a timely manner that encourages collaboration, understanding, and storage throughout the event planning process. These include shared drives, teleconferencing, and Web-based document creation and management applications.

Shared Drive

Shared network drives allow for individuals to post documents and have them accessed by others who have access to the drive. Generally, the shared drives are found within organizations, although access can be made remotely (if allowed). While the least interpersonally interactive system of the three, shared drives have the benefits of storing large amounts of data and having this information accessible in a highly secured environment rather than being Web-based.

Teleconferencing

For event planners who wish to meet and work with individuals across great distances versus across the office, Internet-based teleconferencing opportunities exist. For example, a free teleconferencing service comes from FreeConferenceCall (http://www.freeconferencecall.com). The basic level of service provides around-the-clock access for up to 96 people for up to six hours per time (Free Teleconferencing, 2009). Thus, planners in various locations can be in constant contact with each other at no cost. Another example is Skype (www.skype.com), an Internet-based communications software package that allows communication to occur computer-to-computer or computer-to-telephone. The software also allows video calling, including conference calls and instant message features. An important part of the Skype package is that most of the basic functions/features are available as free downloads. Other online communications software packages exist including offerings from Microsoft's Small Business Center (http://www.microsoft.com/smallbusiness/hub.mspx) and Virtuosity (http://www.virtuosity.com).

Web-Based Applications

Applications are available which provide useful opportunities for event planners to share data and information in near-real time. One example is GoogleDocs (http://docs.google.com). This service, hosted by Google, allows planners to share information and work together on material development (e.g., staffing timelines, event documents, marketing collateral) and have them stored in a place accessible by individuals regardless of their location. The service even includes a template function to help individuals who are not certain where to begin with a document. While multiple individuals can work on a document at one time, materials are securely protected and users can control access. Another, similar example is a wiki. **Wikis** are Web-based pages that can be accessed by multiple parties to create, manage, and store documents. Event planners can either utilize existing wiki applications (e.g., http://www.centraldesktop.com, http://www.wikidot.com) which can be free or subscription-based, or find software that allows them to manage the entire wiki process themselves (e.g., http://twicki.org). The benefit of wikis is that they can be accessed in real time and by multiple individuals. While they do not have the interactivity of a teleconference call, they are useful for collaborative efforts.

Event Management Software

The event planning process has benefitted from improvements in management software. **Event management software** is a package that facilitates different aspects of the event planning process, depending upon the nature of the software. Companies such as Oracle, Sybase, and Microsoft all have event management software offerings. Third-party consulting firms also have their own proprietary software to offer event planners. For example, Microsoft's EventManager software "is a single-user Microsoft Access database that can be used to manage many of the administrative and communication tasks associated with events such as company or organizational meetings, educational and training seminars, customer events and wedding planning" (Event-Manager, 2009a, ¶ 1). In addition to preparing reports and managing customizable communications applications, it can print name badges, produce invitations by email or regular mail, and manage travel needs (EventManager, 2009b).

Database Structure

Creating and managing a database system is a complicated but potentially lucrative task. A **database** is "a shared, integrated computer structure that stores a collection of end-user data . . . metadata, or data about data through which the end-user data are integrated and managed" (Rob, Coronel, & Crockett, 2008, p. 7). Event planners must make a decision whether or not database construction and management will be done in-house or outsourced. Access by individuals, security concerns, and cost are all important considerations when making such a decision.

Databases are useful to event planners because the data collected from a Web site or event location can be used in a number of ways. One example is to create an email list for post-event follow-up and preparation for the next event. Another example is the way in which database information can be searched or segmented in order to understand who participates in events and how this information can be useful when soliciting sponsors and partners. Such interactivity is important to post-event evaluations of the event and preparations for future events. In relation to payment processing, databases can be used to process payments in groups created within defined parameters (e.g., daily) or as the payments come in.

Database design, then, becomes a crucial issue for event planners. "A good database—that is, a database that meets all user requirements—does not just happen. . . Proper database design requires the database designer to identify precisely the database's expected use" (Rob, Coronel, & Crockett, 2008, pp. 10–11). As with other aspects of a database, it can facilitate information searches about the data submitted by those registering. However, given security concerns of personal and financial information, the event planning staff must decide who will have access to the database as well as how often this access will occur. Further, the number of individuals with access to the database at any given time is a critical issue depending on the size of the event, the event staff, and the need for individuals to have access to the information or just reports generated from it.

The ease with which event information can be stored for future use eliminates the need for costly paper handling and storage. Further, access by planning staff members is improved because information remains at a person's fingertips rather than in piles of boxes. This information is also portable in that it can be accessed at the site of an event, making for easier interactions with participants and media members. For example, if a person arrives at an event and the registration list shows he or she is not eligible to participate, a quick search into the registration database will address the problem on the spot.

Some caution must be exercised in relation to utilizing database systems. For mega events (e.g., Super Bowl), expenditures to hire professionals to develop sophisticated database systems are warranted. For smaller events, especially infrequent or one-time events, such elaborate systems are less necessary. In fact, applications such as Microsoft's Excel can be used to handle many database management functions, including preparation of email and regular mail materials via mail merges. Finally, event planners can purchase information from database companies that collect general information about specific groups (e.g., people of a city by zip code). This alternative might be less expensive than creating a database system, but it might also prove problematic because of outdated information and incomplete or inaccurate personal information (e.g., names, addresses).

MONETIZATION OF EVENTS

Whether the goal of the event is to generate revenue or raise money for a charitable cause, understanding how to monetize an event, specifically the technologies involved with the event, is a critical skill for today's event planners. **Monetization** describes the efforts made to utilize Web site space for revenue generation, even if the revenues are not for profit purposes.

Event Sponsorship and Partnership

For those events seeking to generate revenues for profit purposes, the use of Web sites and other technologies offer a chance to maximize revenue generation and increase sponsor or partner presence at the event. For purposes of this chapter, a **sponsor** is an entity that provides cash or in-kind products or services in exchange for a presence within the event. A **partner** can be a sponsor, but the relationship to the event might be over a longer period of time, carry a higher monetary value, or might just be named differently. In this section, the role of a sponsor or partner in an event is examined. In addition, a brief discussion is included regarding the connection between offline and online monetization opportunities.

Sponsors or partners are secured to help fund an event in exchange for promotional considerations (e.g., advertising). Often, there is a range of opportunities to participate as a sponsor or partner including title sponsor opportunities (e.g., Tostitos Fiesta Bowl), locations at an event (e.g., National City Bank Pavilion), or simple advertising signage. Varying rates are charged for these opportunities, with the most lucrative opportunities being the most expensive. For event managers, the notion of value, adding additional benefits for a sponsor or partner, is important when identifying, approaching, and working with sponsors and partners. In addition, a Web site presence costs less compared to terrestrial signage because the digital information can be provided by the sponsoring company with little production cost to the event managers. Today, event planners can leverage the value of the online world to enhance a sponsor's or partner's relationship with an event.

Value Through Online Opportunities

While event managers are well-versed in offline sponsorship and partnership opportunities, attention must be given to ways in which technology can add value to these relationships and provide unique and interesting activities for participants. In this section, a brief overview of how to integrate offline and online sponsorship or partnership opportunities is provided.

A sign at an event can draw attention to a sponsor's or partner's name. Advanced levels of recognition might result in individuals being able to recall what a sponsor or partner does and/or experiences one had with the organization. However, in order to maximize a sponsor's or partner's presence (and the event planners' ability to raise revenues), more creative activities must be undertaken. The following list is a set of key points related to linking offline and online sponsorship and partnership activities:

1. Message dissemination (sponsor/partner and event)

2. Interactivity (encourage user participation)

3. Drive traffic (utilize the site within the promotion and encourage return visits)

4. Establish long-term relationships with sponsors and partners

The purpose of sponsoring an event is to raise awareness for the sponsor or partner. Making the sponsor or partner visible at the event is a time-tested activity. However, creating a space for those same organizations on the event's Web site poses a new set of challenges. First, event planners must determine what the monetary value is for various types of sponsorship opportunities on a Web site. These opportunities range from various standard banner advertisements to the sponsorship of specific items (e.g., title sponsorship of a video player showing event highlights from the previous year). Once the values are determined, sponsors and partners can be identified and pursued.

Interactivity and driving traffic are two related aspects of offline-online sponsorship opportunities. Ideally, event planners can link offline activities to the Web site via a need to look up information, find a clue, or provide a series of answers to a trivia test. Whatever the means, the end goal is to ensure that individuals are taking part in activities in the terrestrial and online worlds. For example, a minor league baseball team could place 25 bobbleheads of its mascot at various locations around a city. Each bobblehead has a sticker with a code on it. Two of the codes are for a special trip for two to a vacation destination provided by the sponsor, a local travel agency. The rest are for team merchandise. Clues to the locations of the bobbleheads are placed on the team's Web site (the locations can be sites for other sponsors or partners, such as a grocery store chain). To obtain the first clue, visitors must register with the team's Web site. Thus, the promotion encourages visits to offline locations and online traffic.

Finally, the purpose of such relationships is to establish long-term sponsorships and partnerships. However, the success of the relationships depends upon the sponsors and partners and the event planners' abilities to maintain productive, unique, and entertaining offline/online promotions.

Offline/Online Promotion Cautions

When establishing a sponsor's or partner's presence on a Web site, the same considerations given to event location placement should be given in cyberspace. The attractiveness of an event can lead to a number of potential organizations wanting to be affiliated with it, and thus, its Web site. Poorly prepared Web sites will end up filling the Web site with a multitude of event and sponsor messages and advertisements. Visitors should not be bombarded with advertisements, pop-up screens, and information collection points. Conversely, sponsors and partners should be visible and not hidden away under a link that the average visitor might not recognize or click on.

The result of a poorly structured Web site could be one that is overcrowded and unpleasant to visit (or remain at for any significant period of time). Targeted sponsor placements are important. As stated earlier, event managers who visualize and prepare their Web-based sponsor and partner strategies will have a set inventory of space available, ideas for online and offline opportunities, and a clear vision for their sponsors and partners in hopes of establishing long-term relationships.

Tickets and Technology—Flash Seats

Technological advancements extend into to the world of event ticketing. It is becoming apparent that soon we will be able to obtain and manage tickets without having to print them or carry them to events. Flash Seats, a company owned by Cleveland Cavaliers owner Dan Gilbert, made headlines when it challenged Ticketmaster's control over event tickets, but subsequently lost in court (e.g., Krause, 2008). Conceived as a paperless ticket management system, Flash Seats heralded several significant breakthroughs for event ticketing. First, it introduced a marketplace for tickets where individuals can buy, sell, or transfer their seats (Flash Seats, 2009), resulting in new advantages for ticket holders, especially those with season tickets. Second, no paper ticket is needed to enter participating events because individuals can use their credit card or state driver's license. Third, it spawned an emerging e-ticket environment complete with online buying and selling of tickets (e.g., StubHub.com) that provides many options to ticket holders.

For event planners, e-ticketing might be able to save time, effort, cost, and the environment by making event access more convenient for attendees. Flash Seats is used by several professional sport organizations (e.g.,

Real Salt Lake, Houston Rockets, Lake Erie Monsters), but while they cannot allow their ticketholders to sell or resell tickets, the concept has advanced ticket purchasing and dissemination forward at a rapid pace. Even for small events, invoice-like *tickets* can be printed and brought to events if completely paperless ticketing is not an option in order to bring significant savings and efficiencies.

ENTERTAINMENT AND EDUCATION OF VISITORS AND PARTICIPANTS

So far, this chapter has examined issues related to the use of technology in the event planning process. Different sections have touched on issues of information dissemination and interactivity. However, this section will focus on how the Web site and other technologies can serve to provide entertainment and education to visitors and participants alike, before, during, and after events. **Entertainment and education** in this sense means that the event planners provide additional experiential opportunities surrounding the event through the use of different technologies, but mainly the Web site. While often thought of as separate entities, entertainment and education are used together in this section to highlight the ways in which information can enhance individual experiences with an event. These ways include location and directions and community development.

Location and Directions

While the location of the event seems like a mundane aspect within the overall planning process, it should not be taken for granted. Providing as much location-specific information as possible on a Web site allows individuals to plan and prepare for their event experience. Driving directions, facility plans, event maps, or other items can be placed on the Web site to aid visitors. If the event is a running, cycling, or combination event, posting the route is recommended. For example, posting a graphic that plots the route a 5K run will take through a local community can help participants prepare their training regimen. Family and friends of the runners can also use the information to decide where to watch the race. Providing links to online map services such as Google Earth (http://earth.google.com) allows individuals to actually see the event location in *reality*. These services can have significant limitations to their usefulness as, for example, Google Earth is generally limited to providing coverage of mainly urban areas.

If the event utilizes tickets, then a seating diagram of the event can be used in several key areas including an information section, ticket sales section, or elsewhere. Technology allows visitors to see computer three-dimensional views from seats or even actual photographs. At the very least, a basic seating chart with price categories, restroom and other facilities, and parking areas clearly marked is recommended. Table 4-4 contains a list of teams that provide different types of seating views for their stadia.

Table 4-4. Example Team Arena Seating Views

League	Team	Web Site	Type of View
National Football League	Cleveland Browns	http://www.clevelandbrowns.com	Seating Chart and Photograph View
National Hockey League	Minnesota Wild	http://www.wild.nhl.com	Seating Chart
Major League Baseball	Houston Astros	http://houston.astros.mlb.com	Seating Chart and Photographic View
National Basketball Association	Sacramento Kings	http://www.nba.com/kings	Seating Chart and Photographic View
Southeastern Conference	University of Florida (Football)	http://www.gatorzone.com	Seating Chart
Major League Soccer	Colorado Rapids	http://www.coloradorapids.com	Seating Chart
Women's Professional Soccer	St. Louis Athletica	http://www.womensprosoccer.com	Seating Chart
Italian Serie A	A.C. Milan	http://www.acmilan.com	Seating Chart

In addition, it is recommended to have directions to the event from a number of key transportation perspectives (e.g., air, highway) for visitors and participants. The directions can concentrate on key routes to the event and provide links to local airports, hotels, restaurants, or map services (e.g., http://www.mapquest.com, http://www.earth.google.com). Parking for the event can also be woven into this section to assist visitors.

Community

In addition to the basics of event location, planners can take extra steps to provide space for interactive activities designed to entertain and educate visitors and participants about an event. A secondary effect of such a strategy is to encourage return visits to a Web site after an event ends in order to keep individuals interested and engaged with the event until the next time it is held. In other words, the event planners can lay the foundation for community development via the event. Thus, visitors can have a multileveled engagement/experience with an event, especially if they are not able to attend it; the game is an experience, attendance is a second experience, and the interactivity offers a third experience level. Two common ways to create community include providing space for user-generated content and interpersonal interactions.

User-Generated Content

A first step in the creation of community is the use of **user-generated content** (UGC). User-generated content refers to pictures, video, podcasts, and text (e.g., blogs) contributed by individuals for others to see regarding their experiences at an event. The UGC revolution came into its own with the development of YouTube (http://www.youtube.com). Today, while technology allows users to upload videos directly to a Web site without needing a link to YouTube, the emergence of a space for people to create, post, and share video content on the Internet was an important point in the development of Web interactivity. Allowing individuals to post pictures, videos, podcasts, or personal accounts of event experiences not only adds additional educational and entertainment opportunities for visitors to a Web site, but also provides the posters with an enhanced participatory experience in an event. Effective UGC areas require that proper evaluation and approval procedures for all submissions (i.e., managed by event staff) are in place for UGC opportunities to remain free from abuse.

The event planners can create a section of a Web site that includes upload capabilities. Once registered (another information capture point), individuals can post their video, photographs, or narrative descriptions of an event. This section can be informal in that there is little structure for participants to follow, or it can be highly organized to allow for categorical searches or other organizational criteria. Once loaded, the different media allow visitors and other participants to read about and view the experiences of their fellow event attendees. It might even encourage others to post their own materials.

In some cases, event planners can utilize professional photographers to wander the event taking photographs of visitors and participants. These photographs can then be placed on the Web site for individuals to download (free or charged) after the event. When a photograph is taken, a code is given to the photographed parties, which then directs them to the Web site where they register and, if necessary, pay for the photograph to be downloaded. This activity also offers an additional sponsorship opportunity (e.g., camera shops or companies).

Functions can also be added to alert registered users (another information collection point) when changes to their favorite poster or blogger are made. These alerts can be emailed, texted, Twittered, or all of them.

In all cases, a visitor is educated about event experiences and entertained by the experiences of others (or even themselves). The USA Swimming case illustrates these points.

USA Swimming and Blogs

USA Swimming has embraced the concept of their swimmers sharing experiences in meets and championships around the world. Not only does this allow the swimmers to keep in touch with friends and families at home, but also, they are able to share individual insights into being a swimmer, competing in these events, and engaging with swim fans from all around the United States and the world. At www.usaswimming.com

(search for *blog*), visitors can see USA Swimming's Biomechanical Director, Russell Marks, sharing information about his experiences at the International Swim Meet 2007 in Japan, or USA Junior Team swimmers at the Junior Pan Pacific Championships 2009 in Guam. There is even a case study of the Winston-Salem YMCA's efforts to better develop their swimmers by uploading and utilizing video of the swimmers to enhance practices (educational and entertaining for coaches and swimmers). Further, USA Swimming's Web site has sections devoted to pictures from swim events around the world and even "swim cams" located at sites around the United States. For a fan of swimming or individual who swims at any level, such opportunities allow for an enhanced experience (entertainment) and increased understanding of USA Swimming and its members (educational). By adding different opportunities for self-expression regarding an event experience, visitors and participants can enhance their event experiences.

Interpersonal Interactions

A second aspect of community development is to allow more personal exchanges between the event planners, visitors, and/or participants. This dialogue can take the form of a suggestion submission form. Having a voice in the event process, however slight, might be a way to enhance a participant's experience and offer insights to the event planners. The form is similar to a registration form in which some demographic and personal information is asked for and then the individuals can submit their question or comment. As stated earlier, the time necessary to monitor and address questions and comments submitted by participants and visitors can take away from the overall planning process. Thus, strategically, event planners must take this into account when developing their online presence.

A final community development initiative is the use of forum areas and/or chat rooms. These areas allow individuals to exchange information about each other, the event, and anything else they deem important. NASCAR, long known as a customer-friendly organization with a devoted fan base, has made certain to include community development opportunities at its Web site. "NASCAR's Web site offers fans NASCAR screen savers, ring tones, chat rooms, bulletin boards, profiles of drivers, race information and much, much more" (Plunkett Research, 2008, ¶ 7). While NASCAR continues to have a strong core community of fans, its Web-based community continues to develop new communities throughout the United States and the world.

These sites take time to monitor (e.g., for offensive language) and manage. However, if the event is large enough and the traffic to the Web site is significant enough, event planners might wish to utilize such a community-building initiative.

SUMMARY

This chapter aimed to provide readers with an overview of various ways technology can impact the event planning process. While it is certainly not exhaustive, the chapter does raise a number of important and interrelated issues central to determining what technology elements to use, and how, when planning an event. Strategies related to information dissemination (external), information management (internal), the monetization of events, and entertainment and education opportunities for visitors and participants can all be generated during the event conceptualization phase of event management.

The forthcoming chapters delve into the specific areas to be addressed in the event development phase of event management. Readers should keep in mind the different technological issues raised in this chapter as they continue through the text. While no single source can address all technology issues related to events that vary in scope and size (e.g., a local charity baseball game or the FIFA World Cup), it is hoped that the reader is now more aware of the impact of technology on an event, the participants, and the overall event management process.

Student Challenge

STUDENT CHALLENGE #4

In Challenge #4, explore the various types of technology that can be utilized to manage and promote the event.

QUESTION 4-1

Create a document outlining the pages (e.g., Home Page, About Us, etc.) of a possible Web site for the event. Please provide a minimum of four Web pages.

a) Provide a 2–3 sentence description of each page of the Web site and the section(s) that will be on each page.

b) Diagram a site map for one Web site. Two different examples of site maps are available at http://gatorzone.com/misc.php?p=sitemap or http://www.nycmarathon.org/help/site_map.htm

Event Web Site Page #1 Description and Sections:

Event Web Site Page #2 Description and Sections:

Student Challenge

Event Web Site Page #3 Description and Sections:

Event Web Site Page #4 Description and Sections:

Site Map Diagram:

Student Challenge

QUESTION 4-2

Research two events—preferably sports events, but entertainment events are also acceptable—since 2007 that have had success using technology (e.g., instant messaging, Twitter, blogs, Facebook, etc.) for promotion of the event. Describe how technology was used.

Event #1 and Use of Technology:

Event #2 and Use of Technology:

QUESTION 4-3

List three possible types of UGC (user-generated content) that can be generated to help in the promotion of the event and the creation of an event community. Describe, in detail, how to utilize each type of UGC to establish a community around the event.

UGC #1:

How to Establish a Community:

UGC #2:

How to Establish a Community:

UGC #3:

How to Establish a Community:

SECTION II

EVENT DEVELOPMENT

Michelle Wells

The second section of Event Management Blueprint (Chapters 5–11) concentrates on event development and some of the behind-the-scenes and business areas leading up to the event. Event managers are not directly responsible for some of these elements, but understanding them will give event managers the well-rounded perspective necessary to see the big picture. Additionally, many of these areas are revenue-generating functions of the event.

The authors of these chapters provide insight based on their experiences, ranging from selling major sponsorships to designing safe sports facilities. Tools for budgeting are introduced, along with an explanation of the major expense categories of events. The chapter covering event marketing provides information on various forms of marketing, gives guidelines for choosing the right type of media, and provides a foundation for understanding media buying. Students will then learn about event sponsorship and are exposed to industry research that provides data on what is important to event sponsors, which may help in the selling of sponsorships. Additional key revenue areas of participant registration and event ticketing are also addressed.

The last chapters in the section focus on items that are vital for the success and proper execution not just of sports events, but of every size and type of event: communications and safety. Readers will learn how to write effective press releases and how to leverage relationships with media. Finally, the chapter on safety and security emphasizes that creating the safest environment possible for participants and spectators is the number one concern for all event managers. Specific guidance is then provided related to safe operations, risk management, and emergency planning. These chapters lead into the details of event execution that follow in the next section.

CHAPTER 5

EVENT BUDGET

Michelle Wells

One of the most essential aspects of creating any event is the budget: How much is it going to cost and how much money can the event make? Creating a budget is one of the areas that allow event managers to determine the scope of the event. They can add specific items that can take the event from a mere well-organized and functioning event to an over-the-top festivity that creates a WOW factor for everyone involved. Conversely, the budget may require scaling back on certain areas to ensure it meets the financial goals of the organizers. Creating the initial budget when assessing feasibility is one of the factors that will help event managers determine if an event gets the signal to go or no-go. This chapter provides a framework for drilling down into the budget detail that is necessary as the event is developed. **So that it does not have to be noted in each of the following sections, every budget item presented is going to vary by event depending on the type and scope of the event.**

REVENUE STREAMS

In most cases, sports are a business and events are usually in business to make money. Hopefully that is not a surprise at this point. In order to make money, an event must have revenue streams that exceed costs to put on the event. The exception relates to those events that have a mission that is non-revenue related (e.g., participatory in nature, charity, or community involvement), or those that are focused on generating economic impact to the locale. If a community believes that an event that is brought into a community will generate a significant amount of money via economic impact, they may be willing to cover the cost of producing the event. The event makes money, but in a slightly different way that is not direct revenue.

Registration and Processing Fees

For participation-driven events, the obvious revenue stream is the fee that participants pay to enter competition, or **registration fee**. This amount may determine whether an event should occur; it depends on how confident the event organizers are that they can bring in money from other revenue sources, especially sponsorship. If an event is very popular and has a cap on the number of participants, there is another revenue stream that an event may charge—a processing fee. A **processing fee** is the amount charged to participants for the right to enter the lottery or other selection process associated with the event. Some events will accept a large number of applications and then have a drawing or lottery to determine which registered participants gain entrance to the event. The event still has to process those prospective entrants' applications and all of their information, and there are costs associated with that work. If the event managers are using a third-party company for online registration, part of that fee will likely go to the registration company as part of their payment. It is money that the event will bill immediately and it may be $3–$7 for the fee, for example. An event in this situation of having a waiting list will not bill the participant for the actual registration fee unless or until that person is chosen in the lottery. They would not want to incur the administrative cost of refunding the fee to the person, plus the event probably would have already paid the processing fee to the credit card company, hence in net, they could lose money. The processing fee, however, is billed immediately when a participant registers. The lottery selection could be several months after a participant registers, which means that it will impact the event's cash flow. The processing fee is charged at the time that a person registers and is non-refundable. This allows the organization to increase cash flow in the buildup to the lottery selection. For example, if a marathon has a cap of 20,000 runners, the event may get 35,000 applicants. With a $3 processing fee, that is an additional $105,000 of revenue for the event, and with a $7 fee it is an additional $245,000 of revenue.

Merchandise (and Concession) Sales

Merchandise sales can be a significant contribution to an event's revenue. Well-designed souvenir T-shirts, hats, jackets, and pins can bring in large amounts of money. People often want a souvenir to show where they have been and where they have competed (or where their family member has competed).

Along with merchandise sales, concessions can be a lucrative revenue stream. Generally, people purchase food and beverages when they attend sports events. When reading through the merchandise information, be aware that a lot of the information is similar for concessions.

Per Caps

When a new event is created, it is often hard to determine what the merchandise sales will be. For existing events, the rights holder should be able to provide the event organizer with data on past merchandise sales. Taking the amount of merchandise sales and dividing by the number of participants gives the per capita amount of merchandise sales, or merchandise per cap. **Per capita spending, or per cap**, is the amount of money spent per person during an event. Per caps for concessions are calculated the same way. Most times, though, it is important to also know the ratio of spectators or family members to participants. This total ratio of people attending to the amount of merchandise sold will give the best number for merchandise per cap. For the event's rights holder, this is an important number to track for each event. When the event is up for bid, merchandise sales is a significant figure for the rights holder to be able to relay to the bidder. Often, percentage of gross sales agreements are made, and both parties will receive a percentage of merchandise sales. The revenue generated by each party depends on the agreement between the two parties. The bidding city may even have a third-party vendor provide the merchandise sales, but they would still have to honor the split in the agreement with the city. Even with the lower amount that the city will receive because of its agreement with a third-party vendor, this may be the best choice if the venue does not have merchandise sales capability. Merchandise revenue split percentages with third-party companies are going to vary from deal to deal, depending on the negotiated terms.

Types of Financial Agreements

There are three main types of financial agreements with respect to merchandise: flat fee, per person fee, or percentage of gross sales. In a **flat fee agreement**, the facility or city charges the event a flat fee for the right to set up and sell products. This arrangement is the easiest for both the venue and the event manager to keep track of, since it is a one-time payment. A **per person fee** agreement is structured so that the event is charged a small amount for each person in attendance. The rationale is that the larger the event, the more likely it is that the event will generate more revenue from sales. This is difficult for events such as a road race, where accurate attendance figures may not be available and the main purchasers will be participants and not spectators. Any time a per-person fee is being considered, research into past events related to per cap spending is critical. Event managers should not enter into these agreements without a solid understanding of expected sales. In both the flat fee agreement and the per-person fee, the venue has little involvement in the operation and accounting related to sale. These functions are passed on to those involved in the event. In a percentage of gross sales agreement, this changes a bit. Percentage of gross sales is the most popular type of agreement for sports events. In **percentage of gross sales** agreements, the event splits their gross revenue with the venue (or city in the case of many non-traditional venues). Common splits can be 70% to the event and 30% to the venue, or 80% to the event and 20% to the venue. Since the amount earned by each party is determined by sales figures, this type of agreement requires involvement of both venue or city personnel and event personnel in accounting for and reconciling sales figures to ensure agreement.

Specialty Merchandise Types

Souvenirs to "prove" that a person attended or participated in an event can amount to significant sales with the right type of products available. Merchandise pieces are also great souvenirs to allow people to hold on to the memories associated with the event. The obvious sales are at the event itself and of gear associated with the event, merchandise that simply has the event name on it. There are other merchandise revenue streams. For road races and triathlons, events that in most cases only require a person to register for the event rather than qualify for it, an event can create "In Training" gear. This line will often only be a couple of pieces, such as a T-shirt and maybe a cap or jacket. This can be sold beginning when registration opens. It allows participants to let others know of their commitment and intention to participate. Another line of gear is "Finisher Gear." Particularly for notoriously challenging events, being a finisher is a significant accomplishment. A similar merchandise line for team events are products with the score on them or "champion" title. These special lines of merchandise are completely different lines of merchandise and should not cannibalize the sales of the regular merchandise. Limited edition or collectors' items may not be as popular as general merchandise, but can still generate revenue. Items that may fall into this category include such things as trading pins and artwork. For more traditional sports events that have extraordinary importance, ticket display frames or acrylics are very popular with spectators. T-shirts and/or signs available immediately after the event noting the final score or the winning team also sell well as exuberant and often intoxicated fans are eager to spend money on their way out of the venue.

Transportation

Another potential revenue stream, dependant upon the event, is transportation. If the event has to provide any sort of transportation or shuttle, the event may choose to charge a fee for the service. This fee may not cover the entire cost, but it can help offset what may be a huge expense.

Ancillary Events

Ancillary events add to the atmosphere of an overall event and are a great way to include family and friends in the festivities. They can also be additional revenue streams. Some events may require a ticket for admission, such as a pasta party, a concert, or an after-party celebration. Others may collect a registration fee, such as a fun run, slam dunk contest, or kids' race. Some events add ancillary events without the expectation of making money. The organizers may view them as benefits to the participants and consider them a success as long as the costs are covered, or they may even absorb the costs in the overall event.

Housing Packages/Travel Packages

Housing packages or travel packages generate revenue for an event based on the number of hotel room nights and/or rental car days booked by participants and spectators. At one time, airline tickets were included as a revenue item in travel packages. Recently, airlines have stopped paying a commission for ticket sales. Most events are not going to have their own travel department. They will often contract with a travel partner to perform the booking functions, even with online booking. The travel partner will negotiate with hotels and reserve a block of rooms around the event date(s). The travel partner will negotiate rates with the hotels, airlines, and car rental companies and will be responsible for the block of hotel rooms reserved for the event. The travel partner will have deadlines in their contracts that allow them to drop a certain percentage of rooms by specified dates if they are not selling as anticipated. This is called **attrition**.

How do the event and the travel partner make money from these packages? The travel partner negotiates rates with various hotels, choosing hotels in various price ranges and star rating ranges to appeal to different budgets. The travel partner makes its commission from the room rate that they have negotiated with the hotel, usually 10% of the event's published room rate. The travel partner and rights holder will negotiate the amount of the commission that each group receives. The 10% commission may be split 50/50 or 60/40 (in favor of the travel partner). Another way to look at a 50/50 split of the commission is to say that the rights holder is earning 5% of the commission.

Event managers work with the travel partner to assist the travel partner in determining how many people the event managers think will be attending the event. This is one of the reasons it is important to track attendance and bookings for events. This number may come from past data or from booking numbers taken from a comparable event. CVBs and sports commissions can be helpful in obtaining this data from past host sites for the event organizers. For a first year event that will be repeated, a rights holder may want to pay for a survey that will provide data on the attendees and determine how many are "booking around" the travel packages, or making travel arrangements on their own. This information can also be collected at the event registration/check-in.

Event organizers may package the entry fee to the event with theme park tickets, hotel room nights, or special events tickets and require that an individual or team purchase the package in order to enter the event. This is known as **package-to-compete**. Forcing participants to purchase a package may seem like an easy revenue stream, but it can cause ill will and may backfire.

Another way to build a package involves simply inserting a fee that reverts back to the rights holder and the travel partner receives the commission for the rooms and/or they may also build in their own fee. Payments from the travel partner to the rights holder are made at various stages throughout the booking period (monthly or quarterly) or after the event, depending on what was negotiated between the parties.

Room Nights

What is the difference between rooms booked or sold and room nights? Simply using the term rooms will tell how many rooms have been sold or are occupied, but not for how long. The term **room nights** refers to how many total nights' stay were sold for an event. This is an important figure to know because it affects economic impact in the area and can provide leverage for event managers in securing free rooms, discounted rooms, commissions, hotel sponsorships, and/or additional services from the hotel based on the number of anticipated room nights.

Let's use the example of a three-day basketball tournament for girls in Miami that will bring in teams from around the Southeast. The tournament will begin on Thursday evening and continue with games on Friday, Saturday, and Sunday. The championship game will be held on Sunday afternoon at 4:30 pm. For simplicity's sake, assume that there are 40 teams in the tournament, that each team has two coaches, twelve players on its roster, and that each coach and player/family on the team will book one room each.

$$40 \text{ teams} \times 14 \text{ people (12 players/families and 2 coaches)} = 560 \text{ rooms sold}$$

When teams travel, though, they are going to have different travel schedules. A team driving from Orlando may choose to arrive the day the tournament starts and leave Sunday night, even if they make it to the championship game. A team driving from Charlotte, however, may drive to Miami on Wednesday and would then need a hotel room that night. For the return trip, they may decide to stay overnight on Sunday and drive back to Charlotte on Monday. Let's look at an example for each of these teams and assume for the example that all of the teams, players, and coaches behave the same.

Orlando team: arrives Thursday and checks out of the hotel on Sunday, which amounts to a three night stay (Thursday, Friday, and Saturday).

$$14 \text{ people (rooms)} \times 3 \text{ nights} = 42 \text{ room nights}$$

Charlotte team: arrives Wednesday and checks out of the hotel on Monday, which amounts to a five night stay (Wednesday, Thursday, Friday, Saturday, and Sunday).

$$14 \text{ people (rooms)} \times 5 \text{ nights} = 70 \text{ room nights}$$

In this basic example, assumptions about the number of rooms, length of stay, and uniform behavior patterns of the team members were made. For real events, these numbers and behaviors are going to vary even among individual teams. Some are going to arrive early or stay extra days for vacation, some families will need more than one room, some athletes may travel with another athlete's parents, and so on.

To show the difference between rooms and room nights at the macro level, let's take our example showing the static total number of rooms booked and make an assumption that every team will stay three nights.

$$40 \; teams \times 14 \; people = 560 \; rooms \; booked/sold$$

$$40 \; teams \times 14 \; people \times 3 \; nights = 1,680 \; room \; nights$$

While the event participants may only occupy 560 hotel rooms in the Miami area, the event has booked 1,680 hotel room nights. As demonstrated, slight alterations in the team travel can significantly alter room nights. The event schedule can help increase room nights, but event managers should be cautious about creating a schedule that puts an undue hardship on traveling teams. The critical concept with room nights is that event managers must be aware of how many room nights the event is generating within the community and at each local hotel.

Adding a room rate to these formulas would also show the revenue that the hotels are making from the event. Using a room rate of $140/night, the hotel would have revenues of $5,880 from the Orlando team and $9,800 from the Charlotte team. If the average room rate for all of the hotels with packages were $140/night, local area hotels would make $235,200 for this event (1,680 room nights × $140/night). Numbers like these provide a strong selling point for communities to host sports events, especially during times that are slow for hotel bookings.

Tickets

Chapter 9 covers Event Ticketing in depth, but there are parts of ticketing that relate to the budget that event managers should bear in mind. If the event managers are not responsible for managing ticket sales, it is important for them to work closely with the ticketing manager to determine the ticket prices for the event. Good ticket managers can provide valuable input to make sure the event does not price itself out of the market. They will also make sure event managers are aware of the associated costs of ticketing, such as staffing, printing, technology equipment, and so on.

Sponsorship

While there are costs associated with fulfilling the sponsorship, for many events sponsorship is a primary revenue stream. The percentage of the revenue spent on fulfillment varies, but the majority of the sponsorship is usually revenue to the event. Pricing a sponsorship and fulfillment are covered in Chapter 7, but event managers need to know that not all of the sponsorship amount will be revenue to the event. The entire amount will be entered as revenue for the event, but the corresponding costs (e.g., printing signage, activating the sponsorship) of fulfilling the sponsorship will be tracked in expenses. The net difference between the sponsorship amount and the fulfillment costs will be the sponsorship revenue for the event. As with ticketing, event managers will partner with their sponsorship sales team if the event managers are not selling the sponsorships themselves.

EXPENSES

Expenses are something that every event has to balance with revenue. There may be a lot of great ideas for events and various aspects of events that are developed, but if the money is not there to pay for them, they are not going to be put in place. Calculating and managing expenses is one of the necessary, but not always fun, parts of event management. Being fiscally responsible can help boost event managers' careers. Several big-ticket categories are going to make up a vast majority of an event's budget. Those categories include: venue rental, accommodations (hotels), meals, transportation, ancillary events, equipment, and staff salaries. Big-ticket items, though, are not the only items that go into an event budget. Some of those additional cost areas are covered with a few notes that may be helpful to event managers as they create their budgets.

Venue Rental

Whether an event takes place in a shopping mall parking lot or a multi-million dollar arena, the venue where it is held is more than likely going to charge a rental fee. This amount could not only take up a significant piece of the budget, but could also impact cash flow for the event. Depending on when the contract with the venue states that deposits and/or payments have to be made, the event could be required to pay out cash before revenue streams come into the budget. Those details of the rental contract are important for event managers to know and understand as they work on the budget so they can calculate how much up-front money will be required to be spent on the event.

Housing/Accommodations

Various groups require housing and accommodations. If elite athletes participate in the event, the organizers often pay for their hotel rooms and travel. When a sports commission or event organizer hosts an event, part of the contract with the travel partner will include receiving complimentary room nights based on the number purchased by attendees. The travel partner will often include in the contract that they keep a small amount that is used to house their staff on-site during the event. In the contract with the rights holder, the rights holder will usually require a certain number of complimentary room nights at the host hotel.

Large events may have costs before they even know whether they will be selected to host the event. For a city that bids to host events owned by rights holders, there are expenses associated with the bid. Depending on the rights holder's specific bid requirements, the city may have to pay for travel, accommodations, meals, or some combination for rights holder representatives to tour the proposed event location(s) and meet city officials. The bidding process could encompass several trips. Once a city is selected, the event organizers may still be required to pay for regular planning trips for the rights holder's staff.

For events that require hotel rooms, the event selects one or two host hotels. The deal they, or more likely their travel partner, negotiate with the hotel is to give the event organizer a certain number of complimentary room nights (comp rooms) for every room night booked that is associated with the event. The general ratio ranges anywhere from one comp room per twenty (1:20) to fifty (1:50) room nights booked, depending on the city, the hotel, and the event. This ratio applies to all hotels where the event has created packages. The sports commission or event organizer either has to pay for the rooms they have agreed to give various groups or they will have to use comp rooms.

If the number of comp rooms received is not large enough to cover the allotted rooms, the event will have to pay for the additional rooms out of its budget. They may be able to negotiate a rate that is lower than the rate provided to participants. Often, events agree to pay for rooms for rights holders, officials, and some out-of-town staff. The event may also pay for rooms for its own staff. For multi-day events, staff members are usually required to be available for long hours. It is beneficial to have them near the event site rather than worry about them commuting on little sleep or getting stuck in traffic.

Meals

Meals can be a difficult item to justify, but create a lot of goodwill. They are often a necessity during planning meetings, especially with the rights holder. When the rights holder comes to town, there may be several people in both groups and several meals over a number of days. Do not overlook these in the budget. With event planning meetings, it is important to realize that if the first planning meeting has food, even if it is only snacks and soda, the expectation will be that all of them will have food provided. These various items will start to add up and must be accounted for in the budget, or they will use up the contingency money.

During the event, staff members have to eat and it is not easy for them to break away to go get food. Even when they can, the cost often comes back to the event when employees charge the meals on their expense report. It is easier for the event to pay for their food by providing catering or boxed sandwiches. One area where food is going to be required is for volunteers. Volunteers are covered more thoroughly in the staffing chapter, but remember that volunteers are not "free," they are just less expensive than part-time staff. Meals are usually one of the expense areas related to utilizing volunteers. Another food cost may be for participants. For long races, such as marathons, half-marathons, or triathlons, runners usually expect some type of food at the end. Even for many youth events, the competition days are very long and participants should have access to water and possibly high-energy snacks throughout the day. The goal for an event is to have a sponsor provide the product, but if that does not happen, the event will have to pay for it. The best practice is to put the amount in the budget at the beginning. If a sponsor provides the product, that amount will be a budget savings.

Transportation

Transportation is not something that every event supplies, but when it is provided, it costs the organizers a great deal of money. In addition to the obvious cost of paying for the vans/buses, it is also necessary to pay for the staff that helps manage the transportation during the event. Companies that manage transportation have the expertise required to plan and manage the routes. Different transportation plans are often needed for different groups. Staff may be asked to park at a distant location and take a shuttle to the site. At an event like the Daytona 500, spectators park in many different lots and take buses to the track. Even a college football game may provide ancillary parking at a local mall with shuttle service into campus in an effort to alleviate game day traffic. Participants may be provided with transportation from host hotels to a marathon starting line. Within that group, elite-level participants, sponsors, and VIPs may all have separate transportation. For team events, police escorts may be needed to help buses negotiate game day traffic in a timely manner. Some municipalities will provide this service at no cost, while others will charge for it. There are multiple combinations, and they can all be very complicated to execute. Having the right plans developed by professionals is vital, but as with the buses themselves, they are part of expenses.

Ceremonies

Ceremonies and special activities or parties add a great deal to the atmosphere and image of an event. Along with those great benefits, though, come the costs of putting on the activities. Ceremonies could be large, entertainment-filled productions such as the opening ceremonies of the Special Olympics World Games and a Super Bowl half-time show, or smaller, straightforward affairs such as trophy presentations after a soccer tournament. For a party or ceremony, the three biggest cost items are usually the food and beverage (especially if alcohol is involved), entertainment, and labor.

At first thought, it may seem that the venue would be one of the largest expenses. For large ceremonies, that may be the case and the venue will need to be booked for rehearsal (and the rehearsal included in the entertainers' schedules). For most venues that host special events, the venue is free as long as a certain amount of food and beverage are purchased. If an event has sponsors who provide beverages in-kind (alcoholic and/or non-alcoholic) as part of their sponsorship, event managers need to be certain to ask the venue what companies have pouring rights at the venue. This also goes for hotels where an event might host a lounge or suite for VIPs, sponsors, and elite athletes.

Just because an event's sponsor(s) has pouring rights at a venue does not mean that the event will not be charged. A key factor to determine is whether the venue will charge corkage fees on sponsor products and how much. **Corkage fee** is a charge exacted at a hotel/venue/restaurant for every bottle of beverage (liquor, water, soda, isotonic drink, juice, etc.) served that was not bought on the premises. If sponsor food products are approved by the venue to be brought in, the event may still be required to purchase a certain amount of catering from the venue or pay a venue rental fee.

Expo

Some events hold an expo (short for exposition) as part of their activities, particularly larger road races and triathlons. An **expo** is a sponsor and/or vendor display that often ties into a larger event. It offers an additional way for sponsors and/or vendors to connect with their expanded target audience. An expo is going to be an expense, but could also potentially be a revenue stream. The biggest expense categories are going to be the venue, drayage, labor for the build out, shipping, and the design, artwork, and signage. **Drayage** is the monetary charge for pick-up and hauling of containers. As it relates to an expo, the containers usually hold the display equipment that exhibitors set up at expos. When event managers evaluate whether to have an expo, they need to first determine the purpose for their expo. If they determine that it is a fit for their event, the next step is to determine where to hold it. The venue selection, location, accessibility, flexibility, and number of booths it can accommodate will all impact the cost of the expo and contribute to its revenue generation potential.

Equipment

Equipment is going to be a big expense for most events. There are several considerations that will impact equipment expenses. One of them is whether to rent or buy equipment. This is covered in more depth in Chapter 14, Event Operations. For this chapter it is more important to know that equipment costs could be one of the event's major category expenses. Chapter 14 contains a detailed list of possible items that event managers may need to have for events. This list is not exhaustive, but it is a start to help event managers as they begin to plan and create their event budget.

Staff Salaries

Full-time, part-time, or intern, staff must be paid. The regular schedule of their pay will impact the cash flow of the event organizers and require that money is on-hand and/or regularly available to meet these payment demands. In addition to the salary, benefits have to be calculated into the cost for the employees receiving benefits (generally this only applies to full-time employees). As a guideline, the cost of benefits above salary is about 30%–35%. As an example, if an employee earns an annual salary of $40,000, the actual cost of that employee to the company is $52,000–$54,000.

Staffing Areas

Chapter 13, Event Staffing, will cover the details of the actual staffing. This section will highlight staffing related to the event's budget and what items event managers may need to include in a budget. The quantity will be determined by the specific characteristics of each event and the contract with the venue.

Officials

There are various levels of officials. This category may include referees for actual events, master schedulers, tournament oversight officials, and/or NGB officials. Costs may be set per game, per day, or a flat fee for the event. Either separately or in conjunction with those costs, the officials my require travel, housing, parking and/or food compensation. The event will also usually provide officials with the appropriate attire (e.g., shirt, hat, and/or jacket). In the case of officials for sports that have standard uniforms (e.g., basketball, football), they will usually at least receive a T-shirt or other attire as a souvenir.

It is important to know the format for the competition when preparing the budget. Otherwise, there is no way to know how many officials to budget. In a multi-game tournament, officials will generally be scheduled to officiate more than one match/game/event. If it is a sport that the event managers are not familiar with, it may be beneficial to hire a master scheduler for officiating who can determine how many games one official can work on a given day and schedule accordingly. As examples:

- An inline hockey tournament may only require one official for the U8 age group, but two officials for all older age groups.

- A Gus Macker basketball tournament may be self-officiating until the semi-finals and then have one official for each game from the semi-finals through the finals.

- A tennis tournament may be self-officiating for all rounds of each age group until the quarterfinals. For the quarterfinals and semi-finals it may have a chair umpire and for the finals it may have a chair umpire and two linesmen.

General Labor

Staff from any number of areas can be represented in this category. Setup and strike crew (also often called teardown, changeover, logistics crew) is going to be a main area. For hourly staff, plan for some of their hours to be overtime pay. Event managers should try to keep the costs down, but overtime may be unavoidable, especially if there are not a lot of staff members. When scheduling hours, a general rule of thumb is that it takes about half as much time for teardown as it does for setup. When working with a facility that is providing the general labor, event managers should work closely with the facility manager to ensure costs are managed appropriately.

Volunteers

Contrary to what logic might imply, volunteers are not free; they are just less expensive. Someone on the staff is going to have to work to recruit the volunteers, manage the communication and assignments, and then manage the volunteers during the event. This is an expense to the event. In exchange for their assistance, it is customary that volunteers receive at least a T-shirt. At many events, volunteers receive a meal coupon to use at a concession area or a meal for volunteering. If events have sponsors in attire, food, and/or drink categories, the contracts can be negotiated for the sponsors to provide these items. If not, they have to be budgeted.

Marketing and Creative Materials

Various pieces of marketing collateral are created for events, printed and/or electronic. Each of these different pieces has an associated cost. Chapter 4 provides more information on using technology to manage some of these costs for the event. Some of the details to factor into the budget are included here.

Print Collateral

A variety of print pieces may be created. It can include a print registration form, promotional materials, participant instructions/handbooks, ticket printing, and many other items. In addition to the actual printing costs, event managers must budget for the services of the creative staff designing the pieces. Most events are moving away from paper, but there may be some print materials that are still required.

Photography

Multiple areas within an event will need to have useful photos, and event managers have to budget for the appropriate number of photographers to get those photos. For small events, it may be adequate for volunteers to take photos to avoid the cost of a professional. The marketing department uses photos for collateral pieces to advertise and promote future events. Sponsor account service managers need them for sponsor recap reports to document the fact that items agreed to in the contract actually happened. The external relations and media staff are able to provide them to media outlets and the Web master posts them on the Web site. For event managers, photos are useful to record the setup, look, and/or flow of the event.

If the event is a multi-day event, it is helpful for future years if photos are taken each day of setup to document the progress by day. Photos taken on event day keep a record of the setup and are especially valuable to show spacing. Photos to document flow will not be necessary for every event, but for mega events, they can provide very valuable information to event managers. To document flow, photos are taken at a designated location(s) at set time intervals to detail the size of the crowd and/or number of vehicles. Another option is to set up video cameras in these locations that can capture flow. This helps establish arrival and departure patterns and provide information on crowd size and space utilization.

It is important to have (or hire) a photographer who can take the type of pictures that specific functional areas request. The view that the marketing team needs is going to be different than what event management needs. Marketing will likely want to show people participating and enjoying the event. The event managers may be fine with photos taken hours before the event even starts. One way to ensure that everyone gets what is needed is by creating a shot list. A **shot list** is a document registering each photo/view that should be captured during an event by a photographer(s). When event managers hire a photographer, it is important to agree on certain requirements and get them in writing, preferably in a formal contract after consulting an attorney. Event managers should specify:

- Who owns the photographs (usually the event),
- Whether the photographer is allowed to use the photos for advertising of his/her services,

- If so, whether advance approval is required from the event,
- The timeframe required for advance approval (e.g., two weeks before needed),
- The format in which they will be given to the event (e.g., JPG, TIFF) and in what medium (e.g., disk, print, both),
- If prints are provided, the size of prints and number of copies.

Whatever the size of the event, photos are going to be a valuable asset whether for historical, promotional, or revenue sources. With the prevalence of inexpensive, easy-to-use digital cameras that are available, a tight budget might mean that volunteers are given the responsibility of photographer.

Web Site

Most events today cannot function if they do not have a Web site (see Chapter 4 for detailed information). The Web site may only be informational, or it may serve additional purposes, such as event registration. Whether the person creating the Web site is internal or the work is contracted to a third party, event managers have to budget for the creation and actual hosting. If the Web site is created and updated by a third party, any changes to the Web site are usually charged on an hourly basis. Event managers will have to conduct research to determine the cost and possible hours involved.

Communications Equipment

One of the most important things event managers do in both the planning and execution of sports events is to properly communicate. During the event, this communication can be imperative to the event's success. Having the proper equipment to do this is not an option, but a requirement. Depending on the number of people working the event and the size of the event, communication equipment could be its own category in the event budget.

Cell Phones/PDAs

Connection today is 24/7. During event time, event managers are often expected to be available at all times. Cell phones and PDAs have become ubiquitous. They are an easy way to reach event staff, whether via voice or email. Sometimes it is best to let the event staff use their own phones and simply reimburse them for their expenses. For large events, it is often easiest from a budgeting perspective to rent phones and pay the services. This way, the event does not have to account for the different cell phone plans and rates that staff may have. It is one consistent and standard amount for service and equipment.

Phones/Landlines

Not every event will need landlines. Any event that sets up temporary offices and/or a communications center, though, will need to have landlines. When budgeting for this, what is not often obvious is to include the phone. Do not assume that because a landline is connected the phone company will automatically provide a phone. The event will need to rent or purchase the actual phones to connect to the landlines. One of the additional elements to include is long-distance service. Event managers need to have access to make whatever calls are necessary, regardless of whether long distance or not.

Two-Way Radios

With the pervasive presence of cell phones and direct-connect communication devices, many events may move away from the use of two-way radios. If event managers decide to use two-way radios, some of the key items to include in the budget are extra batteries (at least one extra per event manager), individual chargers, adequate accessories (e.g., headsets, earpieces, microphones), and multi-bank charging stations.

Awards

Each event has its own requirements for awards, whether established by the event itself or the rights holder. If an event can create a unique award, it can become a fixture—and sometimes even a marketing piece—

for the event. When working with an NGB, though, they may have specific requirements that the event must follow.

Trophies and Medals

If sanctioned by an NGB, the event may be required to use—or more likely purchase—awards that are standard for the NGB. If an event creates them, one of the ways to reduce per unit costs is to create a medal, plaque, or trophy that is consistent from event to event or from year to year. The specialization can be created for less money by making the medal's ribbon or trophy's plate specific to the date and/or location.

Prize Money

Events establish and state in advance the amount for prize money, the requirements to win the prize money, and the collection procedures. If checks will be written on-site, a member of the finance staff, or other designated staff member with the proper authority, will need to be available to write the check.

Broadcast

Broadcast costs can be significant if an event has television coverage or records the event to create a broadcast production. The details of broadcast production costs are beyond the scope of this book, but event managers should be aware that they might have to be factored into the event budget.

Contingency

Contingency plans are created for all different areas of sports events. Contingency is a future event or circumstance that is possible, but cannot be predicted with certainty. With regard to budgets, contingency is money set aside in a coded account, called a **contingency account**, to cover costs that may arise due to an unexpected event or circumstance. While 10% of the total budget amount would be an ideal amount to set aside, for a large event or mega event budget that may be several million dollars, it will likely not be possible to receive sign-off for a 10% contingency account. In the case of mega events, 5% of the total budget is more probable to be approved or available.

USING MICROSOFT EXCEL TO CREATE A BUDGET

There are various event software programs that have many useful features for planning aspects of events, including the budget. For events that do not have event software, Microsoft Excel is a very useful program. Excel has the capability to do so many things that if event managers could only choose one piece of software for their computers, Excel would be a good choice. Many of Excel's uses for event managers are covered in Chapter 12, Event Documents. This section will look at Excel's use in creating and managing an event's budget. Many of the items in this section will be "how-to" items related to formatting and formulas. Basic assumptions have been made that readers know how to copy, cut, paste, and perform some other basic tasks. The same action in Microsoft products can often be performed by several different methods: drop-down menus, shortcut keys, and/or right-mouse click menus are some of the most common. How each action is accomplished is the choice of the reader. The method stated in this section may be just one way. Readers may know other ways to perform the functions addressed here. This section only covers a few of the things that event managers will likely use in Excel. As with any software program, the best way to become familiar with what it can do is by using it.

Workbooks and Worksheets

An Excel file is also known as a workbook, while each tab at the bottom of the screen is a worksheet or sheet. According to Microsoft, the number of worksheets that a workbook can contain is only limited by the amount of available computer memory. For various areas of a budget, especially for mega events, each worksheet can serve as a specific section of a budget (e.g., equipment or labor) rather than having the entire budget in one worksheet.

Worksheets can be renamed by double-clicking the tab. This activates the tab to allow changes, and event managers can then type in the new name, up to thirty-one characters. In newer versions of Excel, right-clicking on the tab and selecting "Color" can change the color of the tab. Event managers may want to use color to show summary sheets in one color, revenues in a second color, and expenses in a third color, color-code them by which event managers are responsible for each area, or for other reasons. The order of the worksheets in a workbook can be changed very easily. Simply click on the worksheet tab and drag it to the preferred location in the sequence.

Worksheets are an easy way to keep a lot of information in one file. If different sections have different budgets, they can be set up individually, but all of the information can be set up in one location.

Budget Sections

When creating a budget, there will be three areas or columns that event managers will create and monitor: budget, forecast, and actual. The **budgeted amount** is the expenses and revenues that the event managers think the event will have. At a time when everyone agrees to the budgeted amount (usually at the go/no-go decision point), the budget will be locked down, meaning that no changes can be made to the budget moving forward. From that point, event managers will use the event forecast to note any variances in the projected revenues and/or expenses. The **forecast** should be updated regularly in order to show any positive or negative variances. A positive variance may be earning more in sponsorship sales than budgeted or equipment costing less than originally anticipated, and negative variances would be the opposite of those examples. The third area will be the actual costs. When concrete expenses or revenues begin to occur, those amounts will be entered into the event **actual** section.

Each of these sections should also have columns denoting variances—variance of budget to forecast amounts and budget to actual amounts. Some event managers may also choose to note variance of forecast to actual. It is useful to include an explanation section or column after both the forecast and budget columns, clarifying why the variance is projected to occur or why it did occur.

Budget Summary

An event budget is going to be made up of several different segments, those segments mentioned earlier in the chapter and possibly others. The first worksheet in a budget should be a **budget summary**, or one-page synopsis showing the total from each segment of the budget (e.g., equipment, labor, marketing) and the grand total of those segments. It should show the budgeted, forecast, and actual amounts. When evaluating a budget, having this high-level snapshot will give event managers a quick glance as to where the event stands compared to what was planned. To see the details, event managers can look at the information on the individual segment worksheets. With links from each of these specific worksheets, any changes in the detailed numbers will be reflected on the summary sheet.

Accounting Codes

On the budget summary sheet, accounting codes may be included next to the segment names. **Accounting codes, or a chart of accounts,** are identification numbers assigned to specific categories (accounts) of revenues and expenses and are used for record keeping. They allow event managers to monitor the budget by account. In addition to viewing the column of actual costs that should be updated, event managers can check the accounting software to see what dollar amounts have hit the event or organization's books. They will know exactly how much is spent or yet to be spent in that category. Established organizations will already have these codes set up as part of their general accounting system, and the number of accounts could be extensive. For smaller events or companies, twenty to thirty accounts are usually enough.

Formatting Cells

The formatting functions covered in this section can be performed on an individual cell, a row, a column, a group of cells, or an entire worksheet, depending on what the user selects. Formatting these areas with one look creates uniformity for the budget, allowing event managers to review the budget without being distracted by aesthetic inconsistencies.

Right-clicking and then selecting "Format Cells" opens a window that allows event managers to set up the format for a myriad of different items. In the bar across the top of this window the two main areas that will be addressed here are "Number" and "Alignment." By clicking on "Number," this window enables event managers to designate how, for example, currency will be displayed. Event managers can select the number of decimal places that will show. When dealing with budgets and large numbers, it is too detailed to have cents displayed. The exact dollar and cents can be entered for Excel to calculate, but Excel can show the amount rounded to the nearest dollar. They can also select whether to show dollar signs ($) with the number or not. How a negative number, or loss, will show can also be set up from this window. In order to highlight the significance of such a number to the event budget, it is often useful to select the format that shows negative numbers in red and in parentheses.

The "Alignment" window can help with many items, but for budget formatting purposes this window is important because it enables event managers to wrap text or shrink it to fit in a cell. These features become relevant when entering the names of budgeted items or the names at the top of the columns. Rather than stretching out columns to fit a long name, simply click "Wrap text" to get the text to flow to the next line(s). The cell will expand and the words will fit within the existing width of a column. Another options is to click "Shrink to fit" to reduce the text size to fit within the given space. With this feature, though, the text could end up too small for most people to be able to read.

Formatting Worksheets

Different event managers will have their own preferences for the specific format of their budgets, but whatever the format of the worksheet, there are easy ways to copy that format to the rest of the document rather than setting up worksheets individually. To insert an additional worksheet, place the cursor over a worksheet tab and right-click. From the right-click menu, select "Insert" and then select "Worksheet." Set up the format of the worksheet. Once the user likes the format, including column width, number format, and so on, click on the diamond in the top left corner of the workbook display (to the left of column A and above row 1). Clicking the diamond selects the entire worksheet. Select copy, click on the worksheet tab where the information is to be copied, select either the diamond or the topmost left cell (cell A1), and click paste. The content from the original worksheet will be copied to the new one, but so will all of the formatting. If only the content cells had been selected and copied rather than the diamond selected, the content would have been copied, but none of the formatting.

An additional way to format the entire workbook is to format one worksheet and then right-click on the worksheet tab and select "Move or Copy." Once "Move or Copy" is selected, a drop-down list will show the file name to which the worksheet is to be moved or copied. By default, the name listed is of the current file. (The worksheet can be moved or copied to an entirely different file.) Below this is a list of the names of the worksheet tabs. Select the name of the sheet before which the copy should appear, check the box "Create a copy," and the worksheet will be copied. The name of the worksheet will be the same with (#) after that name, with the number in parentheses depending on how many copies have been made.

Linking Worksheets

One of the most useful features of Excel (and any spreadsheet) is the fact that cells can be linked throughout the file and with other Excel files. This ensures that when changes are made to numbers, any related information in linked cells or formulas that use that number are updated throughout the workbook. This text will not cover formulas in Excel, but they are vital to creating any budget. Readers should use the Help menu on Excel or read through a text on Excel if they are not familiar with how to use formulas in Excel.

As an example, if event managers are looking at different scenarios for possible number of entrants for a road race, that number will impact expenses for T-shirts, food, and medals, and revenues for registration (among other items). By linking number of participants into the formulas used to calculate those expenses and revenues, any time the number of participants is changed, those numbers will be updated. In this example, when the event managers create the budget, they would go to the cell indicating number of items, put an equal sign to start the formula, =, click on the worksheet tab name that has the number of participants, click on the specific cell that has the participant number, then press Enter. The view will then switch back to the worksheet where the formula originated and the participant number will now appear in this cell. Excel will use the number from the linked cell for calculations that identify the number of items. Links to other files are created in the same manner. With both files open, after entering the equal sign to start the formula, simply switch the view to the file from which the number will come, click on the appropriate cell in that file, and then hit Enter. Again, the view will go back to the view in the original spreadsheet.

There are entire books written on the many features of Microsoft Excel. It is a program that can help event managers calculate budgets efficiently and accurately. The few topics covered here will hopefully help event managers begin to explore the many facets of Excel.

SUMMARY

Generating an event budget is going to focus primarily on calculating the revenues and expenses for the event. There are various sources of both for events. Even if event managers are not responsible for managing revenue streams, it is helpful if they understand the nuances of the various types of revenue in order to partner better with those areas. For expenses, it is useful to know what categories may be the big-ticket cost items and what other expenses the event will encounter. Using Excel or an event software program to create the budget will make it much easier for event managers to create the budget and monitor it throughout the stages of the event.

NAME _____ DATE _____

STUDENT CHALLENGE #5

In Challenge #5, create the financial pieces associated with the event. Establish both the revenue and expense categories associated with each side of the budget. Also, use Excel to create a full and detailed budget for the event.

QUESTION 5-1

List all of the (realistic) probable revenue streams for the event, detailing the anticipated revenue for each item and category.

QUESTION 5-2

List all of the expense items for the event detailing the anticipated cost for each item and category.

Item	Quantity	Cost per Unit	Total Cost

QUESTION 5-3

Using Excel, create a budget detailing the revenues and expenses (breaking down the items on individual category sheets). Using links, produce a summary sheet with the individual total of revenue and expense categories.

CHAPTER 6

EVENT MARKETING

Jim Kahler

This chapter is intended to provide students with an understanding of how to put together an event marketing plan, and the various types of advertising that are available to market an event. To get started, let's put together a simple definition for an event marketing plan as it relates to this text. The event marketing plan includes the production and coordination of all advertising, promotional, and publicity campaigns for the event with the goal of maximizing paid attendance.

When it comes to advertising, a lot of event managers and promoters really do not know what they want, where to get it, or what to do with it after they have it. This chapter will show event managers the different options available to them and how they can use different forms of media to obtain the advertising exposure needed to promote their event. It will show a number of ways to make advertising more cost efficient.

THE MARKETING PLAN

The promoter for any event is typically responsible for putting together an event marketing plan that should include three basic campaigns, including the advertising campaign, the promotional campaign, and the publicity campaign.

The Advertising Campaign

The **advertising campaign** for an event is simply a plan that can utilize all forms of media, including, but not limited to, television, radio, newspaper, outdoor, direct mail, and online advertising to promote ticket sales for the event. Advertising budgets typically represent anywhere from 10%–15% of projected gross ticket sales (sales before any entertainment or sales tax). For example, the Harlem Globetrotters might project $200,000 in gross ticket sales for a game at Quicken Loans Arena in Cleveland, Ohio and set aside a cash advertising budget of $30,000 (15%). Any time cash is spent in return for the specified form of advertising, it is considered a form of **paid advertising**. In addition to cash advertising budgets, many event promoters will extend their media buys with trade advertising.

Trade or in-kind advertising represents any additional advertising that is secured in exchange on a dollar-for-dollar trade with tickets or something else of value to the event. Many media outlets (radio stations, television stations, and newspapers) will use event tickets to build deeper relationships with their existing advertisers. They can afford to run trade advertisements when they are not completely sold out of their advertising inventory, and will often make good use of the tickets provided by the event manager.

The Promotional Campaign

The **promotional campaign** might consist of special discounts, giveaways, theme nights, and other publicity that are sponsored by a media outlet and not a part of the paid advertising campaign. In the example from above, if the Globetrotters had a cash adverting budget of $30,000, their regional promoter would try to leverage the investment and secure another $20,000–$30,000 worth of measurable media for the game. They might do this by working with all media outlets that received a portion of the paid advertising budget. For example, let's say WUAB TV agrees to be the presenting sponsor of the Harlem Globetrotters game at Quicken Loans Arena in Cleveland, Ohio. In exchange for being the primary television station and receiving $15,000 of the $30,000 advertising budget for the event, the station gains the right to be the presenting media sponsor and will run an incremental 100, 30-second promotional spots in support of the game.

In this example the Globetrotters and the television station might offer a $3.00 discount to the game with coupons being made available at a mutually agreeable third-party location that is a paid advertiser of the station and also a promotional partner or local sponsor of the Globetrotters. Let's assume that 7-Eleven becomes the third-party sponsor of the discount and has 45 locations in northeast Ohio. The Globetrotters also receive extra visibility with in-store posters promoting their upcoming engagement and distribution of the $3.00 discount coupons as early as four weeks outside the event.

The Publicity Campaign

Once the paid advertising and promotional campaigns are put together, it is time to generate as much publicity as possible. **Publicity** can be defined as any news coverage for the event that is generated with some type of announcement or interview and is not paid for. Announcements come in the form of press releases for the event and need to be newsworthy. In the past, event promoters would hire local publicists to put together their publicity plans. Hiring a local PR agency made sense because of the working relationships that would exist within given cities, especially when the event or attraction is traveling and does not have a year-round local presence in the market.

Today, most major arenas, stadiums, and convention centers have someone that serves as a full-time director of public relations and will work closely with the event promoter to maximize publicity of the event. Referring back to the Globetrotters example, they use Phyllis Salem, Sr. Director of Public Relations at Quicken Loans Arena to generate publicity for their upcoming game in Cleveland.

Phyllis has over 20 years of experience working with the media in Cleveland and designs a plan that includes taking former Globetrotter Joe Cunningham, who now serves as an advance ambassador for the team, out into the community for a day of promotional appearances. Joe arrives one week before the game against the Washington Generals and makes several school visits to reinforce the importance of teamwork. The Cleveland Public School System is happy to have a former NBA player and Globetrotter deliver the message on teamwork, and the local news media turns out in strong numbers to cover the clinic. The result of this community outreach effort is free publicity for the upcoming event.

Pulling all three components together (the advertising, promotional, and publicity campaigns) requires a lot of work and expertise. Today, many facilities have an in-house advertising and public relations agency that provides this type of service for the promoter. An in-house agency will also take the lead on any events that are produced and promoted by the facility.

Guerrilla/ Grassroots Marketing

Guerrilla marketing is an aggressive way to market an event and could best be defined as "taking the message to the streets." **Grassroots marketing** is marketing an event on a local and personal level as a way to get the word out on the event by using a street team or group of volunteers to help promote the event. Event managers have the ability to do the following:

- Hand out flyers and, in some cases, discount coupons for the event in high traffic areas, including other events, shopping malls, and university campuses.
- Display mini posters for the event with area merchants willing to provide exposure in their window fronts.

Event managers need to be careful where they hand out flyers, as they may need permission ahead of time to distribute materials outside another event or on private property. In many instances promoters and street teams will ask for forgiveness as opposed to permission, hence the reference above to guerilla marketing.

Displaying mini posters that are typically 22″ high by 16″ wide in store fronts along high traffic areas has proven to be a very successful way to increase exposure for events, and works best when asking local merchants to display the event's message. This strategy works better with independent shop owners as opposed to shopping malls with nationally owned stores.

From Personal Experience

I was fortunate in my career to become the Director of Marketing at Cincinnati's Riverfront Coliseum at the young age of 25, and had the opportunity to run Coliseum Productions, the facility's in-house advertising and public relations agency. I believe the experience that I gained in this position helped me later in my career when I became the Sr. Vice President of Sales and Marketing with the Cleveland Cavaliers and Gund Arena. Much of what I learned in Cincinnati was garnered by working closely with a wide variety of family shows and regional promoters for such events as Ringling Brothers Barnum and Bailey Circus, Disney on Ice, Longhorn World Championship Rodeo, Sesame Street Live, the United States Hot Rod Association, the Harlem Globetrotters, and the Ice Capades. Each of these events, with the exception of the Harlem Globetrotters, was a show with multiple performances that made up a large percentage of our 100+ events per year. Each event required Coliseum Productions to handle the advertising, promotional, and publicity campaigns.

CHOOSING THE RIGHT MEDIA—TRADITIONAL MEDIA

While a strong promotional and publicity campaign can enhance awareness for the event, strategic decisions will also have to be made about the best way to utilize the cash advertising budget established for the event. Event promoters are faced with three key questions as they begin to put together their advertising campaign:

1. What is the best media to use for the particular event?

2. How important is creativity to get the message across to the targeted audience?

3. Is there a way to buy space and time that will stretch the advertising budget?

Advertising is an investment in the success or failure of the event, and like any investment, it is important for event managers to find out as much as they can about how to reach their target audience. This should be done before they start spending their advertising dollars.

Purchasing advertising is like buying many commodities, as there is only so much television, radio, newspaper, and online advertising available at any one given point in time. It is important to point out that all electronic advertising (television, radio, and online) becomes very negotiable, and that the rate card used in each of these mediums is just the starting point when putting together your advertising plan. A radio or television station's **rate card** is simply the rates charged for advertising during different day parts or during specific programming on the station.

So how do television and radio stations come up with different rates for different programming? The two most common methods of establishing rates for television and radio advertising are based on a **cost per thousand** (**CPM**) or **cost per rating point** (**CPP**). Both the radio and television industry are monitored and measured by a company called Arbitron (www.arbitron.com). Through its research methodology, Arbitron can determine the demographics of the audiences that are watching and listening to advertisements. The boxed glossary of terms on page 110 provides some other key terms as they relate to radio advertising.

Traditionally, events have used three main staples of advertising (television, radio, and newspaper) to promote ticket and admission sales. Each medium offers advantages and disadvantages for promoters to consider when putting together their actual advertising campaign.

Television Advertising

Television advertising is often referred to as the "king" of all advertising because the majority of people spend more time watching television than listening to radio or reading newspapers combined. Television allows event promoters the ability to combine the use of sight, color, sound, and motion to get their message across to a targeted audience. According to the latest research from The Nielsen Company, a global marketing research firm that specializes in measuring TV, radio, and newspaper audiences (2009) reports that the average American spends more than 4 hours a day watching television. This ends up being the equivalent of 28 hours per week, or 2 months of television viewing per year.

Reach

While television advertising has proven to be an influencer in driving ticket sales for events, it is also the most expensive form of media available to promoters. One television commercial during prime time viewing (8:00 pm until 11:00 pm) can cost $3,000 and ten times more than one radio spot during morning drive on the most popular radio station in any given city. For example, one thirty-second commercial during American Idol could cost Ringling Brothers Barnum and Bailey Circus $3,000 in Cleveland. Conversely, one thirty-second radio commercial on WTAM, Cleveland's number-one-ranked AM radio station, might cost $300 during the morning drive spot. However, the television commercial can reach ten times (or more) as many prospective customers.

Production Quality

Producing a quality television commercial becomes an important variable for any event producer to consider. Many of the events enjoy an economy of scale by producing generic commercials that can be used across a multiple-city tour schedule and simply be tagged at the end of the commercial with pertinent information on the dates, venue, and ticket information for the event. This would allow a touring event like Ringling Brothers Barnum and Bailey Circus the ability to invest more money into a series of three or four standard commercials that could be divided over a 40 city tour, as opposed to a single event that only plays once in a particular city.

Today's television audience is very sophisticated and has come to expect quality commercials. A poorly produced commercial could adversely impact ticket sales for a single event and leave a bad image in the mind of a prospective ticket buyer.

Cable

Cable advertising is a lower-cost alternative to traditional broadcast television, as it does not reach as broad an audience. However, it can often deliver a targeted audience that has real interest in an event. For example, the Gatorade Rock-N-Roll Shootout is a major college basketball doubleheader in Cleveland. The event relied heavily on the purchase of cable advertising on ESPN and Fox Sports Ohio to reach the college basketball crowd in northeast Ohio.

The only downside to cable is that it will not reach every household with a television set and the viewing audience can be much smaller. Today, most major markets have close to 52.5% cable penetration (The Nielsen Company, 2008). In the case of the Gatorade Rock-N-Roll Shootout, the event organizers felt that the cable audience watching college basketball was a perfect fit for the doubleheader and the teams playing in the shootout.

The approximate cost of a cable spot for an early season college basketball game was much more affordable than a radio spot on morning drive radio in Cleveland ($75 per cable spot vs. $200 for an average radio commercial in 2008). While the size of audience reached with a 30-second commercial on cable was much lower than the radio audience, it certainly was much more targeted for the event the organizers were promoting.

Cost

For event promoters to generate positive results and ticket sales with television advertising, they must have enough money to cover the cost of producing a good commercial. The Cleveland Cavaliers, for example, have their own in-house broadcast production crew and could produce a quality commercial for under $2,500. Using an outside agency to produce the same commercial could have cost the organization two to three times that amount.

For commercials that run in the Super Bowl, it would not be uncommon for an advertiser to spend in excess of $250,000 in production cost. With the average cost of a 30-second commercial in the 2008 Super Bowl at $3 million, the ratings and stakes are high for advertisers to get their message across in a very competitive environment (Sports Business Daily, 2008).

In addition to covering production costs, the promoters need to have a large enough budget to reach their targeted audience multiple times during their advertising campaign to be effective. Properly done television and cable advertising is the most effective medium available for an event. However, it is major league advertising and should not be included in the plan unless enough money is projected in the budget. Remember, the general rule of thumb is 10–15% of the anticipated ticket revenue should be reinvested into the advertising budget.

Radio Advertising

Radio offers a form of entertainment that attracts listeners while they are traveling, in the work place, or just relaxing. It can provide a targeted way to reach the audience and offers a wide variety of formats, including rock and roll, sports talk, news talk, country music, rap music, jazz music, classic rock, and others. Radio also provides up-to- the-minute reports on news, weather, and traffic conditions. Between 1991–2001, the Cleveland Cavaliers would often purchase commercial air time within the morning traffic updates, as the research showed the targeted audience, men age 25–54, were heavy listeners to the traffic updates on their way to work.

Radio vs. Television

Compared to television advertising, radio is a relatively inexpensive way to reach an audience. Dr. James Lavery, a former professor in the Ohio University Sports Administration program, once referred to radio advertising as "theatre of the mind" because voices, sounds, and music can be used effectively to create moods that would be too expensive to produce in a television commercial.

Radio can also become a personal advertising medium. Joe Tait, the radio voice of the Cleveland Cavaliers, has a huge fan base, and by using his voice in radio commercials the Cavaliers connected with their targeted audience. In many of the radio commercials they would take some of Joe's greatest play-by-play calls from the previous season to evoke the emotion of a fan being in the arena seeing the action he would describe.

Reach and Research

While radio can be an effective medium, it does come with some disadvantages. Since most major markets will have multiple stations, the total listening audience for any one station is just a small piece of the total listening audience. With a recent move to satellite radio, podcasting, iPods, and MP3 players, the traditional radio audience is starting to shrink.

Event managers need to work with an experienced media buyer who not only understands the event, but the market and the best stations to invest the event's advertising dollars with. From 1991–2001, the Cavaliers and Gund Arena used Scarborough Research extensively to find out what stations Cavaliers fans were listening to.

As an event organizer, keep in mind that prospective ticket buyers do not listen to the radio all the time. It is important to know when your customers are listening. For example, if an event wants to reach a large portion of its audience by advertising during morning drive when they are commuting to work, the event will have to specify that time period to the radio station when it places its advertising schedule. Two of the most popular times to reach people are during their commute time to work with morning (6:00 am–10:00 am) and afternoon (3:00 pm–6:00 pm) drive times. Event managers can expect to pay a premium to advertise during these two drive times because research has shown listening levels are at their highest for the day.

Radio is a personal advertising medium. Station personalities have a good rapport with their listeners. If a radio personality announces an event's commercial, it is almost an implied endorsement. Since prospective buyers will not be able to automatically recall the commercials, event organizers will need to design a schedule that provides them the opportunity to hear the same commercial four to six times before the message sinks in.

Radio Advertising Glossary of Terms

Knowing the terminology used in the measurement of radio listening is essential to a better understanding of audience estimates. The definitions that follow are generally accepted by the radio industry.

Cost Per Rating Point (CPP) The cost of reaching one percent of the target population. CPP is calculated by dividing the cost of the schedule by the gross rating points. National and regional advertising buyers frequently use this cost efficiency measure, since it can be applied across all media.

Cost Per Thousand (CPM) The relative cost of a schedule of announcements may be calculated by dividing the cost of the schedule by the sum of the average quarter-hour audiences of the announcements purchased.

Frequency The average number of exposures to the commercial or song heard by the average listener, or a frequency distribution revealing the number of persons estimated to have heard the commercial or song one time, two times, three times, four times, etc.

Format Programming of a radio station aimed at a specific audience such as Country, Adult Contemporary, Urban, Rock, etc.

Rating The percentage of the population listening to a given radio station during a day part. Ratings apply to both average quarter-hour and cumulative audiences.

Reach The total number of different persons exposed to a commercial or song during a specified day part. Reach can be calculated using a computer for a single station, multiple stations, or across media using formulas generally accepted by the advertising industry.

Share The percentage of people listening to a specific radio station in a particular day part compared to all those listening to radio in that day part. Share answers the question: "What percentage of the radio audience is listening to a specific station at a particular time?"

Time Spent Listening (TSL) The amount of time the average listener spent listening to a radio station during a day part. The estimate may be expressed in number of quarter hours or in hours/minutes. TSL answers the question: "How much time does the average listener spend with this station?"

Source: Arbitron Inc., (www.arbitron.com/radio_stations/tradeterms.htm) and Research Director (www.research directorinc.com/Glossary.htm)

Newspaper Advertising

Every advertising medium has characteristics that give it natural advantages and limitations. Looking through any newspaper will demonstrate that there are some businesses that advertise regularly. Observe who they are and how they advertise their products and services. More than likely, their advertising investment is working if it is selling. Events can reach certain types of people by placing their ads in different sections of the paper. Most events will end up advertising in the entertainment or sports section of a paper.

People expect advertising in the newspaper. In fact, many people buy the paper just to read the ads from the supermarket, movies, or department stores. Unlike advertising on TV and radio, advertising in the newspaper can be examined at a person's leisure. A newspaper ad can contain details, such as event ticket prices, charge by phone telephone numbers, and performance times.

There are many advantages to advertising in the newspaper. From the advertiser's point of view, newspaper advertising can be convenient because production changes can be made quickly, if necessary. Often, a new advertisement can be inserted on short notice. Another advantage is the large variety of ad sizes newspaper advertising offers. Event promoters may not have a large budget, but they can still afford to place a series of small newspaper ads. Advertising in the newspaper offers many advantages, but it is not without its inherent disadvantages.

Today many major daily newspapers are going out of business. Others will be changing their publication schedule to come out on a three- to four-times-a-week basis. Newspapers usually are read once and stay in the house for just a day. The print quality of newspapers is not always the best, especially for photographs that event managers might want to capture the true essence of their event. So, simple artwork and line drawings produce the best results. The page size of a traditional daily newspaper is fairly large and small ads can look minuscule. Remember that in the entertainment or sports section, the ad has to compete with other entertainment ads to gain the reader's attention.

Cost and Format

Newspaper advertising is typically sold by the column inch, with most daily newspapers working with a six-column-wide format. For example, an ad that measures 4 columns wide and 6 inches in height would be the equivalent of a 24-inch ad. If the per column inch rate for the newspaper is $45.00, the ad would cost $1080.00 (24 column inches × $45 per column inch).

Historically, newspaper circulation drops on Saturdays and increases on Sundays, which is also the day a newspaper is read most thoroughly. Create short, descriptive copy for the event's ad. Using a less-is-more approach, event managers can develop an uncluttered ad that will increase readership. Do not try to crowd everything possible into the layout space. If the newspaper or an agency helps with the layout, be sure to request a proof of the final version so the event organizers can approve it or make changes before it is printed. Always make sure everyone is satisfied with what the advertising says and how it looks before it goes to print.

CHOOSING THE RIGHT MEDIA—NON-TRADITIONAL MEDIA

While television, radio, and newspaper have been the staples for event advertising, it is important to consider other alternatives to traditional advertising formats. Online advertising, outdoor advertising, and direct mail are other alternatives that can produce good results for events.

Online Advertising

Today, promoters are using online advertising at an increasing rate to hit target audiences and get the word out on their events. Online advertising utilizes the Internet and World Wide Web to deliver messages, and can be a very cost-efficient medium. In most cases, the Web site with the highest traffic in a given market is typically owned by the daily newspaper. Cleveland Live, www.clevelandlive.com, is a very well read Web site that redistributes most of the articles contained in *The Cleveland Plain Dealer* and is an effective way to reach an audience that is looking for entertainment options.

When event organizers think of online advertising, they should not limit their options to simply banner ads on high-traffic Web sites, but also the boundless opportunities to connect with their intended audience through cross-promotions with email marketing. Many arenas today have built up databases with previous customers who want to stay informed on upcoming events and are always looking for special discounts. The US Airways Center in Phoenix is a good example where the facility and Phoenix Suns have teamed up to let customers sign up for an entertainment/newsletter program called Downtown Live. Members of Downtown Live receive notices when events go on sale and exclusive discounts, and provide the promoter with the opportunity to run commercials and showcase their event. For more information on Downtown Live visit www.downtownlive.net.

Connecting with an event's past and prospective customers via email has many advantages to the event promoter, starting with the ability to distribute information to individuals who have purchased tickets online. When an event contracts with a ticketing company like Ticketmaster, the event will receive the right to all names and email addresses of any customers who purchased their tickets online. Today many live events are incentivizing their customers to purchase tickets online, as it helps build a long-term relationship once they have that customer's email address. Compared to direct mail, electronic mail is much less expensive and allows event organizers to link potential customers back to their Web site, where organizers can provide much greater information on their event. With targeted offers through email, the event organizers can also measure a direct return on their investment.

Outdoor Advertising

When most people think of outdoor advertising, they tend to envision billboards along a busy highway; however, do not exclude other forms of advertising in this category. Others forms include, but are not limited to, transit advertising (buses, light rail, taxi cabs), posters, and municipally owned electronic displays. Outdoor advertising connects with the audience as an element of the environment and does not have to be invited into a person's home, apartment, or college residence hall. It is part of public domain and represents a form of media that consumers cannot simply switch off or throw away. As a result, outdoor advertising represents a captured audience that works on frequency, as most outdoor contracts run a minimum of thirty days.

One of the advantages of outdoor advertising for an event promoter is that there is usually plenty of unsold space in most markets. Outdoor companies are open to trade agreements and will provide space in exchange for an equal value of tickets to an event. These companies can use the tickets to entertain paid advertisers without adding money to their travel and entertainment budgets. The event promoters will still need to pay for the price of producing items like billboards, bus cards, and taxi top signage. In some cases a blend of cash and trade is a good way to extend the event's advertising budget with an outdoor advertising company. The more desirable locations are typically not available for trade, so if the event organizers really want one high-traffic billboard location, they can purchase the unit at rate card and leverage their outdoor reach with other locations.

When considering outdoor advertising, event managers have to keep in mind some of the disadvantages as well. The event's message has to be short and to the point, as the average reader will only have 3–5 seconds to focus on the message. While event managers might be able to negotiate a rate for one month, most outdoor companies will start with a three month commitment. Remember that media is one of the most negotiable services, and if the event has cash and tickets to work with, event organizers should be able to work out an agreement that benefits both parties.

Direct Mail

What makes "direct mail" any different than the regular mail someone might receive from a friend or family member? Nothing . . . it is just a way that the advertising community describes a promotional offer or message that circumvents the traditional forms of media (TV, radio, and newspaper) that were described earlier in this chapter.

The advantage of direct mail is that it can be very targeted if an event keeps records of individuals who have purchased tickets in the past. Event managers might want to consider an early bird offer by sending a direct mail piece to past purchasers of the event before tickets or entry slots go on sale to the general public. This is a great way to reward fans that have attended or participated in the event in the past and let them know that the event appreciates their past support. In some cases the event may even consider a special discount and deadline depending on the overall demand for full-price tickets to the event.

Today, event marketers are using special agencies to help them design direct mail campaigns that help them find likely individuals to target for a direct mail campaign. Traditional response rates for direct mail come in at the 1–2% response rate, and it is becoming increasingly important to develop the right target list to mail to. For example, if an event finds that its past sales indicate that a particular zip code represents 25% of its buying audience, it may want to do some additional research within the zip code to find other consumers that match the profile of these past attendees.

The cost of a four-color promotional direct mail brochure can be expensive, and event organizers need to look at the return on investment before deciding to use direct mail. As compared to email, where the expense can be next to nothing, direct mail does allow an event to stand out from the clutter if the design of the mail creates excitement around the event.

Additional advice on direct mail:

- Define the target audience and determine who the event wants to reach.

- Determine the offer the event is prepared to make on the campaign.

- Estimate the return on investment and use a 1–2% return rate to be conservative.

- Secure the right mailing list and bring in an outside agency to help determine who to mail to and help the event create an exciting looking mail piece.

- Use clear and concise language with the promotional offer that provides good direction to the audience.

- If event organizers are not prepared to invest in creative services, they may want to eliminate direct mail from their media mix.

- Make sure to coordinate the timing of the mailing with the other forms of media that the event organizers choose for the event.

SUMMARY

From this chapter, students should gain a fundamental understanding of the aspects that are important in creating a marketing plan for events. Knowing about the various types of traditional media, and the terminology associated with each, will better enable event managers to make the right media decisions for their events during the planning process.

Student Challenge

STUDENT CHALLENGE #6

In Challenge #6, develop plans around media exposure, advertising, and promotional campaigns for the event. Additionally, create a plan to monitor these activities.

QUESTION 6-1

Develop a basic advertising plan for the event. In 250–500 words, list all appropriate advertising outlets including, but not limited to, television, radio, print, outdoor, grass roots, and Internet. Additionally, indicate *why* each outlet is a good fit for advertising the event. Take notes here and then type up the advertising plan.

Student Challenge

QUESTION 6-2

Choose and examine two prospective media partners for the event. Determine how to work with these partners to maximize promotional exposure (e.g., sweepstakes, contests, etc.). Hint: Most events have a local radio station partner at a minimum.

Media Partner #1:

Ideas to maximize promotional exposure:

Media Partner #2:

Ideas to maximize promotional exposure:

CHAPTER 7

EVENT SPONSORSHIP

Jim Kahler

This chapter provides students with an introduction to the concept of event sponsorships and the key principles associated with sponsorship. Sponsorship has been defined many ways, but for the purposes of this chapter, the International Events Group (IEG) definition will be used. IEG defines **sponsorship** as a cash and/or in-kind fee paid to a property (typically in sports, arts, entertainment, or causes) in return for access to the exploitable commercial potential associated with that property (Ukman, 2008).

EVENT SPONSORSHIP

International Events Group (IEG) was founded in 1981 with the primary goal of helping to establish sponsorship as the fourth arm of marketing along with advertising, publicity, and promotions. Although this chapter will only touch on the broad aspects of sponsorship, event organizers will find IEG to be a useful resource if they are interested in learning more about sponsorships. Feel free to visit their Web site, www.sponsorship.com, for additional information on sponsorships.

According to IEG, worldwide spending on sponsorships was more than $35 billion in 2008, and North America led the world with over $16 billion spent on sponsorship in 2008 (Ukman, 2008). Events in the United States make up most of this spending with traditional sponsorships in the four major sports leagues (NBA, NFL, MLB, and NHL) along with NASCAR. With the recent success of the 2008 Summer Olympics in Beijing, China, and World Cup Soccer, the rest of the world is closing in on this form of marketing. So what is it about sponsorships that today's marketers are finding attractive enough to invest a large portion of their marketing budget to connect with consumers? The inefficiency of traditional media (television, radio, and newspaper) has caused many companies to look for new ways to interact with their existing and targeted customers. It is becoming increasingly difficult to reach customers today with the decrease in circulation of newspapers, the invention of TiVo, and the proliferation of satellite radio. Sponsorship provides a targeted way for a company to reach an audience and can also provide live experiential interaction between the product and customer.

Reasons for Company Sponsorship

Companies have traditionally invested in sponsorship for one of two primary reasons:

- Build brand awareness with a targeted audience;

- Increase sales with a targeted audience.

The proponents of event sponsorship will point out the positives associated with the ability of a live event to create interaction between the event and consumers. When event organizers can create an atmosphere at their event that allows attendees to interact with a sponsor's product or service, they are creating a unique experience for their sponsor which traditional advertising cannot deliver. This interaction could best be described as **experiential marketing**. Today, experiential marketing in the sport of NASCAR has become part of the live event, with sponsors often competing for the attention of race fans on the day of the event.

Gatorade's sponsorship with the National Football League provides the company a dominant amount of space at the NFL Experience, the Super Bowl pre-game festival that runs a week in advance of the game. The experience for a young child to attend such an event leaves a lasting memory that allows Gatorade the opportunity not only to build brand awareness, but also increase brand loyalty, as the children who attend this event are likely to play youth sports and consume some type of isotonic sports drink on a regular basis. While not everyone can obtain a ticket to the game, over 100,000 football fans in the Tampa Bay area attended the NFL Experience in 2009 (Green Events Group, n.d.).

So how can Gatorade use its sponsorship with the Super Bowl and the NFL to increase sales? Let's go back to the definition of sponsorship provided by IEG at the beginning of this chapter. In this case, Gatorade acquires the right to exploit, on a commercial basis, the logos of the NFL and Super Bowl XLIII. Gatorade would then have the right to build special displays in supermarkets across the state of Florida and run a sweepstakes providing fans with the opportunity to attend a private reception at the NFL Experience, throw a touchdown pass on the field, and meet Peyton Manning (one of the company's star athletes featured in Gatorade's television commercials). Having the opportunity to utilize special promotions like this would allow Gatorade's sales team the opportunity to generate special displays and increase sales for a 30-day time period. This example of a sales promotion would allow Gatorade the opportunity to measure incremental case sales in the Tampa Bay area over the same period of time from a year ago, when the Super Bowl was being played in Phoenix, Arizona. This gives the company the ability to then measure the impact of its sponsorship and increase case sales.

Creativity with Caution

Dan Hauser

Creativity and excitement are important elements that every sport entity attempts to accomplish in the execution of sporting events. A primary goal for event managers is for their customers to have a great time and a positive experience at their events. The fan experience is the one element that event managers can control and influence. Wins and losses are out of their control, but they can have an influence on the environment. Sport is entertainment, and in the competitive consumer environment creativity is one tool event managers can use to gain an edge.

Creativity can be very powerful, but event managers must use this power with caution. When creativity goes wrong it can result in a very public and enduring embarrassment for event managers. To illustrate this, let's investigate a Villanova men's basketball game and a Western Michigan minor league baseball game.

Villanova vs. #7 Pittsburgh—January 29, 2007

The game was a huge Big East men's basketball battle that was broadcast live on ESPN Big Monday, the type of game that gets every event manager excited. The game was very close and filled with a lot of excitement through halftime. With around eleven minutes left in the second half, the horn sounded for a media time out. Out came the event managers to the floor, setting up a promotion for a regional grocery store chain. There were two contestants located at half court and two grocery carts located around the free-throw line. The objective of the contest was for the contestants to attempt to throw a grocery item and land it in the shopping cart. The contestant who got the most items into the cart won.

It was a creative contest with strong sponsorship branding until the event managers provided the contestants with heads of lettuce as the item to throw. For two minutes, contestants threw heads of lettuce that exploded on impact with the floor and shredded into pieces when they hit the grocery cart. Lettuce was everywhere when the horn sounded for the end of the time out. Dust brooms were brought out to get all the lettuce off the floor, but the lettuce was stuck to the floor. An army of event managers and referees had to scour the court, picking up every piece of lettuce. The game was delayed for five to ten minutes while ESPN broadcasted images and comments about the debacle to a national audience.

Western Michigan White Caps vs. Southwest Michigan Devil Rays—April 15, 2006

The majority of sports fans have probably attended a minor league baseball game. Event managers in minor leagues are the kings and queens of creativity and entertainment. They have to be, because the majority of their customers cannot name a player on their team or the team's current record. Minor league baseball fans want to be entertained, and this game was like most typical Saturday games—with one twist. At the conclusion of the game there would be a $1,000 cash giveaway for kids. The promotion was set up with children lined up on the outfield fence. The cash was dropped from a helicopter over the ballpark, and the kids scrambled to pick up as much cash as possible. It was a very creative game day promotion to attract families to a minor league game, but with the excitement of the cash, the promotion turned dangerous. The kids' ages ranged from 5 to 12, and the old adage "the strong will survive" prevailed. In the mayhem, a 7-year-old boy was trampled and taken to a hospital. Additionally many children left the outfield with bloody faces. The news was a national story picked up by ESPN; luckily the events were not more tragic.

The aforementioned examples were not provided to stifle event managers' creativity. Instead, each was presented to show the importance of using caution when being creative. Here are ten creativity control measures to assist event managers with their event management:

1. *Practice:* Always execute a promotion on the court or field with staff before it is performed live at an event. Event managers should never roll out a promotion that they have not executed or practiced.

2. *Control:* Event managers have control of everything. Control the number of contestants, ages of participants, apparatus, rules, etc. Review every detail with the contestants so they know what they are to do during the promotion. A great tip is to draw out the contest on paper to the contestants.

3. *Questions:* Create a think tank with the rest of the event staff and ask questions. Are there health and safety risks? What could go wrong with this promotion?

4. *Sell Contests:* The event managers are the experts. Sell contests to sponsors; do not let the sponsor make up the contest. What may seem creative to sponsors may put event managers and/or contestants in danger.

5. *Steal:* Observe what works with promotions and contests at other sporting events and implement these ideas at your events. If it works for their fans, then be creative and steal the idea. In an academic setting this might be plagiarism, but in the sports industry it is called benchmarking best practices.

6. *Adjustments:* A promotion or contest is never perfect. Always evaluate, make adjustments, and observe fan reaction.

7. *End:* Make sure there is an end to your promotion: time, number of attempts, tie breaker situation.

8. *Fresh:* Keep the promotions and contests fresh. Change the contests annually. Do not sell season-long promotions; instead, sell opportunities (10 out of 15 games) so the promotions are rotated and the event has variety. Fans want variety and new elements.

9. *Complement:* Use creatively matched music, video board displays, or lights to complement the promotions and contests.

10. *Go:* A common mistake is to spend too much time talking or telling the rules of a promotion or contest. Fans are smart and they can figure it out. Always keep a fast mentality: Ready. . . Set. . . Go!

NATIONAL SPORT FORUM RESEARCH

As IEG and other sports marketing experts will point out, there are a number of other reasons that companies sponsor events, but increasing sales and building brand awareness seem to be at the top of the priority list. Every two years, the National Sports Forum (www.sports-forum.com) examines the motivations of companies that sponsor sports. In 2008, faculty and staff at Ohio University's Center for Sports Administration conducted over 50 telephone interviews with some of the largest sports sponsors in North America, including Anheuser-Busch, Coca-Cola, Gatorade, and Southwest Airlines. Relevant to this discussion on event sponsorship are the results related to which aspects of sponsorship proposals are most important to sponsors.

Research Analysis

For the most part, sponsors valued the same things in 2008 as they did during the 2006 study when evaluating sponsorship proposals, with the notable exception of a rise of four slots in the rankings for "Create a common bond between your fans and my consumers" up to number one. Conversely, "Become a trademark association within the community" fell four slots, from number five to number nine.

Although it is very interesting that marketers have placed a priority on creating a common bond between fans and their target consumers, the margin of difference between slot number one and number four is small in total scoring.

Most interesting to the research team was that items such as sampling and hospitality that are common to event sponsorship proposals are not valued highly by sponsors. On the other hand, the top categories selected by sponsors were things that are designed into the activation of a sponsorship proposal, such as common bond between fans and consumers and driving quantifiable sales into area retailers (see Table 7-1.).

While each of the companies interviewed have benefitted from their involvement with sponsorship, three key trends emerged: turnkey activation, creativity, and research.

Table 7-1. Corporate & Industry Survey Results

What do sponsors and advertisers consider to be the most important elements when evaluating a good sponsorship proposal?

(**EI** = Extremely Important; **I** = Important; and **NI** = Not Important. **Total Score** is determined on a scale in which EI's get 5 points, I's get 3, and NI's get 0 points.)

Element	EI	I	NI	SCORE	'06 Survey Rank
Create a common bond between your fans and my consumers	39	16	0	243	(4)
Has the flexibility to fit within my budget	41	12	2	241	(1)
Tap into new markets and new customers	41	12	2	241	(2)
Drive quantifiable sales into my area retailers	42	9	4	237	(3)
Helps retain my customer base	32	18	5	214	(6)
Ability for turnkey execution by the team/event	25	24	6	197	(7)
Having a team program that ties into my marketing theme	21	24	10	177	(9)
Hospitality opportunities	13	27	15	146	(8)
Become a trademark association within the community	14	25	14	145	(5)
Ties into our current ad campaign	18	16	21	138	(10)
Opportunity to distribute product samples	9	24	22	117	(11)
Social networking opportunities	13	16	26	113	N/A

Turnkey Activation

There is a need for events, sports properties, and teams to provide additional staff to help execute and activate promotions centered on the sponsorship. Sponsors are currently valuing the ability of the event staff to provide turnkey activation (e.g., event personnel able to activate the sponsorship from start to finish with little involvement from the sponsor). Over time, the word sponsorship has become synonymous with **partnership**, and it is incumbent on the event organizer to treat a sponsor like a true partner where together both parties can benefit from a successful event. One highly respected sponsorship executive indicated that teams and other rights holders are leaving incremental sponsorship dollars on the table by not hiring enough service representatives within their sponsorship department.

Creativity

Event organizers need to be creative and allow sponsors the opportunity to create unique programming and stand out from what often becomes alphabet soup, with too many sponsors taking part in the same event. The example of Home Depot's sponsorship of College Game Day on ESPN—ESPN College Game Day Built by the Home Depot—was cited by several sponsors in the study as an outstanding example of building a unique partnership centered around college football.

Research

Event organizers need to do their homework prior to taking a sponsorship opportunity out to market. They should not assume a one-size-fits-all approach with the promotional ideas for a specific sponsor category. For example, if an event is looking for a bank sponsor, the event organizers need to understand what is important to each particular bank. They cannot simply change the masthead of their proposal as they create sales pitches for various banks. One bank may be more focused on building business with individual consumers with special offers to sign up for a new checking account, while another may be more interested in hospitality at the event where they can entertain their corporate account holders.

TARGETING SPONSORS

As event managers look to target potential sponsors for their event, it will become increasingly important to ask one very significant question: What's in it for you? In this case, the "you" is the sponsor and this key question can be referred to as the WIIFY. Individuals trying to sell the sponsorship need to put themselves in the position of the company they are trying to bring on board as a sponsor. Then they should ask themselves what they might do if they were sitting on the other side of the negotiating table. By doing this, whoever is selling will put themselves in position for success.

Listed below is a series of 22 questions that have been developed to help event managers look for the right sponsors for their event. These questions are what sponsors will be asking themselves as they review countless opportunities for sponsorship.

22 Questions That Sponsors Ask Themselves

1. Does the event line up with the image the sponsor is trying to project?

2. Does the audience at the event meet the target audience of the sponsor?

3. Will the event extend the reach of the sponsor with television coverage?

4. Will event organizers provide the sponsor with the right to bring a retail partner on board? (Example: Would the event allow Coca-Cola to bring in a third-party retailer, such as a grocery store, to create a sweepstakes like the one outlined previously with Gatorade and the NFL?)

5. Would the prospective sponsor think enough of the event to convert a portion of their existing advertising to showcase the partnership? (Example: Coors Light's television campaign that helps celebrate their sponsorship with the NFL via post-game press conference footage with former coaches.)

6. Will the event receive media coverage?

7. Will the hospitality benefits of the sponsorship be attractive to the clients of the sponsor?

8. Is the event willing to place the sponsor's logo in all of its advertising for the event? If so, what is the size of the advertising budget and how many other sponsors will be featured in the advertising? (Note: Be careful that not too many sponsors are included in the event's advertising, resulting in alphabet soup.)

9. If the event provides the sponsor with the right to exploit the event logo, will the sponsor take advantage of that opportunity outside of the four walls of the event?

10. Does the date/timing of the event line up well with the sponsor's promotional calendar, or will it conflict with another event that the sponsor is already involved in?

11. Is the event willing to provide the sponsor with exclusivity? If not, be prepared to share the overall plan and the number of competing sponsors that the prospect might see at the event.

12. Does the event have the ability to showcase the products or services of the sponsor at the event?

13. What is the projected attendance at the event and is it believable?

14. Can the sponsor drive incremental sales by being involved with the event?

15. Will the sponsor be able to measure their return on investment with the amount of extra visibility obtained through the sponsorship and incremental sales driven through the relationship?

16. How will the sponsor's boss feel about the sponsorship?

17. Does the sponsorship have the opportunity to be a long-term partnership? Has the event offered the sponsor the right to enter into a long-term partnership with first right to renew?

18. Will the event be able to deliver everything outlined in the sponsorship proposal?

19. Will the event organizers provide a recap of the sponsorship after the event concludes that helps justify the cost?

20. Will the sponsor get lost in the clutter of other event sponsors?

21. Does the sponsorship provide a competitive advantage to the sponsor over their competition?

22. If the event managers were sitting at the desk of the prospective sponsor, would they enter into the partnership?

This list is not necessarily exhaustive, but will help event managers understand the questions that potential sponsors are asking internally. Reviewing the answers may result in revisions to sponsorship proposals to ensure they are tailored to the specific prospective sponsor being approached. Ultimately, this will help in securing a sponsor.

Outsourcing Sponsorship Sales

Executing a successful event and the ability to sell event sponsorships are two different skill sets that a young promoters need to understand. In some cases, it may make sense for event promoters to hire an outside sales agent to sell their sponsorships. This has been the trend with college athletics over the last ten years, with athletic directors at major universities negotiating for guaranteed sponsorships from companies like ISP Sports (www.ispsports.com), who now represent sponsorship sales for over sixty colleges across the country. An operations staff for a university's athletic department can successfully execute a football game, but would not necessarily have the sales ability or time to secure sponsorships.

Hiring an outside agency typically comes with a price of anywhere from 15–25% of the gross total generated through the sale of sponsorships. If the event or organization is big enough, like a college athletic department, it can require an up-front guarantee from the agency that receives the right to sell sponsorships. This would be the case with the NCAA's Men's Basketball Tournament when it secured an up-front multi-million dollar guarantee from CBS Sports for the air time and sponsorship inventory associated with the tournament.

PRICING OF SPONSORSHIPS

How do event organizers determine what the sponsorship of their event is worth? One formula to establish the cost of an event sponsorship is:

Total Measured Media for the Event / 25% = Cost of the Presenting Sponsorship.

To illustrate this formula, the Avon Tennis Championships in Cincinnati will be used as an example. The Avon Tennis Championships with $100,000 in measured media (print, television, and radio commercials of the event, along with some of the other elements already outlined in this chapter) would be priced at $25,000. In addition to the measured media that Avon received in conjunction with the event, they also received a number of other benefits. The benefits included arena signage, complimentary tickets, opportunity to provide up to 12 ball boys/ball girls for the event, and the right to host a cocktail party for their top customers with some of the top names in women's tennis. Run through the 22 questions provided earlier in this chapter to see that this ended up being a good investment for the cosmetic company.

While the tennis tournament was heavily attended in Cincinnati, it did not include any regional or national television coverage. The seven-day tournament resulted in attendance of over 50,000 fans coming to downtown Cincinnati. If they had the benefit of additional coverage on television, the cost of the sponsorship would have been higher. The general rule of thumb with televised events would show a correlation between the amounts of on-camera exposure a sponsor receives with their event signage and the cost of commercial time on the same network. This type of formula is often used to help determine the value of courtside signage for an NBA team. Listed below is an example that might help show the correlation.

Cleveland Cavaliers Courtside Signage on Fox Sports Ohio (FSO)

- Guaranteed exposure time on FSO of 3 minutes per game

- Multiplier: 40 home games × 3 minutes = 120 minutes

- 120 minutes equals 240 30-second commercials (120 minutes / 30 seconds = 240 commercials)

- Average 30-second commercial on FSO = $600

- Total value of time exposure on FSO = $144,000

In the example listed above, let us assume that Coca-Cola wants 3 minutes per game of exposure on the scorer's table and is looking at a more comprehensive sponsorship in excess of $1 million. The Cavaliers can represent that the commercial time Coca-Cola's logo will receive in the local broadcasts is worth $144,000 on FSO. This is based on the rate card for a 30-second TV spot on Fox Sports. In their negotiation, Coca-Cola will argue that while their logo will indeed receive 120 minutes of on-camera exposure, they will not be able to run the same type of creative exposure as a typical 30-second commercial. Thus, the two parties will agree on a price that is typically discounted by 20–50%. This type of metric could be used for any event on television that provides a sponsor with exposure within the broadcast.

A much larger example would be the Tostitos Fiesta Bowl in Phoenix, Arizona. With the tremendous national television coverage and ratings that the Fiesta Bowl receives each year, it is able to leverage the on-field logo exposure that Tostitos receives as the name in title sponsorship of the game. The end result is a multi-million-dollar sponsorship of the game. The same could be said for other national events like the FedEx Orange Bowl and the Sprint Nextel Series in NASCAR.

Value In-Kind and Budget Relieving In-Kind

A sponsor may be able to provide needed items and services to the event in lieu of a cash sponsorship. If so, the products and services will be categorized as Value In-Kind (VIK) or Budget Relieving In-Kind (BRIK).

Proactive Communication with Sponsors

I can recall a national concert tour with Michael Jackson that was being sponsored by Pepsi when I oversaw all of the sponsorships at Gund Arena (now Quicken Loans Arena). While we knew we would benefit by having two sold-out concerts with Michael Jackson, we had to negotiate hard with the concert promoter to protect our facility sponsor (Coca-Cola) and still come up with some exposure for the national tour sponsor (Pepsi). The solution was limited signage for Pepsi that was attached to the front of the actual stage. We were very proactive in communicating this situation with Coca-Cola, and they appreciated our reaching out, as some other arenas with similar provisions within their Coke sponsorships did not take the time to call Atlanta and make them aware of the concert.

Value In-Kind, is a sponsor's product or service that is provided in exchange for specified marketing rights to the event. The product or service does not necessarily have to be in the event budget. BRIK, or Budget Relieving In-Kind, is a product or service that an event had budgeted that is now being provided by a sponsor in exchange for specified marketing rights to the event, and it mitigates the amount the event had budgeted to spend on that item.

Let's look at an example of the difference. A phone company, such as Sprint Nextel, signs on as a sponsor for the event one year out from the event. The event did not have it in its budget to supply and pay for a company-provided cell phone for staff members. Sprint Nextel, as part of its sponsorship, has agreed to supply a certain number of cell phones and service as part of its sponsorship agreement. This is VIK because although it is a service to staff, it is not something that will alleviate a budgeted cost. It would not have been provided to staff if the sponsor had not given it. If that same event had budgeted a dollar amount to provide certain staff members with a cell phone and related service for one year prior to the event, and Sprint Nextel then agreed to provide it as part of their sponsorship deal, it would be BRIK. The event would be relieved of paying that budgeted amount.

Conflicts/Facilities & Event Sponsorships

Event promoters need to be aware of possible restrictions that they may encounter when renting an arena or stadium to host an event. It is not unusual for facilities to negotiate exclusive sponsorships with companies like Coca-Cola that include exclusive pouring and signage rights within the venue for the soft drink company. The key for any event promoter is to be aware of such provisions with facility sponsors and never promise any benefits that may not be deliverable.

SUMMARY

Many promoters consider event sponsorship to be the icing on the top of the cake and would not recommend placing sponsorship dollars into the overall projections for any new event that event organizers might consider starting (unless the event is going to be on national or regional television). With that being said, the example provided earlier with the Avon Tennis Championships in Cincinnati could be considered a successful event if it covered all related expenses and was able to put the entire $25,000 of sponsorship toward the bottom line of profit for the event. Successful events should be able to turn a profit without sponsorship through revenues associated with ticket sales and/or participant registration, concession sales, parking, and merchandise sales.

Student Challenge

NAME _____ DATE _____

STUDENT CHALLENGE #7

In Challenge #7, evaluate the sponsorship potential for the event and create a proposal(s) targeting potential sponsors.

QUESTION 7-1

Create a list of at least ten benefits (e.g., in game promotions, signage, etc.) available to potential sponsors.

Benefit #1:

Benefit #2:

Benefit #3:

Benefit #4:

Benefit #5:

Benefit #6:

Benefit #7:

Benefit #8:

Benefit #9:

Benefit #10:

Student Challenge

QUESTION 7-2

Evaluate the event needs to determine four potential sponsors that are a good fit to provide VIK/BRIK products/services. Discuss why there is a fit between what each company can provide and the needs of the event.

Sponsor #1:

Sponsor/Event Fit:

Sponsor #2:

Sponsor/Event Fit:

Sponsor #3:

Sponsor/Event Fit:

Sponsor #4:

Sponsor/Event Fit:

Student Challenge

QUESTION 7-3

Make a list of four potential sponsors with target markets that reflect the target market (participants and/or spectators) of the event. Discuss the benefit to each company if they choose to sponsor different aspects of the event.

Sponsor #1:

Company Benefit:

Sponsor #2:

Company Benefit:

Sponsor #3:

Company Benefit:

Sponsor #4:

Company Benefit:

QUESTION 7-4

Using the companies identified in 7-2 and 7-3, write two basic sponsorship proposals. Use the space provided to take notes and then type up the proposals. One proposal will be for a VIK/BRIK sponsorship and one proposal will be for a cash (or combination) sponsorship. Each proposal must be for a different company.

Proposal #1 Notes:

Proposal #2 Notes:

CHAPTER 8

PARTICIPANT REGISTRATION FOR EVENTS

Roy Edmondson

Often an afterthought, but most definitely one of the most important aspects of participant-driven events, is the registration. The registration form (online or paper) will contain all critical information pertaining to the event. If this information is incorrect or incomplete, it can lead to endless amounts of frustration for event managers and participants. For purposes of registration, a **participant** is anyone taking part in a sports event. This includes everyone associated with a team taking part in a sports event who will be on the field of play (including, but not limited to, players, coaches, statisticians, athletic trainers, managers); volunteers; participants in promotions; and so on. In the examples below, "participant" may refer strictly to athletes and coaches, but event managers should remember that, generally, other groups are included in the term "participant." On-site registration is the first face-to-face contact between participants and the event. If everything runs smoothly and all information necessary has been provided, then the participants' first experience is a pleasant one, and that will go a long way. It is almost certain that if the experience with registration is bad, then it will take a long time to recover and possibly even cost the event future business.

When to Start?

The most important factor in determining when to disseminate registration information is to understand the sport and its customers. Each sport is different as to when participants determine in what events they will take part. For example, many travel hockey teams will decide in early fall what tournaments they will play for the entire season (September–April). This way, they can include any tournament entry fees in the player team fee once players have been selected for the team. On the other hand, many summer basketball teams are not even formed until late spring, so to have registration out any earlier does not make sense. The most important thing is to have all the event information confirmed before releasing anything. Once information is communicated to the public, it is impossible to take it back. Sending out bad information will make event managers look unorganized and unprepared.

Online Registration vs. Paper Registration

To determine which direction to go, there are two very simple formulas to use: 1) cost of man hours re-entering all the information into a database multiplied by the number of events run over the course of two to three years, divided by the cost of creating an online registration system, or 2) the cost of man hours re-entering all the information in the database, divided by the cost of outsourcing registration to a third-party online company. There are additional factors that could be involved in making the determination, such as whether the event will be using electronic registration on-site. How much time is spent processing payments? Does the customer base have access/ability to use computers? At the end of the day, the world is continuously moving to electronic everything, which saves time, money, and the environment!

Online Registration

For a nominal fee, there are a number of companies that will handle all of an event's online registration needs. The process is often seamless to the point that participants are not even aware they have left the event's Web site. If an event does not have the capital to create its own online registration system, this is a great alternative. Remember to use the formula presented when computing cost analysis.

Registration Form/Page

An event's registration form should be a "no-brainer" when participants begin to complete it. This is not the place to leave participants scratching their heads. Perception can become reality. If an individual or team perceives that an entry form is unprofessional or lacks information, they can make the leap to believing that the event will have those same characteristics and will be run the same way. Basic information that needs to be included on a registration form includes:

- Date
- Time
- Location
- Fee
- Rules
- Waiver/Release
- Divisions or age brackets
- Awards
- What is included in the registration/entry fee
- Spectator information (costs, viewing, parking)
- Facility rules (cameras, external food & beverage, etc.)
- Cancellation policy
- Refund policy
- Required membership information (e.g., NGB affiliation)
- On-site registration/Check-in/Packet pick-up times and what they need to bring (e.g., ID, birth certificates, etc.)
- Local hotel/attraction/restaurant information (for events with out-of-town participants)
- Weather policy
- Number of games guaranteed
- Forfeit policy and/or mercy rule
- Tie-breaking policy
- Any deviation from NGB rules
- Protest policy
- Cooler policy
- Contact information for questions

The more information included, the better the participants are informed and the less time is taken out of event managers' days so that they can focus on what is most important: getting the maximum number of participants for the event!

Confirmation

All athletes that register, whether on paper or online, should receive a confirmation of exactly what they registered for, how much they paid, and a reminder of the time of site check-in and what they need to bring to check-in. This is another extremely important process that is often overlooked, but the better the communication to participants, the smoother the process and the less likely there will be issues or confusion during the event.

Web Registration Made Easy

Michael Pfahl and Bryan Weigel

The Ohio University Sport Marketing Club (OUSMC) is a student-run organization designed to provide applied experiences and social opportunities for undergraduate sport management students. One of the applied experiences is to manage a 3-on-3 basketball tournament called the B.A.M. Tournament. Conceived as a way to commemorate Bradley Allan Moorhead, a sport management undergraduate student who passed away, the tournament is a campus-wide event held each spring.

After several successful events, the club saw a decline in registrations in 2008 and decided to reexamine how it organized the event. In terms of the plan to solicit participants, the club decided to utilize a few new marketing and registration methods. First, in order to quickly reach out to all Sport Management students, the club utilized email through a listserv that included nearly all of the 400 undergraduate students in the major (subscription to the listserv is optional, but recommended by the faculty). Second, in order to better serve the participants and streamline event planning, the decision was made to utilize a Web-based registration system from www.cashnet.com. There were two main reasons for this decision.

The first was the simplicity the online system offered the event planners in terms of handling registration materials and database management of all participant information. The event planners were busy undergraduate students themselves, so they embraced the possibilities offered by www.cashnet.com. For example, the club would now have a significant number of names and contact information available to market its other events as well as itself. After removing the names of any OUSMC members participating in the tournament, the club would have a sizeable mailing list to use when reaching out for new members.

Second, registration for the event required students to pay upon registration. This meant that interested students would need to carry at least $30 with them. As undergraduates themselves, the planners thought this was unlikely, especially when staffing tables at the university's recreation center. So, it was decided that the Web registration allowed students the best opportunity to find information about the tournament, register their team, and be able to pay all at once. In fact, the students could even designate the cost of registration go directly to their student e-Bill to be paid with other expenses later.

Minimizing the effort required to register for the tournament then influenced other aspects of the event planning process (e.g., sponsorship) as the planners worked to streamline as many aspects of the event as they could. The result was a more sophisticated registration process than in previous years. Numerous teams registered and the event was another successful one managed by the OUSMC.

On-site Registration/Check-In

How long should on-site registration and check-in remain open? Each sport is accustomed to different policies, so again, it is important to know the market. Many sports provide team captains/individuals a very small time frame. Other events allow a much longer period of time so that participants do not have to make an extra trip, but can arrive just before the start of the event or their first game. For events like marathons and triathlons, check-in will often open a few days before the event, in conjunction with an expo. These advance days also enable participants coming from out of town to arrive early and rest. In the case of triathlons, it also enables participants to check in their equipment at the transition location(s) and go on a course preview.

Generally, the rule of thumb should be to make it as easy for the customer as possible. Why make someone come a night early if they do not have their first game/event until the next afternoon? Participants become frustrated if they feel an event is forcing them to spend extra money on travel packages. Event managers need to weigh the benefit of requiring participants to arrive early with the potential downside of them being so frustrated that they do not attend the event the following year.

Sometimes staffing of registration becomes an issue if the person overseeing the registration is one of the event managers. Event managers cannot be two places at once, and trying to both manage an event and run registration is not a good idea. It is highly recommended that event managers always dedicate at least one staff member to registration until all participants have checked in. If an event starts on a Friday afternoon or Saturday morning, make sure to schedule check-in to allow enough time for all teams competing in the first event to complete registration and have 45–60 minutes prior to their first game/event. For example, a soccer tournament using 12 fields has first games at 4 pm on Friday. It takes 10 minutes for each team to complete registration and the event has two dedicated registration staff.

$$12 \text{ fields} \times 2 \text{ teams} = 24 \text{ teams} \times 10 \text{ minutes} = 240 \text{ minutes}/2 \text{ staff} = 120 \text{ minutes}$$
$$+ 60 \text{ minutes prior to first game} = 180 \text{ minutes}.$$

Using this formula, registration should start at 1:00 pm. Another good policy is to open registration 30 minutes earlier than the time posted. This is known as a **soft opening**. Soft openings allow guests who arrive early the feeling that they have been rewarded, and it will also cut down on the typical rush at the start of check-in. This will also allow some time to work through any possible kinks before the majority of participants arrive.

Staff

This is simply a numbers-driven factor. If event managers are limited in the number of people they have, then the previous formula should be used. If they have access to volunteers or a large staff, then the proper way to calculate would be by the following method:

Take the number of participants needing to register, times the time needed to register, divided by the total hours planned for registration to be open.

$$\frac{Number\ of\ participants\ needing\ to\ register \times Time\ needed\ to\ register\ each\ participant}{Total\ hours\ planned\ for\ registration\ to\ be\ open}$$

For example, a basketball tournament has 48 teams and registration is from 4:00 pm until 8:00 pm and the check-in process takes 15 minutes per team.

$$48 \text{ teams} \times 15 \text{ minutes} = 720 \text{ minutes}/240 \text{ minutes (total registration time)} = 3 \text{ staff}$$

OR

$$\frac{48\ teams \times 15\ minutes = 720\ minutes}{240\ minutes\ (total\ registration\ time)} = 3\ staff$$

Using this example, event managers would use no fewer than three staff, but it is highly recommend to increase to one to two dedicated staff for registration and at least one additional staff member to answer general questions. If an event is allowing on-site registration, then depending on the expected volume, they can use the same formula. Another good recommendation is to increase staff, especially if the event can use volunteers, for the start of registration. The opening times are the busiest and event managers can always let people go if they are not needed, but they can almost never get extras to start.

Location

On-site registration/check-in should be held in a location that can accommodate the proper number of staff, expected volume, proper power, ample ingress and egress, and be convenient to the participants. One thing that is important about the location is that there should be a separate entrance and exit if at all possible. Having one entrance/exit tends to form unnecessary backup and could disrupt the flow. Registration/check-in is typically held where the event is being held, at a host hotel, or at a local sponsor's location (restaurant/attraction/retail store). For almost all circumstances, hosting registration indoors or under significant cover is most desirable. Hosting outdoor registration/check-in introduces too many variables event managers cannot control and could make for a very messy time. Rain, wind, lightning, lack of power, lights, secured storage, land lines (phone and fax) are all concerns that event managers could find outdoors, but very rarely are issues indoors.

Flow

Event managers do not want participants to draw upon the analogy of an amusement park where they waited far too long for a ride that lasted 30 seconds and then walked away, vowing never to return. To avoid the same pitfalls, ensuring the proper flow of event registration/check-in is fundamental. If event managers expect to have 10 people in line at any given time, they should have a queue that fits four times that amount. This serves two purposes: 1) if there is an unexpected backup they are prepared to have participants wait in an orderly fashion, and 2) when the participants walk in, go through a line and walk right up to the front, they feel like they must have missed the rush and are pleasantly surprised at how quick the process is. Make sure participants

Figure 8-1. Adjustable Event Registration Queue Setup

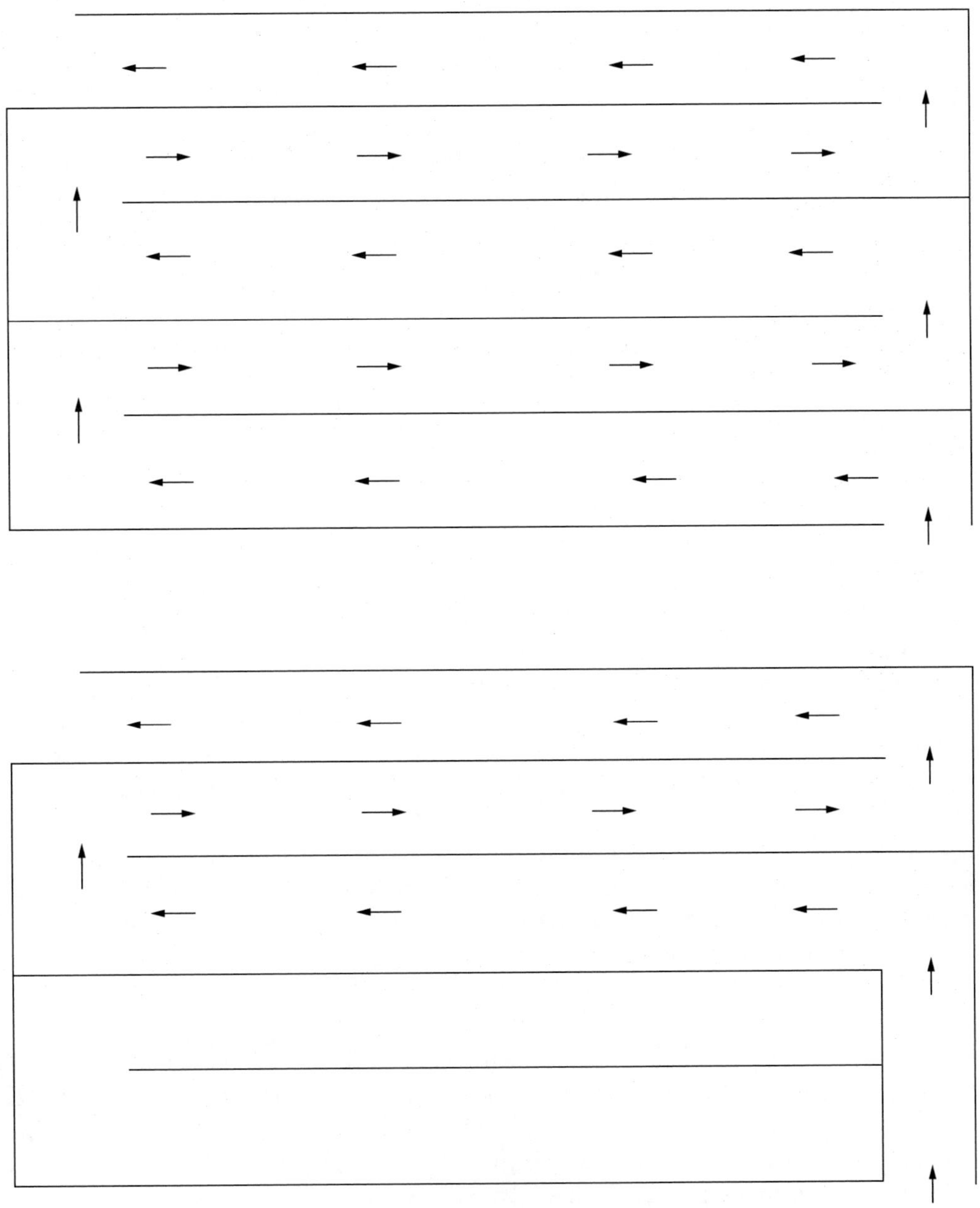

do not have to walk back and forth through a long queue unnecessarily. Adjust the queue to accommodate the flow; otherwise, people will be ducking underneath and possibly knocking down stanchions or hurting themselves, which is not good for anyone (See Figure 8-1 for queue set-up diagrams). Event managers should also have a separate line for any on-site registrations, since this process will typically take longer than simply checking in already registered participants. Those who have already completed their registration should not have to wait for those who are registering at the last minute. Finally, try to set up registration/check-in so that participants only make one stop. Having multiple stops can only cause confusion and add the potential for participants to miss a step.

Check-In

When conducting a large registration, it is best to sort check-in materials alphabetically. By using an alphabetical sort, event managers can divide each station with an equal number of participants. Each station does not have to have every single participant's information. The smaller the number of teams or participants that are entered, the easier it becomes to have multiple stations, all of which can check in any participant versus breaking participants down by designated groupings.

Exchange of Information

When participants arrive at check-in, all necessary information is exchanged. Staff/volunteers should collect any and all waivers, money due, local contact information, and more. Before completing participants' check-in information, ascertain how many people are in their party, how many hotel rooms they have booked, and how many nights they are staying. This information can all be used by the local sports commissions and CVBs to conduct a post-event economic impact analysis, which can result in receiving supporting funds for the event in the future.

Participants should also receive all information relating to the event, if they have not already, such as schedules, captains' meeting information, rules, and gift/goodie bags. If anything of value is given, participants should sign a form acknowledging that they have received the item(s). This is a good way to control inventory and to make sure event managers can verify if someone comes back and says they have not received something important.

Waiver

Every participant should sign a waiver. A parent or guardian must sign for participants under eighteen. A **waiver, or release of liability**, is "a contract in which the participant or user of a service agrees to relinquish the right to pursue legal action against the service provider in the event that the ordinary negligence of the provider results in an injury to the participant" (Cotten, 2007, p. 85). A waiver by no means is security that an event will never be sued if someone should unfortunately get hurt during the event. However, a waiver does mitigate damages and is a very valuable piece of paper in those circumstances. One challenge with waivers is that the laws that govern them are at the state level, thus event managers must be aware of the requirements and general enforcement of the waiver in their state. Make sure all parties involved are included in the waiver, along with release for use of participants' images in photo and/or video. Consult a legal expert to write the waiver in order to make sure it adheres to state laws. Also make sure when collecting waivers that no changes have been made to the waiver, such as participants crossing out statements with which they do not agree. The waiver was drafted for a particular reason and any changes are not acceptable. It is a very simple choice for the participant: sign the waiver as-is, or do not participate. Event managers do not want to be calling the lawyer in the middle of registration to see if the change is acceptable.

IDs

It is a good idea to collect a copy of all participants' identification pieces during the registration process. This will eliminate any future questions regarding a player or participant's status, and also show that the event is serious about making sure the competition is being conducted fairly. Unfortunately, not every person/team has integrity and, believe it or not, some teams actually try to sneak a player onto their roster after registration is complete. Having this information on file makes it easier to solve protests that are filed by other teams.

Sample Participant Waiver

* Be aware that each State is different with respect to their requirements for enforceable waivers. It is highly recommended to seek legal counsel in the development of any specific participant waiver.

First Name: _____ **M.I.** _____ **Last Name:** _____

Date of Birth: _____ **Gender (M/F):** _____

Emergency Contact: _____ **Phone Number:** _____

Event Information

Event Date(s): July 12, 2009

Event: Fun Run ABC

Event Host: The City of XYZ and Fun Run Inc.

Sport Type(s): walking, jogging, running, and any other activities associated with the Fun Run

Please Read Carefully Before Signing

(**Adult** – 18 years of age or over; **Minor** – under 18 years of age)

In consideration of my and/or my child or ward's participation in the Sport Type(s) and Event referenced above and any related activities (collectively, the **"Event"**), wherever the Event may occur, I agree to assume all risks incidental to such participation (which risks may include, among other things, muscle injuries and broken bones). On my own and/or my child or ward's behalf, and on behalf of my and/or my child or ward's heirs, executors, administrators and next of kin, I hereby release, covenant not to sue, and forever discharge the Released Parties (as defined below) of and from all liabilities, claims, actions, damages, costs or expenses of any nature arising out of or in any way connected with my or my child or ward's participation in the Event and/or any such activities, and further agree to indemnify and hold each of the Released Parties harmless from and against any and all such liabilities, claims, actions, damages, costs or expenses including, but not limited to, all attorneys' fees and disbursements up through and including any appeal. I understand that this release and indemnity includes any claims based on the negligence, action or inaction of any of the Released Parties and covers bodily injury (including death), property damage, and loss by theft or otherwise, whether suffered by me or my child or ward either before, during or after such participation. I declare that I and (if participating) my child or ward are physically fit and have the skill level required to participate in the Event and/or any such activities. I further authorize medical treatment for me and/or my child or ward, at my cost, if the need arises. For the purposes hereof, the **"Released Parties"** are City of XYZ and Fun Run Inc. and their respective parent, subsidiary, affiliated or related companies; the Event Manager referenced above, all Event sponsors or charities, and each of their respective parent, subsidiary, affiliated or related companies; Affiliate #1, Affiliate #2, Affiliate #3; its Board of Supervisors; and the officers, directors, employees, agents, contractors, sub-contractors, representatives, successors, assigns, and volunteers of each of the foregoing entities. I further grant the Released Parties the right to photograph and/or videotape me and/or my child or ward and further to display, use and/or otherwise exploit my and/or my child or ward's name, face, likeness, voice, and appearance forever and throughout the world, in all media, whether now known or hereafter devised, throughout the universe in perpetuity (including, without limitation, in online webcasts, television, motion pictures, films, newspapers, and magazines) and in all forms including, without limitation, digitized images, whether for advertising, publicity, or promotional purposes, including, without limitation, publication of Event results and standings, without compensation, reservation or limitation. I further authorize distribution by the Released Parties of my contact information, including my email address, to third parties for promotional purposes, or for any other purpose whatsoever, without compensation, reservation or limitation. The Released Parties are, however, under no obligation to exercise any rights granted herein. This Waiver and Permission Form shall be governed by the laws of the State of XYZ, and any legal action relating to or arising out of this Waiver and Permission Form shall be commenced exclusively in the Circuit Court of the First Circuit in and for Blue County, State XYZ. State XYZ (or if such Circuit Court shall not have jurisdiction over the subject matter thereof, then to such other court sitting in such county and having subject matter jurisdiction), and I specifically waive the right to trial by jury. I certify I am 18 years of age or older and, if I am executing this Waiver and Permission Form on behalf of my child or ward, the information set forth above pertaining to my child or ward is true and complete.

Date _____

Signature of Participant (if over 18) or Parent (if Participant is under 18) or Court

Appointed Guardian:_____

Print Name of Participant (if 18 or over) or Parent (if Participant is under 18) or Court Appointed Guardian:_____

SUMMARY

Every year there are new events created, and event managers have to do everything possible to keep their past customers. In a sporting event, there is very little event managers can control over the duration of the event. Most everything is decided on the field of play, so it is important for event managers to make sure the elements they can control are efficient, timely, and professional. Even if a team/participant does not win, the event managers' efforts to ensure an organized event will go a long way and will equate to repeat customers, and the word of mouth is invaluable.

Student Challenge

STUDENT CHALLENGE #8

In Challenge #8, create a registration form and determine the setup of the registration/packet pick-up area.

QUESTION 8-1

Produce a registration form that contains all of the information that needs to be collected from participants. If the event is not participant-driven, please use a 20-mile charitable bicycle race in the community as an event to create a participant registration form. Use the section below to take notes about the sections needed on the form and then type up the final registration form.

Sections:

Student Challenge

QUESTION 8-2

Draw a diagram detailing the setup and flow of registration/packet pick-up for the chosen event. If the event is not participant-driven, please use a 20-mile charitable bicycle race with an expected 1,200 cyclists as an event to create a registration diagram. Half of the participants generally pre-register while the other half will need to register on-site. Determine the number of staff needed based on the opening time of registration/packet pick-up and the estimated time it will take to manage each person/team through the process.

CHAPTER 9

EVENT TICKETING

Robb Wade

This chapter discusses important concepts in ticketing and how ticketing fits into the overall event management process. There are a number of important issues to be considered that relate to the organization, sale, and distribution of tickets for various events. For some events, there might be one or more staff members specifically responsible for ticketing, and the role of the event managers may be minimal. In the case of other events, however, the event managers may wear multiple "hats" and also be the ticket manager. In either scenario, it is important for event managers to have a thorough understanding of the ticketing process and the decisions made along the way.

Due to logistics, ticketing is mainly a topic in traditional spectator-driven events held in traditional sport venues. However, there are some events in non-traditional venues that do ticket the event. Ancillary events, such as a concert associated with a NASCAR event or a fan fest linked to a championship game are two examples of events that are commonly ticketed.

Ticketing an event is a more in-depth process than many people realize. There are questions related to seating arrangements, ticket format, design, sale, and price that have to be addressed for any ticketed event. This chapter will address these topics and others, as well as discuss the role of the customer, how the venue impacts ticketing, premium tickets, parking, credentials, special interest groups, and reconciliation.

TICKETING BASICS

A ticket is considered a limited contract between the sport organization and the spectator. The money the spectator paid for the ticket means that he or she is afforded the rights associated with the purchase of that ticket. Specifically, a **ticket as a limited contract** means that the ticket buyer receives the right to attend the event and the organization has an obligation to provide the event as advertised and promoted.

The ticket holder is also owed the ability to observe the event in a safe and enjoyable environment. The person attending the event is not guaranteed a victory for his or her team or a result that he or she might find favorable, but the ticket holder does have the right to expect to see the teams that were advertised and to witness the event. The ticket buyer also has the right to voice his or her opinions about a team's or player's performance. Again, this could be in a positive or negative manner.

The ticket is also a **revocable permit**. This means that the organization reserves the right to take the ticket back from the purchaser (usually with a refund) if he or she is interfering with the enjoyment of others. These concepts go together, in that to ensure that the majority of patrons can exercise their right to see and enjoy the event, others may have to have their tickets revoked. Often, when alcohol is served at events, there are instances where security and/or police must get involved to remove spectators from the venue.

Ticket holders also have the right to know what to expect when they get to their assigned seats. If an obstructed view seat was sold without telling the purchaser that the view of the playing surface was not clear, this would limit the visibility and enjoyment of the event for the spectator. Some refund or accommodation (e.g., relocating the spectator) should be made for spectators that are not able to see and enjoy the event. This has nothing to do with liking the performance, and everything to do with accommodating the guests so they can see the show free from major impediments.

There may be some situations which involve a change in the event after tickets are bought. This is more common in entertainment events. A high-profile team could, however, get snowed in and become unable to travel to the event, and the event organizers might have a local team substitute for them. This changes the event, and ticket holders requesting refunds should receive them (or a ticket to the rescheduled event if applicable). There are some sports, however, where schedule changes are likely. In these cases, the information must be clearly spelled out at the time of purchase, and preferably on the ticket itself. Baseball is commonly rained out and games are cancelled or rescheduled, sometimes multiple times in a season. It must be clear what the ticket holders' rights are in a rain-out situation. If a rain out is called before the game even starts, is that different than a game that makes it to the fifth inning? What about if it is a double header where one ticket is used for both games and the second game is cancelled?

The ticket as a limited contract and a revocable permit are both important concepts. Event decisions might have to be made at some point with this in mind. If a traveling show cancels at the last minute, ticket managers must have the money available and a plan for refunding to all of the customers.

THE CUSTOMER

Most, if not all, sport professionals are familiar with the service industry phrase, "The customer is always right." While that is an admirable and somewhat functional motto under which to operate, it may not always ring true. What about the instance in which the customers want a refund because their seats were further away from the action than anticipated? How about the customer that arrives late and wants a refund on his ticket because he missed the beginning of the game? What should be done about a ticket holder that wants money back because she arrived for a game intoxicated, used profanity, disrupted others, and had to be asked to leave? In each of the preceding scenarios, there is a risk of angering the ticket holder and possibly losing business.

Loss of business means loss of revenue. As is the case with any business, the cost to the organization of attracting new business is about five times greater than the cost of retaining current customers. In other words, it is much more cost efficient to keep the current customer base than it is to continually have to go into the market in search of new ticket buyers. What does this have to do with the three scenarios previously mentioned? The answer is that while these customers were not "right," they are still an important part of the business equation, as they are still adding to the bottom line for that particular event. Quite simply, they are still customers.

For many events, the only contact spectators have with the organization is the ticket office, ticket takers, parking attendants, ushers, concession, and merchandise staff. These groups with face-to-face contact with the public are known as the **front of house** staff. This is in contrast to **back of house** employees such as the public address announcer, the scoreboard operator, operations personnel, truck dock employees, and even the event managers in some circumstances. Supervisors, such as the ticket manager, must ensure the front of the house staff understand and appreciate their valuable role in conveying the desired image for the entire organization. In most cases, game day workers are part-time employees or volunteers who should not be expected to know this on their own. So, it is the responsibility of the event managers to provide these members of the team with all of the necessary tools and information to be helpful and knowledgeable when approached by patrons.

Although each event and facility is different, it is likely that paying customers will be one of the most important revenue streams for the event. There may also be sponsors, television contracts, boosters, and advertisers that all contribute to the bottom line of the event. In many cases, however, the people purchasing tickets are the most important and largest stream of revenue that the event can realize. For that reason, the ticket buyers must be considered when making decisions about the ticketing process. For the purpose of this book, a new motto will be adopted. Rather than saying that the customer is always right, decisions and conversation will be based on a different phrase: "The customer is not always right, but the customer is always the customer."

THE FACILITY

The size and configuration of the facility will dictate much of the decision making about ticketing. Basic facility information will be obtained in the feasibility portion of event conceptualization. This will include how many seats there are, the availability of accessible seating, and premium seating options. Early in the process, event managers will also work with the venue on specific set-up information for the event. As event development progresses, the venue information needed to make ticketing decisions becomes more specific, such as knowing about any obstructed-view seats. For venues that are constructed specifically for the event, there is usually more flexibility in creating the appropriate seating. However, there is also more work involved, since the venue is being created from scratch.

It is particularly important that those who may respond to media inquiries or that have direct interactions with participants be knowledgeable about the facility regarding seating and beyond. Having the entire sport organization or event management team on the same page (e.g., giving consistent answers to questions about seating), will help to ensure the same message is conveyed by all. Plus, administrators, coaches, promoters, and members of the press will for this, and a host of other information, expect answers quickly. Moving forward in the ticketing process, educated decisions can be made related to pricing, point- of-sale locations, date of on-sale, and use of technology based on the venue constraints.

Seating Configurations

Event managers that work within a traditional sport venue may have the opportunity to work with and for a number of different entities, acts, promoters, agents, teams, and sports. For example, college campuses may host numerous athletic events, as well as indoor concerts at the basketball arena, outdoor concerts at the football stadium, and cross-country meets on the golf course. In addition, on-campus venues may host various post-season tournaments and games at both the conference and national level. For each and every one of these events, the seating configuration might be different. There could be a concert, basketball game, hockey game, and graduation all within the same week. Event managers working in this type of facility must know the different possible configurations, and how each will change the opportunity to sell tickets. Once the configuration is established, then it must be decided whether seats will be reserved only, general admission only, or a combination. In some venues, the option of having some general admission, standing-room-only tickets might be available.

Reserved Seating

Reserved seating is very common in sports. The ticket holder is assigned, or chooses, a specific seat in the venue for the event. There is little confusion for ticket holders in reserved seating scenarios, as the seat is essentially "theirs" for the event. Often there is also a prestige associated with getting "good seats" in the venue that can be leveraged into charging higher prices for the reserved seats that are considered "the best."

Reserved seating models will require an usher at each entry point to a reserved section. Therefore, for many events, there simply may not be enough available staff for a reserved seating arrangement, or it may cost more to staff the event than can be realized in financial gain. A local youth basketball game would not use reserved seating because it just would not make sense. However, if the Harlem Globetrotters were performing in a 2,000-seat local area, reserved seating would be an important component to the ticketing strategy. The demand for the Globetrotters will probably exceed capacity with effective marketing techniques, so the market for reserved seats would be strong. Unless the layout of the venue makes it impossible, any event with high demand should have some reserved seats as part of the seating arrangement.

General Admission

Along with configurations, there may be events which are better suited to an arrangement that calls for all seats to be **general admission**. This means that seating is open and patrons with a ticket are able to sit in any unoccupied seat, but they are guaranteed a seat. There are a few inherent problems with general admission seating that should be kept in mind. This type of seating is, for all intents and purposes, first come, first served. The first people in the door and to the seats get the "best" seats. These could be closest to the stage, the field, or center court. In any of these cases, it is likely that a number of people want to be first to the seats, and therefore, there could be some pushing, shoving, running, and possibly even some violence. Plus, when people are not bound to one specific seat, they tend to spread out and leave unused seats in the venue. If a group of three attends an event with general admission seating, they will probably leave one seat between them and the next group or couple which will then go unused, since very few people attend events by themselves.

General admission seating also does not give consideration to the loyal fan, large donor, or season ticket holder. Part of the reason people purchase season tickets or contribute significantly to sport organizations is to choose the seats they want. For season ticket holders, it means they can sit in the same seat for every contest and not have to worry about getting to the venue hours in advance of the start of the contest to claim their seat. General admission seating eliminates that option. It may mean that some of the best supporters and biggest donors are relegated to the seats in which nobody else is willing to sit.

Staffing for general admission is less than for reserved seating, because there is less concern with access control. Since spectators are able to choose their seat, there is no need for ushers in each section.

General admission seating works well for low-demand events where there is little risk of spectators becoming aggressive while trying to obtain seats. A recurring event such as women's volleyball at an NCAA Division II institution may draw a few hundred people in a venue that could seat a few thousand. In that scenario, general admission seating should be adequate, as even loyal supporters will have access to quality seats since the demand is generally not high.

Festival Seating

Festival seating refers to a ticketing process where no seats are assigned and people stand to experience the event in a large open area. Festival seating is common for concerts where there is a wide-open area close to the stage in which people are admitted. Ticket holders generally rush towards the stage to get the best possible view of the act, which can result in pushing and shoving in the crowd. An example of an event where festival seating might be used is at an outdoor concert prior to a championship basketball game. Often, these concerts are held in a downtown area that has been fenced or roped off for the concert and that does not have any seating.

It might seem like festival seating would not require very many staff, but often the opposite is true. There is risk associated with a large group trying to move forward towards the stage, and a lot of security is needed to ensure people act in an orderly fashion.

Standing Room Only (SRO)

The final type of seating arrangement is **standing room only (SRO),** and is defined as a ticket to enter the venue with access to specific areas where there are not seats, but where the event can still be viewed. Although not a new phenomenon in sport, few venues have adequate areas for standing-room tickets, and there can be problems with the fire marshal if standing-room tickets impede the ingress or egress of other patrons. Generally, if standing-room-only tickets are sold, it is in addition to other types of tickets. Different from festival seating, standing-room-only tickets could be anywhere in the venue where patrons can gather without seats to view the event. In a few venues, there might be areas designed for this purpose, such as picnic areas, patio areas, or balconies.

Combination Seating Arrangements

It is possible to have a combination of general admission and reserved seating. Based on the configuration of the facility, a portion of the seats can be reserved while others are general admission. This is commonly done, for example, by making end zones general admission and sideline seats reserved, or by making the upper level general admission while the lower level is reserved.

Finally, it is worth mentioning here that there is also a financial consideration when looking at seating arrangements. Reserved seats will command a higher selling price than general admission. Many fans are willing to pay for the privilege to sit in a desirable seat and know it will be available when they arrive at the venue. However, other fans do not mind the crowds in a general admission area. They would rather spend less money, arrive early to get a seat, and take their chances on where that seat might be.

The Ticket Manifest

A **ticket manifest** is needed for all ticketed events, and identifies how many seats are in each row and section of the venue. Generally, the manifest is "built" within a ticketing software program and is used to set prices, print tickets, and keep track of how many and which tickets are sold. However, the information entered must be accurate. It is a major problem if the ticket manifest is not the same as the actual venue, because non-existent seats could be sold or the event could miss out on potential revenue.

For some events this is simple, because the venue does not change much from one event to another. In other cases, the venue will be new to the event managers, or it will be altered for the event. For example, a college wrestling meet may use only one or two mats and might not need all of the existing floor space available. In this case, it might behoove all involved to add floor seating to the setup. This will increase capacity, allowing for more tickets to be sold and move the spectators closer to the action. This alteration in the normal seating configuration requires that the event managers, if not serving as the ticketing director, work closely with those in tickets to ensure that they are aware of the available seats.

The Seats

For all events, the seats must be checked prior to the event. In traditional sports venues or for recurring events, this might occur at regular intervals prior to, and during, the season instead of before each event. When checking seats, the event managers are ensuring all seats are in good repair, are numbered, and do not have an obstructed view. This involves having someone sit in every seat, and although not glamorous, it is an important task. If there are seats that are damaged or missing, these should be replaced or repaired as quickly as possible. The labeling of seats is also important, as keeping up on maintenance contributes to a positive event environment. Imagine a situation in which the season opener rolls around and a major sponsor of the event arrives to find his or her seat broken. The time to remedy the problem is not at half time of the game; it is before the customer knows the problem exists.

Recognizing if there are seats with obstructed views is often part of this process. In many venues, the ticketing staff is well aware of seats in which a pillar, wall, or other obstruction is between the spectator and the competition area. There will also be times when media presence creates obstructed views for some spectators, as TV cameras are often set up in front of existing seats. For non-traditional venues or unique setups, obstruction might not be as obvious. Obstructed view seats can be **killed,** which simply means the seat is removed from the ticket inventory for the event. The other option is to sell obstructed-view seats at a discount. In this case, it must be made clear to customers that there is an obstruction prior to their buying the seat.

Lessons Learned in Ticketing . . .

After spending 11 years as a ticket manager, I have a list of lessons I learned the hard way. In 1987, and then again from 1993 to 2003, I was involved in ticketing for a professional hockey team, as well as at two different universities. At one of these universities, major events were a regular occurrence. There were some situations we could have handled better. As a result, I learned a great deal about ticketing and event management, and want to share a few short examples about my experiences. As you read these, consider how closely the operations of the event mesh with ticketing.

Seating Configurations

On campus, we had an old basketball facility that rarely got used since the team had moved into a new facility. In an effort to continue to use the venue, we contracted with an artist to perform in the building. The facility could accommodate 13,000 people for a basketball game. When a stage was added at one end blocking seats, the seating capacity shrank considerably.

The feeling from our standpoint was that it made the most sense to make all seats reserved. What we did not realize was that this particular group was famous for having a mosh pit directly in front of the stage. Unfortunately, nobody on our staff was familiar with the group, we did not do our own research, and the promoter did not tell us about it. So, on the day of the concert, we set the facility with all reserved seats in all locations.

As the concert was about to begin, the band realized what was happening and expressed to us that it could potentially be a very bad situation if the seats were not rearranged allowing for a mosh pit. One hour before the doors were supposed to open and in a panic, we were removing chairs from the floor to create the mosh pit. As it turned out, the event was a success and the fans never even knew there was a problem before the concert. However, by doing our own research and asking the right questions of the promoter, we would not have had to change plans and scramble at the last minute.

Projecting the Right Image: Parking

For football game days, we were fortunate to have an excellent parking situation around the football stadium. With about 5,500 assigned parking spaces for donors, it was critical that each person parked in the correct spot. In fact, an error in parking in the wrong spot resulted in their car being towed. As you can image, we had to hire a lot of people to staff parking entrances and help direct people to their assigned parking spaces. It would not seem like parking would fall under the ticket office's purview, but it did. In my case, the ticket office was heavily involved in parking because passes had to be issued for each of those 5,500 spots, similarly to the ticketing process.

For the fans that came to every game, they knew and understood the process because they were used to it. But for visitors who were unfamiliar with a game day on campus, it could be a nightmare. Imagine their frustration when they arrived at the stadium and asked the parking attendant for directions, and the attendant had none to give. Imagine my frustration when the attendant that did not have the information was also wearing a hat or t-shirt supporting our biggest rival or the team that we were scheduled to play on that particular day. The experience for those interacting with our parking attendants was negative and needed to be fixed.

As much as I would have loved to rely on the parking attendants to remember our verbal instructions, it just did not seem to be working. So, the resolution was fairly straightforward. We decided to post signs at each aisle of parking spaces. Each parking lot attendant was given a map that showed the numbers of each spot that were located in each row. Each parking attendant was given a hat and golf shirt from our institution and was expected to wear it each and every time they came to work. There was a cost involved in outfitting all of these people and printing off all of the material, but in the end it was better to present the right image to all of our customers and start their event experiences off in a positive way.

Two Concerts, Two Different Strategies

We had a rare chance to host two major outdoor concerts in our football stadium within a short period of time. The two shows were very different. The first was a country concert that featured George Strait and seven additional acts. The other concert was Jimmy Buffett. That particular summer, ours was the only outdoor stadium concert that Jimmy Buffett was going to perform. From an event management standpoint, these two shows could not have been more different.

All indications were that the country show would be a very successful concert and that tickets were very likely to sell out. The decision was made to outsource ticket sales so that they could be purchased around the country immediately as they went on sale. This was just as online ticketing was becoming popular, but many people still were buying tickets through ticketing outlets instead of online. As most of us know, a service charge generally applies when a ticket agency is used, and can vary from minimal to substantial. Therefore, a group of people wanting to purchase tickets for the show could be faced with "service" or "convenience" charges of $10 per ticket. However, those who purchase tickets at the venue do not pay the service fee.

The country show was a day-long event. That particular day was extremely hot and humid. The promoters and the facility staff had to work together to acquire and setup mist tents to keep people cool. The concession stands sold every bottle of water they had midway through the afternoon. In addition, alcohol was also being sold at a somewhat alarming rate. The combination of all of these factors led to a number of tense situations. Problems included everything from patrons wanting the tower of speakers on the field to be angled differently to complaints about long restroom lines.

The Buffett show could not have been more different. This particular show was an evening show. Since we have a relatively good parking situation at our stadium, it meant that the Parrotheads, or loyal Buffet followers, spent much or most of the day on campus preparing for the show. As the show opened up, so did the skies. It was as close to a torrential rainstorm as there could be. It rained from the start of the show to the end. We did not experience a single problem that night. In fact, most people stood up in the rain and sang along to every song.

These two shows were both revenue sources for the department. Both concerts sold out and had very large crowds in attendance. Both, however, created a very different set of circumstances for the staff members involved in working the two concerts.

Football Bowl Game Ticketing

Our ticket office had a situation in which our football team was going to a bowl game, which was very exciting but also created a lot of work in the ticket office. As a result of the short turnaround time between receiving the bowl invitation and the actual game, we decided not to mail any tickets, and instead had tickets available for pick up at the game. There was one particular customer that ordered tickets and picked them up. A few weeks after the bowl game, we received a notification that he was disputing the charges, saying that he did not receive the tickets. We were able to produce the envelope that the customer had signed when he picked up the tickets as confirmation of receipt.

On a side note, we did not play very well in that particular bowl game and ended up losing by quite a bit. There were a number of fans that were very disappointed with the performance and quite vocal about their feelings. It is possible that this particular patron was so upset by the game that he was trying to figure out a way to get out of having to pay for the tickets. In this case, we had a system in place that did not allow him to do that and allowed our ticket revenue to remain the same.

The Rival Game

In my first year in the ticket office, our team boasted one of the greatest players the conference has ever had. In fact, in this player's final year, we set attendance records at eight of the nine conference away games. As you can imagine, home games were also very popular.

I clearly remember the game that we played against our arch rival. People were begging for tickets and going to any means to attempt to secure them. Our office sold every possible ticket that we could. One week before the game was played, we were completely sold out. There was not a single ticket to be found at any location in the building.

Three days before the game, the call came. The president of the university needed four more tickets for some members of the Board of Trustees. Needless to say, the president's office was not impressed with my explanation. I managed to save my job, but I learned a valuable lesson about games being sold out. There was never a game from that point on that I did not have a small stash of tickets hidden away somewhere for emergency situations. For an event that is very popular, any tickets that I held thereafter would be sold as the event approached.

THE TICKETS

There are a number of considerations related to the actual tickets, and many of them evolve along with technology. Decisions about the type of ticket needed, ticket design, ticket printing, and security are all part of the ticketing process.

Types of Tickets

The type of ticket refers to whether the tickets will be punched, collected, stubbed, scanned, or whether some other method will be used to denote that the ticket holder has entered the facility. Event managers need to decide if it is important to know how many and which tickets were used prior to deciding on the ticket format. For some types of tickets, information can be gathered about which tickets were used, while other formats do not even allow for an accurate count of spectators. Another consideration is whether any part of the ticket will be used for sponsor advertising. A coupon for a local fast food restaurant printed on the ticket is a great idea, but not if tickets are collected as spectators enter the facility.

Punching Tickets

Punching tickets is the simplest way to indicate whether a ticket was used. It is simply using a hole punch or ink stamp to indicate the ticket has been used. However, it does not allow the organization any record of which tickets were used for the event.

Collecting Tickets

Collecting the tickets will allow for reconciliation of how many tickets were used, but cannot be used for reserved seating events. If the ticket is collected, the spectators are not left with anything denoting their seat as they walk into the venue.

Stubbing Tickets

Stubbing refers to creating a perforated section on the ticket when printed that is torn upon entry to the facility. If the tickets are going to be stubbed, then the seat location must be printed on both the torn and retained portion of the ticket. This will allow for the spectators to have the information needed on their part of the ticket, and the organization to be able to reconcile exactly which tickets were used for that event.

Scanning Tickets

To scan tickets, the event or facility must have the equipment to do so. This includes the scanners for the gate workers, and the technology infrastructure that allows the information gathered by the scanners to be communicated back to the ticket office. The scanners are efficient because they allow the ticket office to keep track of which tickets were used. Scanning also eliminates the hand counting of thousands of ticket stubs. Once a ticket is scanned, it is invalidated. If a fan tries to pass the ticket through the fence to a friend, the friend will not be able to enter because the scanner will recognize the ticket as already being used.

For scanned tickets, barcodes, RFID (Radio Frequency Identification) embedded chips, or magnetic strips are used, with barcodes being more popular at this time. Often, for season tickets, the ticket looks similar to a credit card. The spectator then does not have to worry about keeping track of multiple paper tickets for the entire season. Paper tickets can be scanned using a barcode as well, and one big advantage to using this method is that ticket purchasers can buy their tickets online and print them at home. They can also email tickets to someone else, who can then print the ticket and attend the event. This method eliminates people needing to meet in person to transfer tickets, or using will call to leave tickets for someone. It is extremely convenient.

Even more advanced is the ability to scan tickets directly from a cell phone or PDA. In this case, the spectators are able to use their ticket account online or open an email with their ticket attached on their cell phone or PDA. The ticket can be scanned directly from there, and no paper ticket is ever printed. Whether paper, plastic, or electronic, the scanning of tickets is becoming very popular.

The AT&T National: Leveraging an Event Web Site for Ticket Sales

Mike Rielly

Many PGA Tour events are introducing robust event Web sites designed primarily to: a) provide general information to the public, b) sell tickets, c) recruit and coordinate volunteer logistics, and d) facilitate various media issues. Tiger Woods has created Web sites for each of his major events, including the Chevron World Challenge, Tiger Jam and, most recently, the AT&T National. One of the newest PGA Tour events, the AT&T National has fully integrated the event Web site into the operations of the event. For the purposes of this discussion, the focus will be on selling tickets and the media, but event managers should be aware of the many other functions a well-planned Web site can serve.

The inaugural AT&T National was one of the first PGA events to sell all of its tickets online. The title sponsor, presenting sponsor, and television revenue are the top three largest revenue sources for golf events. However, next on the list are ticket sales, so an effective online ticket sales program, like AT&T National's, is essential for streamlining the process for the consumer and for the tournament office. Online ticket sales also eliminate human error. The traditional method of transposing credit card information over the phone can lead to dozens, if not hundreds, of credit card billing errors, and multiple problems at Will Call on the day of the event.

Another important function of the AT&T National event Web site is media coordination. Most PGA Tour events which do not feature Tiger attract approximately 100 media (mostly domestic), but those events that feature Tiger attract 300 to 400 media (including many international media). There is a substantial amount of coordination required to register, approve, provide press kits, and deliver credentials to this number of media. All of these functions are handled online for the AT&T National. With many of the needs of the media met online, costs are reduced, paper is conserved, and the international media have much easier access to information needed to prepare for the tournament.

It is important to note that, unless the title sponsor of the event is an international company who requires (and pays for) a multi-lingual Web site, most event Web sites function well in English for the international community. If, however, the event anticipates attracting international spectators, event organizers must ensure that the online transaction service for buying tickets is able to process international currency-based credit cards (most service providers offer this feature). So, in today's sport event marketplace, a well thought-out and implemented Web site can save the event manger valuable time and money, as well as help the event move into the international marketplace.

Ticket Design

Ticket design can be simple and inexpensive or detailed and expensive. There are a number of considerations when the time for designing the tickets arrives, such as how much information to include, whether or not to sell advertising on the tickets, and what the graphic should look like. In general, the front of the ticket should at least provide information on the opponent or name of the event, date, time, place, and price. It is also helpful to include entry gate information for venues with multiple entrances. Legal disclaimers and the ticket refund policy are often printed on the back of the ticket, along with any coupons or advertisements from sponsors.

A major part of ticket design is image. Every time customers receive a piece of correspondence, walk into the facility, interact with staff or look at their tickets, they are forming an opinion about the organization. The ticket design is an opportunity to make a positive impression on the customer. There is also a difference when printing single-event versus season tickets. Season ticket designs can include pictures of players, coaches, facilities, or mascots. Single-event tickets are typically less expensive and feature a less complicated design. They are designed more for functionality than flair.

If the ticket is for a one-time only or special event, there is a good possibility that the customer will want to save the ticket as a memento of the event. Given this, it is important to design a ticket which the person can be proud and display. Events that fall into this category would include a Super Bowl, the Master's, many concerts, the opening or closing of a particular facility, or a night in which a particular athlete or coach is being recognized. There are many other examples—the important factor is that it is going to be a memorable night that will never be repeated, and the ticket should reflect that.

It is critical that the information on the tickets is accurate. Once ticket proofs have been created, have at least three other people look at every bit of information provided on the tickets to ensure accuracy. In some cases, information will be left vague or incomplete on purpose. For example, if there is a chance that game times could change or be altered for any reason (primarily television), then it makes sense to leave the time as "TBA" and announce it when it has been finalized. It is easier to leave information off the ticket and inform customers at a separate time than it is to tell customers a wrong time and then try to reach each and every one of them to inform them of a change.

If communication about a time change is needed, information must go out to every ticket purchaser, all media outlets, and be posted on the Web site. Despite all of these efforts, it is likely that some people will not get the message and will show up at the wrong time. Needless to say, this leads to hard feelings, disappointment, and, in some cases, loss of revenue if the situation is not handled properly.

Ticket Printing

Depending on the type of event and availability of resources, ticket printing is either done prior to the event as hard ticketing, as customers purchase tickets, by the customers themselves, or a combination of these. For small and mid-size events, hard printing or printing as tickets are purchased is most likely. The combination approach is common for larger events, as it is able to meet the needs of the most people.

Hard Ticketing

There may be certain events for which all tickets are printed in advance. This practice is known as **hard ticketing**. It has the advantage of giving the ticket seller complete control of the ticket inventory. The sellers can distribute the tickets in the manner and method that they determine, as they are the sole source of obtaining tickets. The disadvantage of hard tickets is keeping records of purchases, and that customers can only get tickets from one entity. A lack of computerized records means that the seller must make other arrangements to keep sales records, assign seat locations, and distribute sales receipts.

Printing As Purchased

For those venues with access to ticket software or that outsource their ticketing to a company such as Ticketmaster, printing can be done in house. In this case, a customer can order a ticket in person, on the phone, or online. The ticket manager can then print the ticket immediately. The software automatically recognizes the specific ticket has been sold and adjusts the available inventory accordingly. This allows for multiple places to be selling tickets at the same time, as the system is networked together to ensure that no duplicates are sold. The computerized records are much more convenient for the ticket manager than hard ticketing, and the ticket office will have the ability to generate a variety of reports related to when, where, and how tickets were sold.

Print Tickets at Home

Having customers print their own tickets at home is certainly the cheapest method for the organization once the technology infrastructure is set up. However, there are still many people that do not want to do this. Some customers want to talk to someone in ticketing as they choose their seat, and others like having a well-designed paper ticket to keep as a reminder of their experience as opposed to something from their home printer.

Besides cost savings in printing and box office staff time, printing at home allows more flexibility for customers. As discussed previously, the customer can electronically send tickets to someone else if they are not going to use the tickets, and might not even have to print tickets at all, and instead simply use their cell phones to display the barcode for scanning at the event.

Combination Ticketing

To ensure that the needs of all customers are met, a combination plan usually works best. If finances and time allow, it is preferred to give customers the option of printing their tickets at home or contacting the box office to purchase their tickets.

While sports professionals may prefer electronic ticketing over other methods, there may not be a choice. For example, when a college athletic team gains a berth into a post-season contest (basketball tournament, football bowl game, etc.), the school often receives hard tickets from the venue. It is still possible to keep computer sales records. One possible solution is to build the facility (or part of it) into the computer and assign the seats as they are sold. It is almost like creating a partial ticket manifest for another facility. Another option is to put the sales through the computer and put a note in each customer's record as to the seat location. In conjunction with this, it may also be prudent to draw the sections, rows, and seats that are to be assigned and to write names of patrons on the chart as the seats are sold. The main reason to keep such records is to have backup information if there is a dispute over charges, or if customers happen to lose their tickets before the contest and have not written down their seat locations.

Cost

There is also a cost associated with the printing of tickets. In some places, this can be of little or no consequence, but in some smaller operations, this can be a major concern. The cost of printing tickets varies greatly depending on the design, type of ticket, the number of tickets being printed, and the company that does the printing.

For those that do not have an unlimited budget, a possible revenue source to cover the cost of the tickets is to obtain a ticket sponsor. In other words, it may be possible to approach a local or national company and offer them the chance to obtain thousands of contacts with potential customers. Often, the ticket backs (or space on the paper from home-printed tickets) may be sold as part of a larger package of advertising by the marketing staff of the organization. When customers print tickets at home, there is even more space for advertising and there is no cost to the organization in printing.

The most likely people to advertise on tickets are those businesses that can put an ad on the ticket that will generate business. Restaurants such as McDonald's or Pizza Hut are a natural fit because they can potentially generate business immediately after the event if they print a coupon on the ticket. Automotive supply stores and supermarkets also commonly use tickets as advertising.

The reason that companies enjoy this type of promotion is that they are able to track their return on investment (ROI). They can count up the number of tickets that get redeemed during the course of the season and, in that way, can get a direct measure of the effect of their sponsorship. Keep in mind that if the ticket manager is selling sponsorships, there needs to be frequent communication with anyone else selling sponsorships to ensure a coordinated effort.

Ticket Security

Another element that should be mentioned is that there have and always will be a certain segment of the population that will try to gain access into events through some sort of illegal and/or immoral means. This may include anything from using counterfeit tickets, to lying about lost or stolen tickets, to giving false information about being left tickets by someone, to simply trying to make up a story to convince a person of authority to allow them to enter the event. While it is very difficult to eliminate this problem, steps can be taken to reduce these occurrences. Computer ticketing systems are very important in these efforts. The ability to search for customers, seating locations, credit card numbers, and mailing addresses can decrease the issues.

It can be important to have a system to identify re-printed tickets. There are occasions when customers lose or forget tickets. They will usually contact the ticket office and ask for re-prints. Some entities charge the customer a fee to re-print the tickets in an attempt to encourage responsible handling of the tickets. When tickets are re-printed, they should be marked in some way. If the original set of tickets was lost and/or stolen and two sets of people show up at the seats with the same tickets, it may be difficult to ascertain who, in fact, is entitled to the seats. Re-prints can be marked with a stamp, initials, a hole punch, or any other kind of defining mark. The idea is that the usher in that section must be able to make a quick determination of the rightful owners of the seats.

There are many new security features that can be used in the formatting of tickets to prevent counterfeit tickets from being reproduced and sold. At the 2006 FIFA World Cup, organizers used extremely high-tech methods to ensure tickets could not be reproduced or transferred. Each ticket was embedded with a chip that was able to link to a computer database containing the spectators' names, addresses, nationalities, and even their passport numbers. Only the purchasers of the tickets were allowed to use the tickets, which caused some controversy since there was no way to transfer tickets to a friend or family member. However, this system served a secondary purpose, in that if there was trouble from anyone in the stands, they could be easily identified and found.

PRICING

The price of the tickets is typically not decided by the ticket office or by event managers alone. However, savvy event managers will realize that input from ticketing specialists is important when choosing the price points. Bear in mind that the organization wants to maximize profits and fill every seat. The promoter, coach, or sport organization wants people in every seat. In order to sell the maximum number of tickets, it is imperative to find the price point that is attractive to the most people and will motivate them to buy tickets.

Certain events will sell most, if not all, of the tickets at just about any price. Games against an arch rival, playoffs, championships, and popular musical artists will have fans eager to obtain tickets. However, the majority of events will not sell out. Look at a simple example of selling tickets for an event.

Imagine a concert in a building being put on by a group that was popular 20 years ago and has had a resurgence in popularity in recent years. For the sake of argument, say that the promoter and the facility have allowed the event managers to determine the ticket price. The venue has 10,000 seats and all tickets will be the same price. There is a core group of fans that will show up regardless. If 5,000 tickets are sold at $40, there will be a guaranteed income of $200,000. Alternatively, the event managers may decide to sell tickets for only $20. At that price, all 10,000 seats would have to be sold to make up the same gross dollar amount that would have been realized at the higher ticket price.

Logic and a bit of conservative budgeting dictate that it is not likely that all 10,000 tickets will be sold, but that there may be some people who would like to go but are not willing to pay $40 for the show. Therefore, the decision that might be made in this case would be to find a price range closer to the middle ($30), and hope to sell 8,000 tickets. This would mean a gross revenue of $240,000. In this example, the correct price, combined with the appropriate marketing strategy, led to an increase in revenue of twenty percent.

If the tickets do not have to all be the same price, the options for pricing are endless. Two or more different prices could be charged, depending on where the seats are located in the venue. Maybe $40 for lower-level seats and $30 for upper-level seats is appropriate. If there were 4,000 lower-level seats and 6,000 upper-level seats, gross revenue would jump to $340,000. This is a greatly simplified example, but it does illustrate the point that price is important. The prices cannot be dictated by what people think events are worth, so much as they are governed by what people are willing to pay.

ON-SALE DATE

The **on-sale date** for tickets is simply the date the tickets are available for purchase, and is determined by a couple of factors. The first is whether it is a one-time event, or part of a season package. In the case of many ticketed athletic events, each event is part of a season, which means several events in the same venue. The consideration here is to maximize profits by selling the most possible tickets. The best way to do this is to use individual events to drive sales for all events.

Take, for example, a college football season. Depending on the year, the season probably consists of eleven games. In this example, that breaks out into six home games and the rest of the games on the road. Among the six games are two that are likely to sell out easily. There are three others that are against reasonably well-known opponents, and one game that will be difficult to sell out. With those thoughts in mind, how would a decision be reached as to when to put single game tickets on sale?

An excellent approach is to obtain a calendar and mark down dates when everything should happen. The calendar should include all pertinent dates, including when renewal forms will be mailed, when the forms are due back in the office, when tickets will be mailed, and when tickets will go on sale. The dates should be based on the date of the first home contest and be built backwards. The premise here is that the popular games drive the sales of all the games. The marketing strategy is to inform fans that the only way to see the one or two marquee games is to buy a full-season ticket package.

In terms of the timeline, the only thing to sell for the first period of time is full-season packages. If tickets are not sold out at the deadline, the next thing to do is to put together a mini-plan or partial package. In the example, this package would be built to include the most popular game, the least popular game, and one of the other three games. The second package would include another popular game and the other two games that will be decent sellers. When putting together these packages, the most important factor is to look at the popularity of the opponent. A secondary factor is to look at the dates of the contests. Avoid selecting and packaging the games that are too close together on the calendar. The ideal schedule would allow each package to have one game at the beginning part of the season, one in the middle, and one toward the end. This way, when people are looking at a calendar and making plans, they can plan to come to the venue and attend the events.

Unless it is a mega event, athletic events are typically most attractive to supporters that are within a 100-mile radius. Ticket sales can generally be handled by the office that handles that responsibility for the team or venue. There are some occasions and events that have more of a nationwide following. Examples could include championship games, professional tennis tournaments, and concerts. There may be a chance to host a concert in a facility that features a nationally known act. In this case, consider using a nationally known ticketing company to assist in ticket sales.

OUTSOURCING TICKETS

Ticketmaster is probably the most well-known company used by organizations to outsource ticketing. Keep in mind that there are some costs involved with using such a company. In addition to the service fee, there is also an option to have tickets mailed to the customer. This can be done through any of the normal shipping/mailing options that are available. This service also dictates an additional fee. The fee can be as small as $1 if the tickets are to be sent through the regular mail, or as much as $20 if the customer would prefer to have the tickets delivered the next day. Communication is very important here. The last thing that the customer wants is to purchase four tickets for $40 each, and then look at a credit card statement and see a charge for more than $200. It is important to disclose any and all charges that will appear on the credit card and make sure that the customer agrees to the specified charges.

A customer who claims charges were not authorized can cause a substantial problem for the ticket operation. A customer that does not agree with charges may contact the credit card company and inform them that the charges are being disputed. The credit card company will then contact the vendor, in this case the ticket office, to inform them of the dispute. The company that charged the card then has a certain period of time to prove that the charges were justified or can be explained, and that the service or good (the tickets) were in fact delivered or picked up and used. The problem then becomes proving that the customer knew what they were being charged and that they actually used the tickets. It is imperative to have an effective system in place for both taking orders, tracking mailed tickets, and/or checking identifications for tickets being picked up at the venue, as well as having the customer sign for tickets that are picked up.

Even when customers are interacting with a third party such as Ticketmaster, they still associate their interaction with the third party as an extension of the team, venue, and event. Therefore, the ticket manager and event managers must be confident that the outsourcer will represent the organization well and provide excellent customer service prior to any agreement.

PREMIUM TICKETS

Premium seating encompasses a variety of seats. Luxury suites, party suites, club seats, loge boxes, field-level seats in baseball, courtside seats in basketball, and any other special section of tickets with enhanced amenities fall into the category of premium seating. For the purposes of this text, the various types of premium seating will be grouped together for discussion.

Premium tickets can be handled in a variety of ways. In many facilities, they are sold for every event in the building. The customer purchases the rights to the particular seats for the year. Once the rights to the seats have been purchased, the customer still must pay for the tickets to each event. There might even be a requirement that the customer must purchase seats for certain events. For instance, the patron may be required to buy tickets for all basketball and hockey games that take place in the building. In addition to those, the customer would also have first right of refusal for any and all other events in the building. Premium seat holders would be given a deadline, and if the tickets are not purchased by that point, the tickets are made available to other ticket buyers.

Some venues do not sell premium seats if their owners do not use them for events. This means that during concerts or other types of shows, these seats may go unused. It can be disconcerting and frustrating to both promoters and building managers to look around and see empty seats during major events, but that is the contractual agreement in place with the customers.

The customers that sit in these seats represent key revenue streams for the organization. In the United States, luxury suite revenues averaged $9.8 million per professional sports venue during the 2006–2007 season, which is a significant source of revenue for most facilities (Lawrence et al., 2007). Even though most professional sport leagues require some sharing of luxury suite revenues, it is still considered a key ingredient of an organization's financial prosperity. Spectators pay a substantial amount of money (often $100,000–$300,000 for a luxury suite) for the right to buy the tickets to the various events. In addition to the annual fee, the tickets that they do purchase are often much more expensive than the tickets that other customers purchase.

The event managers may or may not be involved in the servicing of premium seats. However, it can never hurt for those associated with the organization to take time to get to know patrons that are key accounts for the organization. Providing first-class service is critical in premium seating. Often, premium seats account for a substantial portion of overall ticket revenue.

SPECIAL INTEREST GROUPS

There is another group of people that must be kept in mind when deciding on seat locations. For lack of a better term, these will be called special interest groups. This group includes, but is not limited to: student booster groups, players' families and guests, school or local officials, league officials, promoter's group, major donors, and facility staff. All of these groups will require tickets for seats. Some of them will be paid for, while others will be complimentary.

Depending on the group, they do not necessarily need to be in the best seats possible, but they should be in reasonably good locations. Furthermore, they must be located in seats to allow them to view the contest or event from a reasonable vantage point while not displacing customers and donors that may have paid substantial amounts for tickets.

In some cases, the locations of these tickets may be dictated by an outside agency. For example, a facility that hosts an NCAA Basketball Regional will have the locations of many groups outlined specifically in the tournament manual. Ticket locations for all of the participating teams, bands, NCAA officials, and contestants are among those that are outlined for the host facility. This is an important factor because all of these seats must be held when tickets go on sale. Once the tickets are sold and have been delivered, there is no way to get the tickets back or alter seat locations without having a public relations problem and, most likely, people demanding a refund of their money.

PARKING

A source of revenue for event and facility managers that was overlooked for a number of years is the money that is generated through the sale of parking spaces during an event. Depending on the number of spaces available for use and their proximity to the facility, these can translate into substantial amounts of revenue for the event.

Parking Plans and Passes

There are a couple of approaches that can be taken with regard to parking spaces. When dealing with a particular sport season, it may be advisable to issue parking passes for all contests to be played at the facility during the course of that season. These can be charged automatically, but more likely the customer that purchases the season tickets will be given the option to purchase a season parking pass.

The parking pass that is sold can be for any available lot, for a general area, or for a specific spot. Football is traditionally a sport that is associated with tailgating before and, sometimes, after the games. There are some football fans that like to enjoy their pre-game festivities with the same people each and every game. For that reason, it may be advisable to number every available parking spot and to assign each customer to a specific spot. While there may be some added expense and labor in terms of numbering all of the spaces, there may also be an opportunity to charge a premium price for people to have the opportunity to be able to arrive at any time before or during the game and know that their spot will still be available.

In other cases, the parking situation can be handled much as the tickets for the event are handled. Those that want the "best" seats are willing to pay a premium price. Such is the case with parking. Those customers that want the best possible parking spaces may be willing to pay a little extra to park close to the facility. The parking areas could be broken down into categories such as platinum, gold, silver, and bronze. The per-game prices for these categories might be $15, $12, $10, and $7 respectively. When making a purchase, either prior to or on the day of the event, customers could be given the option of which area they prefer to purchase.

An additional option for parking is to charge a set amount for every vehicle that enters the parking lot. No spaces would be reserved and the cars that arrived earliest would be able to park in the spaces closest to the facility. While this idea may not seem as appealing as the previous two examples, it may have the potential to generate the same or greater net profit. The reason is that this type of general parking requires a minimal amount of staffing. The only staff required are the attendants that collect the money when the cars enter and a few to help direct traffic to the available spaces. In the first two cases, there are people needed to sell passes, to check passes at the different areas, and possibly tow trucks and vehicle movers to move cars out of spots that are not assigned to them.

There is one scenario that guarantees revenue from parking. Most stadiums and arenas have some number of reserved parking spaces for various groups. Average fans are left to fend for themselves in looking for a place to park. Some venues will build an additional fee into the ticket price and allow fans to park on a first come, first served basis. It is basically a general admission parking pass. This eliminates the need for parking attendants to take money on the night of the event. It also generates instant revenue on every ticket that is sold. While it is a reasonable idea in principle, there is one inherent problem. The problem is that there may not be enough parking spaces for all the cars that may come to the game. However unlikely, what would happen if 10,000–12,000 fans all drove their cars to the game and there are only 8,000 parking spaces at the arena (which, by the way, is an unusually large number)? The headache of returning money to people would pale in comparison to the public relations nightmare that would face the venue. Also, regardless of who made the decision, the people that would hear all the complaints and listen to all of the cursing would be the ticket takers and people in the ticket office, since they would be the first people the angry customers would encounter upon entry into the facility. A side note regarding this system of parking: This system may allow for greater concession profits and merchandise. If patrons want to get the best parking spots, they are likely to arrive at the facility quite some time before the beginning of the contest. Logic dictates that the longer people are in the facility, the more likely they are to spend money on food, beverages, and souvenirs.

Considerations

There are a few additional considerations to be kept in mind when making parking decisions. From an event management perspective, one main objective is to get patrons into the parking lots, into the facility, and into their seats as seamlessly as possible. This means that parking attendants must be able to perform transactions quickly. These transactions become substantially easier and more expedient if the price for parking does not require the attendant to make too much change. For example, a parking fee of $6 probably means that the majority of the customers will require some change. If the customer pays with a $20 bill, the attendant must count out the required number of bills. It may not seem like a large amount of time, but imagine a situation where 1,000 cars are entering a particular gate. If each transaction takes 15 seconds as opposed to 10 seconds, the customers at the end of the line are waiting a long time to give their money.

A problem that could arise based on the price of the parking pass is having enough change. In the previous example, with a $6 parking pass, any customer that does not have exact change is going to require at least four $1 bills and, possibly a $10 bill as well. Each attendant would have to have a significant number of $1 bills to be able to make all of the required change.

It is important that there be some sort of accounting system for the parking on the day of the event. While unfortunate, it is possible that there may be an occasional parking attendant that tries to take advantage of the system. The cars that pull in and pay for a parking pass should receive some sort of ticket or pass to be displayed in their vehicle. These tickets should be seen by the attendant helping to direct the traffic. A missing ticket could signal an issue with a person collecting money and not turning it in to the event managers.

The event managers must also keep traffic flow in mind. It is not enough to simply accept parking money and expect people to get in and out of the parking lots without some guidance. The people bringing in the revenue from the parking passes also have a responsibility to direct traffic in and out of the lots safely and efficiently.

CREDENTIALS

The event managers must make sure that everyone has access to the areas where they need to be. Equally, if not more importantly, the event managers must make sure that people are not in areas where they do not belong. Careful consideration should be given to which people will receive which credentials. There are clearly some people that need to have access to any and all areas within the facility, while there are others that only need limited access—despite what they might think or say.

The most critical areas for access include the playing surface or area where the contest is taking place, any areas where money is being handled, the locker rooms, the officials' area, and any areas where food and beverages are being prepared. Beyond that, there are areas where most people need not be, regardless of whether they are ticket holders or workers.

Credentials must be easily seen and easily differentiated. The most common practices for designing credentials is to make them different colors or to print a large number on the credential. In other words, a person with a green credential or with a hang tag with a large number "1" on it has access to all areas. Each different level of access would have a different color and/or number associated with it. After the credentials have been designed and made, sample boards are constructed and placed strategically through the building. **Sample boards** have exact replicas of credentials, tickets, and parking passes on them and provide an easy reference guide for staff. All staff should be charged with helping to keep people out of designated areas where they do not belong, and sample boards help with this.

Keep in mind that the more important or high profile the event, the more elaborate the scheme will be to try to gain access. There have been numerous examples of people trying to beat the system and gain entrance into sold-out games or restricted areas. These include such scams as dressing up as a member of the janitorial staff or a police officer, printing false league official credentials, or even dressing as a member of the team. Also, some people will arrive at certain areas without any credentials and attempt to talk their way into restricted areas. Some of these people will have legitimate excuses, while others will be completely fabricating a story. The bottom line is that the people entrusted with security of certain areas will have to use their judgment and make the best possible decision under the given circumstances.

RECONCILIATION

Each organization and each facility will have a different way to reconcile event receipts. The computerized ticketing systems in use now allow for sales records to be pulled up on a daily basis. Further, depending on the system, it is possible to see which outlets are selling which tickets, how many, in which price category, and how quickly they are being purchased. Complimentary tickets should also be carefully accounted for as part of reconciliation. One thing that is an absolute is that receipts must be reconciled at the end of each business day. In the case of major venues with a professional team as a tenant, this could involve reconciling income from as many as 10 or 12 different upcoming events on any given day. Once the total receipts have been counted, they must be broken out and deposited in the appropriate accounts.

As a rule, this does not take long, but there are times when issues arise. Cash on hand may be inaccurate, or credit card charges might not match those reported in the daily activity journal. This can be a frustrating and difficult situation to work through, and makes it even more important that everyone who has a responsibility to ring in sales is diligent and accurate with all that they do. Extra care and caution during the sale will lead to more accurate reports and more satisfied customers and administrators.

NON-TRADITIONAL SPORT VENUES

For events in non-traditional venues, event managers must examine where seats are needed, establish how many are needed, and decide if ticketing is appropriate. It can be very challenging to control access for spectators to a roadway, waterway, or park where an event is being held. Even golf courses have found that controlling access given the amount of space used is a challenge. However, renting seating is expensive, so the costs and benefits must be examined before ticketing decisions are made. Before any decisions are made, the event managers must know if there is a market for tickets, whether the physical layout of the venue would allow for access control, and if there are options other than selling tickets available to generate revenue.

Think about the sheer number of staff that it would take to control spectator access to any sort of cycling race. Plus, it is more likely than not that the price of admission would drive spectators completely away from an event such as this unless it was a major international event or Olympic qualifier. Many of these types of events have their goals and objectives based in being participant driven, and therefore selling tickets might move the organization further away from the purpose of the event.

There may be other ways to generate revenue that would be more cost effective and make more sense instead of ticketing the entire event. One option is to ticket the start and finish of a race, and another is to create exclusive areas along the course (e.g., Viewing Zones) where amenities such as food and drink are provided for those wanting to purchase a ticket to enter the area. The most common option is to not ticket the event, but to make sure concessions and/or merchandise are available for spectators throughout the course. When this is done, fans may be more willing to spend money on concessions if they have not had to pay for a ticket.

THE SECONDARY TICKET MARKET

The **secondary ticket market** refers to the reselling of tickets after the first purchase. Reselling of tickets is an ongoing concern in the industry. While there are some sellers that offer a valuable and legitimate purpose, there are many who simply undermine the process and can adversely affect the event and the price paid for tickets. At some point in the recent past, the name of these entrepreneurs changed from "scalpers" to "ticket brokers." New ways have been devised to sell game tickets at a substantially higher price than face value.

For example, let us imagine that a fan had an ample supply of money and wanted to go to the Super Bowl. Further, for the sake of this example, suppose that the Super Bowl was being held in a state in which it is illegal to sell tickets for anything more than $2 above face value. A person wanting to sell two tickets that are worth $250 each could not legally charge more than $504. The seller would have to sell a lot of tickets to make a profit. What, then, would allow them to realize profits of thousands of dollars? The answer is quite simple. They would not sell tickets to the Super Bowl. They might sell a hat or a jersey with the logo of one of the participating teams proudly displayed. This souvenir might be priced at $5000. The added bonus is that along with the new piece of gear, the seller would toss in a couple of Super Bowl tickets! It can be a difficult proposition to dissuade people from re-selling tickets.

INCREMENTAL REVENUE AND BREAKAGE

Incremental revenue is revenue that is generated through "up selling." For example, a team might send a loyal fan a $5 coupon for the merchandise store, knowing that the cheapest item in the store is $20. The fan does not want to waste the $5 gift and ends up spending $40 at the next game on merchandise. The team generated $35 that they would not have without the $5 coupon.

This applies to ticketing in that many teams are using the bar coded season tickets to "load" these small gifts on. The advantage of loading money on the ticket is that there is an electronic record for the team of when the money was spent, how much was spent, and on what. That information is then used in future marketing efforts.

This concept can go a step further where the price of the ticket is increased to account for some in-stadium spending money for the purchaser. In this case, a fan decides to attend an NFL game. The normal ticket price is $85, but, the price that the consumer pays is $100 per ticket. Built into the ticket price is an extra $15 that acts like a credit. When the patron arrives at the facility, she can obtain $15 worth of concessions, souvenirs, or anything else that might be for sale.

The added price is not optional, and if the credit is not used that night, there is no refund and the customer may not "save" it and use it at a later game. The difference in the amount that the customer pays and the amount he spends is known as **breakage**. The team or venue receives this "free" money the customer did not spend. Both incremental revenue and breakage strategies are beginning to be commonplace in ticketing strategies.

THE UNEXPECTED

The more events that event managers have an opportunity to work with and around, the more unique situations they will experience. There will come a time when computers and ticket printers will stop functioning at the absolute worst possible time. It could be before the biggest game of the season, the start of the play-offs, the on-sale date for a major concert, or the doors opening for a WWE event. Some of these problems are impossible to anticipate while others can be expected. Some simple steps to prepare to handle a technology crash include:

1. Have a printed list of season ticket holder seat locations available.

2. Have an additional laptop computer available to connect to a network.

3. Have additional ticket stock and possibly a ticket printer and an extra set of tickets.

4. Print a set of tickets with no dates or event on the ticket. Take care to ensure that every seat is printed, and that if there are changes to the seating, the back-up tickets are adjusted accordingly. The tickets can be locked away in the back of a closet, and the hope is that they will never be used.

If there ever is an occasion to use anything mentioned above, everyone involved in administering the event will be glad that someone had the foresight to address the potential problem. Hoping for the best but expecting the worst will prepare the ticket manager and event managers for many of the foreseeable problems that could occur in ticketing.

SUMMARY

One of the goals of event managers should be to know as much as possible about what everyone else involved in the event contributes to the process. Especially in ticketing, event managers and the ticket manager must communicate and work hand-in-hand throughout the entire event management process. By working together, all decisions about ticketing will take into account other aspects of the event that the ticket manager may not be aware of.

A ticket manager who is able to provide exceptional customer service, make the ticketing process as easy as possible for customers, and provide options for customers will contribute significantly to the overall success of the event. Customers often only interact with the ticket office prior to arriving at the event site, so the ticket office sets the stage for what is to follow in the minds of customers.

Student Challenge

STUDENT CHALLENGE #9

In Challenge #9, evaluate existing ticketing companies as well as potential companies for the ticketing needs of the event. Then, set up a parking and credential access plan for the event.

QUESTION 9-1

Research two ticketing companies that provide ticketing services to events and facilities. If the planned event is not spectator driven, use a beach volleyball pro tour event as the event for this question. Generate a list of the services each company provides and then list the pros and cons for each company.

Ticket Company #1 Name:

Services Provided:

Pros:

Cons:

Ticket Company #2 Name:

Services Provided:

Pros:

Cons:

Student Challenge

QUESTION 9-2

Create a ticket pricing strategy for the event. Explain how the pricing strategy was developed and why the strategy works for this event. If the event is not spectator driven, use a beach volleyball pro tour event and assume that the local event organizer has the right to set ticket prices.

QUESTION 9-3

On another sheet of paper, create a credential and parking pass plan (e.g., how many different types of access are needed for credentials and why, how will the parking lot be restricted, what will be charged, and why). Identify the various groups in the plan, and create/design the respective credential and parking passes.

CHAPTER 10

EVENT COMMUNICATIONS AND EXTERNAL RELATIONS

Packy Moran

This chapter introduces concepts of communication and external relations to the framework of event management. At first glance the concepts seem simple. However, when one digs further into what effective communication means in event management and the importance of external relations to a successful event, the challenges emerge. As with other aspects of event management (e.g., marketing, sponsorship, ticketing), even if event managers are not directly responsible for the function, they must understand all areas that make the event come to life. Flexibility in channels and message is important in executing a communications strategy. Even with flexibility, there are guidelines event managers and communications professionals can use to help ensure their message is "heard." The communications strategy will evolve alongside the event, but will always be tied to the overall event purpose, objective, and theme.

External relations is defined as the management process concerning the creation and communication of information through media (both earned and paid) to intended audiences (publics) and is akin to communications, but slightly different. During different phases (i.e., conceptualization, development, execution) of the event, the goals of communications will change. While event communications covers the creation of media-focused and straight-to-consumer pieces, the larger concept of external relations considers integrating communication at all levels of organizational control into a management function.

An organized communications system will help maintain positive relationships with distribution channels (i.e., newspaper, television, radio, Internet) and in return help garner cooperation from those media in the event of a crisis. Definitions for paid and earned media are given and their interdependence explained. In-event and participant-based communications can be a point of differentiation for certain groups and should not be ignored. This chapter will shed light on the event communication process. A brief discussion of media auditing and long-term relationship building and planning is also included.

EVENT COMMUNICATIONS

Event managers can discover the common thread in successful event communications in the answer to the following fundamental questions: Why do people want to work in sports? Why would anyone want to work when others are off, spend holidays and weekends on the job, and make less money than comparable jobs in the financial, medical, and retail sectors?

Sport is a sequence of well-planned and managed events. Shared emotional (and sometimes physical) investment is celebrated and the outcome is uncertain. People gather at an appointed time and place, there is often food, drink, and entertainment, and then people leave when the event is over. Stories are told about the event, some to a few people, and some to a worldwide audience. Some sporting events are forgotten as soon as they are over, while some rise to such legendary status that people who were not even in attendance claim to have been there. This is why, despite the long hours and the low pay, many still want to join those who help make these events happen.

So, how do event managers set an external relations strategy for a sporting event? While not every sports event has exactly the same build-up, most go through the following stages: conceptualization, development (including planning, invitation, and supply), and execution (including the event itself and wrap-up).

As discussed in the prior chapters of this book, event mission, goals, and objectives are the guiding force in making every decision at almost every level. External relations efforts include the communication processes in publicizing an event and the relationship with the media throughout the event cycle. No one would flier the campus or expect media coverage when having a couple of friends over for a pick-up basketball game, just as one could not expect to fill a gymnasium for a big rivalry basketball game without some contact with the campus and outside media. These paths are chosen during event conceptualization; figuring out the basics of the "why" and "what" will narrow the reasonable options for the "who, when, where, and how."

EVENT CONCEPTUALIZATION

Event conceptualization from a communications aspect places the organization and event in relative positions to other organizations and events that occur in the same activity, geography, or time-space. Let's look at various types of basketball as an example. If a person has a gathering to play basketball, it exists in relation to all other basketball games, both on campus and off, both for this game and others before it, as well as everything else that is going on for that afternoon. The fact that this basketball game will be played on a custom-designed hardwood court with NBA regulation backboards and breakaway rims may change its position, but it does not change who and what is involved.

The questions of "why" and "what" become central at this point. The "what" is a basketball game with friends played on a great court, but the "why" will determine in what ways one lets others know about the event. Is it a small gathering where calls and texts will deliver the right attendees? Is it a local tournament where the number of teams playing determines success? Is it a fraternity fund-raising event, where more attendees are better, but a certain level of player is expected and targeted? All three of these scenarios involve a basketball game, a court, and a communications strategy, but have different goals and ideas as to what makes the event successful. Just as a youth recreational league, a high school game, and the World Cup are all soccer, it is the "why" (the goal of the event) that determines the "who, when, where, and how" in terms of external communications.

The organization's relative position to other groups and happenings helps form strategy. Information provided is about facilitating choices. Hosting a successful event—with the right people there at the right time—includes packaging information in such a way so that people can make the choice the organizers prefer them to make. "Where do I want to play basketball?" is the question that all three basketball organizers want to help as many people as possible answer in the way most appropriate to reach the goals of all those involved.

Paid vs. Earned Media

There are two main access strategies to media in terms of getting information out to potential consumers: paid and earned. **Paid media** takes the form of advertising, sponsorship, and activation marketing. The event organizers retaining control over the message characterizes paid media. Also included in paid media are internally controlled or created pieces for official team or league Web sites, in-game use (i.e., programs, scorecards, stat sheets, video board spots) or broadcasts controlled by the league or team (radio announcers hired by the team or regional cable broadcasts controlled in-house). **Earned media**, on the other hand, has gone through an independent editorial source before it reaches the intended audience. A newspaper or online story, a television report, and an ESPN highlight reel are all examples of earned media. The introduction of the intermediary results in less control of content retained by the event organizers.

The event organizers will want to distribute information to as many people as possible that fit their target market. The goal is volume. Preferably, the communication will reach people who will spend money to enter the event, but ultimately, more people results in more opportunities for money. The group's communications will focus on the number of people expected and the opportunities that exist in that situation. They will utilize fliers, radio ads, newspaper ads, Internet ads, and an earned media strategy focusing on sports and entertainment outlets to get the information out to the masses. The goal is that those interested will then use word-of-mouth and personal selling to tell their friends, resulting in a large crowd.

Using the basketball example, a fraternity charity tournament will likely flier campus areas and may run advertising and put an earned-media campaign in place on campus-specific outlets such as the student radio station or Internet home page. But this group will mainly focus on more personal distribution techniques. Word-of-mouth and personal references help give an air of exclusivity to the event. Even with a fraternity charity tournament, the event's place amongst the others is important to consider. In this example, using mass media (print, radio, TV) is unlikely, but a message will need to be disseminated that convinces students to attend. This can be achieved through phrasing personal invitations and referrals in comparison/contrast to what is going on elsewhere (i.e., Why the fraternity tournament is a better choice for the weekend than going to watch a movie or to the library to study). In the fraternity charity tournament organizer's case, whom they do not tell is as much a part of the communication strategy as whom they do.

Communications by Event Type

The four event types listed in Chapter 1, Event Management and the Event Manager, as recurring, traveling, mega, and ancillary events can help define expectations. Each event type is unique in focus and can occur at every level of size and intensity, but event regularity is only one element in the overall conceptualization of a communication strategy.

Recurring Events

As mentioned before, recurring events are the most common, and therefore provide the most opportunity to utilize communication channels toward an organization's goals. The regularity of a "Third Thursday" event allows a media strategy to let more people know about an event, while adding specific details about each date in order to entice return visits. Any sports team with regularly occurring home games draws similarities—the opponent changes, as does the relative position of the team for championships and post-season chances—but the location and general format of the event is consistent. The promoting group emphasizes differences through news coverage and controlled channels—for example, Web site features on opponents and promotions—but the overall tenor and feel of the messaging will be consistent. For example, a hockey team may use the same tag line at the bottom of every press release, flier, newspaper ad, Internet ad, and billboard for the duration of a season. The National Hockey League's Columbus Blue Jackets have used "Ignite the Night" and "Jackets Time" in recent years.

Traveling Events

Consistency of messaging and style can also be important to traveling events. While not as frequent within the same media market—groups of newspapers, radio, and TV stations that serve a similar geographic area or population, such as the New York City media market—traveling events benefit from consistent messaging used at each stop on their tours. Traveling basketball tournaments can range from the more festival-like atmosphere of a Gus Macker or Hoop-It-Up tournament to the more sedate character of an AAU championship, but each and every branded tournament carries an expectation of what will be communicated and how. The former will use the commercial enterprise's approach from the "big game" example—mixing fliers, radio, Internet ads, and earned mass media—while the latter will depend on personal invitations and qualifiers from other tournaments. In the sports and event world, the facility-based communications professional—a person who is employed by the arena, convention center, stadium, or complex—plays a key role in providing the traveling event promoter with information and introduction to the local media market. Traveling outfits are normally on tour for a distinct period of time and dates. They can include concerts, circuses, monster truck rallies, motorsports, family shows (Disney on Ice, Sesame Street Live, Bob the Builder, Clifford the Big Red Dog, High School Musical on Ice, etc.), combat sports, rodeos, and more. To borrow from the Gus Macker Tournament example, the promoter is the Gus Macker Tournament organizer, and the facility is the host.

Ancillary Events

Ancillary events fit within the scope of the larger events they support. Depending on the event that is the main draw, ancillary events can have their purpose defined by the group attending the main event, or a specific subsection of that population. The homecoming football game tailgate sponsored by an academic department is an example of an event looking for a subset, while a charity 5K run and walk scheduled the day before a major marathon may be looking for more attendees from a general group. For a Gus Macker or Hoop-It-Up event, it may be a slam dunk contest, a ball handling demonstration, a 3-point shootout, or a H-O-R-S-E contest. The ancillary events could be additional competitions, or simply to provide entertainment. The type of event and size of the targeted population heavily influence the communication strategy.

Mega Events

Mega events provide opportunities for creating and implementing a media strategy of grand scale for a single group of events. Unlike a recurring or traveling event, the mega event is conceptualized, planned, and executed with a single, specific end-date in mind. Logos and graphics are the easiest example. Each Olympic Games, Super Bowl, and NCAA Final Four has its own logo that suggests the place and year of the event. These marks act as a unifying symbol for all of the events that happen around and as part of those mega events. Communication strategy in those cases often involves an attempt to contextualize the effects or "big picture" of the event. The paid media piece for mega events often falls to the media companies who are capitalizing on the rights fees they paid to carry the sport. The **rights fee** is the payment made by an entity to legally associate with the event. The challenge becomes controlling access and distributing information to the other members of the media who are covering the proceedings for the earned, or "news," side.

Most event managers of mega events consider an event that generates no outside press coverage a bigger disaster than one where only half of the expected participants are there, but all are photographed and interviewed. Sports events have a role to play in generating press coverage, and communication and event managers need to facilitate that role.

News Items vs. Features

Event managers have two main types of stories to offer earned-media producers in dealing with an event: news items and features. These story forms also hold true for in-house paid-media sources, like official team Web sites, features on team-controlled broadcasts, and in-event media, such as programs, yearbooks, and video board productions. **News items** normally surround the event itself and include coverage of what happens at the event, previews of the event, and announcements that the event is going to happen—often by covering a smaller ancillary event related to the main one (e.g., a press conference).

Features are human-interest stories that somehow link back to the event through personalities or elements of the event that are the focus of the story (e.g., a star player on a Final Four team who only began playing basketball at age 14 after moving to the US from Africa). A player on an NCAA Final Four basketball team reading to elementary school kids is a typical feature photo that promotes a positive social message and the team as sponsoring group. Community service projects before college football bowl games are an example of intercollegiate athletic departments meeting several priorities that can be displayed by the media, including rounding out the student-athlete experience and the involvement of non-athlete students with the program.

After event conceptualization, event managers should be able to answer the "when, where, and who" of the communication strategy as defined by the "what" and the "why" of the event. The question that remains is the "how" of getting the message to those who need to hear it.

DEVELOPMENT

Development of the external relations plan is *not* a solitary process for any one department. Although primarily media strategy will be discussed, it should be understood that buy-in and direction from other parts of the event management group will be needed to optimize effect. Coordination with other departments prevents disasters caused by misaligned expectations, which often have their roots in an erroneous piece of information put out by a frenzied and unfocused media campaign. In the public assembly realm, ticket and security policies are paramount for ensuring everyone—especially the authorities, the customers, and the facility—is on the same page. Misinformation in event times, lineups, and promotional activities can cause big headaches.

Information Sharing

In practice, the communications professional needs to be informed in the decisions that surround the event, and vice versa. Ideally, communications managers should be involved in the decision-making process. The five P's (prior planning prevents poor performance) are as true for external relations as they are for the athletes and performers. Maintaining the policy decision's original intent through the media's reporting process—regardless of the level of control of the story—is much more likely when the communications professional is involved in the initial decision making. Familiarity with every aspect of the event is important in offering proper context for paid media and answering any questions of earned media workers. Paid media—print advertisements, radio spots, TV commercials, Internet ads, and so on—have a high level of control from the event organizers.

The group's external relations staff should have final oversight for each ad before it runs, and should follow up with clippings and schedule checks—a log of when a commercial ran on radio or TV and the rating it received—to make sure the group received what it paid for. Earned media—TV, radio, newspaper, and online news items and public service announcements—is subject to less direct control from the event organizers, but information flow and existing relationships with media members can influence the transmission of the necessary information. The basic information for an event is the source of content for both paid and earned media support materials. Consistency between those materials for the two media types is helpful, but allowing the earned media outlets to "do what they do" with the information is key to getting it out through their channels.

External Relations as a Management Function

Proper planning ties paid and earned media—regardless of the outlet it is focused toward—together into a unified program, referred to as external relations. Being familiar with each outlet—TV and radio station, magazine, newspaper, Internet, community post, and so forth—and their particular information schedule on both the paid and earned side of the desk is the only way to put the right strategy in place. For recurring events, such as a team's home season or a series of annual flat shows (e.g., home show, boat show, etc.), event organizers purchase paid media plans weeks, if not months, before the event dates. Delivery of the ad follows closer to the date of publication or broadcast. Overseeing production of the entity's paid media is important because the lessons learned can be directly applied in assisting the news media in doing their job at the event site. A communications director should have a basic understanding of media production—lighting, sound control, delivery systems, and more—in order to manage the organization's advertising and help the news media craft the best possible image of the event. This also comes into play for earned media. For example, at an outdoor basketball tournament or a road race, white signage looks great, but it doesn't show up well on television. If the event managers anticipate television coverage or are targeting it, this is one small item that will help in the promotion and branding of their event via broadcast media.

Communications managers must be able to facilitate the information created by the event as well as document it for future publicity. Statistical record keeping and archiving are important for communication teams to consider because core constituencies (big fans, participants, sponsors, etc.) and key partners (leagues, governing bodies, etc.) rely on locally collected information. A long view of the calendar is also needed to make sure production schedules hit deadlines for media guides, yearbooks, and game programs that the event produces—often with an up-to-the-day statistical insert in a preplaced program.

Processes for participant-based events can eventually be turned over as internal operations, but until they become participants they are an external public, and interact with the event through some media managed by the communications team. Everything from event presentation (race timers, scoreboards, etc. in a race set up) to details on parking and logistics must be communicated through a managed medium. Continuing the race example, runners' numbers and pins are internal to the event, whereas a time clock is external as it communicates to an external audience (runners are both internal and external to the race). The transfer of the runners' information from the timing chips and ultimately reporting of the runners' times is an important operations to communication handoff, as it involves expectations of the runners and possibly some earned media outlets, as well as ongoing archival records of the event.

Ancillary and traveling events will have the general media playing field dictated to them in reference to the event and facilities to which they are related. Communications strategies for these events should consider the input of the sponsors. Traveling events often seek advice and support from facility communication professionals and lean on existing media relationships. Similarly, ancillary events fit within the larger picture of the main draw for the schedule and media positioning—both paid and earned. The other side of the coin is the mega event. While a central theme or logo ties a series of events together, communications strategies will be as diverse as the groups sponsoring the events. In mega events, protecting the main identity and themes of the primary event is a principal concern. One misstep can cloud an otherwise successful event. The NCAA Final Four, for example, is likely to have partners policing the use of their logo in the local community and in the areas surrounding the event itself. Fliers and T-shirts will be destroyed at the least and multi-million dollar lawsuits can result at worst, from unauthorized use of a logo.

There is more to the development phase than individual event strategy. Development involves invitation and supply elements of event management communications. The basketball metaphor can help again. Calling to mind the pick-up game and tournaments, each group planning a basketball event had a different focus group to attend their specific event. The target audience is the result of the invitation process when it comes to external relations. In the world of mass media and instant information, it helps to be aware of as many media outlets as possible. Inviting everybody to every basketball event does not make sense, but knowing more ways to get information to more and different types of people is never a bad thing. Having the appropriate facilities, information, and supplies for media when they arrive to cover the event is one way to improve chances of continuing coverage.

Media Audit

A **media audit** is the process of determining the content, format, deadlines, and contacts at the entire population of outlets that are active in the media market where the group, and/or the event, takes place. The audit is a first "scene setting" exercise that a communications professional must perform when taking a new job or launching a new event. Differences in events—even within a promoting group—will call for different editorial contacts at various outlets. A sports writer may be very interested in a college football game, while a linebacker reading to elementary school children as part of his student teaching will intrigue an education beat reporter. The following are helpful in maintaining a media audit:

- Use a Web search engine for daily alerts from key word searches including the event and group names; archive as many stories and sources as possible. Google News and RSS feeds make this very easy today.

- Include Web resources and editors affiliated with more traditional media outlets (i.e., newspaper Web sites, TV Web sites, etc.).

- Keep a list of bloggers (text-based) and vloggers (video-based) who mention/cover the events.

- Make regular contact with key constituent outlets.

- Update media audits fully every three months.

Invitation

The invitation phase of development is a balance of space issues and expediency for sponsor groups. For some events, working press space will be at a premium, while other events will not have an access problem. Official media credentials are a privilege, and a revocable one at that. The event organizers should use press passes for their greatest good, while maintaining fairness and avoiding political problems caused by limiting one outlet's access in relation to a competitor (more likely referred to as a peer). The group should reserve the right to determine competitors; however, not every TV station is a competitor to a network affiliate, nor every newspaper the largest daily in the area. Space issues may cause choices to be made as to which media outlets can be accommodated. Quantity and frequency of coverage must be balanced with opportunities to reach the most people when making decisions.

Communications professionals should consider these issues with each event, but more often than not will be extending more invitations to events than are used. When the number one team in the country comes to a rural campus for a football game, it would not make sense for the school to exclude its local paper from the press box for three people from the metropolitan TV station 90 minutes away, regardless of how much it is perceived that coverage from the TV station may suffer because of it.

Press passes differ from complementary tickets, in the expectation that some form of news story will be created from the media member's attendance at the event. Reminders that the press area is a working area should be made via announcement in the area and in writing. The Baseball Writers Association of America has specific rules and encourages local oversight of the press box by chapter members (BWAA Constitution, 2007).

Supply

Access to supplies and resources on-site is also an issue for promoting groups to consider. Communications managers and event managers regularly reserve certain places, resources, or experiences for certain media when planning the allocation of space and access for an event. *ESPN the Magazine* may be granted exclusive access to locker room pre-game and halftime observation, or *Runner's World* magazine may have exclusive access to shadow the race director of a major marathon on race day in conjunction with writing a story for the *Runner's World* Web site.

The minimum level of service is the opportunity to perform their job in an efficient manner, determined by the nature of the medium (i.e., TV, radio, print, Web, etc.) and the schedule of their production (i.e., instant, morning, afternoon, weekly, etc.). Communications professionals consider the timing of the media member's product as well as its potential reach in making these decisions. Most press areas in spectator sports offer the best views first to those broadcast journalists who are presenting the game live, next to print journalists with the most subscribers and quick turnarounds (dailies, blogs, etc.), and finally to the rest of the media (radio news, magazine writers, weeklies, etc.). Recently, press areas for the non-broadcasters have been removed from areas immediately adjacent to the playing surface so those areas can yield revenue from customers willing to pay top dollar for the access.

Seating is only one access issue that needs to be considered. Interview space and behind-the-scenes access is also a resource that communications professionals help distribute. The digital information age has created challenges here as sources like YouTube, Rivals.com, and fansonly.com have created outlets for video from "citizen journalists." The communications professional needs to work with the facility and the event operations, as well as sales and marketing departments, to protect the access of more traditional media members whose outlets have proven reach for the event's messages. Press conferences (both pre- and post-event), partner announcements, and other ancillary events that have had a history of exclusivity have an allure to sales-focused people who are looking to turn revenue without adding expense. The lead-up events must have their original function maintained: communicating information to media members who control and program the sources that reach key publics.

Another consideration brought on by the Internet and Web 2.0 acceleration of media content—video on demand and other interactive Web features—is the relationship between in-house sources (which are considered paid media, as resources and reach are traded for control of the product) and more traditional independent sources. Broadcast resources are often at the center of this conflict. Game transmissions of professional sporting events are often the property of the league and teams, but local television and radio outlets, as well as video elements of other resources, will want to produce clips and original content around the event. Balancing these relationships through pool services (a single photographer or videographer, e.g., the Associated Press or the broadcast rights holder) and allowing limited access (defined by time or place) should help every group meet their needs.

Proper planning and invitation goes a long way towards success for an event's media and communication needs, but some needs arise in reaction to things that cannot be frequently expected. While planning for these contingencies is the key to thriving during their occurrence, they will be discussed in the execution stage.

Sixteen Rules for the Press Release

The press release is the basic skill needed for media relations professionals. The format and content are varied and determined by the situation, but the fundamentals are the same, just like shooting a free throw or making a golf swing. The 16 rules have been adopted from Mel Helitzer's "The Dream Job" and Dr. Tim Newman (York College of Pennsylvania), and apply specifically to releases sent via mail or fax, but the underlying principles apply to all communication with the media.

The digital information age has changed delivery, but not the needs of the receiving outlet based on content or structure. When sending out press releases today, the press release may be distributed in Word or PDF format via email and/or virtual fax. Another way that they may be distributed is by using an FTP or other Web site. The communications department gives access to the media at their request, which allows the communications staff to control access. Regardless of how media access press releases, the format for writing follows these 16 rules.

1. Paper choice: 8 ½ × 11 white paper

   The point: Do not let the medium used to convey the message get in the way of the message itself. In digital communication this could apply to the file format of attachments. The widest used file formats are Word documents (.doc) and protected data files (.pdf); use anything else sparingly unless specifically requested by a particular media outlet. Balance must be struck between the look of the release and its ability to be used effectively by the outlet.

2. Margins: two inches on the top and one-inch margins on the sides and bottom

   The point: Press releases are working documents. Media members will take notes on the paper if given in printed format, and the ultimate goal is to make the job of the press easier so they can convey the information in as positive a light to the sponsor group as possible. This is important in electronic documents as well, which are often printed at the outlet for ease of use for the reporter and editor.

3. Headers: pre-printed information that visually identifies the sponsoring organization and delivers the contact information

   The point: Have a template that works like letterhead. The subtle professionalism will not be lost on your media contacts. The header should include the organization name, address, and several ways to contact (Web site address, email, phone, fax, etc.). While this can be extended to html-coded email headers, be careful of how the information looks to those who pick up their email in environments that do not support html. Perhaps a PDF file attachment of the release with the body copied in the email (and formatted for the text-based email) is the safest bet. Be consistent. An outlet should be able to almost instantly recognize the source of the release.

4. Contact person: include a name and phone number that the media can talk to

   The point: Providing a contact name and number where that person can be reached increases the likelihood of response from the media. They know more information is available, and the gesture of assistance in meeting their deadlines will be appreciated. The follow-up by the contact person is as important as having their information listed. They should be available, at the least during business hours the day the release is sent and the next day. Familiarity with a particular contact person increases the chance for earned media coverage because it provides a known quantity.

5. Release date: use "FOR IMMEDIATE RELEASE" unless embargoed to a specific date

   The point: Old news is *no* news. Most releases (97%) are for immediate release, meaning all the information in the release can be used right away. Embargoed releases are sent out to give news outlets a sneak preview of an announcement or an event. The date on the release then signifies when the message can be distributed from their outlet. Hiring a new coach is a good example of an embargoed release, as you want news agencies to be prepared for the press conference, which serves as a formal introduction and place for statements by the organization and the coach. Be specific in whatever medium the release is in as to when the information is to be made public.

6. "Special to" or "Exclusive to": these terms suggest that only the receiver of the release got this information

The point: This is a dangerous but powerful technique that should never be used with "hard" news (hirings, firings, etc.). An organization cannot afford to play favorites amongst the media. This can be used sparingly in terms of feature angles or for pitching personality pieces.

7. Headline: summarize key points in no more than two lines

The point: Just like a newspaper head, the wording should be truthful and emphasize the main points of the release. The font used should be bolded and larger than the body text. A secondary or deck headline can be used if there is a secondary point that can be made quickly.

8. Single space the text of the release

The point: It is a working document and will often be retyped by media members regardless of distribution method; radio or TV will retype into readable copy or into the teleprompter. Single space also allows more information on a single page.

9. The lead: most important information should be stated in the first sentence of the release

The point: Efficiency is important to news organizations. Most will assume that the important information will be in the first couple of lines.

10. The body: inverted pyramid style of writing

The point: Think about each paragraph as a five-second audio clip. If you had only 10 seconds to give your information, what would be included? Specifics and details should be given in subsequent paragraphs; if the news organization wants it, they will find it.

11. Paragraphs: short, but complete

The point: Press release paragraphs include one complete thought. Remember the five second example: If the paragraph is reading long, break it up.

12. Subheads: draw attention to the details

The point: Use a subhead if another topic is being covered, or to introduce a table (such as statistics) or a section of supporting quotes.

In the digital age, the next three rules help let the outlet know they have the entire release.

13. Page numbering: top, center of pages

The point: If a release needs to be longer than one page, number the second page (and subsequent pages) at the top and centered with a convention that will be consistent, such as -2- or {2}.

14. MORE: bottom centered on pages that are continued

The point: The typewritten "MORE" lets the news gatherer know that the release is not just a single page. Most releases are kept to one page.

15. Use ###: bottom centered on pages that are not continued

The point: Acts as the industry's stop sign. Some releases use the old printer's code -30-, or some will change the end key to something that fits their organization, such as *Tigers*.

Finally, a rule that ties a communication skill—press release writing—to the management functions of external relations.

16. Date code

    The point: The date code is an internal organization key that allows files to be tracked by release date and media. A typical code will include the numerical date of the release and the modes by which it was sent. "102309fme" may indicate the release was sent on October 23, 2009 by fax, mail, and email.

EXECUTION

Event execution in external relations shares many principles that are presented throughout this chapter. A realistic and detailed schedule, division of duties by skill set, time, and place, and the limiting of duties for the supervisor in order to provide troubleshooting are all keys to success. Other challenges arise from the nature of the event being conducted. People like sporting events because of the element of the unknown; it is the source of the cliché "That is why they play the games."

Event Day Responsibilities

As discussed above, communications professionals have to manage both the internal collection of information and its immediate dissemination to the earned-media people who need it, all while making sure both operations can function without getting in the way of the core activity—the event itself.

Being prepared for and reacting to this uncertainty is also part of the allure of a career in sport communications. Every event has the potential for something memorable to occur; a fantastic single-game performance or some sort of disaster can strike without warning. Additionally, career milestones and team records should be carefully recorded and updated as part of the process. Having these records and contextualizing facts about the event and the participant is a part of the expectation of the media on event communication professionals.

While the broadcasts and media may be the primary responsibility for the communications professional during the event, several other reactive pieces to an event can add to—or often prevent detracting from—the experience of the attendees. Returning to the basketball metaphor, attendees are often pleasantly surprised by added touches such as free water bottles, gifts, promotional items, or product samples. These are examples of structured ways to enhance experience with information. Events provide ample opportunities to do this from the mass effort (i.e., a scoreboard and video screen) to the more personal (i.e., scorecard or mini-program giveaway). The participant-driven event provides chances as well, such as race timing systems in running races, tracking of runners via text messages, or presentation-sized pledge boards at fundraising events.

These information touches become more important as the event consumer experiences more personalized service in the digital information age. Personalized mailings, emails, and mobile device programming all raise the level of expectation for event attendees. Often the key to activating a sponsorship is found through tagging a brand to a piece of information and delivering it in a measurable and actionable way to the attendee. A more traditional take would be a coupon on the bottom of a free program sheet, while the tech-savvy may prefer to tag a mobile highlight package with a UPC code for a discount in-store. A communications professional has an opportunity to affect not only event experience, but also the financial bottom line through "outside the box" thinking in delivering messages to those in attendance.

Crisis Communications

The defensive contribution the communications professional can make is in coordinating efforts in an emergency situation. Often the external relations worker will be looked to as the spokesperson during or immediately after a crisis at an event—ranging from an injury to a player or an ejection of a spectator, to a building evacuation or an event cancellation. As mentioned above, planning for the contingencies is the key to their effective management.

Communications professionals must have access to several decision makers in case of less-likely occurrences. This includes communication contact and the ability to ask the questions that constituencies (like the media or others) will need to have answered. For example, a contact at the governing body's office is needed, as event cancellation is often not ultimately determined on-site. Good communications personnel will have contacts with the local police, fire, and EMT units, and will coordinate with event managers, facility supervisors, and local authorities to ensure an immediate and unified response to unanticipated negative situations. Certain scenarios, such as building evacuations, should be practiced for operations and communications staff to understand their role in the emergency. Relationship management that began in the event conceptualization phase can pay off during these crisis times. A professional keeps bridges strong before the storm.

Non-natural disasters—things brought on by human error or frailty—can have similar effects to weather or fire on an organization. Planning and management of those instances can therefore be handled in like manners: prepare, practice, and maintain relationships. In sport, there is nothing more heart-wrenching than a life-threatening injury occurring on a large stage. A detailed plan, including who will act as a spokesperson, where and how sensitive medical information will be released, and a chain of command to make decisions on the postponement or cancellation of the event, can increase efficiency and minimize the crisis environment surrounding a major injury.

After an event, a careful recap should be performed. One of the many parts in the recap will be the amount and type of the media coverage the event received. Internal relationships with front-line personnel are equal in importance to those with external constituencies for picking up on what is or is not working. Comments about auxiliary items like information-based giveaways (i.e., programs, roster sheets, or fan guides), public address and scoreboard satisfaction, and event-specific details can often be gleaned from front-line people who were with the consumer throughout the experience. Talking to people in the organization and in the building also saves time and expense compared to surveys.

The communications office should keep a scrapbook of media coverage: newspaper and Internet articles, electronic media Web site coverage, and so forth. The binder (or electronic file) can also contain video footage from the event itself, as well as copies of stories run about the event. Paid media schedules and fulfillment paperwork—the copies of the traffic logs that show when the commercials actually ran on air—are also useful to include. Some media professionals use the time of TV or radio earned media multiplied by the "rate card" cost for the time to determine a value of the coverage. The **rate card** is the publicly available or retail price that an outlet charges for its commercial time. The same technique can be used with "column inches" in the newspaper or magazine. Internet sources are more difficult to judge, but **page view counts**—the number of times the content is loaded into a browser—are often available from the page's publisher.

Media reports from events can be valuable to the sponsor organization, facility, and governing body. They should be kept and reviewed with strategic goals in mind, and should be a source of changes in tactics.

SUMMARY

This chapter used a basketball metaphor to explain the process of developing and implementing a communications strategy for a sports event. How details of an event will be communicated through media and on-site should be considered during the initial event conceptualization. The development stage in communications strategy involves a mix of paid and earned media and providing interesting and compelling background information of the event as thoroughly as possible. The execution phase is where actions associated with the event will test the results of the development stage, and will also include a wrap-up to justify future efforts.

NAME _____ DATE _____

STUDENT CHALLENGE #10

In Challenge #10, identify and research the media that should be contacted for the event. Then, develop the communications strategy to reach each outlet and their audiences with information about the event.

QUESTION 10-1

Conduct a media audit (using Web resources only) for the media market where the event is taking place. List five outlets including at least one TV, one radio, and one newspaper source. Indicate the contact most likely to handle the event's press release.

For "time of production/update" think about the following: When does information need to be provided to fit the outlet's regular schedule? What time are their newscasts? When do they publish? Is the schedule different for their studio news program and their Web site? Is there a difference between the newspaper's printed copy and their Web copy?

Outlet #1:

    Type of media:

    Time of production/update:

    Contact information:

Outlet #2:

    Type of media:

    Time of production/update:

    Contact information:

Outlet #3:

    Type of media:

    Time of production/update:

    Contact information:

Outlet #4:

    Type of media:

    Time of production/update:

    Contact information:

Outlet #5:

Type of media:

Time of production/update:

Contact information:

QUESTION 10-2

Write three press releases for the event. One should be aimed at TV, another radio, and the third newspaper or online newspaper. Consider the details most important for each type of media outlet and how to convey understanding and support of their needs in the release. Please refer to the **16-Step Guide to Writing a Press Release** contained in this chapter.

TV Press Release:

Radio Press Release:

Newspaper/Online Newspaper Press Release:

CHAPTER 11

EVENT SAFETY AND SECURITY

Jon Niemuth, Stephen J. Duethman, Doug Brown, Paul E. Griesemer, and William D. Crockett

Over the last several decades, there has been an increased emphasis on sport event safety and security design and operation. The events of September 11, 2001, along with previous World Trade Center bombings and the 1995 Alfred P. Murrah Federal Building bombing in Oklahoma are just a few high-profile incidents in recent years. Sport venues in the United States, so far, have not been the target of a successful terrorist attack. However, the plaza bomb at the 1996 Olympic Games in Atlanta illustrated to all that sports and entertainment events and venues are not exempt from domestic and/or international terrorism. Even with a high level of security, the possibility of the unthinkable happening must be addressed.

Terrorist attacks and bombings are on one extreme end of security incidents in sport venues. Less severe situations are those such as participant or spectator injuries, unruly fans, earthquake, fire, or power outage that force an evacuation. These are more likely than a terrorist attack to happen during an event, but terrorist activity must be considered. Venue architects, operators, and event managers must be proactive and vigilant in their efforts related to keeping events and venues safe and secure for spectators and participants alike. Everyone involved in events should always be looking for ways to prevent problems before they occur—this is true whether related to security, concessions, or any other operational function of the event. Through these efforts enhanced security is provided to spectators, participants, and employees alike.

Before getting into the specifics of event safety and security, a working definition is needed for what a secure event is. Ellerbe Becket, a world leader in sport venue design, engineering, and construction defines a **secure event** as an event in a venue (traditional or non-traditional) with an enhanced atmosphere for patrons and participants while providing a certain level of safety and an efficient, direct, and unobtrusive emergency response. For the patrons, the feeling is positive and they feel well attended-to, while the level of security intervention will be minimized. The measures required to sustain a safe venue will be focused from a patron service rather than a punitive environment.

There is a certain intangible "feel" to events that are secure and it is apparent to spectators and participants that if something bad does happen, the event staff are capable of launching the appropriate response.

Beyond the basic definition, there are some fundamental aspects and key ingredients for a venue to host a safe, secure, and enjoyable event. Building design, function, and equipment are the first defense against all types of safety threats, while a well-trained staff that reacts appropriately is also crucial. Controlling the venue with respect to spectator management and using technology to protect the building also play roles in how the building functions on event days and non-event days. Event managers must use risk assessment strategies leading up to the event. This process will guide the creation of an appropriate emergency plan that is understood and communicated to all of those involved in event management. Finally, event managers should have a system in place to react to medical emergencies that ensures the best possible outcome for those injured.

VENUE CONTROL

Thankfully, the days of treating public assembly venues as windowless boxes that open only for ticketed events are long gone. Today's best, most secure, and enjoyable venues are transparent and connected to the community and neighborhood. This facilitates clear observation of activity within and outside the venue, and allows for the facility to be part of its surroundings. However, the building also must employ proper infrastructure design, equipment, and technology to ensure control over the entire space.

Infrastructure

The best security infrastructure is that which is positive and effective while unobtrusive. **Infrastructure** refers to the aspects of the venue that are at the core of its operation such as the structure, roadways, access ways, lighting, and utilities associated with the venue. Well designed building security strategies include:

- Site bollards and other physical barriers that impede vehicular attack and direct and isolate safe pedestrian and vehicular flow

- Efficient, dramatic, and energy-efficient lighting makes spaces feel safe while enabling better-quality video surveillance

- Hardening of the building envelope (e.g., using materials that can withstand major structural forces), where required, will mitigate progressive structural collapse and injury to patrons from flying glass, etc., should such an event occur

- Building heating/ventilating/air conditioning (HVAC) systems must be configured with outside air intakes located safely and not accessible to criminal assault

Since control methods may be required in a variety of scenarios and locations, consideration should be given to their appearance and integration with the larger project design. One trend in access, primarily for premium seating customers, is to provide direct access from the individual levels of attached parking garages or adjacent structures (e.g., office building) to specific levels of a facility. While not widespread in its adoption for general entry and exiting of the building, this still is an area that must be considered in security measures.

By reducing accessibility to all utilities (mechanical, electrical, and plumbing), they are less likely to become a target area for chemical terrorism. The position of air intakes and exhaust louvers should be elevated from the ground to prohibit access. A venue could use sensors inside louvers to detect airborne chemicals, but such sensors have cost and reliability issues. All utility lines, including exterior vaults, should be locked and monitored as well. Finally, dual electrical service should be provided when feasible.

Spectator Movement

Access control does not end at the sidewalk or vehicle door. The circulation and approach of event traffic presents many different levels for evaluation and analysis of control strategies. Spectator management and entry has evolved significantly in recent years, with the resulting strategies challenging new and existing facilities alike. While the approach to search and control of spectators entering tends to vary both by event type and geographical location, some commonly accepted methodologies do exist.

Entry Areas

Interior and exterior entry spaces must be unobstructed and direct; clear and gracious; and provide a simple sequence. This will allow for multiple lines for patron screening and security checks. Typically these functions occur some distance back from the venue entry to allow for mitigation of potential concerns. To efficiently manage the associated costs of such measures, newer facilities have limited points of entry and access to single, large entry lobby-type spaces where large populations can gather and multiple functions can occur. Adjacent, secure rooms (holding cells) may be required at mega events to allow for transfer of detainees or to separate individuals requiring special security clearance from the main entry population.

Multiple locations or stations for bag and person/apparel checks should be sequenced and separate from the areas of ticket taking. While event staff typically handle these functions, additional screening via a pass-thru metal detector may be required. Because the cost of these devices and the inabilities of older facilities to handle the multiple power locations can be significant, many facilities have chosen to use hand-held wand devices for both economy and expediency.

Communication

One way to help fans understand how to enter the facility is to communicate it to them. Web sites, mailings, and marketing materials can be used to "tell" people where to go, how to get there, and what to expect. From simply providing information on parking to more detailed security information, good communication can alleviate many event day problems and frustrations. For example, an event that will be using metal detectors should explicitly state that in their materials. Event managers should also communicate that it might take some extra time to screen all fans, and that they should plan on arriving early. Fans can then adjust their schedule and plan on leaving some extra time to get through security.

Wayfinding

Multiple points of access for either entry or egress present a variety of operational and design related issues. Visibility in many forms is important to address. Clear line of sight can improve **wayfinding** within a facility, the ease with which visitors find their way throughout the venue. Well placed, visible entries help people to navigate into the building efficiently.

Sports facilities are typically large-scale structures that can be disorienting for their occupants. The inclusion of glass and views to the exterior, plus other major architectural features of "landmarks" in both concourses and in exit stairs help orient the occupants to the exterior and can assist in the efficient egress in evacuation. The connection to security and wayfinding is that at all times, defensible space must be provided. **Defensible space** refers to using architectural design to diminish or mitigate any tendency toward negative behaviors. No dark corners or places should exist where staff or patrons may feel trapped or lacking in clear visibility or access.

This is also true of non-traditional sport venues. In the creation of a facility for an event, wayfinding and defensible space should be kept in mind. Areas that are considered part of the venue for a road race should be away from heavily wooded areas and provide for ease of accessibility to and from key functional areas of the event.

A facility that is planned to ensure clear line of sight for security (either physical observation or with cameras) will aid in efficient control of a building and its perimeter. Visual obstructions must be minimized or eliminated with thoughtful placement of perimeter enclosure, strategic landscaping, and support structures.

How Building Planning and Design Impact Safety and Security

By The Ellerbe Becket Architect Team

The building design and function is the first defense in protecting against all types of security and safety issues. In most cases, the building is well into the design or already built when event managers get involved. However, decisions made in site selection, planning, and design will impact all events that occur in the venue after the building opens. Thus, event managers need to be familiar with how these factors impact event safety and security.

Urban redevelopment has increased in the last 10 years, with sports facilities being a major catalyst for downtown renewal. With growing concerns about potential security threats and new attitudes towards spectator safety and security, both venue planners and operators are challenged constantly. Among the benefits of developing sports facilities in dense urban settings is the close proximity to live-work-play amenities commonly associated with vibrant city centers. This presents challenges to maintaining realistic safety zones between sports facilities and unprotected public right of ways.

Sports facilities share many of the common operational issues of the surrounding businesses. However, their large scale of structure demands considerations in additional areas and careful management. In addition, venue design and operations must accommodate a variety of events and the collateral implications of the size and demographics of a given crowd. A venue should also be a "good neighbor" or good building 365 days a year, not just during events. To achieve these objectives, certain fundamentals in the building site selection and design must be considered carefully. With proper planning and creative design, potential security issues can be properly mitigated to ensure the continuous fabric of the city development.

Site Selection

When planning a new sport facility, site selection brings many challenges beyond the inevitably large physical size and scale of the building. Specific evaluation of surrounding transportation networks, utilities, and infrastructure is required as part of site evaluation. Transportation access and modes are always a concern, and become even more pivotal as the capacity of the venue increases. Vehicle management is key, not only as this relates to the experience of the fan, but also the collateral impacts event days can and will have on the larger urban context. Architects should evaluate and assign proper importance to the capacity of a road network to sufficiently handle event day traffic and not encumber regional movement. Emergency vehicle ingress, egress, and staging at the facility is an important layer to this evaluation. Event-specific personnel are part of standard event practices (ambulance with EMT, local police, and state patrols). In some cases, additional personnel and vehicles may be necessary in the event of fire, a bombing, structural collapse, or hazardous materials incidents. Venue planners must also consider the capacity of surrounding infrastructure to accommodate this additional loading, as well as potential expedited evacuation.

Site Setback

Facility best practices now include consideration of site safety zone setbacks and associated systems to restrict vehicular proximity to the building and site. **Site setback** refers to the distance between the spectator venue and other structures and/or public right of ways. In urban locations, evaluation of these items is needed. Specifically, designers will examine congruity of the venue with the adjacent development as well as the quality of the environment, while still providing the necessary separation.

Architects must strike a delicate balance between creating a facility design that is seamless with its surroundings versus the "Fort Knox" approach adopted by many early-generation facilities. Planners must identify site locations or building plan configurations that can create safe, operationally functional, and attractive site setback. Meeting these objectives is becoming increasingly challenging as developable sites become more scarce, and are often "four sided" versus "one to three sided" locations that back up against other buildings. Each side of the building that is prominently exposed presents a "public face." Thus, each side will require adequate measures for access control and security. The more exposure, the greater the complexity of the security challenges.

Site Context

Site context refers to whether or not the venue site and immediate areas convey a sense of welcoming, safety, and control. To create a welcoming feel, designers should conceive a site in the context of surrounding neighborhoods, whether they are urban, suburban, or a college/university campus.

Architects and building planners can take some specific steps in site context to enhance the feeling of security, and they include:

- Control and segregation of vehicular and pedestrian traffic
- Ample, inviting site and building lighting
- A sense of vitality and activity around the site and within the building
- Music, messaging, and video displays

- A carefully orchestrated arrival sequence, including ample accommodation to perform security screening in an efficient, customer-friendly manner.

These features create a sense of heightened pre-event anticipation, and encouragement of post-event lingering to savor the event. Simply, the goal is "smiles on the way in, smiles on the way out."

Designing an Invisible Perimeter

Efficient movement of game day spectator foot and vehicle traffic, both before and after an event, contributes significantly to the fan experience. This can also reduce operation costs related to security and traffic management. Grand boulevards, wide sidewalks, and active hardscape plazas are visually attractive means for providing sports facilities necessary setback without undermining the game day experience. Additional techniques involving site grade transitions with structured planter beds, landscape features, and decorative bollard-type elements can all work in concert to create a perimeter that is visually pleasing, harmonious with its surroundings, and, most importantly, an effective deterrent to direct facility vehicular approach.

In the years since the establishment of the Department of Homeland Security, many municipalities and institutions have begun a process of staging mock event scenarios centered on the stadium or arena to test and review preparedness plans. The integration of limited open plaza-type areas and broad perimeter circulation can double as effective staging areas for these activities as well. In areas of pedestrian circulation, there are many alternatives to unsightly yellow-painted steel and concrete cylinders. Careful attention to the design of unobtrusive architectural barriers, curb heights, or low height reinforced walls can all provide similar but more visually attractive methods of security. Where land or adjacent property is present, planning strategies that consider connecting walkways or enclosed bridges can provide the same level of service without introducing similar security concerns.

Parking

Especially in urban areas, existing parking garages in the proximity are commonly associated with sport facilities and deserve attention during planning. Parking garages present a series of challenges to venue security, but are also integral components of venue design. As discussed, efficiency of movement is a primary driver in all facets of sports facility planning and operations. Nowhere is this felt as acutely as parking. Delays in loading or unloading can impact customer event satisfaction.

In many cases, premium seating and hospitality clients are the only customers with parking access in close proximity to the venue. Delays in entry or exit from the parking area become a big concern for venue and event managers, since these individuals represent a significant revenue stream. Being as such, careful attention should be given to remove inefficiencies and unnecessary delays for this important client group that represents a significant revenue stream for the venue.

Architects should evaluate the proper balance in determining operational procedures related to parking. While convenience is important, especially for premium clientele, the proximity of a significant number of unattended vehicles to a sports venue is a security challenge. Most of the major professional sport leagues have implemented safety zones in which no public vehicle can park, regardless of existing garage or surface layouts. Security experts recognize unattended vehicles as a threat because terrorists around the world have put explosives in unattended cars and trucks close to high-profile target buildings.

Structural Elements

The integration of sports venues into urban developments also typically requires a higher level of physical articulation than their isolated counterparts to achieve the optimum level of "fit" and interaction within the urban context. The introduction of elements such as exterior ornament, lighting, large changeable signage, and significant expanse of glass creates an energetic exterior that will integrate and complement its surroundings.

Building planners should also integrate these elements into their overall security management plan. Consideration must be given for proximity of glass to both the ground and adjacent roadways, to acknowledge concerns related to both blast and vehicle intrusion. Design of exterior elements should incorporate reasonable redundancy in structure to minimize failure. Redundancy concepts relate to how safely people can evacuate a total, partial, and segmented collapse of a building, and help to isolate structural collapses to the impacted area. In general, modern building codes address this concern through a variety of categories including occupancy type and separation, fire-resistive construction assemblies, and seismic design considerations. However, the designers are responsible for the creating an overall safe solution.

These requirements create structures more responsive to the needs of maintaining building integrity, allowing for safe evacuation. Blast-resistive construction is very specialized in its application and tends to be more expensive than conventional design. There are many opportunities to incorporate similar or component-specific technology to typical commercial construction to gain the related benefits without paying an extraordinary premium.

Involving Experts

Best practices today bring police, fire safety professionals, and security consultants together into the planning and design process early. They help set expectations and specific technical program requirements that are integral to the building and design process. Security consultants, specializing in technology, should partner with the design team to help make buildings safer for the occupants. These professional experts, in collaboration with the architect, focus on detailed work sessions with owners, operators, and tenants throughout the project to ensure security measures are reviewed and developed fully. An example of the value of involving security experts early in the process relates to communication systems and protocols. Together, the local police and fire agencies can work with the architects and security consultants to integrate a direct communication link from the facility to the local public safety office via a secured communication system. To add this type of communication after the building was constructed would be extremely challenging, but in the planning and design process, it becomes part of the overall building design.

Event managers may never be involved in the planning and design of a new facility, but understanding the design features that help provide a secure event is important. From the strength of the building's structure to the placement of hardscape plazas, event managers need to know the entire building before a security or emergency plan can be effectively developed. The concepts that help to make a major venue secure can be transposed on a smaller scale to any sport event or facility.

Command Center

Command centers are essentially the building's "nerve center," and bring the use of security-related technologies to a central location. All sport facilities, traditional and non-traditional, should have a command center, or an identified area that functions as one, as in the case of smaller outdoor events. A properly designed and integrated command center is the hub of facility security, police, fire departments, and outside emergency responders. It will typically bring all the available technologies of facility monitoring, security video, and audio together into one central location. This enables authorities to give public address announcements, alter directional signage, and send out communications to all the various emergency teams.

The individuals staffing the command center will log and document anything related to safety and security, but they may also deal with other event functions. Deliveries that do not arrive on time, missing equipment, reports of lost items, and staff not at their correct location might all be reported to the command center. All incoming communications to the command center are then routed back out to the appropriate person or entity. To give a non-security example of how the command center might operate, imagine a non-functioning timing display at the finish line at a road race. The staff at the finish line can radio to the command center that the timing display is not working correctly, the command center can locate the on-call timing system contact, and they can be dispatched immediately to resolve the problem.

For large venues, there are commonly two additional areas where safety and security monitoring and logistical functions take place. Besides the main command center, there is generally a separate fire command center. This location is equipped with redundant security technology and life safety systems that can be controlled by fire and police officials. Because it must have direct access from the exterior, it is often located near the loading dock area. The second command center is generally located in the upper portions of the seating bowl to monitor and direct staff during a situation in the event seating areas or on the event floor. Both of these areas must have quick and direct access to the main command center.

For non-traditional venues, the command center may be located within an existing fire or police station. In other situations, a mobile command center will be used which is set up one of two ways. A portable building can be used like those on construction sites, or it can be set up similarly to a television production truck in that it has all of the functioning of a command center in a venue, but it is self-contained.

A full-service formal command center may be beyond the scope of some events, but for all events there should be a central location where all communications are directed. Many college sports events will use the area from which the game is being run (e.g., P.A., sound, stats) as the central point of contact for all communications. Often the event managers are in this area, and if they are not, the individuals in the area can find them quickly.

Technology

Players, performers, fans, and VIPs expect sport facilities to protect them from situations and persons who might cause them harm. Technology and involving the right people during planning increases event managers' ability to control and monitor the facility. Proper use of current technology can help monitor and screen spectators, help to separate the public and private spaces in the facility, and improve the efficiency of overall building operations.

CCTV / Camera Monitoring

Closed circuit television systems (CCTV) have become common elements that help monitor all public areas, especially the ticket-taking area and the seating bowl. Stationary cameras and those that pan, tilt, and zoom are used to monitor areas and alert building security officials of issues needing immediate attention. Cameras can also document and verify events and identify people for post-event investigations. Some facility managers have seen the benefit of having staff dedicated to documenting events with hand-held cameras in addition to CCTV. With this option, security handling of fans or others is documented if it is ever needed following the event, for clarification of situation or legal action. Other common areas that cameras are used to monitor are parking lots, pedestrian access ways, building perimeter, entrances, ticket windows, lobbies, concourses, specialty clubs, team corridors, entry points, and the truck dock area.

Patron Scanning and Ticketing

Frequently, patrons are now asked to go through metal detectors before their ticket is taken or scanned. This process is best implemented before spectators enter the main lobby of the building. Currently, many arenas are using the exterior entrance doors as the point of screening, and patron tickets are then scanned. If possible, event staff should scan tickets before spectators enter the venue. If security staff wand spectators, they should do it in an area that does not impede the flow of spectators into the venue. This must be integrated with a strategy and location for bag checks. The most effective operations for major events have incorporated a 100-foot safety zone for accomplishing these tasks.

In-Venue Texting

Event managers can use patrons' own cell phones, and PDAs can be used to help make the venue more secure. Some venues are providing a number to which fans can text problems in the venue directly to the command center. The service allows fans to help the team and venue in keeping everyone safe. For example, since facility staff cannot be everywhere at once, a fan may be sitting next to a drunken, rowdy fan that is disturbing all of those around her. Instead of having to leave her seat to find a member of security, the fan can quietly text the command center about the problem, and the text can be logged like any other security concern. In 2008, all but three NFL teams provided this service for their fans (McCarthy, 2008). The Miami Dolphins received over 100 texts per game (McCarthy, 2008). Allowing fan participation in keeping the venue safe is a new strategy, but one that does not cost much and puts some of the management in the fans' hands.

Emergency Phones

In and around venues, managers should install emergency phones (often topped with blue lights so they are visible at night) to provide emergency access to patrons without cell phones or in areas where cellular signals are weak. It is the event managers' and facility operators' duty to do everything in their power to ensure the safety of those attending the event. If parking structures are located far from the venue, and/or there are large parking lots, then emergency phones are a good option to enhance safety. These phones allow someone in distress to pick one up and be automatically connected to the local emergency response system. The operator will know immediately which phone was picked up and dispatch help very quickly. Event managers must not assume that all patrons will have working cell phones, and emergency phones are a good alternative to providing security staff in these outside areas of the venue.

Delivery Areas and Truck Docks

Some major venues are locating separate rooms outside the arena footprint to allow for equipment for screening mail, bulk packages, and other items needing to be evaluated before entering the facility. This is a big expense, and unless incorporated into the design at the earliest stages, can be cost prohibitive in all but the largest of venues. Even for those facilities that employ this security strategy, some vehicles need access directly to the venue.

All event production requires load in and load out of equipment and supplies. This creates some risk, as trucks often drive up to or into the building. For non-traditional venues, deliveries often occur on the event course, such as water delivery trucks on a marathon course. Technology continues to advance in the area of real-time vehicle scans for explosives and other dangerous substances. However, currently these applications are not typically considered an economically viable solution for sport venues and events.

Instead, a combination of well-placed security stations and related video surveillance and access controls create an effective deterrent. Special care needs to be given to vehicle control, restraint, and inspection in areas where vehicles are engaging with the event levels, or will come in close proximity to back of house operations (e.g., player parking, service vehicles, and event-related support).

During planning, screening and securing entry points into the truck dock area of the arena is a challenge that needs to be addressed, especially in urban settings. One option is to restrict truck access with movable bollards or electronic overhead doors to validate the delivery before the truck drives close to the building. Retractable bollards and restraint systems both go beyond the typical operable gate. The benefits of these flexible systems are that they retract when not needed. A typical day often requires less stringent security than an event day, and flexible devices allow for a variety of different levels of security. In some cases, screening of all packages arriving at the facility occurs. If this is part of the security protocol, tagging of items should also occur to clearly distinguish screened parcels from non-screened parcels.

Even for events without intricate security systems for deliveries, the areas where delivery trucks will enter or be close to the venue need monitoring. Creating one entry point that is easily staffed by security using removable barricades is sufficient for most events. Separating delivery traffic from spectator and/or participant arrival traffic also helps to keep traffic moving and people safe.

Communication between the event managers and those individuals responsible for monitoring traffic into the delivery area is critical. Event managers will likely have to submit a delivery schedule well in advance of an event. The **delivery schedule** will include the date, time, company, the driver's name, contact phone numbers, vehicle description, and the license plate number of each expected delivery. Additionally, for event days, event managers may issue a required vehicle permit that the driver must have (in addition to all other information) to enter the event site. This puts a lot of responsibility on event managers to be aware of every anticipated delivery prior to the event. For good reason, any deviations from the expected list are likely to incur a delay while event managers work with the security at the truck dock to verify delivery, or security might turn them away and refuse access.

Electronic Access Door Systems

Beyond the standard keyed hardware, a number of devices are used to monitor door access. Venue operators are adding card access readers, door monitors (sensing when a door has been opened or left ajar), key pads, electronically controlled locks, and motion detectors to help secure entries. Beyond entry doors to the facility, monitoring is often necessary for interior doors that separate public and private access (entries to event level, locker rooms, ticketing areas, offices, athletic training areas, etc.). **Biometric scanning** uses individual physiological characteristics such as fingerprints, face recognition, and iris recognition to allow or deny access to doors. Venue managers are discussing the possibility of biometric scanning for sport facilities, but cost and complexity of programming has kept this technology from wide adoption.

As science and technology continues to advance, new systems will become available. Buildings need to be adaptable and flexible in order to embrace future options to secure buildings. Event managers may rely on building operators to implement the preceding security strategies, but they also need to have an understanding of the facility in which the event is being held, and how it operates in relation to building control. Beyond the design of the building and equipment used, there should be crowd management policies in place to create a fun and safe environment for all.

GAME DAY MANAGEMENT

Managing the event, while keeping safety and security in mind at all times, can be challenging. Being prepared for circumstances that may arise will help to set the stage for a safe and secure event. The "What If" game is commonly used to help all those involved in the event think through and share possible responses to a variety of scenarios. For instance, before a skateboarding event at a local skate park, the facility and event staff can challenge each other to brainstorm as many situations as possible that might happen. It might look like this:

- What if it rains?
- What if nobody signs up to compete?
- What if a crack in the skate park concrete is found that day?
- What if a participant is severely injured?
- What if we expect 300 people and 2,000 attend?
- What if a child falls into the competition area?
- What if the parking lot fills up?
- What if there is a fight between spectators?

These are just a few of the many types of situations that might emerge through playing the "What If" game. The game allows event managers to be proactive in addressing each scenario and communicating to staff the appropriate reaction to the situation. Ideas that surface might also remind event staff of things that could have been forgotten during planning. In the skateboarding competition, thinking through what would be done if the parking lot fills up might remind event managers to secure a secondary parking lot at a neighboring business for the day. No situation is too crazy to consider when playing the game. Crowd scenarios will often come up in this game, and managing a crowd is one of the most difficult parts of any spectator event.

An Interview with Christine (Cusick) Moore

Director, Torch Relays Promotions for the Vancouver
2010 Olympic and Paralympic Games
Organizing Committee (VANOC)

The following interview was conducted with Christine (Cusick) Moore, Director, Torch Relays Promotions for the Vancouver 2010 Olympic and Paralympic Games Organizing Committee (VANOC) about her preparations for the 2010 Olympic Torch Relay. It was conducted one year prior to the opening of the 2010 Winter Olympic Games in Vancouver, British Columbia, Canada.

Given the protests that occurred during the Beijing Olympics Torch Relay, what, if anything, has that done to change your plans for the 2010 Olympic Torch Relay?

We recognize that some individuals and organizations may use the 2010 Olympic Torch Relay to draw attention to specific issues they would like to highlight, and we hope that they would do so in a safe way that respects Canadians' desire to participate in and celebrate the 2010 Olympic Torch Relay.

While we respect the right to freedom of expression, we remain committed to finding opportunities to build equity, trust, and respect with the public so that we can create a uniquely Canadian scenario where the 2010 Torch Relay is seen and accepted for what it is: an unprecedented opportunity to connect and inspire Canadians and people around the world through the power of sport, peace, and the Olympic ideals.

Our team continues to work with many partners to ensure the safety and security of those involved in the Olympic Torch Relay. We continue to monitor the situation with organizations and individuals who wish to use the Olympic Torch Relay to draw attention to other matters. As long as these individuals and organizations draw attention to their issues in a peaceful and safe manner, we do not have concerns with their activities. If, at any time, public safety is at risk, we will work with the RCMP (Royal Canadian Mounted Police), local law enforcement, and the Vancouver Integrated Security Unit to ensure that Canadians can participate in their Olympic Torch Relay in a safe and peaceful atmosphere.

As with any event, we always do contingency planning, and this includes contingency due to protest or barriers we may encounter on the relay. We are also going out there and looking at risk mitigation by doing public outreach. We also learn at each event we do. We anticipate that there will be occasions when protests will happen, but we are trying to have more outreach in advance in order to mitigate any issues that may occur while we are on the Relay. Certainly contingency planning and risk identification are something we talk about regularly.

Managing the Crowd

Understanding the projected crowd is the first step to managing it effectively. Certainly, a NASCAR event and a cheerleading national championship will have very different types of fans attending. Experienced event managers realize how different types of crowds tend to behave, and will adjust their strategies to the anticipated crowd. Beyond the type of event, the significance of the event is important to grasp. What might normally be a regular NCAA Division I basketball game can become a heated battle where emotions run high when a conference championship or NCAA tournament berth is on the line.

Using existing relationships with other event and facility managers is a good strategy to help understand the type of crowd that will attend the event. Most event managers are happy to share information with others when asked. A telephone call to the previous host of the event can garner important information related to attendees.

Other policies can help in the management of the crowd throughout the event. Some of the security strategies highlighted throughout this chapter also relate directly to crowd management (e.g., improved wayfinding, in-venue texting, communications, etc.). Examples of other, more direct strategies include:

- Creating a Fan Code of Conduct. It sets behavioral expectations for everyone and is communicated in a way that encourages good behavior and sportsmanship.

- Prohibiting fans from leaving the venue and returning, often known as pass-outs. For events that do not sell alcohol, this keeps spectators from drinking outside the venue and then returning to possibly cause trouble.

- Setting aside pre-game time for the head coach to speak about sportsmanship and behavior. This can be especially impactful at college athletic events, where the head coach is often held in high esteem.

- Using existing in-event communication channels such as P.A. reads, video board productions, and signage can also set the tone for behavior.

- Establishing family-friendly areas that allow those attending the event with children to be able to separate themselves from other fans who might be a little rowdier.

- Ensuring that the presence of television cameras does not draw the crowd down the seating area, creating the possibility of a crush. Cameras should stay well back from crowds and use strong lenses to capture close-up footage.

Policies such as these help to promote a culture of personal responsibility that is important to overall crowd management. By emphasizing good sportsmanship, supporting the team, and respecting the wishes of the head coach, the message is clearly positive. This strategy is more effective than telling people they cannot do something.

Sample Guest Code of Conduct

Team *Successful Sport Management* is committed to sportsmanship among its coaches, athletes, staff, and fans. Sportsmanship has been defined as the conduct becoming to one participating in sport. Team *Successful Sport Management's* coaches, athletes, staff, and fans believe sportsmanship is playing fairly, acting respectfully toward others, and promoting the interests and good name of Team *Successful Sport Management* on and off the field of play.

It is expected that all persons show respect to opposing teams, game officials, and each other while at Team *Successful Sport Management* events.

The following rules apply to Facility Go Big or Go Home:

- Fans are expected to sit in their ticketed seat and be able to show their game ticket if requested.

- No outside food, drink, or glass containers of any kind.

- No bags or backpacks allowed. Purses are subject to search and could delay entry.

- No umbrellas.

- No video cameras.

- No artificial noise makers.

- Smoking is permitted in designated areas only.

- Foul or abusive language will not be tolerated.

- All signs and banners must be in good taste.

- No oversized stadium seats.

- No throwing of objects from the stands.

Guests that become aware of any safety issues or encounter difficulties with other fans are urged to contact a member of the event management staff. Fans violating any of the above rules or displaying poor sportsmanship are subject to ejection from the stadium, revocation of season tickets, and in some cases, criminal prosecution.

Thank you, and GO TEAM SUCCESSFUL SPORT MANAGEMENT!

Staff

The architects and event managers are responsible for setting the stage for events, and the attitude, appearance, presence, and training of event staff is all part of that. Event staff have an enormous impact on security and the behavior of the crowd. First and foremost, background checks of all staff are important to protect the safety of all patrons. The type of event will dictate what type of background (i.e. misdemeanor vs. felony charges) might disqualify someone from working. These decisions should be made on an individual basis with all of the available facts.

Having the correct number of staff is critical to ensuring safety for all. Industry standards call for one trained crowd manager for every 250 patrons. This number should be adjusted based on the results of research conducted about the anticipated crowd. For example, for an important college football game, extra crowd managers are needed in the student section. The number might go to one trained crowd manager for every 150 spectators in this scenario. If alcohol is sold, the number of crowd managers might also be higher. Another commonly used ratio is for staffing the ticket-taking areas. In general, one ticket taker for every 1,000 to 1,200 spectators should be sufficient. By having the entries identified on tickets, event managers can staff each entrance appropriately, because they know the volume to expect at each entrance.

All front of house staff should embrace the point of view that patrons are treasured guests, whose every need must be catered to—and these staff must be sufficient in number to maintain an obvious presence. Workers need to also be continually trained to be on the lookout for activity that might threaten safety or security. Procedures must be established—and continually, rigorously updated via continuing education—so that reactions are quick and effective in any situation that may compromise safety and security.

Event mangers should empower staff to speak up about safety and security issues. Event day staff work throughout the venue, and are likely to become aware of safety issues before upper-level event managers. The same is true of spectators; they are likely to become aware of safety issues before event staff, but they need to know whom to tell. Messages to spectators should include phone numbers and texting numbers which they can use to report safety and/or security concerns. Using all staff (and event spectators) as part of the security team expands the reach of event managers exponentially.

Internal Communication

Internal communication is often overlooked prior to the event. Event manager should regularly communicate with marketing, tickets, concessions, and facility managers to make sure that all the pieces of the event are coming together. This is critical to safety, because if event managers or facility managers are staffing the game, they need to know how many tickets have been sold and in what areas. If the marketing department decided to have a costume contest for a game close to Halloween, it might be a major problem for security, as masks and costumes conceal the identity of people and are not advised from a safety and security perspective. If the facility and security staff were not aware of this promotion and did not let spectators in masks into the event, the possibility of major delays at screening resulting in upset fans is likely. Event managers are the ones that close these communication gaps and prevent promotions such as this from moving forward if they pose a risk. Even if it does not seem directly related to safety and security, often small decisions in individual departments will impact overall safety and security.

Communications Equipment

Having adequate communications equipment on the event day is critical to keeping the event safe and secure from start to finish. Cell phones and two-way radios are commonly used by event staff, but using them effectively with a large group of workers can be difficult. Although it can be costly, communications can mean the difference between life and death in an emergency. There is no excuse for not having appropriate communications equipment.

First, event managers must assess their communications needs before exploring the best type of equipment. How many radios are needed? How many different channels on the radios are needed? How far away from each other could event staff be when needing radio communications? Are there any other local agencies that also need to be on the same frequency for security? For single events, often two-way radios can be rented for the event, and sometimes facilities offer event managers the use of their radios as part of the rental agreement. Answering these questions will help event managers decide on what is needed for the event.

In general, two-way radios communicate directly to one another and can cover a fairly large area. So, an event that is small in nature and only needs coverage at one venue can probably use a few two-way radios with one channel and have adequate communications. The more people using the radios and the larger the geographical area that needs to be covered, the more complex radio operations become. Radio frequencies can be programmed by a communications company in a variety of configurations. The event can have everyone on one channel so that everything said is heard by all, or channels can be assigned by group (e.g., marketing channel 1, medical channel 2, event ops channel 3, etc.). The structure of the channels is driven by the number of people and diversity of their work involved in the event. If the event is loud, then event managers must provide headsets to ensure communications can be heard. Lapel clip microphones allow for communication without removing the radio from the holster, and extra batteries are a must.

The size of the area that the radios need to cover will dictate whether a repeater is needed for communications, or whether exchanges can be radio to radio only. A **radio repeater** receives a low-level signal and retransmits it at a higher power, increasing the distance the signal can effectively cover. A repeater will most likely be needed for golf events, road races, or just to maintain communication within the locale if staff are driving to do errands. The radio repeater is placed in a central elevated location of the event, and increases the range tremendously. One note of caution is that the repeater is generally AC power operated and not on batteries. The radios still need to be configured to communicate without the repeater in the event of a power outage. Radios are most critical in the event of an emergency such as a power outage, and losing communication at that time can be catastrophic.

Often, the local police or fire agency will provide one of their radios for key personnel to communicate directly with them. This means that event managers will be carrying an event radio as well as the emergency radio for police and fire. Codes should also be established for emergency situations so that the specific emergency is not broadcast to everyone on the radio. For example, if there is a kitchen fire that can be easily contained, it would not make sense to announce there was a fire. Merely the word "fire" can create a panic. Using a code, such as "code red—contained to kitchen" will alert emergency responders listening in and the command center of the exact nature of the incident. Concurrently, others will go about their business.

Alcohol Sales

For some sports events, alcohol goes hand in hand with the event. Unfortunately, alcohol also can cause problems related to crowd behavior. The combination of exciting sports, large groups of people in a confined area, often hot or cold weather, and alcohol is a recipe for disturbances. Event managers may not be directly responsible for alcohol sales, but they should be aware of policies that can be implemented to minimize alcohol-related disturbances and problems.

The Techniques for Effective Alcohol Management (TEAM) Coalition is a group of "professional and collegiate sports, entertainment facilities, concessionaires, stadium service providers, the beer industry, broadcasters, governmental traffic safety experts, and others working together to promote responsible drinking and positive fan behavior at sports and entertainment facilities" (n.d., ¶ 1). The TEAM Coalition trains facility and event employees in sport and entertainment (and provides certification) on how to educate their alcohol sales and services staff. It is a great, cost-effective way to help reduce liability associated with alcohol sales, as well as help to reduce alcohol-related incidents at events.

Ensuring that only those of legal age are able to purchase and/or consume alcohol is difficult. A wristband or hand stamp might be provided to those over 21, but as many people know, wristbands and stamps can be transferred to someone else. Often, venues and events outsource alcohol sales to a third party to transfer a lot of legal liability associated with alcohol sales. Regardless of which entity sells the alcohol, event managers should ensure that vendors have adequate training and good policies.

Most sport venues stop selling alcohol at a certain point during the game, often two-thirds of the way through the game. This slows down consumption by fans toward the end of the game, and gives them time to process the alcohol they have consumed before they drive home. Designated driver programs are becoming increasingly popular at sports events. To encourage people to use a designated driver, that person is given a wristband and often some other benefit, such as a free meal, as a "thank you" for staying sober to drive others home safely.

The exact behavior of crowds cannot be predicted, but the general nature of a group of sports fans can be anticipated based on past experiences of others, research, and the specifics of the event. Event mangers can also use specific strategies to encourage good behavior by fans and create a positive atmosphere. However, even with the best strategies implemented, there is always risk associated with a sports event.

RISK MANAGEMENT

Risk can be defined as "a hazard or the possibility of danger or harm" (Mulrooney & Farmer, 2005, p. 309). Risk associated with sports events cannot be avoided entirely, but it can be managed through the risk management process. The entire process of evaluating risk and using cost-effective strategies to reduce and treat risk is known as **risk management**. The overarching goal of event managers with respect to risk management is to protect life, the building, and the finances of the organization. Since events can vary greatly in their characteristics, risk management needs to be considered separately for each event. The uniqueness of each event will result in different risks that are identified and thus, different treatments of those risks.

There are a variety of frameworks available in which risk can be assessed for a facility and/or event in sport. Mulrooney and Farmer (2005) provide a model that is broad in scope and easily applicable to a wide spectrum of events. They explain the risk management process by breaking it into three stages: recognition, evaluation, and treatment (Mulrooney & Farmer, 2005). There are entire textbooks written on the subject of risk management in sport, so the following is designed to provide an overview of risk management for events and is not intended to be all encompassing.

Recognition

The first step in risk management is to identify all possible risks. Recognition of many risks comes with experience, so new event managers should seek out those with experience when beginning this process. For purposes of description, an example of a simple local summer fun run will be used to illustrate the risk management process. For a fun run, some of the risks might include:

- Severe weather (e.g., significant rain, thunderstorms)
- Minor injuries to athletes
- Major life-threatening injuries to athletes
- Vehicle traffic entering the race route
- Lack of event staff to manage the event
- Not enough concessions prepared
- Terrorist attack

Evaluation

The severity of the loss (financial and otherwise), along with the anticipated frequency of occurrences, can be used to evaluate the risk (Mulrooney & Farmer, 2005). A risk matrix (see Figure 11-1.) is often used to evaluate risks by noting the frequency across the top row of the chart and the significance of the loss in a vertical column down the side. The risks identified in the recognition phase of this process are then included in the matrix to allow for overall evaluation of each risk. In the case of the local fun run, the identified risks have been inserted in Figure 11-1. where appropriate.

Figure 11-1. Risk Matrix With Identified Risks

	Very Frequent	Frequent	Moderate	Infrequent	Very Infrequent
Very High Loss					Terrorist attack
High Loss				Major life threatening injuries to athletes	Vehicle traffic entering the race route
Moderate Loss				Severe weather	
Low Loss	Minor injuries to participants		Lack of event staff		
Very Low Loss			Not enough concessions prepared		

Treatment

Once the risks have been categorized appropriately (which will differ by event), event managers can begin to assess how to treat each risk. Commonly used categories in sport to treat risk include avoidance, transfer, and keep and decrease (Mulrooney & Farmer, 2005). A treatment matrix (Mulrooney & Farmer, 2005) (see Figure 11-2.) provides guidance as to how to treat each risk.

Figure 11-2. Risk Matrix—Treatment of Risks

	Very Frequent	Frequent	Moderate	Infrequent	Very Infrequent
Very High Loss	Avoid	Avoid	Shift	Shift	Shift
High Loss	Avoid	Avoid	Shift	Shift	Shift
Moderate Loss	Shift	Shift	Shift	Shift	Keep and decrease
Low Loss	Keep and decrease	Keep and decrease	Keep and decrease	Keep and decrease	Keep and decrease
Very Low Loss	Keep and decrease	Keep and decrease	Keep and decrease	Keep and decrease	Keep and decrease

(Mulrooney & Farmer, 2005)

Avoid

If a risk falls into a matrix cell that is labeled "avoid," event managers should not hold the event and avoid the risk completely. In these cases, the risk is too great to those involved to have the event. For the fun run, no identified risks fall into this category. However, for any event that had a credible terrorist threat, the best option might be to cancel the event to avoid the terror risk completely.

Shift

Event managers can "shift" the identified risk by transferring the risk to a third party. Often this is accomplished through insurance. For many risks, event managers can purchase insurance, which will protect the event organization financially if the risk is realized. There may be cases in which shifting the risk is not an option because the insurance is cost prohibitive. In those situations, the risk should then be avoided and the event should not occur.

For the fun run, a terrorist attack is very unlikely, as is vehicle traffic entering the race route. A successful terrorist attack would result in very high loss, while vehicles entering the race route have a possibility of high loss since they could injure one or more spectators or participants. Major life-threatening injuries to athletes are infrequent occurrences that result in high loss, since a person's life would be in danger with these types of injuries. All of these risks can be insured against for the fun run, and then the event can occur with event managers knowing they are protected from these occurrences. Severe weather will result in losses through decreased participation and decreased spectators, which will in turn decrease registration, concession, and merchandise revenue. Weather insurance is available for events, but event managers should conduct their own research on past weather on the event date, as well as anticipated losses, prior to purchasing the insurance. If an outdoor event that does not offer concessions or merchandise is sold out (with no ticket refunds available), then severe weather may have little to no impact on revenue, and weather would be categorized as low loss which would not result in recommended insurance.

Keep and Decrease

The final category of treatment is those cells in which identified risks fall that are labeled "keep and decrease." These risks are minimal enough that it is more cost effective to accept the risk and take steps to decrease the likelihood of it happening than to employ any of the other treatment strategies. In the case of the fun run, minor injuries to participants can be expected since physical activity is involved. The risk to the event can be decreased by using participant waivers (Chapter 8, Participant Registration for Events) or informed consent documents that inform participants of the possibility of injury. A lack of event staff may make the day tougher on those involved, but the resulting loss is low and thus can be decreased through proper planning and communication with those that do sign up to work the event. Not having enough concessions prepared might impact the event a bit financially, but through estimating attendance and participation, as well as keeping an eye on weather, event managers can provide some estimates of concessions needs to the vendor.

Follow Up

As with any management process, risk management needs follow up and continual updating to be effective. The risk management process should be conducted for each event, with the individual characteristics taken into account each time. For one event, bad weather may have little impact, while for another it will cancel the event (e.g., thunderstorm at an open-water swimming event). There is not one risk management matrix that fits all events. It is a process that is tedious, yet imperative to comprehensive safety and security operations. Risk management and emergency planning go hand in hand, as the emergency preparedness plan is the result of identifying possible emergency situations based on identified risks and developing detailed plans of actions. Even with the best risk management, emergencies will happen and emergency planning is necessary.

EMERGENCY PLANNING

The primary responsibility of any venue management team is to provide an environment where fans can safely enjoy the event. While safety is at the forefront at all times, emergency situations heighten the stakes for event managers and facility operators. Planning and preparation are critical to making the right choices at the right time.

Emergency planning is usually done by the facility, but event managers should be aware of the emergency preparedness plan. The difference between emergency planning and risk management is that emergency planning is related to the reaction of all those involved in the event and facility when an emergency occurs. As discussed, risk management deals with identifying and treating risks, and does not address reaction to them if they are actualized.

All venues, whether traditional or non-traditional, must have an **emergency preparedness plan (EPP)**, which is a document that articulates the policies guiding emergency management and how the organization functions given a specific emergency. The development of a good EPP involves a variety of constituents and will match the level of emergency with the appropriate level of response. Whether the emergency is large or small does not change the planning steps that take place to ensure all involved are ready to handle the situation. Proper emergency planning will also increase the management team's ability to make decisions in a calm and instinctual manner, subverting the potential for confusion and/or accidents.

Emergency Preparedness Plan (EPP)

Event managers should follow certain steps when developing the emergency preparedness plan (EPP). The following guidelines are set up for large traditional sport venues, and can be altered for smaller events. There will be variations depending on the size of the event, size of the venue, location of the venue, and anticipated risks, but three steps provide a general guideline to developing the EPP.

EPP Step One: Assess Risk

The first step in formulating a plan for emergency incidents is developing an understanding of the scale of emergency vulnerability. For large venues and events, this will mean going above and beyond the risk management procedures identified previously and involve sophisticated software analysis. The Department of Homeland Security (DHS) Office of Infrastructure Protection is working to prevent catastrophic events. Owners and operators of sport venues are in the best position to determine the risks to their facilities and how to protect their facilities from such risks. The Risk Self Assessment Tool (RSAT) is available through the Commercial Facilities Sector of the Department of Homeland Security, and was launched in 2009. RSAT is designed to develop risk information by breaking the data collection and analysis into three distinct areas:

- Venue Characterization: Information about the facility, including its major uses, size, and capacity.

- Threat Rating: The DHS has divided threats into two categories, man-made and natural. For example, a vehicular bomb is a man-made threat, while a hurricane is a natural threat.

- Vulnerability Assessment: This is comprised of input from the user about the facility's security preparedness.

Completing this risk assessment provides the venue operator a clear picture of areas in which the facility is vulnerable. Additionally, the program will highlight the facility's strengths and areas for enhancement. Benchmarking is also done through the software, that compares the facility to others that are similar.

Step Two: Plan Preparation

It may seem obvious, but emergency planning occurs best at times of non-emergency. A well-crafted EPP is a result of joining the skills and thinking of every contributor to the emergency situation. Individuals involved in the process may include:

- The facility management team

- Facility ownership (if separate)

- Event managers (if applicable)

- Building security team

- Local law enforcement

- Emergency medical teams (city or private)

- Local hospital

- Local National Guard command

- City Manager's office

- Facility designer or construction expert

The EPP utilizes all these resources to respond to emergency threats internal to an event (via spectators or fire) and external threats (such as terrorist threats or natural disasters). In an emergency, each support team must have their own coordinated activity and have already coordinated those roles with the facility manager and the incident commander for incorporation into the overall facility plan.

Modern building codes have progressed toward addressing the realities of moving large volumes of people in mass, and at times, partially blinded conditions. People will become largely reactionary and follow the crowd when confused by an emergency. A facility EPP must anticipate this and work with the inherent building design to match the crowd's mentality with equal amounts of flexibility and rigidity. Additionally, those with special needs must be taken into consideration with respect to their movement. If elevators are generally used by those in wheelchairs to reach their seats, a plan to ensure they are able to evacuate the building in the event the elevators are not working is needed.

The EPP also outlines the close working relationship between those in charge who are able to make determinations with respect to response, including the senior fire official, the senior police official, the facility manager, and the event managers. The plan must outline a clear delineation of responsibilities, authority, and the chain of command so action can be taken quickly in an emergency. Roles to be delineated would include:

- Incident commander: Generally the highest-ranking fire and safety official on-site will assume the role of incident commander. In cases where this individual is not present, this is often designated to the highest-ranking police official. This person is typically responsible for overall coordination of operations on-scene of the emergency or disaster. This includes coordination of all forces at the scene such as city and outside agencies.

- Agency representatives: Each responding agency and/or military unit must be coordinated by an agency representative. These persons respond to and coordinate resources through the incident commander.

The EPP will identify contact information for each potential agency including:

a. Stadium management
b. Event manager
c. Establishing the unified command center
d. Media operations/public information center
e. Medical operations
f. Ambulance staging
g. Special needs rescues
h. Helicopter landing operations
i. Fire unit staging
j. Police unit staging
k. Prisoner detention area
l. Victims inquiry center
m. Traffic control and monitoring
n. Volunteer coordination
o. Morgue

The above is for major facilities and large events. However, other event managers can take these principles and apply them to their own situations. It is always better to be over-prepared than underprepared.

Step Three: Training/Rehearsals

Every facility where large groups of people gather should have in place an EPP and rehearse it on a regular basis. The best planning in the world is useless unless it is communicated, rehearsed, and understood by those needed to execute the plan. The industry standard is to perform major emergency event rehearsals at least once a year. Through incident simulation with all participating agencies, validating communication and chain of authority can occur. This will ensure that the plan will be an appropriate response during an emergency event.

Small Events

In general, small events (especially those in non-traditional venues) will rely heavily on local agencies in their emergency planning. Much of the response will come directly from police, fire, and EMTs, with event managers making the contact with them. Imperative to this type of plan is up-front and early communication with these agencies. Months or weeks before the event, event managers should communicate all the event specifics (e.g., location of event, age of participants, number of participants, time of warm-up and competition, on-site medical response such as athletic trainers, etc.). Then, event managers should call the week of the event as a follow-up to ensure the local agencies are aware of the event. Providing this information to agencies will allow the local responders to be aware of the event and be ready to respond to the location if needed. It is common that police and EMTs, if not busy elsewhere, will come to the event if they are aware of it as an act of goodwill.

Command Center Function in Emergency Response

The command center is at the core of good emergency response. Operators must first assess if the emergency can be localized. Monitoring a facility properly and responding to situations is centered in the command center. In an emergency, it also functions as a location for briefings, strategy meetings, and training. Because of its critical nature in the event of an emergency, the command center's location in a facility is crucial. Its location should be close to where local police and fire responders will arrive in an emergency, and at the same time have access to the building's main vertical and horizontal circulation (e.g., stairs, escalators, concourses, and elevators).

As discussed earlier, smaller events may not have a command center, but the concepts are the same. Event managers will still establish a specific location where the control of the event occurs. In an emergency situation, event managers will be the point people for the on-site response, but the situation will quickly be turned over to local emergency response through calling 911 or radio communication with emergency response units.

Whether the event is large or small, documentation is critical when any incident occurs. One of the command center functions is to document, organize, and house information related to incidents that do occur. This documentation is important in the event someone is seriously hurt or the launch of an emergency response occurs. The documentation clearly indicates the details of the situation and whether or not established protocols are followed.

Evacuations

Evacuations, on the surface, seem simple: get everyone out of the building. There are a lot of variables that can impact an evacuation procedure, and a full evacuation is not always a necessary response in an emergency. Plus, evacuations are inherently risky because they can cause panic among the crowd that can result in injuries. Event managers have to figure out how to effectively move people out of the building, where people go once they have been evacuated, how people with special needs are identified and assisted, and if there are any issues with getting all the vehicles evacuated in an orderly fashion.

Evacuations are not as simple as they seem. Even a small outdoor event may pose a challenge if people need to be moved quickly away from an area. Event managers commonly use barricades and/or fencing to establish the venue and take tickets at outdoor events. In an emergency evacuation, people need to be able to exit the area quickly, and barricades and fencing can impede their egress. Additionally, people will generally not be as familiar with the entrances/exits, since they might have been created just for that event. Conversely, in a traditional sports venue, the flow is usually logical. For instance, people are in elevated seats in most arenas and stadiums, and they can see the entire venue. Plus, the stairs generally lead to a vomitory, which leads to a concourse, and then to exit doors. Outdoors, people may be in a flat area and unable to see where appropriate exits are, which can cause confusion. In all emergencies, but especially in evacuations with limited sight lines, communication with the crowd is critical.

The P.A. should be used to direct people, and bull horns should be available as back-up in case the P.A. is not working. All communications need to be loud, clear, and calming if there is to be any chance of people following the instructions.

When to Evacuate

There is no single answer to the question of when to evacuate. It depends on the risk to those in the building. Fire, bomb threats, hazardous materials, power outages, tornadoes and hurricanes, and lightning are all common emergencies that may warrant evacuation. In certain situations it will be more dangerous to evacuate people than to have them stay in the building. For example, at an indoor venue, in the event of severe weather such as a tornado, it is likely power will be lost. Evacuations due to power outages are common. However, if there is the possibility of a tornado, all spectators are safer in a dark solid building than outside in the path of a tornado. Common sense and prior planning must prevail in these situations.

In some circumstances, partial evacuations are the appropriate response. In the case of a partial structural collapse of one section of bleachers, those people need to evacuate immediately, while others should stay in their seats so as to not cause more confusion. Once those that are in immediate danger are secure, others can be evacuated.

For outdoor events, severe weather —especially lightning—is a common reason for evacuations. Many outdoor stadiums and bleachers are metal, which are prone to lightening strikes. Amazingly, some spectators will refuse to leave their metal bleacher seats 80 rows up in a stadium, even when they can see lightning approaching. Clear announcements asking people to evacuate and to seek shelter are a necessity. Event managers are responsible for deciding on an emergency response in these situations, prior to the emergency occurring.

Golf tournaments are also prone to lightning and are challenging to evacuate since the course is often spread over a large area. It is the responsibility of the event to address severe weather in both of these situations in the EPP, and to have shelter available. For those in the stadium, it might mean a neighboring building is used as shelter, while the golf course might send people to their cars until the weather passes.

How to Evacuate

With proper planning and the establishment of an EPP, all those working the event will be prepared to assist in the event of an evacuation. The command center will issue the evacuation order following pre-established protocols, and then staff should know what to do from there based on training and drills. It is essential that all event and security staff know where to go and what to do during an evacuation. For example, consider an evacuation due to lightning at a college football game that has a very limited covered concourse area. People will generally make their way to the covered area, but will be reluctant to move out into the rain to the staging areas or to their cars. This can cause significant crowding in exit areas. Since 20,000–30,000 cannot fit in one small concourse, security must move people along to ensure they exit the stadium. A crowd crush can happen quickly if the front of a moving group stops and the back does not.

Just as in risk management, every facility and event is different, but some general guidelines are provided here for evacuations.

- Only evacuate those sections of the facility that must be evacuated.
- Make sure exit doors are unlocked and any gates/fences are quickly taken down.
- Have multiple pre-established staging areas away from the building where people can seek shelter.
- Announcements related to emergency procedures should be written in advance and posted in the P.A. booth or provided as part of every game script.
- Ensure there is clear communication available (that is battery powered or hooked up to an emergency generator).
- Provide information on re-scheduling, refunds, and so forth as quickly as possible via bullhorns or the P.A. system.
- Provide ushers with flashlights for all indoor and/or night events to use to show people how to exit if needed.
- Ensure that a specified number of staff are available to help those with special needs.
- Secure all cash, merchandise, and concessions prior to staff evacuating.
- Media should be provided information as quickly as possible for distribution.
- Identify police that will assist with moving vehicle traffic away from the building.

No event mangers ever want to have to evacuate their venues, but the odds are it will happen—especially with outdoor events. The key is to be prepared so that any evacuation is conducted in a calm and controlled manner by those involved. The EPP will help event managers choose appropriate strategies given specific emergency situations.

MEDICAL

The timeless Boy Scout motto of "Be Prepared" is relevant to the task at hand for a facility operator that hosts hundreds of events each year and attracts a wide variety of patrons from all demographics. It is likely some patrons will face physical challenges on a daily basis, and they must be accounted for in the dynamics of each event that occurs. Event managers will face medical emergencies of some sort on a regular basis, and the way they are handled can be the difference between life and death for someone. All fans want to enjoy an entertainment event and feel secure in the knowledge that the facility that is hosting the event will respond in an expedient and professional manner in the event of a medical incident.

Just as athletes have a game plan, so too should event managers whose goal it is to access the site where a medical incident occurs, make the proper assessment as to degree of emergency, provide the proper care, and minimize risk to the victim and to the facility. Management of information, state-of-the-art life safety features, and proper procedures are the three most important elements in dealing with a medical situation.

Managing the Process

In a facility with tens of thousands of patrons and requisite staff, it is essential to effectively manage the communication and subsequent information that is forthcoming when the call comes in about a medical incident. As discussed, an event should have a command center where communications of all incidents are recorded and handled. As part of any **standard operating procedure (SOP)**, or routine process, "**Base**" is referenced as a person or small group of personnel who field all medical calls and disseminate information during an event at the command center. Event and facility staff should know to call "Base" via radio or landline for any crisis, medical or otherwise. The "Base" representative initially logs the time when the call comes in (actual time and time on game clock, if applicable), the individual who made the call, and the nature of the call. This person then advises the necessary medical personnel, again logging in need, who was assigned, and time services were requested. Upon resolution of the medical incident, the individual performing the service is supposed to call "Base" back and advise them of the status/resolution of the situation along with any additional information that might be needed for the event files. This ensures prompt communication to the first aid provider, as well as documentation of the timeline of events.

These logs are relied upon to determine what the initial call was, who made it, and approximate response times. Most importantly, they provide a timeline of each occurrence that may play a prominent role in any subsequent investigation or legal process. As such, all medical incidents should be reported to the facility's risk manager. A listing of risk managers and their contact information should be provided as part of the EPP and command center materials.

Medical Response Equipment

The ability to mitigate any medical emergency rests in large part with the availability of medical and operational resources, equipment, and forms that are provided on-site. A concerted effort on the part of the facility operator(s) and state, county, and/or local jurisdictions to coordinate efforts related to emergency equipment is vital to the ability to respond to all types of emergencies that may occur at any given event. Also, training responders in the proper use of AED units, radio communication equipment, and other associated equipment will increase the odds of a successful resolution of a medical incident and mitigate any possible legal repercussions. The following is a sample list of equipment and forms that are needed for effective medical emergency response.

- Fire rescue or first aid/ambulance services
- AED (heart defibrillator) units
- 2-way radio communication equipment
- Communications log
- SOP first aid form

- SOP command base form

- Accident report document

Rendering Assistance

Optimally, first responders will be the first on the scene of a medical emergency, but often the staff member who first arrives on the scene must quickly assess the situation and take steps that do not add further peril for the victim. All staff should be CPR/AED certified at a minimum. First responders should be available quickly, and ambulances should be on-site for most events. Only those events with very minimal risk and that are in close proximity to a hospital may not have ambulances on-site. Additionally, it is common to have multiple ambulances on-site. In some cases, one set of responders will be focused on participants while another is responsible for spectators, and for large events multiple ambulances are needed for spectators. If someone is being transported when another medial emergency occurs, a second ambulance is needed, and often the time needed to call an additional ambulance could put the person at risk.

When rendering medical assistance, the following procedures (American Airlines Center, n.d.) are recommended to be followed by all event staff to reduce response time and to provide the victim with the best opportunity for further medical assistance:

1) On-scene personnel are to radio Base on command center channel.

2) On-scene personnel advise the location and nature of the incident, and request for first aid response.

   NOTE: If the incident is life threatening, say so! Radio codes may be used to convey the seriousness of the situation.

   NOTE: Arena personnel and on-site Fire Rescue must respond to all first aid-type incidents involving guests.

3) Base will repeat the information to ensure that it is correct.

4) Confirm that the information is correct.

5) Render first aid until Fire Rescue and/or Risk Management Arrives.

6) Base will contact First Responders and Risk Management and relay the information.

7) Do not leave the incident scene until First Responders and Risk Management arrive on the scene.

8) Provide any pertinent information to arriving Fire Rescue and Risk Management personnel.

9) Make sure that Risk Management and/or event personnel are completing a written incident report detailing the events and conditions that contributed to the incident. This will include the pre-event condition of the injured person.

10) Once the incident scene is under control by Fire Rescue and Risk Management, leave the area unless requested to stay by Risk Manager or other management.

SUMMARY

Whether the event is big or small, the safety and security of all involved is at the forefront of all decisions related to the event. For major sport venues and mega events, many complex security features are now commonplace. Event managers should be current on how the infrastructure and equipment help to keep the venue and event safe. Smaller venues or non-traditional venues face different challenges in providing a safe and secure event. Often, local emergency response systems are adequate for smaller events instead of creating their own in-house response.

Student Challenge

STUDENT CHALLENGE #11

In Challenge #11, evaluate the facility and event for security issues, explore possible situations that could occur during the event, and create a risk matrix for the event.

QUESTION 11-1

Identify five security challenges that event managers will face at the event given the venue characteristics. Describe how the challenges can be overcome.

Security Challenge #1:

Strategy to Overcome:

Security Challenge #2:

Strategy to Overcome:

Security Challenge #3:

Strategy to Overcome:

Security Challenge #4:

Strategy to Overcome:

Security Challenge #5:

Strategy to Overcome:

QUESTION 11-2

Suggest five "What If" scenarios for the event that would impact the safety and/or security of participants and/or spectators. Also, provide information on how each scenario should be addressed if it were to occur.

What If #1:

Strategy to Address Situation:

What If #2:

Strategy to Address Situation:

Student Challenge

What If #3:

Strategy to Address Situation:

What If #4:

Strategy to Address Situation:

What If #5:

Strategy to Address Situation:

Student Challenge

QUESTION 11-3

Fill in the provided risk matrix for the event and identify how each identified risk will be treated. Be specific!

	Very Frequent	Frequent	Moderate	Infrequent	Very Infrequent
Very High Loss					
High Loss					
Moderate Loss					
Low Loss					
Very Low Loss					

Discuss Risk Treatment:

SECTION

EVENT EXECUTION

Heather Lawrence

Event execution is addressed in the third and final section of the book (Chapters 12–16) and encompasses the management of the core event functions. Operations are a key aspect of the management process, and this section includes detailed information on necessary documents, how to staff the event, the specifics of operations, and event settlement and follow up. In execution, event managers get to see all of their hard work pay off as the event comes to life and occurs.

As with most aspects of the event management process, execution will overlap with many of the other functions leading up to the event. The chapters in this section provide event managers structure as to how they might want to approach specific tasks leading up to the big day (or days). Information such as formats for creating a planning timeline, setting up sample boards, finding and training event day workers, equipment purchasing, diagramming event flow, and post-event settlement are all discussed in this section. Supplemental information is also provided by industry experts that describe how to create an environmentally friendly event, what to do if the event outgrows the available space, and some of the challenges associated with event settlement.

The final chapter of the book serves to inform readers of special considerations for events with international competitors, with an international media presence, or that are looking to expand to other countries. With the globalization of sports and the shrinking of the world due to advances in technology and the ever-expanding media coverage of sports, it is realistic to expect more and more traditionally domestic events will become international in nature.

CHAPTER **12**

EVENT DOCUMENTS

Michelle Wells

Information is key to the success of any project. The documents used to communicate information will be a foundation in the planning process. It is assumed that readers have a working knowledge of Excel; being able to use Excel for the organization (and budgeting) of an event is important. There are many types and varieties of event management software that can help in creating all types of planning documents, but for the vast majority of events, Excel is sufficient and helps to control costs.

For all events, planning documents are vital, but they are especially so if an event does not have a permanent venue. Items can sometimes slip through the cracks. During an event held in a permanent venue, small items can often be easily fixed. For example, if a table is forgotten, the venue likely owns more and can provide them. In a venue on city streets or a local park, getting additional equipment can be more difficult. The planning documents covered in this chapter include:

- Planning Timelines
- Day of Timelines
- Checklists
- Contact Sheets
- Fast Facts
- Staffing Positions/Call times
- Diagrams/Maps/CADs/Google Earth
- PA Scripts
- Parking Passes
- Credential Boards/Ticket Boards
- Production Binders
- Emergency Plans

PLANNING TIMELINE

Planning timelines are used to set up and track detailed tasks by functional area. They ensure that event managers can account for each detailed item, who is responsible for specific items, and whether the event is on schedule. By filling in a completion date as well as a due date, event managers can use this information the following year (or for the following event) to evaluate if the planning timeline dates were realistic or if there were trouble areas. A common format for a planning timeline is shown in Figure 12-1. and is easy to create in a spreadsheet program such as Microsoft Excel.

Figure 12-1. Sample Planning Timeline
Event Date November 15, 2008

Days Out	Date Due	Task	Functional Area	Task Owner	Date Completed
-240	20-Mar-08	Initial course drive-thru	Events	Smith	
-1	14-Nov-08	Final pre-event course drive-thru	Events	Smith	
-150	18-Jun-08	Signage creative design first draft	Creative	Davis	
-75	1-Sep-08	Signage creative design final selection	Creative	Davis	
-45	1-Oct-08	Course split timing mat locations tested for interference	Timing	Ross	
-45	1-Oct-08	Exact course split timing mat locations noted on drive-thru	Timing	Ross	
-8	7-Nov-08	Course split timing mat locations marked with spray paint	Events	Thompson	
5	20-Nov-08	Recap report format sent out	All	Thompson	
10	25-Nov-08	Recap reports due back	All	Thompson	

At the top of the planning timeline is the EVENT DATE. If the event is over multiple days, this date will be the first day of the event. The DAYS OUT column lists the standard number of days before the event that the task is due to be completed, and is determined before the timeline is created. In the DATE DUE column, a simple formula will calculate the date based on the number listed in the days out column and the date in the event date cell. TASK is the actual work that needs to be performed. The FUNCTIONAL AREA lets everyone involved know which department is responsible for that task, and the TASK OWNER is the person within that department who is accountable to complete the task. DATE COMPLETED is filled in by the person responsible for completing that task. Some event managers will also add a COMMENTS or NOTES column to account for any details about that task that may be important to record during planning.

At the top of the spreadsheet, event managers can fill in the EVENT DATE with the day that the event will begin. The DATE DUE will automatically fill in activity due dates, which will be calculated based on the date in this cell of the spreadsheet and the number of days out listed for the activity. For those not familiar with Excel, it may be helpful to open Excel and go through this process while reading this section. The formula for this task will start in cell B4, the cell location of the first DUE DATE, and assuming that the EVENT DATE is in cell B1 and that the DAYS OUT start in cell A4, the formula would be: =B1+A4. Then, copy the dates exactly like copying any formula in Excel. In the formula, it is important to make sure to put the dollar sign ($) before the letter and also before the number of the cell that houses the EVENT DATE. This ensures that the DATE DUE is being calculated from the same cell each time (EVENT DATE). It "locks" the formula to that one cell (EVENT DATE) as the reference point.

If multiple people are working on this document, it is a good idea to have an AS OF date in the header or footer. The AS OF date denotes the last date on which the document was changed to ensure all those with access to it are working off the most recent version. If the date feature on Excel's header/footer is used, that date changes each time the document is opened, whether changes have been made to the timeline or not. Thus, the best option for this is to enter it manually. As the event gets closer (or even just the deadline for completing the timeline) and multiple changes are being made, it may even be necessary to include a time stamp. It will dramatically help the team's productivity if it can be quickly and easily determined what the most recent version of the timeline is.

With seemingly constant changes in technology, it is easy to share these documents, even for teams working in different geographic locations. Google Documents is one of the easiest ways for an entire team to be able to edit and view the same document if the team is not on the same mapped drive (commonly also called a shared drive) for saving documents (see Chapter 4, Technology and Event Planning, for more information).

DAY OF EVENT TIMELINE

The day of an event involves a flurry of activities. Staff and volunteers report, deliveries are made, signage is set up, and everything that was done has to be undone. A countless number of things happen, and all of them need to be accounted for in one place so that the team managing the event knows what is happening throughout the day. This is where the **day of event timeline** comes into play. Each activity for the day should be noted on this timeline. Event managers may choose to customize the categories, but a basic setup for a day of event timeline will include most of the same categories as the event planning timeline: TIME, TASK, FUNCTIONAL AREA, TASK OWNER, and NOTES/COMMENTS. Putting each activity as an individual item helps event managers see each activity as it will occur chronologically. Some event managers will create two columns for time: START TIME and END TIME. As an example, let's use some activities related to a band playing on the main entertainment stage, looking only at the TIME and TASK columns.

In the two-column format for time, it would look like this:

START TIME	END TIME	TASK
6:00 am	4:00 pm	generators on site for band on main stage
7:00 am	8:00 am	sound check for band on main stage
9:00 am	3:00 pm	band plays at main stage

The challenge with this format is that people have to search through the timeline for an activity to determine its end time. They may also have to make some assumptions. If the generators are on site until 4:00 pm, does that mean that they will be gone at 4:00 pm, or is 4:00 pm when the generator company will start loading out? If they are in at 6:00 am, is that when the company arrives, or when the generators are functional?

The one-column format for time requires more initial entry of information, and sometimes more information in general, but it allows the staff to simply flip through the pages on the event day timeline and check off tasks as they occur. Let's take the same example and put it in a one-column format, which is the format recommended by the author.

START TIME	TASK
6:00 am	generators arrive on site for band at main stage
7:00 am	generators set up and functional
7:00 am	start of sound check for band on main stage
8:00 am	end of sound check for band on main stage
9:00 am	band begins play at main stage
3:00 pm	band set ends on main stage
3:00 pm	rental company arrives for load out of main stage generators
4:00 pm	rental company finished loading out main stage generators

The load-in time, start time, run time, end time, and load-out time are all separate items in this format. With Excel, information can be entered in any order and then sorted very easily. Each functional area can enter its own information in the master document, and the lead event manager can sort the information by time. The information can also be sorted by functional area and printed for staff in each respective functional area. Timeline information should be distributed on a "need to know" basis. For example, certain staff need all of the information from the timeline, but student interns helping at the finish line of a race only need a copy of the timeline related to their position. These position-specific timelines can be set up so they are small enough to fit in a pocket for reference.

If detailed activities, such as load in, are starting a couple of days before the actual event, the day of event timeline may need to be expanded. If that were the case, a field for DATE would need to be added. It may also be best to use a 24-hour clock (see Figure 12-2) to avoid any confusion or typos with "am" and "pm" as staff enter their timeline items.

Figure 12-2. Sample Day of Event Timeline

Time (24-hour clock)	Task	Functional Area	Task Owner	Notes/Comments
6:00	Generators arrive on site for band at main stage	LOGS	Harris	
7:00	Generators set up and functional	LOGS	Harris	
7:00	Start of sound check for band on main stage	ENT	Black	
8:00	End of sound check for band on main stage	ENT	Black	
9:00	Band begins play at main stage	ENT	Black	
15:00	Band set ends on main stage	ENT	Black	
15:00	Rental company arrives for load out of main stage generators	LOGS	Harris	
16:00	Rental company finished loading out main stage generators	LOGS	Harris	

Checklists

Often, event managers are responsible for managing various areas within an event. Checklists are an easy way to keep track of "to do's" for an event. For a large event, the day of event timeline will often suffice as a checklist, although event managers may still want to have a separate checklist for themselves. Some of the things included on a checklist may be for the event managers to specifically check in with an area supervisor or to meet a person at a location. These are not items that all event day workers need to see or that should go on an overall event timeline. They are tasks, however, that should be tracked and documented: (1) in case someone needs to step in and work the area for that person, and (2) for future event planning purposes.

The format of the checklist may vary depending on the preference of the event managers. Some may list the items by time, some by task sequence, others may break down the items on the list by functional area, and still others will utilize a combination format (see Figure 12-3). Functional areas for a marathon could be: Entertainment—Main Stage, Finish Line, Awards, and so on. For a college football or basketball game, the functional areas could be: Field of Play (Court), Equipment, Concessions, Custodial, Ushers, Tickets, and so forth.

For recurring events and events in a fixed venue, checklists are essential. It is too easy for event managers to become so familiar with the steps and nuances of their events and/or venue that they check off the tasks in their heads. Even if they do not formally use a checklist and check off the items, they should create and regularly update checklists for the event and/or event type. Checklists preserve the procedures for the organization in case the event managers leave, they help to train new staff and interns that are hired, and can be vital if ever requested for legal action or other reasons to demonstrate procedures and actions.

CONTACT SHEETS

The footprint of many events will be so large that event managers are going to need to use communications equipment to speak with one another. There are also people that event managers might need to reach who will not be on site at the event, especially if an emergency situation occurs. Having documents on hand with the phone numbers or radio channels where people can be reached allows event managers to contact them more quickly.

Internal

It is hard to think of any organization that does not have its internal contact information available via its email system, internal Web site, or even its external Web site. Even with this information readily available and the common use of cell phones that can access the information, it is still a good idea for event managers to have a printed **call sign list** that they keep with them during their event. This is also sometimes called a **contact list** or **call sign sheet**. If nothing else, it serves as a backup in case they cannot access those other pieces

Figure 12-3. Sample Event Checklists

Checklist by Time or Order of Operation

_____	test communications equipment (radios, Nextels) with finish line crew
_____	ensure timing mats are set up at finish
_____	confirm arrival of main stage entertainment
_____	deliver 3 event jackets to main stage for entertainers to wear
_____	verify with timing crew that timing mats are functioning
_____	meet and greet the person who will deliver official results to awards stage
_____	confirm location of over-sized check for awards ceremony
_____	ensure two Sharpie markers are with the over-sized check and that both markers work
_____	verify that awards for top 3 men, women, wheelchair-men, wheelchair-women are at the finish line
_____	check awards stand area to make sure it is clear of leaves, debris, etc.

Checklist by Functional Area

Finish Line

_____	walk-thru area and greet staff and volunteers
_____	ensure timing mats are set up at finish
_____	verify with timing crew that timing mats are functioning
_____	test communications equipment (radios, Nextels) with finish line crew
_____	meet and greet the person who will deliver official results to awards stage

Entertainment

_____	walk-thru area and greet staff and volunteers
_____	confirm arrival of main stage entertainment
_____	deliver 3 event jackets to main stage for entertainers to wear

Awards

_____	walk-thru area and greet staff and volunteers
_____	confirm location of over-sized check for awards ceremony
_____	ensure two Sharpie markers are with the over-sized check and that both markers work
_____	verify that awards for top 3 men, women, wheelchair-men, wheelchair-women are at the finish line
_____	check awards stand area to make sure it is clear of leaves, debris, etc.

of information for any reason. A call sign list keeps all of the information in one place where it is easy to find and access.

The call sign list should include anyone who may need to be contacted for any reason. Different levels of the event staff may have different numbers on their call sign list. For example, event managers at a venue at a Division I NCAA school may have their direct supervisor's cell phone and home numbers on their list (and the common list that everyone has), while their boss will probably have the numbers of athletic department staff who are much higher in the organizational chart. Some events will rent communications equipment (e.g., two-way radios and/or cell phones) rather than requiring staff to use their own. In this case, the call sign list should have both the permanent and rented cell phone numbers listed, along with specific radio channels used for different operational areas.

Call Sign List

For large events, event managers often need to create a call sign list or event call sign list that is reduced to the size of a credential, is laminated for weatherproofing, and then worn on a lanyard. The font is usually small,

Figure 12-4. Sample Call Sign List

Name	Functional Area	Event Cell	Personal Cell
Ben Harris	Logistics	(555) 555-9999	(123) 555-0000
Erin Davis	Aid Stations	(555) 555-7766	(123) 555-3344
Heather Lawrence	Start Line	(555) 555-3333	(123) 555-4444
Jane Smith	Awards	(555) 555-1111	(123) 555-2222
Joe Black	Entertainment	(555) 555-7777	(123) 555-8888
Michelle Wells	Finish Line	(555) 555-5555	(123) 555-6666
Mike Ross	Course	(555) 555-1212	(123) 555-7788
Peter Thompson	Timing & Scoring	(555) 555-4433	(123) 555-1122
Regan Adams	Timing & Scoring	(555) 555-9988	(123) 555-5566

and only essential information can fit. The least amount of information a call sign list should include is: name, area(s) each person is supervising, event cell phone number and/or personal cell phone number (see Figure 12-4). If the event team is using two-way radios, the radio channel each person will be operating on will also need to be included. The reason to include the area the person is working is that events often have people working—both volunteers and paid staff—who were not involved in the conceptualization or development of the event. They likely will not know the event staff or which event managers are leading which areas. With the call sign list, if they have an issue related to a specific area and cannot reach their immediate supervisor, they can call the person on the call sign list who can help them. Excel is often the best software to create the call sign list if event managers are creating it themselves.

Whether the call sign list is on a lanyard or will be in a production binder, it is advisable to list the names alphabetically by first name rather than last name. Especially when volunteers and event day staff are brought in, people often remember other workers' first names, but not necessarily their last. In fact, they may not even know last names. Let's say a volunteer is told, "Call Ted at the finish line and ask if everything is all set up." If a volunteer does not know Ted's last name and the call sign list is alphabetical by last name, it will be cumbersome to search through dozens of names to find his contact information on the list.

External

In the sports world, many events occur on weekends or after normal business operating hours, and delivery/setup of equipment may occur at a time before normal operating hours. If vendors are on the contact list for the event, such as tent companies or ice delivery companies, event managers should make sure that the company provides the name and cell phone number of the driver making the delivery. If it is 6:00 am and a vendor was scheduled to make a delivery at 5:30 am, a call to the office is likely only going to lead to the manager's voicemail, and waiting until 9:00 am when the company opens—three-and-a-half hours after the delivery was due—is likely to severely hamper the event. Frequently, this is not only an organizational issue, but is also important if there are security check-points for deliveries. Even if the delivery is for setup of equipment the day before the event, it will impact the setup schedule and could have a domino effect on the setup of other items. For example, assume the tent and flooring rental company is late. The tents and flooring have to be put up before the tables, chairs, and linens can be placed. The audio-visual company will also have to wait to set up any speakers, rigging, video screens, lighting, and soundboards. The company providing the themeing and decor cannot decorate a tent that is not set up. The more complicated the event, the more dominoes that could fall because one vendor is late. Whereas if the event managers have the driver's cell phone number and the vendor manager's cell phone number, they can contact the driver directly to see what the problem is, contact the vendor manager to work out a solution (if they cannot work it out directly with the driver), or start adjusting the day's schedule. At a minimum, the event managers can start notifying other vendors of the situation so they can schedule around the delay, a delay that has hopefully been shortened by being able to contact the driver.

Trick of the Trade

There is a very small, but helpful, thing that event managers can do when creating a call sign list that will make the call sign list easier to read when on a lanyard. When laminating a two-sided call sign list, format the two sides in opposite directions, meaning the top of the front side of the list will be lined up with the bottom of the back side. When the hole is punched in the list to hook the laminated list to the lanyard, punch it at the bottom of the front side of the list. This way, when a person is looking down at the lanyard, the text will be readable without having to twist the call sign list around, and to see the other side, the person only has to flip the card over vertically rather than twist it around on the lanyard.

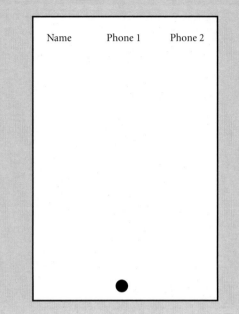

FAST FACTS

Fast facts documents are just what the name implies—a fast way for staff and volunteers to find pertinent facts about an event. The information listed will be common questions that participants and spectators are going to ask about an event, and not everyone working the event will know the answers (see Figure 12-5). Fast facts are useful prior to the event for "front of house staff," which is anyone in direct contact with patrons and that routinely speaks to the public. Instead of front of house staff having to say, "I don't know," they should be able to find the answers to the most common questions in the fast facts. The information that is on this document should be information that anyone in the public can see. This is not the place to put sensitive or confidential information such as personal contact numbers or emergency protocol. Assume one of these will be left lying around and will be picked up by a member of the general public.

For printing, if the fast facts can be folded so that staff can carry the document in their pockets, they will be more likely to hold on to it and utilize it. If an event has the budget for fast facts to be professionally produced and printed, this document can be created to look more like a marketing piece, but it is not necessary just to create a functional document. It can simply be produced in Excel and printed on 8.5"×11" standard size paper or on 8.5"×14" legal size paper. If event managers produce and print the document themselves and it is a multiple-day event, they can re-work the document and print new ones each day. This will allow event managers to add any new items that staff members were asked on the first day of the event. Each day's fast facts could be printed on a different color paper to help avoid confusion as to which version is the most up to date. After printing the fast facts, it is easy to then copy any maps/diagrams onto the second side of the sheet.

Figure 12-5. Sample Fast Facts*

Fast Facts	Race Schedule for Sunday	First Aid	Lost and Found
2009 BLUEPRINT MARATHON **September 20, 2009** **Event Managers:** **Heather Lawrence** **and** **Michelle Wells**	6:00 am - buses begin departing 6:30 am - first runners arrive at start 8:00 am - runners move to start line 8:40 am - wheelchair athletes start 9:00 am - race starts 9:20 am - last runner crosses the start line 10:00 am - male wheelchair winner est. to cross finish 10:10 am - female wheelchair winner est. to cross finish line 11:15 am - male winner estimated to cross finish line 11:30 am - female winner estimated to cross finish line	Spectators needing first aid can go to any of the tents with a red top for assistance. Tents are located on both the north and south sides of the race finish line. For athletes needing assistance, medical staff will be throughout the finish and post-finish area and will be wearing red shirts and red hats.	Found items can be turned in to any staff or volunteer member in a blue shirt or jacket or taken to the **Information Tent** next to the ticket kiosk on the corner of L Street and W Street. Lost items can be picked up at the **Information Tent** next to the ticket kiosk on the corner of L Street and W Street. **Results** All results will be posted on the event Web site by 10:00 pm Eastern time the day of the race.

Tickets	Awards	Statistics	Volunteers
Tickets for the 2 seating sections closest to the finish line (both north and south sides) are sold out. Spectators wanting to purchase tickets for other seating areas can purchase them at the kiosk on the corner of L Street and W Street beginning at **6:00 am on race day.** The kiosk will be open until 12:00 pm. After 12:00 pm, seating is first-come, first-served.	The awards ceremonies will begin at 12:00 pm. Male and Female top 3 places will be presented first (12:00–12:15) Male and Female wheelchair first place winners only will be presented next (12:15–12:25) After awards are presented, athletes will pose for photos in the awards area and then be escorted to the media room for media interviews.	There are over 20,000 runners participating in the 2009 Blueprint Marathon. The event has runners from all 50 states and 17 countries. The race sold out 2 days after registration opened. 8,500+ volunteer shifts are needed throughout the week to produce the Blueprint Marathon. This is the 14th year for the Blueprint Marathon.	Volunteer sign-in and sign-out is located at the Volunteer tent on the corner of L Street and Bank Street. Unfortunately, all of our volunteer positions are full and we cannot take day-of sign-ups for volunteers. Only those already registered and confirmed can volunteer. To sign up to volunteer for next year's race, go to www.blueprintmarathon .com/volunteers.

*By using the layout shown in Figure 12-5, the Fast Facts can be folded once horizontally and then three times vertically to create a pocket-sized information sheet.

If event managers are not sure where to start with information that should go on the fast facts, some of the most common items include:

- Schedule: opening and closing times; competition start times

- Tickets: prices; where they can be purchased; whether they are required or not for all areas

- Parking Information: parking lot locations; drop off locations; disabled parking areas

- Media Information: If the event is on the radio or television, list which station and if it is live or delayed; location of media entrances and work areas

- Lost and Found: where to turn in lost items; where to collect lost items; the hours of operation

- First Aid: location(s) of first aid personnel; times first aid will be open

- Results: where they can be viewed; how soon after an event that they will be posted on site; the Web site address for results

- Statistics: how many people or teams are entered; how many states and/or countries are represented; what is the capacity of the venue, etc.

- Maps/Diagrams: inside the foldout is a great place to put a diagram(s) of the event layout

STAFFING POSITIONS/CALL TIMES

No matter how much planning is put into an event, plans cannot be properly executed without people. People are the backbone of an event and what allow the carefully thought-out plans to be fully executed (staffing is discussed in Chapter 13). Sometimes, inexperienced event managers can overlook this fact. Again, many of the people working an event will not be involved in the detailed planning. What is second nature to the event managers may be brand new information to the staff. This is why it is important to provide this information to them.

The staffing schedule and call times should ideally be completed two weeks in advance, sooner if possible. If the event is being held in a union venue, staffing needs may need to be submitted even earlier, depending on

Figure 12-6. Sample Staffing Positions

2009 Blueprint Marathon Staffing and Volunteer Positions		
Position	**Contact**	**Description**
Ushers	Elliott Stevens	- check tickets and credentials at bleacher access points
		- direct spectators to their bleacher section
		- serve as crowd control at the finish area
		- answer general questions from guests
Medal Distribution	Jane Smith	- unpack and unwrap medals and hang on medal racks
		- clean up area of all trash and breakdown boxes before finishers arrive
		- distribute one medal to each finisher by placing the medal around the runner's neck (not handing it to them)
		- pack up remaining medals at the end of the event and stack boxes
Post-Finish Water Station	David Keter	- set up tables for water distribution
		- unpack bottled water and place on tables
		- clean up area of all trash and breakdown boxes before finishers arrive
		- distribute one bottle of water to each finisher
		- clean up area of discarded bottle caps and bottles
		- place bagged garbage in dumpster in the post-finish area

the requirements of the union's collective bargaining agreement with the venue. Producing documents detailing the schedule of the staff and volunteers enables event managers and the managers of other functional areas to make sure there are not any gaps in coverage. They can see what areas are covered, at what specific times, and how many people are scheduled to work each area. If there are any gaps in coverage, they can be caught early and corrected. An example of a staffing position document is shown in Figure 12-6.

DIAGRAMS/MAPS/CADS

Diagrams are useful in many different areas. They can be employed to show equipment for logistics, staffing/volunteer placement, signage placement, participant flow, and more. When it comes to diagramming event details, **CADs (computer-aided design/drawing)** provide the ultimate detail for events and are great because the information is to scale. The downside is that they usually require an expert to create them. If the foundational information does not already exist, such as the layout of the state park the event may be using, the foundational CAD will have to be created. CADs are intricate and complex. Learning to use the software to create them is often time consuming and expensive. It is not a skill that can be picked up in a short time period. Hiring someone to create CADs can also be expensive.

There are other options event managers can utilize for creating diagrams. Visio is a Microsoft program that allows users to create diagrams for many different purposes. Diagrams created from scratch can be drawn to scale relatively easily. In the ideal scenario, event managers want diagrams that are to scale, but it is not a requirement. For smaller events it is not always possible or economical. For those situations where general layout is the biggest need, easier options are PowerPoint and Google Earth. With PowerPoint, event managers can use the drawing tool to create diagrams of event areas (see Figure 12-7). These can be very detailed, but event managers need to note that the diagram is not to scale. With the option of saving the diagrams as PDF files, the documents are easy to share without worrying about someone making unauthorized changes to them. Google Earth is one of the newest tools that can be added to event managers' toolboxes. Google Earth can help show exactly where equipment, for example, needs to be placed, where a start and finish line will be set up, and any number of other things by using drawing tools on satellite photos. Rural areas may not be as easy to map. Often, the satellite pictures for rural areas are not available or are not clear at the level of zoom that is available for metropolitan areas. A word of caution on Google Earth is that some of the satellite images can be dated (up to a few years old) and thus not be as accurate as needed.

PUBLIC ADDRESS/VIDEO BOARD SCRIPTS

Public address or PA scripts should be written and distributed to announcers in advance of the event. The **PA script** includes the specific details of what is being said when. For events in permanent venues, there is often a person who regularly serves as the announcer. For events where an announcer is less familiar with the script, it is helpful to give them plenty of advance time to review the announcements. If there are any tricky names, make sure to provide a pronunciation key. Write out the announcements exactly as they should be read. Do not abbreviate the event name or any other names. Make sure to include sponsor names where appropriate, and provide instructions on how often the announcements should be read. Many sponsor agreements will contain specifics about how many PA reads are required, and the event managers should ensure that this is executed per the sponsor contract.

In addition to sponsor reads, other information that patrons or spectators need to know should be included in the PA script. Examples include where concessions are located, good sportsmanship information, how to exit the facility, and when the next event is being held. Finally, emergency announcement information should be printed on the back page of the PA script (or posted in the PA booth/area) in the event it is needed. If an emergency situation should occur, the PA announcer has the correct announcements readily available instead of having to wait for the announcement to be communicated.

For events using video board displays, oftentimes the PA script is combined with a video board script which contains information on which graphic, sponsor advertisement, or public service announcement is shown when.

Figure 12-7. Sample Event Diagram

2009 Blueprint Marathon
Finish and Post-finish Area

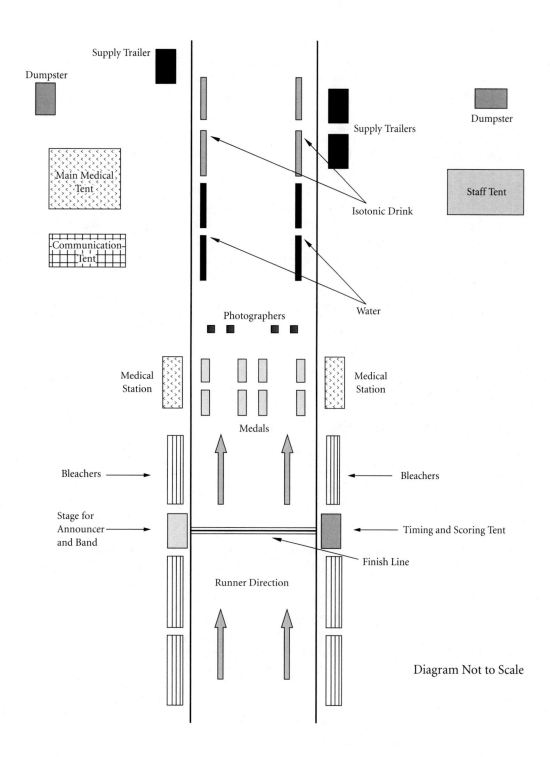

Diagram Not to Scale

This will ensure that a sponsor graphic will be shown on the video board at the same time the PA announcer reads the sponsor announcement. The technician responsible for the video board will have all of the graphics and video clips pre-programmed and ready to go on event day, but the script will dictate what is shown and when.

PARKING PASSES

Parking can become a complex aspect of event operations. As such, the creation of parking passes can take up a lot of time for event managers because the passes must be easily identifiable, different for each parking area, communicate other information to patrons, and not easily copied.

Parking passes should be large enough so that they can be identified when put in the window of the vehicle. If there are different parking areas, it may be wise to have the passes in different colors. Utilize both sides of the pass and put the directions and/or a map on the back for the driver. A couple of ways to help prevent people creating counterfeit passes by copying them is to number them and/or to have a hologram put on them when they are made. The parking staff should have a list of the numbers and the names associated with the passes. If the passes are issued to one person and are not transferable for the owner's friends or family to use, the staff should have the vehicle description and license plate number as well. This may be harder for repeat events because people may simply drive different cars each time. These are also added security measures for large events to track who has access to certain areas. For large events, local law enforcement will likely request this list in advance, which also means that event managers have to create, produce, and distribute parking passes according to that requirement.

Make the job of the parking staff as easy as possible. Create a sample board or document that shows what all of the parking passes look like and which lot(s) they allow the person to access. This should be done by either attaching actual passes to a coroplast board, or by scanning color versions of the passes into a computer for printing. This is something that should be reviewed at the pre-event staff meeting, and should also be included in the production binder.

CREDENTIAL/TICKET BOARDS

Credentials and tickets allow access to areas of the event. Credentials are usually for staff and may also be given to VIPs and/or media to access certain areas. As with parking passes, credentials should be numbered and/or have a hologram where security is tight. There should also be a list of which credentials are given to specific people or groups. For smaller events and areas of an event where security is not as tight, numbering and holograms are probably not necessary.

There are companies whose entire business is geared around creating access control and credential plans. For intricate events, it may be necessary to consult with one of those companies. These companies can offer security measures such as printing credentials on site with photos on them, RFID chips on the credentials to track them at access points, and many other high-security measures. For the types of events covered by this text, let's consider three very simple methods of determining how to assign credential types and access. (1) The credential type or color can indicate the group to which the person belongs (e.g., staff, VIP, volunteer, medical, vendor, etc.) and then the access code can specifically indicate where they are allowed access. For example, purple credentials indicate staff, green credentials indicate volunteers, red credentials indicate medical, and the codes on the credentials indicate where they can gain access. If it is a road race, AA could mean all access to all areas; FA could mean access to all areas of the finish, F1 could mean all areas of the finish except the finish line proper; S1, CA and F1 could mean access to all areas of the start except the start line proper, all access to the course, and access to all areas of the finish except the finish line proper. Again, the color of the credential would indicate the group to which the person belongs. (2) The type or color can indicate the area and the access code can specifically indicate where they are allowed access. This method works better if people are not crossing over to multiple areas. For example, let's say that the finish area is indicated by a yellow credential and the start is indicated by an orange credential, then the specific codes to allow a person to access areas is put on each credential. If people are at both the start and finish, such as sponsors, for example, they may require multiple credentials to access areas. The person may have a finish credential with FA and a start credential with S1, as an example. (3) For an event such as a college football season, each game may have a different color. The parking passes, tickets, and credentials would all be color-coded for that game. Game one may be the red game, game two the pink game, game three the yellow game, and so on. Everything for that game would be the same color, but the access granted would be letter or number coded onto it. For events similar to a college football game, this often works best because it allows ticket holders to pass on their tickets, parking passes, and credentials to another person without having to get them back for access to the next game. For the staff working the college football season, their credential may be striped, indicating that it is good for all of the games that season.

Sample boards should be created and hung at access points showing staff which specific credentials and tickets will enable access at that point. As defined in Chapter 9, Event Ticketing, sample boards have exact replicas of credentials, tickets, and parking passes on them, and provide an easy reference guide for staff. It can also be created in a document format and distributed to staff in those areas. This is something that should be reviewed at the pre-event staff meeting and should also be included in the production binder.

Production Binders

Many events carve up the responsibilities for supervision of functional areas during an event. Staff and volunteers who have not worked on planning the event may also be brought in to work. In order to facilitate the integration of information from various functional areas for all of these people, event managers create production binders. A **production binder** is a book or collection of detailed information (e.g., parking maps, event day checklists, fast facts, staffing positions, maps and diagrams, etc.) about the event that can be carried with event staff during the event. The binders are distributed to staff so that they will have most of the information about the event if they need to look up details, especially in areas they do not manage. The documents covered in this chapter are often the ones collected and put into production binders.

EMERGENCY PLANS

Emergency plans are something event managers need to create, but something they hope they never need to put in action. This topic is covered in greater detail in Chapter 11, Event Safety and Security. Event managers need to consider major scenarios and then develop a plan to account for what actions will be taken. For major scenarios, event managers may be able to name a few of the potential situations, but will never be able to come up with everything (dangerous weather, terrorist action, complete power loss, natural disaster, etc.). It is important for the plan to include actions that will be initiated in any major situation. This should be discussed, finely honed, and the response practiced with the appropriate staff members and with city or municipal authorities. There will be results of many scenarios, though, that may be the same, and to some extent, event managers can plan for those results. For example, if a road race has to be stopped mid-race due to lightning, what is the best point (or points) geographically to do this or to try to re-direct people? Is it an area that has public transportation close by? If not, is it an area where buses can easily reach? Is there a plan in place to easily get transportation to that location to return runners to the finish area? Is there adequate room to store backup supplies (e.g., bottled water for runners) in that location in case the race has to be stopped?

In any emergency situation, communication is going to be paramount. The plan for how communication will be handled, who will be in charge of communication, and who will be authorized to speak to the media should all be worked out in advance. Event managers renting venues and/or working with city agencies for their event will also need to partner with the venue and the city to answer these same questions.

As introduced in Chapter 11, Event Safety and Security, related to crowd management, "What If" sessions are a key to planning for a variety of situations. Alternate scenarios need to be developed and reviewed in detail. It is helpful to come up with the four or five most likely scenarios and work out the specific elements of each, what actions will be taken, and who will be responsible for each one. For the relevant staff members, it is important to go over these few scenarios and the action plans in great detail. Maps and diagrams of alternate routes or locations have to be created and fully understood by everyone involved. Staff should be able to immediately go into action and lead their teams without having to think or ask what should be done. In contingency planning, event managers may have to spend money to prepare for a situation that never happens. What they need to ask themselves is what the opportunity cost is of doing nothing. If it costs $50,000 to have an adequate backup plan, that is a lot of money, but what would be the costs—and not just in terms of money—if something happens and there is no backup plan?

SUMMARY

There are many tools that event managers have in their tool bags. Tools that facilitate information sharing are some of the best ones. Planning documents vary in purpose and complexity. Event managers change the format dependent on their personal taste or the event for which they are working. There is rarely only one right way to do something. It is the same with planning documents. Using one particular format is not nearly as important as the information that is conveyed and the timeframe in which it is distributed.

NAME _____ DATE _____

STUDENT CHALLENGE #12

In Challenge #12, construct three different planning documents related to the event.

QUESTION 12-1

Draft a planning timeline for the event beginning at least three months before the event and encompassing at least eight different functional areas (e.g., logistics, marketing, staffing, entertainment, etc.). Take notes here on the functional areas, the event start date, the tasks for each area, and the number of days out (days before) the event that the task will need to be completed. Using this information, create a version in Excel with the full details as described in this chapter. See Figure 12-1, Planning Timeline, for an example.

QUESTION 12-2

In the space provided below, sketch a diagram of the setup of the event's field of play (FOP). Then, using the drawing tool in PowerPoint, create an electronic diagram.

Student Challenge

QUESTION 12-3

Create a Fast Facts for the event. Make a list below of the eight to ten information items that should be included on the Fast Facts for the event. Select from this list when completing the final document in Excel.

Information Item #1:

Information Item #2:

Information Item #3:

Information Item #4:

Information Item #5:

Information Item #6:

Information Item #7:

Information Item #8:

Information Item #9:

Information Item #10:

CHAPTER 13

EVENT STAFFING

Colleen McGlone, Michelle Wells, and Heather Lawrence

The structure of the sport organization responsible for the event will dictate much of what is needed with respect to event staffing. There are some sport organizations that host hundreds of events per year, while others may convene only to host one event every few years. Thus, the organizational structure will impact the staffing needs of the event, the availability of staffing, the role of event managers in staffing decisions, and the resources and expertise available to event managers.

Event managers understand that some level of staffing is needed at all events. While the event manager is responsible for the overall operations of the event, other individuals need to be available to ensure the needs of the participants and spectators are met. The options for staffing events are many. However, figuring out how many workers are needed, where they are needed, and for how long, are at the core of the challenges associated with staffing an event. Event managers can rely on event staffing companies, use local agencies (EMT, police, fire), hire part time workers, use volunteers or volunteer groups, provide academic credit or practical experience to college students, or use any combination of these. There are advantages and disadvantages to each type of worker that will be discussed in this chapter.

Beyond obtaining event staff, event managers must be skilled in leadership and motivation as they lead their event staff during what are often long events. There are also organizational skills that can help event managers to effectively manage their work teams. Oftentimes the event manager also is responsible for hiring, training, and evaluating the various workers for their specific positions, and needs to know basic human resource-related laws. Leadership, management, and legal aspects in this chapter will be discussed specific to the time period leading up to, and during an event.

STAFFING BASICS

Knowing who is responsible for what is critical. When contracts are being negotiated and signed for the facility, the basics of staffing are decided upon. The venue contract will specify, in detail, whether the venue or the organization provides staff, which entity decides how much staffing is needed, and who is paying for the staff. Medium to large sports venues often either outsource their event staffing or have a pool of workers to pull from to provide staffing services. Thus, the contract might indicate that staff would be scheduled by the venue, but the expense charged to the renter. However, there are smaller venues and non-traditional venues where event managers might have to establish staffing levels and secure personnel independently from the venue. These are pieces of information that event managers must have early in the process so that the budget can be developed accurately and all those involved can understand the expectations related to staffing.

Once it is clear whether the facility or the event is providing the staff, then the type and volume of staff need to be determined. The type of staff refers to the various positions that need to be filled during the event. The level of expertise and knowledge needed to fill a position can vary greatly from someone involved in ensuring the restrooms remain stocked to a customer service representative that must be educated on all aspects of the event. The volume of staff will depend on many factors including the type of event, the location, the venue size and type, the anticipated crowd, and the budget. Even if the venue is wholly responsible for staffing, the event managers should be aware of and involved in the decision making related to staffing. If the venue does not schedule enough staff to successfully handle the event, the event managers will be vicariously at fault for this failure, as they should know about and approve all staffing plans.

TYPES OF STAFF

Human resources can make or break the event. Even if all else goes well, the way staff handle each situation will impact the satisfaction levels of stakeholders (consumers, vendors, sponsors, entertainers). Think about why a team that has a losing record year after year is still able to fill the stands every year. It all revolves around creating a positive experience, in which staff is a critical element. To that end, understanding the various roles of the event management staff is important. This section focuses on event day staff, as other positions have already been discussed in previous chapters (e.g., ticketing, safety and security, marketing, and sponsorships). The event managers need to treat each event day staff member in a respectful manner regardless of their role, as it will help them envision how they should interact with spectators and participants. It is usually these individuals that are "creating" an experience with the consumers. If the person giving directions, registering participants, or helping people park is not friendly and professional, this sets the tone for the overall event.

The Importance of Customer Service

As discussed in Chapter 9, Event Ticketing, the customer is critical to the success of any organization, sport or non-sport. For many sports events, ticket sales or participant registration are the largest sources of revenue for the event. The customers that either purchase tickets or participate in the event should feel like their needs are being met before, during, and even after the event.

An organization's customer service philosophy should become a part of the everyday atmosphere. For managers, it is necessary to communicate the customer service expectations and train full-time, part-time, and volunteer workers on those expectations. It is much more expensive for an organization to obtain new customers than it is for the organization to keep the customers it already has.

There are two categories of workers involved with the event: front of house and back of house. **Front of house** workers are in direct contact with spectators, such as ticket takers, box office personnel, ushers, concessionaires, and merchandise sales people. **Back of house** staff is generally working behind the scenes and has responsibilities such as setup, teardown, and taking care of a lot of the "nuts and bolts" of making the event happen.

Front of House Staff

Contact with the front of house staff is often the first encounter that spectators have with an event. This group can quickly "make or break" a person's experience. Good customer service should not be something that takes a lot of effort on the part of staff. It may involve solving a problem for someone or doing something to make the experience more pleasant, such as alleviating lines. Interaction is another way to increase customer service, and it does not have to take a lot of time. It can be as simple as smiling when talking to people. A two- to three-second interaction with a customer can make a big difference. Front of house staff might ask a child wearing a Yankees #2 jersey if she thinks Derek Jeter is going to hit a home run today, and the child will associate an interest in her with the event for years to come. People want to be treated with respect and treated as individuals. While spectators realize they are one of thousands in attendance, acknowledging them with a simple "Welcome to the game," and "Thanks for coming, see you next time," makes them feel as if they are important, and can go a long way in giving them a memorable experience.

Back of House Staff

Back of house staff do not have the direct interaction with spectators that front of house staff have. However, depending on the event, they could have significant interaction with participants. Participants often turn to the closest event day staff member when they need something. For participant-driven events, that staff member is usually related to the operations of the event. The interaction between the participants and the back of house staff should be as customer service oriented as those taking place between front of house staff and spectators. Back of house staff also have an impact on customer service through the regular performance of their jobs, even when participants or customers do not come in contact with them. The event managers should ensure that back of house staff understand how important they are to creating a memorable, first class event for everyone who attends. For example, when they view the event as a whole, they will understand why it is important that they wipe off the bleachers before games, or why a field should be well prepared. As such, event managers must emphasize the role back of house staff play in creating a good event experience for everyone.

Regardless of whether workers are front of house or back of house, they generally fall into a few categories: part-time staff, volunteers, students/interns, and contracted services. There are advantages and disadvantages of each that are discussed in the following sections.

Part-Time Employees

When event staff is hired, they are most frequently hired as part-time employees based on the nature of events. Since many events only last a short time or only exist during certain seasons, it is difficult to hire many full-time employees. Part-time employment has many pros and cons. Part-time work allows for a greater work force than having to hire all full-time people. There are many times when help is needed at peak times and requires a lot of staff, but these "peak hours" may only be eight hours a week. Part-time employees can get the job done and do not come packaged with the compensation issues of full-time employees. In addition, a lot of people like part-time work because it offers a chance to be involved in the event without compromising their other endeavors. Furthermore, part-time employment allows individuals to test the waters of event management to see if it is a viable career option, as they can see what other types of opportunities and positions may be associated with event management.

Volunteers

Sports and recreation events often rely on a strong volunteer force. A **volunteer** is typically defined as an individual who takes on a task or duty with no expectation of monetary benefits. In fact, the entire event day staff could be made up of volunteers! Most people volunteer because they support the event or the cause, or because they want to give back to the community or sport organization. Volunteers can help in any area and can be used before, during, and after the event. It is a good idea to have an estimate or plan on how many volunteers will be needed in order to recruit and find the appropriate number. When that number is determined, add on another one-third for volunteers who change their mind and will not show up. For example, if 300 volunteers are needed, recruit 400. A recruitment plan is important because, unlike paid employees, volunteers do not often come knocking down the doors to help. For recurring events, recruitment of volunteers is a continuous process. Word of mouth may be helpful, but the most productive places to find volunteers may be to seek out groups (Kraus & Curtis, 2000).

Whether individuals or groups are volunteering, it is important to understand that volunteers are not "free" labor. Just like other types of labor, volunteers require training, and training costs money. Uniforms may need to be provided, or shirts that designate the area they are volunteering in. Volunteers need to be screened prior to being allowed to volunteer in certain areas, to make sure they are qualified to perform the tasks they will be asked to perform. In addition, event managers need to be aware of Workers Compensation laws and how they affect volunteers. Furthermore, while the use of volunteers can be very rewarding for all parties involved, there is a potential for the event to be held liable or even negligent if volunteers are not trained appropriately or act in a manner outside the scope of their assigned duties (Fried, 2005).

Revenue sharing may be a way to attract groups of volunteers as opposed to individuals. Often, a group will volunteer to help out at the event if they concurrently can do some fundraising for their organization. For example, a local high school team may be willing to come and clean up the stands after an event in exchange for the event making a donation to the team. This creates a positive for both groups, as they both get something they need from the relationship: the venue gets cleaned and the team earns money. Another example would be when a group staffs the concessions areas in exchange for a percentage of the profits from the sales they make during the event. Even when groups do not ask for some type of revenue sharing, it is a nice gesture to make a donation to the group, or at a minimum write a thank-you note to the group supervisor after the event to show appreciation for their help. This also will help retain their services in the future.

One area of caution with respect to groups of volunteers is to establish specific age requirements and supervision ratios for those volunteering as part of the group. A high school group could arrive with 14-year-old freshmen and only one parent to supervise them all. The parent might also bring along a younger child assuming they can help work as well. Or, a group could arrive where everyone is too young to work (e.g., young Boy Scout and Girl Scout groups). So, establishing ratios for adult supervision and having age requirements can help ensure the work groups are adequate for the job.

Volunteers should be supervised similarly to other employees, but may need closer attention, as they may not be as familiar with all the logistics of the event. Good volunteer training will overcome this potential obstacle. It is also important to remember the event may rely on volunteers, so volunteers should always be treated in a courteous and friendly manner, with their efforts recognized. A thank-you letter, providing event memorabilia, announcing the volunteer group names during the event, providing a thank-you dinner, or having a post-event party may go a long way in letting volunteers know they are appreciated.

Students/Interns

The use of interns is also a way to help staff the event. Usually, student interns are energetic and eager to get involved and help. Interns are students interested in event management trying to gain experience in a variety of areas, and it is important to note that they may not fully understand or have the complete skill set to do all of the tasks at hand. They, like volunteers, will need to be trained in the areas they will be assigned to work. When using interns, it is important that they receive an education while they work. This may not be formal education, but they need to gain experience in event operations and should be assigned work tasks that help them meet their goals and that add to their educational foundation. Interns should be asked to do more than basic tasks, and an explanation of why each task is important and how it fits into the overall event operations plan will be beneficial. By utilizing interns, event managers are able to capture and use a specialized work force in a variety of areas (e.g., broadcasting, media relations, merchandise sales). In addition, these interns have knowledge in areas where some volunteers, or even part-time employees, may not be as proficient or skilled.

Contracted Services

In some cases, event managers need to hire specialized services through a contractual agreement. These types of specialized services include, but are not limited to: officials, medical personnel, and vendors. In most cases these contracted services will be set up as an independent contractor arrangement. **Independent contractors** are people or businesses that provide products or services to another person or business based on the terms of a contract. They do not work on a regular basis as employees do.

Officials

Depending on the type of event, officials may need to be hired. The duties assigned to officials include keeping time; officiating the game; or verifying distance, place, or statistics. Officials may be hired as an employee or an independent contractor. Most officials are paid as contractors who are hired and directly contracted for their services by the event organization or league.

Medical

Event staffing should include a medical emergency plan and staff. Event managers need to make sure staff is trained in emergency first aid and CPR/AED (automated external defibrillators). Medical personnel must also be aware of how to access additional medical assistance from outside the event if needed. Some events will need more medically qualified staff than others. In addition, some event insurance policies will require a certain number of qualified medical caregivers on site throughout the event. This will be detailed in the contract.

Vendors

When considering vendors, event managers need to decide which vendors are needed. For example, event managers must choose whether or not to procure their own concessions and merchandise inventory or bring in outside vendors to provide it. Either way, the staffing needs should be fully understood prior to the event. If the event is using vendors, the contract should detail how the area will be staffed and by how many people. In addition, whether the staff will be paid or volunteer, as well as who is responsible for paying the staff, needs to be addressed. When contracting the services of vendors or setting up vending and concessions, the walk-thru is critical to ensure the venue layout will be able to perform as needed. There is nothing worse than needing an electrical outlet and finding out that there is not one that is accessible. A careful walk-thru will avoid this and other potential problems.

Another area to keep in mind when vendors are used is to ensure that whatever equipment will be provided by the venue is detailed in the rental contract, and that work orders are done well in advance to ensure that all equipment is available and is on site prior to the time of setup. If vendors are provided by the venue, event managers need to make sure there is an understanding of who is responsible for staffing, providing the merchandise and food, paying the staff, and understanding how any funds raised through sales will be distributed.

All of the various types of event day staff need those above them in the hierarchy to provide leadership to them throughout the event. Event managers will develop their own leadership styles with experience, but there are some simple tips that will help to create a work environment where event day staff feel valued.

STAFFING NUMBERS AND COST

There are no clear-cut formulas that apply to all events related to the number of staff needed. As discussed throughout this text, communicating with other event managers that have hosted the event previously is a good strategy to obtain information about expected crowd behavior and staffing needs. All events have a **baseline staffing** number. This number takes into account the bare minimum of staff required to accomplish the management of the event. For example, an arena may have eight entrances, but the event could occur with only two of those doors open for ticket taking, one near each parking area. This baseline number of staff is where all staffing plans begin, and then are built up from there.

Once information on the expected behavior and size of the crowd is obtained, event managers can begin to add staff to the baseline numbers. First and foremost, the staffing numbers must be adequate to ensure the safety of the crowd. Second, there needs to be adequate staff so that spectator and/or participant flow is good, even during the busiest times. Finally, the staffing plan must stay within the established budget, while also providing for the previously mentioned items.

Anticipating the Crowd

Even with proper research, there are some events for which the number of expected spectators and participants are very difficult to predict. Participant-driven events that accept event day registrations, as well as spectator events with event day ticket sales, do not know the exact number of participants/spectators until the day of the event. By that time, it is too late to adjust staff very much, so staffing levels need to be established with the "best case scenario" in mind for high participation and/or ticket sales. For events in non-traditional venues, participant numbers can be capped based on the number of people that the facility can accommodate, and participants turned away if/when that number is reached. Although this strategy helps control participant numbers, it does not solve the problem of the number of spectators, and it takes revenue away from the event.

Even with proper planning, there are times when an event may be understaffed based on a tremendous spectator turnout, and event managers must recognize it immediately when they are in an understaffed situation. If an event is understaffed, workers will need to be repositioned during the event. For example, registration staff may normally be done working once registration is finished, but they could be asked to help work another area once registration is closed if they are needed. Other workers in less critical areas such as ushering might be asked to cover two sections while one person is moved to assist at the entrance gates. Post-event workers should also be called in early, and police, if they are willing, can help cover certain areas. This can become a serious problem, since many venues are only certified to hold a certain number of people by the local fire marshal. Safety is important all of the time, but with an understaffed event, it is even more critical that event managers are aware of everything going on at the event in case an incident occurs, due to the crowd, that puts people at risk. As with all other times during the event, safety is the first priority.

Safety

Event managers need to understand the safety and security needs of the event, which are discussed in detail in Chapter 11, Event Safety and Security. This includes areas outside the venue as well as inside, and involves positions ranging from security at venue entrances, to crowd managers, to EMTs. Even though some positions will have direct responsibility for safety and security, all those working the event can play a role in keeping the event safe and secure. The event managers should emphasize this with all staff, and provide detailed information on how to identify potential issues, report problems, and respond to guests.

There are only two areas in event day staffing in which industry standards exist: ticket taking and crowd management. Crowd management is directly related to safety and will be discussed here. Within the seating bowl in traditional venues, or the spectator area in non-traditional venues, industry standards call for one trained crowd manager for every 250 occupants. A **trained crowd manager** is defined as someone who has been educated in crowd management techniques, the responsibilities of his or her job, as well as emergency procedures. Not only is this a guideline that will help to ensure a safe event, but if something were to happen where the event managers had to legally defend their staffing numbers, this is considered adequate for a typical spectator-driven event. Common sense must also prevail. The physical layout of the facility, along with the type of event and anticipated crowd, will help to dictate the number of trained crowd managers needed. An event that serves alcohol, anticipates patrons drinking prior to the event, or has a history of aggressive patrons, needs to increase the number of trained crowd managers.

Unfortunately, numbers of staff in other positions are not as clear cut. Through experience and communication with other event and facility managers, staffing levels can be established. It is clear that it is always better to be safe than sorry. Even if it costs a bit more, providing adequate staff to ensure the safety of all is critical.

Flow

The movement of spectators through the facility in an orderly and efficient manner requires that event managers understand peak times and have staffed those areas appropriately. **Peak times** are periods in which specific areas will have a surge in spectator/participant traffic. For example, sports that have a half-time will see a surge to concessions during this time. For half-time concessions, workers can be moved from other positions to the concession stands to help handle the rush at half-time. Being prepared for the peak time that will occur entering the parking lots, participant registration, ticket sales locations, entry gates, seating areas, merchandise areas, and concessions is part of understanding the staffing needs of the event.

As indicated above, there is an industry standard for ticket taking ratios, and adhering to this ratio can help manage flow at the event entrances. For every 1,000 ticket holders, one ticket taker should be employed (City of Cincinnati Task Force on Crowd Control and Safety, 1980). Beyond just knowing how many tickets were sold, the distribution of tickets will help to ensure ticket takers are placed at the appropriate entrances to meet this ratio. For example, at a regular season college football game, the gates may open two hours before the game, but from experience the event managers know that the flow of fans will peak 30 minutes before kick-off until 15 minutes into the game. In this scenario, the event managers can staff the gate with one ticket taker from the time the gates open to 45 minutes before the game, and then increase staffing to the appropriate level given the number of tickets sold from 45 minutes before the game to 30 minutes into the game. Strategies for all positions that incorporate the peak and non-peak times will keep patrons moving efficiently throughout the event.

One strategy to prepare for peak times is to use jump teams. As discussed in the sidebar, **jump teams** consist of event day workers that are available to fill in at a variety of staffing positions throughout the event day. They may be used during peak times, or at other areas when it is recognized that more help is needed. Being prepared for both peak and non-peak times will keep the flow of the event smooth and the spectators and/or participants content.

Jump Teams!

Michelle Wells

One of my previous jobs in sports was working for New York Road Runners (NYRR) as the Director of Event Development and Production. NYRR is a non-profit organization that promotes long-distance running and puts on over 55 road races each year. One of their biggest races (after the ING New York City Marathon) is the NYC Half Marathon presented by Nike.

The inaugural NYC Half Marathon presented by Nike was held in 2006 and had over 10,000 runners. One of the areas I managed at that time was the Volunteers Department. Because this was a new event on a new course, we wanted to make sure we were prepared to address any unexpected staffing needs that may have come up during the race. One of the managers in the volunteer department, Steve Boland, came up with the idea to create what he termed "jump teams" for the event. We created a team for each of the three main areas of the race course—Central Park, Midtown, and Downtown—and staged them in those areas. In the volunteer recruitment information, we assigned ten slots per jump team, anticipating that seven people would show up on race day. The description posted on the volunteer section of the NYRR Web site explained the possible responsibilities of the shift, where volunteers would check in on race day, and the fact that they could end their day at another area of the event.

During meetings, we communicated to other staff that we had formed these jump teams. If a location had a shortage of volunteers at their site or needed someone to perform a previously unanticipated task, the area would let the volunteer managers know how many people they needed, and jump team members would be deployed to that location. The jump team members were given a map that showed the specific locations of the cross streets, subway lines, mile markers, fluid stations, medical stations, entertainment zones, and so forth. If they were directed to go to fluid station #2, for example, they knew where they would be going. Steve had secured a van and driver to transport jump team members to locations that were outside of a reasonable walking distance. The van had an "official vehicle placard" in the window, as other race vehicles did, to make it easier for the van to get through areas near the race course. Being in New York City also provided the possibility of utilizing the subway system if necessary.

These teams were deployed to various areas that needed help, and some were even re-deployed to a second area after completing their tasks. The volunteer managers were given jump team lists for all of the areas, and could sign out any of those volunteers no matter where they started or ended their day. For volunteers who liked the idea of being on the go and "fighting fires," this position was appealing and provided something a little different from the usual roles. More importantly for the event, they helped alleviate potential problems that could have developed due to needing additional staff in some areas.

Budget

Deciding upon staffing numbers and paying for those staff is a major undertaking for event managers. Managers that have experience with a lot of events are very good at estimating staffing needs accurately, based on the type of event which allows for the most efficient use of the budget. For new event managers, seeking advice from those with experience will prove worthwhile when trying to determine staffing numbers and preserve the available budget.

The budget number can vary widely, even for specific dates in a traveling event. The hourly rate that a traveling event will pay for part-time staff in New York City will likely be different than the rate it would pay for hourly staff in a city the size of Columbus, Ohio, for example. Federal and state minimum wage requirements will apply, and event managers should become familiar with the rate of pay considered fair in their locale. Sometimes, event day staff can be paid in equipment in lieu of cash. The contract with the person would stipulate payment type and date. For example, let's say a person is hired to manage one sport within a mega event, such as table tennis. If that person is the local expert on table tennis competitions, and she is affiliated with a local club that may not have funds for equipment, she may agree to take payment in a comparable amount of table tennis equipment. It may also be presented as a donation to the organization in exchange for event day staff to run the table tennis competition. If the mega event organizers know that they will not be hosting any other table tennis tournaments where they will need the equipment, they may offer the equipment as payment. It alleviates the issue for the event managers of what to do with the equipment after the event, and allows them to work with an expert as the table tennis competition manager.

Cost restraints will almost certainly come into play with any staffing plan. The balance between providing enough staff to accomplish keeping people safe and providing good flow must be balanced with what the budget can handle. As discussed in Chapter 5, Event Budget, the cost of staff can add up quickly—whether part-time or full time. The University of Florida incurs event day costs for home football games of about $250,000 (DiRocco, 2009). This includes security, ticket taking, ushers, concession workers, medical support, clean-up, and other game day services (DiRocco, 2009). Luckily for Florida, their revenue far exceeds their costs associated with home football games. However, for many events, staffing costs can eat up a majority of the revenue, or even exceed revenue generated.

HIRING, FIRING, AND THE LAW

As previously stated, successful events require good employees. Finding and keeping them is often easier said than done. Just how do event managers go about acquiring the best people for the job? Recruitment, selection, and hiring are key elements for any event. This often creates a challenge because every event is different, and diverse skill sets are needed because of the variety of tasks often involved in events. The first principle is to find people who have positive attitudes. Too often, event managers wait for people to come to them instead of being proactive in recruitment of staff. Frequently, game day staff can be easily found by thinking about creating "win-win" situations. How can the event help others gain experience or meet a need for potential future employment? Recruiting, screening, training, evaluation, and termination are all aspects of staff management that event managers may find themselves responsible for. Legal issues also play a role in how staff is managed, and some of the relevant legal issues associated with hiring and management are discussed here.

Recruitment/Advertising

When considering recruitment for event day staff, getting an early start on recruiting is optimal. Once event managers know what roles need to be filled, they will be able to identify where to go to recruit. Some simple potential staffing sources are often overlooked. For instance, the local high school ROTC unit might be a great resource for a local fun run for traffic control. There are many high school groups that are required to "volunteer," and many are willing to assist local events when given enough lead time to do so and organize themselves. Another place to recruit game day workers is local colleges. Again, different majors and groups may need to gain experience in several areas related to their course of study. Church and local community groups (e.g., women's clubs, Kiwanis chapters, retirement groups) are also good sources for staffing. Other examples of possible recruitment sources include the event Web site, social networking sites, and newsletters/Web sites of partner/sponsor organizations or community groups that are associated with the event.

When going to local groups is not enough, or if more specialized help is needed, a job announcement may be very beneficial. A written announcement should be prepared based on the job description and skills needed.

Be careful not to leave the description or announcement so broad that the event gets (OR the recruiter gets) more people who are not qualified than those who are. On the other hand, being too specific may result in not getting any applications or interest at all. A good job description/announcement will contain the essential skills needed and the minimum qualifications for the position(s) to be filled. For any position requiring training or additional certifications, the requirements should be stated in the posting.

Once the position announcement is written, a decision on where to post it needs to be made. In today's electronic age, there are more options than just in the newspaper or on the mega job boards. If looking for specific skills, sending it to a profession-specific electronic listserv or bulletin board will disseminate the information to the targeted group. If the skill sets are less specific, placing the advertisement electronically in the local or community news publications, which many cities offer for free or a minimal charge, sending a press release to local television and radio stations to put on their job sites, as well as asking current employees to help get the word out about staff needs, are all options to consider.

Screening

Depending on the size and scope of the event, the selection process may be simple or complex. In any case, selection of staff may involve one or more of the following components:

1. The applicant filling out an application that includes background information and previous employment, and references if desired

2. Conducting a personal interview (either in person or on the phone)

3. Conducting a background investigation (this is particularly important when working with children, the elderly, or the disabled)

4. In some situations, having the applicant perform or display their skills by completing some type of performance test

There are a variety of human resource laws that can come into play during the screening process. Many are mentioned in the following section, but human resource professionals and attorneys can provide more detailed legal information specific to hiring.

Training

Training sessions should be built into the event schedule for event staff. Training will vary for each position, because the job functions vary. Every employee needs to know the details of the tasks he or she will be doing, no matter if it is providing security, taking tickets, ushering, directing traffic, or working in the media center. Each area will have a different set of requirements and may require different use of equipment, and staff in each of those areas should be given directions and training prior to the event getting underway. If possible, this training should include both verbal and written instruction and a trial run. Training and skills that staff receive helps each staff member grow, as well as shows that the event managers care about them. In many cases, it will be necessary to pay for staff training time. This is often overlooked in the event budget, and can be a significant cost.

During training, staff needs to be trained on basic functions of the organization. This may include understanding the mission of the organization and the event, understanding how the timekeeping system works (e.g., time cards, time clocks), and the issuance of keys, uniforms, and equipment as needed. Event managers should strive to provide uniforms that staff is proud to wear, but still are obvious that they are associated with an event worker. It is important to provide both men's and women's sizes in uniforms. Organizations do not require men to wear uniforms sized and cut for women, so women should not have to wear men's sized uniforms. It is common for event managers to assume that because men's shirts will also fit women, it is okay to only provide men's sizes. All workers feel better when they are proud and confident in their uniforms, and having shirts that fit well is part of that, so a variety of sizes for both genders should be available for workers.

Other areas in which training is needed include when and how shift changes occur, how to deal with difficult customers (and employees), and what to do if an issue arises that requires security. Moreover, each staff person should know what is to be done in case of a medical emergency, security emergency, or other emergent problem that requires managerial response. If the venue is available, a walk-thru should be scheduled with event day staff to familiarize them with the area and how it will be set up for the event. This will be beneficial when spectators ask for directions or where something is located; all staff should at least be able to point them in the right direction.

Oftentimes, staff members will require training in order to perform various duties, or they may require refresher training. This could range from updating or acquiring new technological skills, such as new video editing equipment or timing devices, to updating CPR/AED certifications. Other areas, such as security, may require on-site training to familiarize them with the flow of the event, the location of cameras, alcohol policies, and the command center. Many large events may require advanced training in managerial concepts or in areas that lead to certification. Examples of these include pyrotechnic certification for firework shows, athletic training, security, crime prevention, and certifications offered by the International Association of Assembly Managers (IAAM).

Evaluation

Evaluation of performance is an important aspect of event management, but is sometimes overlooked in the grand scheme of the event. All event staff should be evaluated on overall performance based on the job description. Evaluations should always take place in a private area and be performed in a non-threatening way (Kraus & Curtis, 2000). Time should be set aside to discuss the areas of performance that may need improvement, as well as strengths in performance. In terms of event staff, the focus should be on problems and opportunities (Prosser & Rutledge, 2003). This does not have to take a long time, but should be done in a way that demonstrates they are cared for by the event managers. Event day staff should also be given the opportunity to evaluate the event managers and the overall operations of the event. These individuals are closer to the action than event managers, and can provide important feedback on many aspects of operations. This can be used to improve the event in the future.

Termination

When considering terminating event staff, event managers need to keep the overall picture in mind. Retaining staff is less costly over time than having to obtain and train new staff. Therefore, if a staff member or volunteer is performing unsatisfactorily, the event managers need to decide if it is worth the time to try and retrain or re-motivate an individual in order to retain the person. A person may need to be "let go" or dismissed from duties for a variety of reasons, including not performing duties in a professional manner or not completing the assigned tasks. While it is no fun to terminate employment or a contract, it is often in the best interest of both parties. Remember too that this will create an opening for a new person or vendor to come in, which may enhance the event by bringing new ideas and experiences into the mix.

Legal Issues

Although it is outside the scope of this chapter and book to go into detail about all the human resources laws that may affect an event, there are a few basic laws, legal concepts, and situations that event managers that hire event day staff need to be informed of. In addition to these, event managers should refer to Chapter 3, Event and Facility Contracts, for more information on contract law.

American with Disabilities Act (ADA)

The ADA prohibits private employers, state and local governments, employment agencies, and labor unions from discriminating against qualified individuals with disabilities in job application procedures, hiring, firing, advancement, compensation, job training, and other terms, conditions, and privileges of employment. The ADA covers employers with 15 or more employees, including state and local governments. In addition to applications in labor law, ADA has a variety of stipulations related to equal access to facilities for people with disabilities (United States Department of Justice, n.d.).

Civil Rights Act of 1964

This act is a comprehensive legislative plan that prohibits discrimination. The goal of the act is to eliminate discriminatory practices in employment and places of public accommodation (Moorman, 2007). It provides the framework regarding many employment laws, including sexual harassment, and discrimination under Title VII.

Child Labor Laws

Event managers should familiarize themselves with the **Fair Labor Standards Act (FLSA),** which restricts the employment of child workers. "Child labor provisions under FLSA are designed to protect the educational opportunities of youth and prohibit their employment in jobs that are detrimental to their health and safety. FLSA restricts the hours that youth under 16 years of age can work and lists hazardous occupations too dangerous for young workers to perform" (United States Department of Labor, n.d., ¶ 1). There may also be related state laws on using teenagers for labor purposes, as some have more restrictive policies.

Occupational Safety and Health Administration (OSHA)

OSHA outlines the specific conduct that is required to ensure that a safe work environment is being maintained. There are several areas in which event managers need to be aware of OSHA standards, including noise levels, chemical use, and dealing with blood-borne pathogens.

Worker's Compensation

Worker's Compensation, also referred to as Workman's Compensation, is a series of laws aimed to protect injured workers. These laws provide the framework to deal with an employee that gets injured on the job to ensure he or she receives appropriate care and treatment.

Sexual Harassment

Sexual harassment is a form of sex discrimination that violates Title VII of the Civil Rights Act of 1964. It states:

> *Unwelcome sexual advances, requests for sexual favors, and other verbal or physical conduct of a sexual nature constitute sexual harassment when this conduct explicitly or implicitly affects an individual's employment, unreasonably interferes with an individual's work performance, or creates an intimidating, hostile, or offensive work environment (United States Equal Employment Opportunity Commission, n.d., ¶ 2).*

Unions

Some areas of the country have a strong union presence which impacts all types of events and facilities. If union labor is involved in the facility, event mangers must know the limits and restrictions placed on work by the union. For instance, many unions specify the number of workers needed to load in a certain type of event, while others have strict rules on how many hours union employees can work, or how much of a break is needed between shifts. Using union labor for the setup and teardown of an event is not necessarily better or worse than non-union labor. However, it can be different, as event managers will lack some of the control they are used to and would like to have when union employees are working.

Event managers need to understand that the local labor unions and their practices will match up with the **National Labor Relations Act**. This law restricts an employer's ability to interfere with employees in the execution of their job duties by offering coercive incentive such as higher pay, better work conditions, or a more comprehensive benefits package in order to sway an employee away from joining a union (National Labor Relations Board, n.d.). Unions are restricted in interfering with organizations by trying to influence personnel decisions such as who to hire, promote, or fire.

As indicated, the concepts addressed are specific to areas that commonly involve aspects of event managers' jobs. There are certainly other legal issues that human resources departments deal with on a regular basis. Event managers that are solely responsible for human resources need to obtain additional information from a qualified professional.

LEADERSHIP AND MANAGEMENT

Leading a team of event day staff throughout a sport season or for a single event can be more difficult than it seems. With all of the other responsibilities event managers have related to the event, providing quality leadership to event day workers is often not a priority. However, an investment in creating a positive work atmosphere can go a long way to increase overall morale of the group, which will translate into better customer service.

Work Teams

There will likely be some event day workers that exhibit exceptional leadership potential early in the hiring process. Delegating some of the management of event day workers to these people can lessen the load for the event managers, as well as help these exceptional workers to develop further. For example, event managers might choose to have a position called Director of Ticket Takers. The Director of Ticket Takers then becomes responsible for the ticket-taking work team using this strategy. This individual can also schedule ticket takers, provide supervision throughout the event, and respond to customer concerns more quickly than the event managers might be able to do.

Motivation

People have a variety of motivations as to why they might work a sports event. Some may be there exclusively for the paycheck, while others are there because they care deeply about contributing to the success of the event or being a contributing member of the community. These reasons for being there will impact the way event managers should interact with individuals. No motivational strategies will directly result in better performance from all employees, but the goal of motivational strategies is to create an environment that is positive and brings out the best in event day staff.

Event managers need to understand these different motivations and use a variety of strategies to reach as many event day workers as possible. Some examples of ways to create a climate of motivation include:

The Environment
- Provide a nice area for workers with snacks, water, and chairs.
- Make sure worker areas are clean and well kept.
- Ensure staff have ample time to use the restroom and take breaks.
- Provide meals during long shifts or water during shorter shifts.
- Post communications near the staff entry doors or in the area where snacks are offered.

Swag/Gifts
- Purchase T-shirts or other gear as gifts for workers.
- If there is a sponsor give-away, purchase/request extras for event day staff.
- If it is a recurring event, provide tickets to employees and their families for those games they are not working.

Recognition
- Implement "Employee of the Game" or "Employee of the Month" type recognition occasions.
- "Catch" people doing things well and congratulate them at staff meetings.
- Send thank-you notes to home addresses of workers to ensure their families also know they are appreciated for the work they do at the event.

- Especially for volunteer groups, include a "thank you" P.A. read during the event. It will provide good community recognition for their efforts.

Treatment

- The "golden rule" applies here: "Do unto others as you would have them do unto you."

There are volumes of published management theory, but in event management, a few simple acts will go a long way in motivating much of the event day staff. Sport is different than other industries because people generally have an emotional attachment to the event. Event managers can use this emotional attachment to their advantage with little cost to the organization. Unsold tickets, sponsor freebies, and treating people well can create an energetic work environment where the event day staff looks forward to getting to work and feels like part of the team.

Game Day Organization

No matter how much planning is put into an event, plans cannot be properly executed without people. People are the backbone of an event and what allow the carefully thought-out plans to be fully executed. Sometimes, inexperienced event managers can overlook this fact. Again, many of the people working an event will not be involved in the detailed planning. What is common knowledge to the event managers may be brand new information to the staff. This is why it is important to provide this information to them.

Call time is the time that staff is expected to be on-site, signed in and ready to go to work. Call times for events will vary. Generally, events and venues want their staff at their stations and ready to go at least thirty minutes before doors open or participants and spectators start arriving. Working backwards, this often means that staff members have to arrive at least an hour-and-a-half before that time. Staff check in and are directed to one location for a call time meeting. During the **call time meeting** (see Sample Call Time Meeting Agenda sidebar), event managers review general information about the event, key issues they foresee that might come up and discuss how to handle the issues, and answer any questions workers have. Topics that might be discussed include such things as:

- It is a big game, and if the home team wins the fans may try to rush the court or field;

- How to handle ADA special seating requests;

- Counterfeit tickets are being sold on eBay, and how to tell what a counterfeit ticket looks like.

This is also a good time to hand out the fast facts and review it with everyone. There should be plenty of time allotted to answer questions from staff. All staff needing uniforms will also receive them at this time. Event managers can address what will happen at the end of the shift or end of the event day. For example, staff need to know if they will return to an area to check out on their own, or if event managers will come to their area to release them when their shift is finished. Information on whether or not to return uniforms and any specific post-event information is also provided during the call time meeting.

Especially with volunteers, it is important that they know what they will be doing. Too many times, volunteers are dropped of at their assigned location (or simply directed where to go), and are not given enough information about what they will be doing. People should have a good understanding of what is expected of them on event day. Event managers should write up what each general area is responsible for, as well as review the specific positions that people may hold on that day. For example, ushers should help people find their seat, answer customer questions, and ensure that everyone admitted to their area has a ticket for that section. Clarify the name of the supervisory contact for each area in case a worker has questions, wants a restroom break, or needs other assistance. Ideally, area contacts should be at the call time meeting to so that staff can see and be able to recognize them.

To ensure that the call time meeting runs smoothly and that all event day staff is aware of their responsibilities takes a lot of preparation and planning on the part of event managers. During the event, event mangers should regularly check in with all event day staff to ascertain if they need anything. Providing water, food, and breaks to staff working long shifts will help to keep their energy level high and motivation to work strong. Event day staff should be released as soon as they are no longer needed at their positions. Not only will releasing people save the organization money, but event staff will be frustrated if they are working an area where they are not contributing to the operations of the event. For instance, parking workers may arrive earlier than other staff, and should be released shortly after the event begins. There is no reason to have workers guard parking lots after the vast majority of spectators are parked and inside the venue. There may be a few people that are able to park for free with unguarded parking lots. However, it is still cheaper for a few folks to park for free than to pay multiple parking guards.

Sample Call Time Meeting Agenda

The following is a sample call time meeting agenda for a college softball tournament. If the first game of the day is at 11:00 am and the gates open at 10:00 am, this meeting would take place from 9:00 am to 9:20 am, with all staff in place at 9:30 am.

1. General
   A. Review of schedule.
   B. The officials are the only ones that can call a weather delay/cancellation.
   C. All event staff will receive a meal voucher.
   D. Fast Facts distribution.
   E. CUSTOMER SERVICE IS KEY!
2. Facility
   A. Fields Prep Teams will work between EVERY game.
   B. ADA seating is available in section 10, 12, and 14, and extra companion chairs are in the concessions area.
3. Tickets
   A. Spectators must have a ticket. All tickets available at entrance gate.
   B. Tickets are torn at main entrance.
   C. All tickets are reserved seating.
   D. There are no pass-outs (people cannot leave and return on one ticket).
   E. In the event of a cancellation, tickets will be good for the re-scheduled game.
4. Programs
   A. Programs are available from the entrance gate ticket area.
5. Credentials
   A. All those entering the field of play must have a credential (no parents allowed on the field).
   B. Example of what they look like.
6. Parking
   A. Parking is $5 and is collected as fans enter the lot.
   B. Team buses can park for free. We are expecting approximately 6 buses.
   C. Officials and event day staff (with the parking pass I sent ahead of time) do not have to pay.
   D. Example of what parking passes for teams and officials look like.
7. Safety/Security
   A. City Police are on-site and available if you need help with spectators.
   B. Beer is being sold, so beware of intoxicated spectators. Sales will end during the 5th inning of the last game of the day.
   C. EMTs and ambulances are on-site and are located along the right field fence of Field #1 and Field #3.
   D. Fans must act respectful at all times (police will help enforce this).
   E. In an emergency, listen to the P.A. for instructions.

8. Marketing
   A. There are no promotional contests today.
9. Media
   A. All media should be directed to the press box.
   B. The games are live on FM 99.9.
   C. No television coverage.
10. Concessions
    A. Located in the middle of the complex.
11. Merchandise
    A. Located at the entrance gate.
12. Hospitality
    A. Coaches' hospitality is under the tent by Field #1.
    B. Athlete hospitality is located in each dugout.
13. Other issues for discussion?

Leading and managing staff on the event day can be both challenging and fun. Event managers have the opportunity to create good memories and experiences for event staff, just as event staff create those memories for spectators and participants. Taking care of event day staff and treating them well does not take much effort, but will reap great rewards in the quality of work the event staff will provide during the event.

STAFF POSITIONS

Helping all event day staff to understand their roles during the event is the responsibility of the event managers. Many times, it is a lack of communication that results in people underperforming their jobs, as opposed to them being unable to complete the required tasks. Developing simple job descriptions will help event managers to organize their staffing plan, and also help them to communicate with the event day staff about what their responsibilities entail. Some event day staffing positions require more skills than others, but all should know what is expected of them. Job descriptions should be specific to the event. For example, a police officer at a youth soccer tournament will have a very different role than a police officer at an NBA All-Star Game. The following information was compiled to help event managers in the development of their own job descriptions for event day staff.

Professional Staff

Medical Director: A medical director is often required by the rights holders of an event. Sometimes it is part of the sanctioning requirements, and other times it might be tied into insurance requirements for liability protection. The primary duty of a medical director is to plan for medical coverage for participants, spectators, and staff. This includes arranging for how medical care will be accessed and how care will be given. This person will be intimately involved in all risk management plans, emergency preparedness plans, and emergency responses.

Athletic Trainer: Athletic trainers conduct initial assessments of injuries or illnesses to determine whether athletes should be referred to physicians for diagnosis and treatment. Athletic trainers should be present at most athletic events. Often, elite-level teams and athletes will bring their own athletic trainers to the competition site. For other events, the event managers should work to contract with local athletic trainers to cover the event. Often, athletic trainers are able to direct injured athletes as to whether or not their injuries require emergency care, or if they can seek medical care from their primary care physicians when they return home.

Security (Police, Agency): Event security personnel typically provide a variety of duties including crowd management, security scanning, door monitoring, and protecting access points and barricaded areas. Furthermore, security officers assist with customer relations by providing patrols, assisting with compliance and enforcement of alcohol policies, and helping to direct traffic pre- and post-event.

Video Board/Audio: The video board operator and/or audio editor develops, records, produces, and edits programs, features, and show imaging. They also might operate the control panel of the radio station during live and taped broadcasts, and other times as required.

Web Site Design: The Web designer creates and designs the look and feel, graphic elements, page layout, and navigational templates for multiple types of sites, products, and services. This individual helps to shape the visual direction for online sites, products, templates, and graphic elements.

Video Streaming: Those working in video streaming must have specialized technical knowledge. Video streaming involves recording an event using specialized video equipment and converting it into a digital and electronic format for viewing over the Internet.

Non-Professional Staff

Ticket Taker: The main responsibility of a ticket taker is to ensure that no one is admitted to an event without permission, either by showing proof of paid admission or event credentials. This person may also assist in ticket sales and customer relations.

Usher: Ushers assist patrons by performing duties such as collecting admission tickets and passes from patrons, assisting in finding seats, searching for lost articles, and locating such facilities as rest rooms and telephones.

T-shirt security: Patrols assigned to monitor an area on foot, or in motor vehicles, as assigned, to ensure personal, building, and equipment security. Informs and warns violators of rule infractions, such as loitering, smoking, or carrying forbidden articles.

Concessions: Concession workers may have a variety of duties, but generally interacting with patrons by selling concession items, processing sales as cashiers, and maintaining inventory controls are the primary tasks.

Gate Supervisor: The gate supervisors oversee their assigned areas. A gate could be an entry area to parking or the main venue. Tasks may vary, but include supervising ticket takers and parking staff, as well as interacting with customers.

Ticket Seller: Ticket sellers are responsible for selling event day tickets. Tasks typically include interacting with customers by helping them to choose seat locations for the event. They may also have to use specific software to process payments and complete ticket sales.

Parking: Parking staff is outside, often located away from the primary venue. They are involved in setting up parking areas and providing traffic direction. For restricted lots, they are responsible for confirming patrons have the correct type and number of passes. In addition to helping people park, some events may need parking staff to sell parking passes, process sales, and interact with customers.

Program & Merchandise Seller: Program and merchandise sellers are responsible for selling a variety of merchandise. Tasks typically include selling programs and merchandise, and serving as cashiers.

Scoreboard Operator: A scoreboard operator requires a basic knowledge of the event operations, game statistics, and technology. The primary responsibility is to keep event statistics up to date in real time for spectators, teams, officials, and the Internet.

How to Conduct Event Management Meetings

Athena Yiamouyiannis

Event managers are responsible for conducting a variety of meetings. There are internal meetings to figure out what type of staffing is needed; external meetings with staffing agencies, police, and volunteer groups; and event day meetings/call time meetings with staff to ensure pertinent information is communicated. A meeting that is conducted well can be a great forum for productive collaboration and sharing; if done poorly, it may be perceived by attendees as a waste of time. It is up to event managers to conduct internal, external, and event day meetings effectively and efficiently so they are productive for all involved.

The first step in meeting planning is to determine what type of meeting is needed (its purpose). Will the meeting's purpose be solely to share information? Will it be to brainstorm or problem solve? In event management, one of the primary purposes of conducting meetings is to share specific event details with key individuals who will be managing the event.

Who needs to be in attendance at the meetings? Good event managers will identify the individuals who should be present during the meeting so that they can be informed and/or contribute to the discussions. If an event team is being put together, care should be taken to ensure the team is comprised of the individuals necessary to get the job done effectively and efficiently.

Where should the meeting be held, and what resources might be needed at the meeting? A location should be identified, along with any equipment needs and documents, including the preparation of a meeting agenda.

The following is a meetings checklist used by the National Collegiate Athletic Association (NCAA) staff (NCAA, n.d.) for pre-, during, and post-meeting activities.

Before the Meeting:

1. Determine objectives.

2. Select participants.

3. Determine date and time.

4. Ensure room size and seating arrangements suit group size and activity.

5. Prepare meeting agenda and send to participants before meeting.

6. Collect necessary data.

7. Reserve and set up facilities and equipment.

Starting the Meeting:

1. Be on time (leaders and participants).

2. Confirm objectives and review agenda.

3. Review prior meetings.

During the Meeting:

1. Keep on track with the agenda and items.

2. Encourage sharing of ideas; discourage clashing of personalities.

3. Summarize decisions/conclusions.

Ending the Meeting:

1. Review the action plans.

2. Set date, time, and objectives for the next meeting.

3. End on a positive note—thank participants for their time.

After the Meeting:

1. Prepare and distribute summary/minutes.

2. Follow up on action items.

3. Check on progress.

4. Evaluate leadership methods and effectiveness.

5. Plan the next meeting.

As indicated, the meeting organizer should develop and send out a meeting agenda to attendees prior to the meeting. Oftentimes, the meeting organizer will send out a request for agenda items several days before the development of the agenda, so that new issues/problems that arise can be added to the agenda.

At the meeting, someone should be assigned as the scribe (note taker). The scribe is responsible for drafting the "minutes of the meeting," which is a summary of the key points of the meeting. The meeting minutes should clearly specify what needs to be done, the name of the person(s) who will be held responsible for getting the projects/tasks completed, as well as applicable deadlines. The scribe should have the meeting organizer review the notes, and then send out the minutes of the meeting to committee members, generally within 24 hours of the meeting.

Although meetings may be viewed as tedious by those required to attend, they are necessary. If they are run properly, meetings can be extremely beneficial. They provide an opportunity for event managers to work out some of the details of planning the event. One of the biggest errors that event managers can make, though, is to utilize meetings to try to make all the major decisions for an event. Event managers—both the lead event manager and the ones managing specific functional areas—should be using the time between meetings to work out plans and secondary options to problems. Group meetings are for updating everyone on the progress of these areas and to ensure that there are no unforeseen conflicts with things that have been discussed.

In summary, the meeting forum itself offers a great venue for event managers to get various staff members and constituents on the same page regarding event information and implementation strategies. The use of the meeting planning techniques described above (pre-meeting preparation, meeting protocol, post-meeting follow up) can be used as a roadmap by event managers to assist in the planning and implementation process. By conducting efficient and effective event meetings with internal and external constituents, not only will communications be enhanced, but staff morale will be higher, issues minimized, and the quality of the event improved.

Public Address Announcer: A public address announcer typically reads the P.A. script, announces important information, and becomes the voice of the event. The announcer may also assist in marketing and promotions, especially for events with a half-time.

Staff positions and their descriptions may seem obvious to event managers, but it cannot be assumed that all those working the event are familiar with the expectations of each position. Clear instructions, along with adequate training, will ensure that the event day workers will excel in their positions.

SUMMARY

As with many aspects of event management, staffing is not glamorous; it is challenging because every event has different staffing needs. The management of human resources can make or break the overall success of any event. As discussed, event staffing is multi-dimensional and impacts contract negotiation, customer service, security, media, and revenues. Event managers need to be able to make difficult decisions, and direct and understand a variety of situations and personalities, all while keeping a perspective on the entire event. Understanding the differences between the various types of staff, positions, and duties is important. Every member of the event staff, whether front of house or back of house, plays an important role in the event. To the participant and spectator, the event day staff are representatives of the event and need to provide excellent customer service to ensure the event is a great experience from the beginning to the end for all involved. It is a difficult task to determine how many staff are needed and which positions are required for a successful event. The combination of research and experience can help event managers as they try to balance controlling cost with providing adequate staffing levels.

Event managers need to have a basic knowledge of what responsibilities should be assigned in each position, and when specialized training or certification is required. In addition, it is important to understand the basic rules, regulations, and laws that may impact the event staffing and operations, based on the type of staff being utilized. Event managers should rely on human resource experts or attorneys to clarify the specifics of employment law as needed.

NAME _____ DATE _____

STUDENT CHALLENGE #13

In Challenge #13, examine the staffing needs of the event. Some job descriptions will be created, an overall staffing plan will be established, and a call time meeting agenda will be produced.

QUESTION 13-1

As part of the overall event plan, write detailed job descriptions for four event day positions required to successfully run the event. If the positions are similar to what is provided in the chapter, the descriptions must be significantly expanded to fit the event needs.

Position #1 Title:

Job Description:

Position #2 Title:

Job Description:

Position #3 Title:

Job Description:

Position #4 Title:

Job Description:

QUESTION 13-2

Develop a detailed staffing plan for the event. In order to do this, take the staffing positions from Question 13-1 and determine the hours they will be needed at the event—allowing for meetings, breaks, meals—and the number of people needed in those positions based on the event setup. (If there are additional jobs needed that were not listed in Question 13-1, please include them in this plan.) Determine how many supervisors will be needed for those positions. Based on this information, set the call time(s) for the various positions. Take notes here and then type up the staffing plan.

Position #1 Title:

Number Needed:

Call Time:

End Time:

Position #2 Title:

Number Needed:

Call Time:

End Time:

Position #3 Title:

Number Needed:

Call Time:

End Time:

Position #4 Title:

Number Needed:

Call Time:

End Time:

Supervisor(s) Needed:

What position(s) will each supervisor oversee?

How many individuals will each supervisor oversee?

QUESTION 13-3

Draft an agenda for a call time meeting that directly reflects the items that need to be addressed for the event. The sample agenda in the chapter is for a softball tournament, but can be used as a guide. Take notes here and then type up the agenda.

CHAPTER 14

EVENT OPERATIONS

Heather Lawrence

Event operations begin once the event is scheduled, and conclude when the last piece of trash is picked up (and recycled), the lights are turned off, and the gates are locked. Essentially, this encompasses making the conceptualization process of the event come together for the execution of the event. Facility management and event management need to be examined as a whole, not as separate parts, when planning for the event. This is when it all comes together. The event experience of participants, spectators, officials, and staff will be lacking if either the facility management or event management is poor. There will always be some unanticipated occurrences during the event, but with attention to detail and proper planning these can be minimized.

This chapter will describe the details of event operations such as facility setup and teardown, procuring and managing equipment, and event flow. Facility management deals with different spaces, and ensuring each space meets its intended need and is ready for the event. Equipment is used as either a core component to the execution of the event or to support the core function, and may or may not be available from the facility. The flow of the event is the seamless integration between the people involved in the event (i.e., participants, spectators, and officials) and the facility. It is an abstract concept, but event managers can recognize whether the flow is good or not in an instant. People will move in a natural and easy way and the operations of the event become invisible to the spectators if the flow is conceived and executed well. Customer service is also an important aspect of operations that should not be ignored, but details on customer service were discussed in Chapter 13, Event Staffing.

THE FACILITY

The facility can be broken down into the primary space and the ancillary spaces. The **primary space** is the area of the venue where the main activity takes place. The field is the primary space in a football stadium, and the ice is the primary space in a hockey rink. For non-traditional sport venues, the primary space may have to be created, as in the case of the ING New York City Marathon or a ski race. For the vast majority of the year, the streets of New York are filled with cars and pedestrians. However, during marathon time, those same streets become the primary space of the marathon venue. For a ski race, the mountain may be open all year to skiers of varying abilities, but during a race week, the course is set up on a particular slope and creates a primary space on the mountain.

Ancillary spaces are all of the areas that support the primary space. A football stadium has locker rooms, concourses, storage areas, lobbies, press areas, loading docks, offices, restrooms, security areas, merchandise shops, maintenance shops, control booths, concession areas, restaurants, luxury suites, club seating areas, and maybe even an outdoor gathering place. For a marathon, the ancillary spaces are similar, but may have to be constructed. There could be a participant registration area, staging area, starting line, water stations, restrooms, spectator seating, a command center, broadcast areas, and sponsor hospitality. Event managers are responsible for deciding how each area needs to function to result in a successful event.

Facility Walk-Thrus

A pre-event walk-thru of the facility is an important piece of event operations. A **walk-thru** is exactly what it sounds like, a literal walk around the building or site examining in detail how everything will look, function, and flow for the event. All of the key event and facility managers, along with representatives from the rights holder, from television (if a televised event), and major sponsors should be part of the walk-thru. For big events, multiple walk-thrus will occur at different points of the development process. However, for all events there should be at least one walk-thru during the month prior to the event. Discussions of television camera placement, sponsor activation, hospitality needs, access control, flow, and the event timeline are all part of the walk-thru. Event managers should schedule the walk-thru allowing plenty of time between it and the event day for any modifications in plans that result.

COURTS, FIELDS, AND COURSE SPECIFICATIONS

Knowing the correct layout, setup, and specifications for courts, fields, and courses can be complex. There are different requirements depending on the rights holder involved. For example, the dimensions of a basketball court vary from 94' x 50' for professional/college courts to 84' x 50' for high school courts (Athletic Business, n.d.). Imagine being ready to host a high school tournament, only to realize that the professional arena that was rented only has lines for a professional court. This is an issue easily correctable with temporary lines if it is known in advance, but on the day of the tournament it becomes a very difficult problem. Specifications for most sports are available online from the national governing body (NGB) of the specific sport, but they can also be obtained from the rights holders of the event.

Setting up and certifying road race courses are even more difficult than dealing with courts. To have a race course certified by USA Track and Field, it is recommended that a professional be hired to measure the course (USA Track and Field, n.d.). For participants to be able to compare their race times to other courses and for any record to be set, the race course must be certified (USA Track and Field, n.d.). USA Track and Field provides a database on its Web site of known course measurers to assist event managers in finding someone to measure a course. Specific procedures on how to certify the length of swimming, running, and bicycling courses are usually included in the sanction application and/or bid documents. For events without standards, such as a local fun run, it is up to the organizers to create a course that is fun, safe, and meets the needs of the event.

Not only do published recommendations and guidelines provide activity area information, but some also have guidelines for safety areas between the playing area and spectators. For example, in high school and college basketball, the industry standard is to provide three feet of clear space on the side of the court opposite the team benches, with ten feet recommended (Athletic Business, n.d.). Recommendations and guidelines set forth by professional organizations are important to heed because if something were to go wrong and a spectator was injured resulting in a lawsuit, the legal system will look to adherence to industry standards as a guide in assigning fault.

FACILITY SETUP AND TEARDOWN

For many event managers, the physical setup and teardown of the venue are the most difficult portions of the event. **Setup** is the process of preparing the venue for the event, and **teardown** returns the venue to the pre-event condition. Needs in these areas will vary depending on the type of venue, type of event, and staff availability. However, there are some things that are constant. For all events, allowing plenty of time for setup and teardown, making the venue as user friendly as possible, and providing for maximum sponsor exposure are important.

Depending on the event and venue, setup could take five minutes, 24 hours, or even several days. A rule of thumb is that it takes half as long to teardown as it does to set up. Event staff and volunteers are generally more enthusiastic during setup than during teardown. Many times, people that have worked hard all day are tired, and are ready to go home at the end of the event. Event managers must be clear in their expectation as to who is required to stay for teardown, and use the management strategies discussed in Chapter 13, Event Staffing, to motivate volunteers and employees.

Customer service is at the core of ensuring that the venue adds to the spectator experience and does not detract from it. Making the venue user friendly through good flow is also important and will be discussed later in this chapter. People will remember if they got lost between the parking lot and the field, if their seats were soaking wet when they got to the game, or if the gates did not open on time. In the case of facility setup, it is generally good to not be memorable.

Planning for maximum sponsor exposure is the final key point in venue setup. As discussed in Chapter 7, Event Sponsorship, event managers need to make sponsors visible. If there is a live activation, then the event manager needs to set up that area with as much precision and attention to detail as the rest of the venue. Plus, it needs to be in a high-traffic location. If signage is part of a sponsorship deal, then the signs should be placed in the correct locations and be as visible as possible to spectators and media.

Primary Space Setup

The primary event space should receive the most attention during setup because it is the focus of the event. All eyes will be on this area, as will any media presence, so detailed setup according to the pre-established needs of the participants and spectators is crucial. For some events, especially those held in single-purpose venues, there will be little primary space setup. However, for others, there is a tremendous amount of work to be done in creating this area. An ancillary event such as an interactive golf experience and trade show associated with a golf tournament will still have a primary space associated with the interactive golf experience, in that a large area will have to be set up to make the ancillary event a success. There will be vendors arriving, possibly a check-in area to set up, large pieces of equipment and displays to set up, and significant power needs in the area. This is in addition to the golf tournament primary space setup on the course that will probably occur at the same time. So, within one major event (if there are ancillary events associated with the primary event), there could be more than one primary space, and both need attention.

Basic primary space setup could include a changeover. A **changeover** is the process by which the primary space in the venue is converted from functioning for one purpose to another (e.g., flat exhibit space to basketball). There is also an element of participant safety in setting up of the primary space. A soccer field should be checked for holes and other dangerous conditions, just as the area around a basketball court should be checked for sharp corners that could pose a danger to players. Examples of other common set-up items for events include the scorer's tables and sideline chairs for basketball; leveling the ice and cleaning the glass for hockey; and installing and checking the touch pads (part of the timing system) and checking the pool chemicals and temperature for swimming. There will probably be sponsor agreements related to signage that must be executed during setup. Ensuring signs are hung in the correct places may seem trivial, but sponsors will notice and be unhappy if they are hung incorrectly.

Warm-up time may be provided to participants in the primary space and needs to be taken into consideration when planning setup. Warm-up is when the athletes get a feel for the environment, so the scoreboards should be on, signs hung, and lighting should be the same as it will be for the event. If a temporary logo needs to be affixed to the basketball court, it should be done prior to all practices so the court is exactly the same during practice as it will be for the game.

For non-traditional sports venues, the setup will be extensive. For example, creating a course, keeping spectators separate from the course, securing the area, and moving the required equipment to the course are all time-consuming activities. It is not unusual for a marathon that is starting at 9:00 am to have workers out at 2:00 am setting up. Beyond the primary space, there are supporting areas that also require set-up attention.

Organization Is Everything!

Bren Stevens

I just wrapped up my sixteenth season as the head volleyball coach for the University of Charleston. The University of Charleston is a Division II member of the NCAA, and is also a member of the West Virginia Intercollegiate Athletic Conference. It is not uncommon to find staff at smaller institutions that wear many hats, and often, head coaches must assume the event manager role for their own games or matches. Trying to solicit help on a game day is like looking for the proverbial needle in a haystack.

Organization is everything to a head coach. An event manager for an intercollegiate sport will help to take a significant burden off of the head coach and his or her staff. This allows the coach to concentrate on the game, the athletes, and ultimately winning. Throughout the years, I have developed my own checklist for the purpose of setting up the gym for a home volleyball match. I am confident that all coaches would rather come across seemingly too organized as compared to the alternative.

I am including a copy of the checklist that we now utilize at the University of Charleston for our volleyball match setup and tear-down. It can easily be adapted as a model for almost all other intercollegiate sports. In addition, the event manager should expect to meet with the head coach on the day of a game or match about specifics for the day. Some of the below tasks may be completed by other individuals on campus, but it is the event manager's responsibility to provide oversight for each of the seven areas listed on the check list.

University of Charleston—Volleyball Match Checklist

I.   **Publicity:**

_____Campus advertisement

_____Statistics and talking points

_____Post game media/score calls

II.   **Court Preparation:**

_____Sweep and damp mop floor—utilize electric scrubber

_____Assemble scorer/stats table

_____Set up chairs for team benches

_____Hook up scoreboard and test

_____Hook up computer and printer and test

_____Set up National Anthem Tape or CD

_____Put out paper stat sheets, pencils, score sheets, libero tracking form

_____Turn on gym lights and balcony lights

_____Lock side doors of the gym

_____Clean/lock officials/team locker rooms

_____Dry erase markers and erasers in each of the locker rooms

_____Check bathrooms for cleanliness and toilet paper supply

_____Set up volleyball net system and referee platforms

_____Place balls on to the volleyball court for visitors and home teams

III. **Parking:**

_____Make sure that campus security knows that there is a home match

_____Contact security for assistance with general parking

IV. **Ticket and Program Sales:**

_____Poster that contains ticket prices

_____Money box with change for ticket and program sales

_____NCAA Pass gate list

_____Programs

_____Secure one money taker

V. **Pre-Game Details:**

_____Host to meet and greet visiting teams

_____Host to meet and greet officials

_____Gather drinks for the officials

_____Towels and checks for the officials (if applicable)

_____Give the PA script to the PA announcer

_____Game details (copies of stats, box scores to visiting teams)

_____Secure two line judges—Give out flags

_____Secure one timer

_____Secure one libero tracker

_____Secure one "official" score keeper

_____Secure one PA announcer

VI. **Emergency Medical Care:**

_____Make sure that there is a Certified Athletic Trainer (ATC) assigned to the match

_____The ATC should place ice, cups, towels, and water coolers for both of the visiting teams and the home team

VII. **Clean-Up:**

_____Put volleyballs and net systems away

_____Unhook scoreboard and put away

_____Lock all gym doors

_____Turn in ticket money

_____Put away the PA system

_____Pick up trash around the benches and the scorer's table

_____Turn statistics in to the sports information director

Division II has come up with a strategic plan, which in part addresses the game day environment. The NCAA lists priorities such as:

> *3.1: Provide game environments and atmospheres that are competitive, safe, fun, positive, respectful and entertaining.*
>
> *3.2: Enhance and increase the opportunities to strengthen the experience for game day, conference championships and national championships for Division II student-athletes, coaches, officials, fans and spectators. (NCAA, 2009, p.6).*

The individual that assumes the responsibility of the event manager is instrumental in assisting the NCAA with the associated priorities for their strategic plan. All of us play an important role in making the game day experience positive, and providing organized steps that ensure fluidity and make people feel welcome on our campuses.

All coaches would like to be able to devote more time to the details of coaching, and they will certainly be appreciative of having an event manager that is capable of creating a proper game day atmosphere.

Ancillary Space Setup

Although counterintuitive, the ancillary spaces may take longer to set up than the primary space. The setup of these spaces can be spread over a large area and involve coordinating with various people to ensure each area gets set up according to plan. Moving from place to place and meeting up with different people can be very time consuming. To ensure spaces are available to the users when they need them, it is common to set up areas in the order they are needed by all involved.

Parking

Parking lots are the first locations to receive setup attention. Even those working the event need to park, so it is important that procedures are in place to ensure parking lot security and staff are the first to arrive. Barricades, chairs for parking attendants, and parking signage should also be set up early. Some major events will require that parking is staffed the night before the event to ensure cars do not sneak into the lots. One car parked where a media satellite truck is planning to be the next day can cause major problems, resulting in towing and an upset patron. No matter how much effort is put into securing parking lots, it is likely that cars will need to be moved by tow trucks if reserved lots are being used. Establishing a relationship with a towing company before the event is recommended so trucks are available if they are needed.

Weather can also play a role in parking setup. Some events expand their available parking by using grass fields, which creates issues if it rains. Being prepared is the key if rain is in the forecast. The heavier the vehicle, the more challenging parking on grass in rain can be. Plywood sheets are one strategy to create "lanes" for cars to enter the parking area to avoid it becoming a mud pit. Plywood can be laid out end to end at major entrances to these areas.

Tailgating

For events with tailgating, that area should be set up next. Tailgate setup includes signage, the delivery and setup of port-a-potties, marking tailgate spots, if needed, and tent setup. Golf carts are a must for events that have large parking or tailgate areas, as they allow event managers to quickly move from one area to another to deal with any issues that may arise. In the event of rain, severe cold, or snow, event managers can expect that the number of fans tailgating will significantly decrease, and that fans will arrive closer to game time. However, in spring and fall weather, or for events with a lot of meaning to fans, tailgaters will arrive early and event managers must account for that in their planning.

Participant, Media, Vendor, and Staff Needs

Other facility spaces used by event workers, participants, media, and vendors are set up after parking and tailgating. These groups all arrive much earlier to the event than spectators. For all facilities, this means that worker, media, and participant entrances/registration are open early while the rest of the venue is secured. Also, the command center (if applicable), locker rooms, participant hospitality, media work rooms, and press row/press box should be open and accessible as early as possible. Members of the media generally set up early and can work for hours after the event concludes.

Communication with all of these groups is important, but ensuring vendors have specific information is especially important. Whether the vendor is a concessionaire bringing in a stand-alone trailer to a snowmobile race, or a charity group collecting money for a good cause at the event, all should have the same rules. A time prior to the gates opening should be established for all vendors to be set up and ready to open. It can cause significant disruption to the event flow if a vendor arrives late and needs to drive into the event area after the perimeter has been established and gates are open for patrons. Simply transporting a folding table through a crowd of people to accommodate a late-arriving charity group can be dangerous and will interrupt the event flow. Event managers need to be ready to turn away vendors that arrive late and/or do not follow established protocol.

Sponsor, Official, and Spectator Needs

The last wave of setup is those areas used by sponsors, officials, and spectators. Event managers should meet officials in a designated area and escort them to their locker rooms and answer any questions they may have. Weather can also impact setup in spectator areas. For outdoor venues, simple actions such as drying off wet seats or having ponchos for spectators when it rains will help to create a good atmosphere. In hot weather, umbrellas and/or misters can be used to provide a place for fans to cool off.

When the gates open, everything should be "open for business." Concessionaires should have the hot dogs hot, sponsor areas should be established and appropriately staffed, scoreboards should be on, and music should be playing to create the event atmosphere. Once setup is complete, it is not long before teardown begins.

Teardown

Teardown is simply the reverse of setup, and event managers should strive to leave no trace behind. During teardown the facility is restored to its pre-event condition. This means that every sign and every piece of trash is removed from the site, and all tables, chairs, and other equipment are returned to storage. Some venues may not require this much attention to teardown, but event managers that put in the extra effort in teardown will impress rights holders and venue management. When relying on volunteers, it is difficult to motivate them to stay for teardown. Generally, they have worked a long day and are ready to go home at this point. The management skills and enthusiasm of the event manager will be essential to make sure teardown is as smooth and as quick as possible.

In general, the different groups involved in an event tend to leave in the same order they arrived. Again, the teardown process will take about half as long as setup. The parking lots are the first to be torn down. Midway through the event, barricades can come down and parking staff released. Event staff will also be released in shifts as the game progresses. The ticket taking and gate security areas are generally shut down one-half to two-thirds of the way through the event. Vendors will begin their teardown prior to the conclusion of the event as well. For instance, a temporary concessions setup will probably sell until the last quarter of the event, and then shut down as business winds down. This allows for adequate time for clean-up and financial reconciliation, without losing much revenue in the final minutes of the event.

Spectators will leave at the conclusion of the event (barring any unique circumstances), and teardown of any special seating can begin at that time. Participants (unless there are post-event press conferences), the bulk of the event staff, and game officials follow the spectators. Special attention should be given to the safety of game officials. They should be escorted to their vehicles as they exit the facility. The last group to leave is usually the media. The working media area should be available for a few hours after the conclusion of the event so they can finish their work without having to change locations. The event manager should stay until the media have finished working. Usually, during this time, event managers are finalizing all teardown and ensuring the venue is as clean as possible.

A running or cycling course will be different than a traditional venue. For a course, teardown will begin immediately after the last athlete has left the starting area. The starting area is torn down immediately, and the teardown team will follow the last athlete, taking down water stations and barricades as the race progresses. As the majority of participants pass the fluid stations on a course, the tables and cups will begin to be consolidated. The number of tables that were set up at the beginning will slowly begin to be reduced, those tables broken down, and the area cleaned, even as the last runners are utilizing the fluid station. A systematic approach to teardown will keep it from distracting from the main event. Whether the event is in a traditional or non-traditional venue, a good teardown operation will be invisible to the spectators and participants.

Creating and Managing *Green* Events

Michael E. Pfahl

There are several key points to keep in mind when integrating environmentally friendly practices into the event planning process, no matter the size of the organization or event. While specific events have different levels of environmental planning needs, these keys are applicable across all events. First, an organization's sustainability policy must be integrated into the mission of the event, indicating the planning members' commitment to *green* practices. Once the mission is identified and understood by all constituents, then specific action points can be developed for the overall event plan and the sub-plans that comprise it. Second, like any other aspect of the planning process, the environmental initiatives should have clear implementation, control, and review guidelines developed as part of the overall event management plan. These guidelines must be developed in conjunction with the broader strategy to ensure success. Further, integration helps to foresee complications during the event due to poor planning of green objectives, or to identify potential roadblocks to the success of the green initiatives. Placing the green objectives under the same rigorous criteria as any other aspect of the event plan sends a clear signal as to their importance to the overall event and adds accountability for the event managers. Third, clear and consistent communication of the green objectives to internal and external constituents alleviates uncertainty and encourages individual ownership in the success of the green objectives and overall event. In addition, the external constituents involved in the event are directly encouraged to act in environmentally responsible ways after the event concludes.

In order to accomplish the key points outlined above, a set of *Environmental Levels of Activity* are provided below. These levels are meant to guide event planners toward their desired goals for green planning.

Level 1: Basic Environmental Planning

- Recycle bins for paper, plastic, cardboard, and other materials used during the event
- Goals and procedures to reduce the paperwork associated with the event (internally and externally)
- Moderate environmental language in external relations channels (e.g., press releases, promotional materials) to engage the public in the event's green goals in addition to the event itself
- Commit to environmentally friendly practices as a team; develop an incentive-based reward system for members of the event planning staff and event attendees for their contributions to the green goals
- Obtain any food, beverages, and other materials from local sources (as applicable)

Level 2: Intermediate Environmental Planning (Level 1 plus the following items)

- Partnerships with local community groups to promote green initiatives at the event and to manage the collection and removal of recycled items
- Use of electronic means to advertise and promote the event
- Use Energy Star rated electronic equipment wherever possible

- Utilization of biodegradable or recyclable materials for food and beverages service (e.g., biodegradable cups, utensils, plates)

- Unused food donated to local food banks or charitable/community organizations

- Use of Green Seal cleaning products for event clean-up and removal

Level 3: Advanced Environmental Planning (Levels 1 & 2 plus the following items)

- Paperless internal planning, promotion, and implementation processes

- Paperless registration and dissemination of promotional and other information to external constituents

- Corporate and community partners to promote green initiatives at the event and to manage collection and removal of recycled items

- Activism through placement of advocacy organizations and corporate organizations at the event to promote awareness and behavioral change among participants and the broader community (through media exposure)

- Encourage carpooling by event attendees with possibility of reward (e.g., discounted fee) for such actions

- Use of biodegradable and recyclable materials in any promotional giveaways (e.g., wallet card with environmentally friendly tips included in re-usable gift bag)

- Development and utilization of vendor guidelines including requests (and preference) for vendors with environmentally friendly product offerings.

EVENT DAY MAINTENANCE

Maintenance is not glamorous, but it is critical to a successful event. Event day maintenance does cross over with concepts from setup and teardown. Field, court, and course event day maintenance is often left to a grounds crews and facility management staff. However, all event managers should have basic knowledge of the maintenance requirements for fields, courts, and courses. For traditional sport venues such as outdoor sports-plexes, stadiums, and arenas, it is likely that the event day maintenance will be included in the contract to use the venue. Turf management and field maintenance is a highly specialized area, with many turf managers having advanced degrees in horticulture or related areas. However, savvy event managers will be ready to step in and help whenever needed.

The event day maintenance of courses is the most challenging due to the course being used for other functions until the event starts. A race course may be open to vehicle traffic until the lead group of runners approaches a specific intersection. Maintenance issues can range from having to fix temporary directional indicators that get inadvertently moved, to having a manhole cover go missing.

Indoor surfaces require minimal attention. Keeping the court clean and dry so it is safe for the athletes is the main concern for indoor courts. It is not the intention of this section to prepare event managers for all possible maintenance issues during an event, but to provide some examples of areas that require attention before, during, and after events.

Natural Grass Fields

Generally, event managers will not be responsible for extensive field maintenance. If the grounds crew does a good job up until game day, there should not be too much to worry about. However, during a multi-day event where fields are getting heavy use, the event managers will want to keep an eye on wear and tear and be knowledgeable enough to help with maintenance. Even after a long day of games when everyone involved is exhausted, taking care of the fields is important to ensure some recovery overnight.

Baseball and Softball

Baseball and softball fields require the most attention of outdoor fields because they are a mixture of grass and dirt. Most coaches and players are also knowledgeable about field maintenance and are used to helping with the fields. Event managers should not exclusively rely on coaches and players, but often these groups are willing to help.

Game day maintenance for baseball and softball will vary with the weather and the number of games being played. If a multi-game tournament is being held on a field, re-lining will take place approximately every third game (or other designated number of games appropriate for the conditions). The time required for this must be factored into the day's schedule. Budgeting for supplies and staff to perform the function is also important. Some common pre- and post-game maintenance tasks include:

Pre-Game Routine

- Remove tarps

- Mow grass

- Scarify the dirt areas using a spiker

- Drag the skinned areas smooth

- Water the infield area

- Set the chalk lines

- Place pitcher's mat on mound for batting practice

- Set up safety screen for pitcher for batting practice

- Paint/wash bases, pitching plate, and home plate

- Place bases

Post-Game Routine

- Remove bases and cover base anchors

- Drag skinned area and baselines

- Recondition mound and home plate area

- Replace, fill, and pack loose divots in turf

- Tarp if needed (The Baseball Tomorrow Fund, n.d.)

Baseball fields do not tolerate rain very well and can become unplayable quickly. In the event of rain immediately prior to or during the game, a rain delay is often called. To combat wet weather, most fields (except youth fields) will have tarps available to protect the infield. Drainage installed in the outfield, the soil composition, and a crown will also help handle the water. A crown refers to the slope of the field, and helps drain the field. In baseball and softball, the field slopes slightly away from the baselines to the warning track area to aid in drainage.

During a game, the tarp needs to be easily accessible and a "tarp crew" established. Some newer tarps with a lifting and rolling device may only require a few people, but in most circumstances, the players are the "tarp crew" and 15–20 of them are needed. It can take 10 minutes or more to tarp the field and get it protected, so the longer officials and event managers take to decide whether to call a rain delay, the more damage is done to the field. If lightning is a concern, the safety of the tarp crew far outweighs the need to get the field covered.

Tarps are either edged with chain, use sand bags, or use spikes to hold them down. It is important that wind is not allowed under the edges, as a blowing tarp allows for water to get to the field. If the game is able to resume, the tarp is removed, drying agents are used where water has pooled on the dirt, and the field is dragged before play resumes. Extra sod, chalk, drying agents, and even green paint to fill in dead spots on the grass will all come in handy during a long event.

Football, Soccer, Lacrosse, and Field Hockey

Football, soccer, lacrosse, and field hockey fields rarely require much attention from event managers. Besides mowing, striping, replacing large divots, and general field setup, there is little to do pre-game if the field is well cared for. Most of these fields will be crowned, with the highest point on the field running down the center of the field from end zone to end zone or goal to goal. Thus, water is propelled towards the sidelines to aid in overall field drainage. If the field is unable to drain as quickly as the rain is coming down, damage to the field can be expected. If any field becomes slippery and dangerous, game delays and/or cancellations are an option.

At some point in the career of event managers, it is likely that painting lines on a field will be required. Many outdoor sports require that the field be lined for both practice and competition. If a grounds crew is available, this task will fall to them. However, event managers should know the basics of how to string and line a field. For natural grass fields, choosing the right paint, preparing the field, and having proper equipment are keys to success. To keep the grass in good condition, water-based paints are preferred (LaRue, LaRue, & Sawyer, 2005). String, small spikes, spray paint, and a field striper are all essential equipment. In some cases, more complex field stripers use pour-in paint as opposed to spray cans. Even a simple soccer field requires specific instructions, attention to detail, and patience to line it correctly. To line a field, the dimensions and layout of the field, string, spikes, a hammer, a tape measure, a paint liner, cans of paint, and a few people are all needed (Cecil Soccer, n.d.). The outside field lines are measured, staked, and strung first, with the goal boxes and other field markings following. Although the dimensions and layout will change, the principles are the same for painting all natural grass fields.

For those fields requiring more complex logos, call in the experts. Heavy plastic stencils are the most common way to paint a logo on a field, but using a drawing and then creating a scaled grid on the field is also a frequent approach. A projector can be set up and the logo projected onto the field and then painted in as well. Logos can be painted free hand by artistically talented people, but with this method comes a lot of room for error. The majority of outdoor fields are natural grass, so event managers need to be familiar with all aspects of maintenance, especially related to needs during inclement weather.

Synthetic Fields

Synthetic fields have become extremely popular in recent years. They do not require mowing, are more durable than natural grass, can easily handle heavy rains, do not require recovery periods, and the quality continues to improve. However, they do require care. Most new synthetic fields are top dressed with infill that is some combination of sand, rubber, recycled tires, or other plastic material. This material must be evenly spread on the field using small tractors to ensure a level playing surface.

Synthetic turfs do retain more heat than natural grass and can be over 30° warmer than a natural grass field (New York State Department of Health, 2008). Not only is the heat retained within the turf, but it radiates to the playing area, with temperatures in one study at head-level reaching 138°F on a 98°F day (New York State Department of Health, 2008). Watering the field can lower temperatures temporarily, but due to good drainage, the field returns to being hot quickly. Event managers need to account for this increase in heat for summer events on synthetic fields in their emergency medical planning.

Lines on synthetic fields will generally be permanently "painted" through the use of white turf. If temporary lines or logos are needed, there is removable paint available. The application is similar to that for natural grass, but it needs to be tested on a small and out-of-the-way section of turf prior to using it. The paint is usually designed to be washed away with a remover solution, a bit of agitation from a brush, and a light pressure wash. The advent of improved temporary paint products allows synthetic turf fields to be used for a variety of sports.

Courses

Courses can be maintenance free or they can be a massive maintenance nightmare, depending on the characteristics of the event, the location, and the weather. As indicated throughout this book, venues that are created specifically for an event are more difficult than traditional venues to manage. This can also be true with respect to maintenance. It is helpful if a line is painted (usually blue) on the course of a race several days before the race so that participants can easily see where they are supposed to go. This may require traffic to be shut down for several hours, which will likely require the event organizers to work on the municipality's timetable. Often, painting is completed in the middle of the night when there is less traffic. Given the large area covered by many courses, there is a lot of space that cannot be controlled all the time by event managers. Imagine trying to anticipate road conditions, set up barriers for spectators, and organize a bicycle race on a 100-mile stretch of road. Now, imagine trying to set up and manage that same race while the road is open to vehicles on the same day.

The many unknowns are also what make races a lot of fun to manage; anything can happen. A water main could break 10 miles into the course and flood the road, and it is up to the event managers to make sure they know who to call, and to be there to help resolve the issue before the cyclists arrive at that spot (or re-route them). As for general course maintenance, the course conditions are at the mercy of the weather. Since most events that use a course are endurance related, where athletes are exerting themselves at a high level for long periods of time, the event managers should have a good handle on the expected weather and possible impact on the participants. In heat, extra water and medical personnel should be called in; and in rain, event organizers should be ready for slip-related injuries. In wet conditions, event managers should be especially careful with any banner or chip mats that runners will actually run over during the race. These plastic surfaces can become very slippery and dangerous in the rain.

With evolving technology, there is also maintenance to go along with timing systems. It is common practice for major road races to use microchips for more accurate timing. These chips are worn by runners, and when the runners pass over chip mats that are spread out on the course in intervals, their time at that point in the race is recorded. In some major races it takes more than 10 minutes for the back of the pack to cross the starting line after the gun goes off, so chips allow a runner's net time to start only when he or she passes the chip mat located at the starting line, whereas the runner's official time is recorded from the time the race starts. However, these systems are not without problems. Experts on the timing systems should be on hand to address any issues that may arise. There is little room for error when dealing with timing systems.

Other Surfaces

Indoor surfaces (except ice) are less troublesome than most outdoor surfaces. For wood floor playing surfaces, a dry sweeper and towels need to be on hand to dry the court if needed and remove any debris. The event managers should also know how to tighten a volleyball net or adjust any equipment that is part of the game they are managing. It may sound simple, but often special equipment is needed to do it correctly.

Sports played on ice have specific maintenance needs that are probably beyond the expertise of the event managers. Large and expensive ice resurfacers, such as Zambonis and Olympias, are required to keep the ice clean, at a consistent thickness, and smooth for the athletes. Prior to the event, the ice crew will take measurements of the ice thickness in a variety of areas and then reshape the ice, if needed, to ensure a consistent thickness. It is common to have the edges of the ice rink become thicker than the middle due to the ice resurfacer driver slowing down around the edges (which puts more water on the ice) and driving faster down the middle of the rink (limiting the amount of water put down).

Outdoor tennis courts do not require much maintenance during an event unless it rains. In the event of rain, event managers need to have a lot of people ready to work hard to dry the courts as soon as the rain stops. There are specific squeegees made for drying tennis courts, and many should be available for event staff at any tennis event. The goal after a rain delay in tennis is to get the courts dry as quickly as possible so play can resume.

Maintaining all playing surfaces throughout an event allows athletes to perform safely and at their best. Additionally, for natural turf fields, post-game maintenance is crucial to allow for field recovery overnight.

General Facility Maintenance

Besides playing surfaces, event managers should be aware of the entire venue and its maintenance. It would be impossible to mention every maintenance scenario in this book. However, once event managers are thinking about the facility as a whole as well as each space individually, they will notice maintenance issues in a timely manner and be able to react to each appropriately. By walking around the venue and listening to patrons, maintenance issues will be identified. A spill at concessions, a clogged toilet, or broken seats are examples of common maintenance issues that occur at events.

Event managers should have a facility management point of contact that is available to address these types of general facility maintenance issues. Prior to the event, event managers should make sure the facility has trained maintenance personnel either on-call or on-site so that problems that arise can be resolved quickly. Especially for areas that impact the operation of the core event activity (e.g., timing systems and scoreboards) personnel should be on-site and available. Maintenance personnel that might need to be available, depending on event needs and equipment use, include a plumber, electrician (scoreboard, lighting, timing system, etc.), sound specialist, elevator/escalator specialist, and telephone repair.

A good maintenance plan, although not a direct responsibility of the event managers, will help the event to run smoothly. The list of items that could need maintenance during an event is endless, but common areas have been addressed here related to playing surfaces and the facility to help event managers plan ahead for maintenance issues they might be faced with.

My Event Is Too Big

Mauro Palmero

As an event manager at a major sports complex from 2005–2007, I learned how to handle an event that was too big. Among other areas, I was responsible for managing the boys' and girls' basketball and baseball events for a large client. During that time, such events where quickly outgrowing our venues.

My responsibilities included finding extra venue space, coordinating the logistics of holding multiple and simultaneous events outside our facilities, and ensuring that the event was a success. That encompassed: (a) establishing a relationship with all the schools and private sports venues in the area; (b) reserving dates at each venue; (c) getting contracts signed for each venue; (d) hiring site supervisors; (e) coordinating equipment and supply delivery to each site; and (f) being the liaison between our client and the off-site venues before, during, and after every event. These tasks occurred on an annual basis.

I began the event management process in October for events occurring the next summer. I traveled around visiting all middle and high schools that had a gym and/or a baseball field, plus any other privately owned sports venue in the area. After that, I met with our client's sport managers to discuss the feasibility of events at each site.

November through May, my job consisted mainly of establishing new relationships with sites that had been added from the previous year (the incremental growth in number of teams participating demanded more space every year) and strengthening existing relationships with the schools continuing to be involved. The relationship management process included the negotiation of space usage (who, what, when, equipment needed), rental price (every school had a different price and fees), and contract issues (insurance, indemnification, waivers). Simultaneously, I was monitoring all space reserved and making adjustments to reservations based on the needs of the venue and needs of our client. Even with the best planning, scheduling conflicts would arise because the venues had other events and/or our client had increasing space needs.

By mid-May, I had most of the venue contracts signed and started working on the logistics of each event. Many details were important for the success of each event. To ensure success (and less headache for me during the events) I would: (1) make sure every off-site venue had a copy of our client's insurance policy; (2) make sure every off-site venue had an updated schedule they were comfortable with; (3) make sure the site director for each venue was contracted (including amount and form of payment) and he or she was aware of his or her responsibilities; (4) make sure each venue was scheduled to receive the appropriate equipment at the right time and in the correct amount (estimate based on prior years); (5) make sure that medical assistance for each venue was contracted and scheduled; (6) make sure the coordinator of officials had an updated schedule and directions to each venue; and (7) make sure that our client had updated directions to each venue to provide to teams and spectators.

By June, I held training sessions for all our staff, event coordinators, and interns assigned to work the summer events. Training included an explanation of daily responsibilities (e.g., checking equipment inventory, contact site director, pickup score sheets, etc.) and what to do (or who to call) in scenarios outside their responsibility area. For example, event coordinators were supposed to call me if it was a venue-related issue, and if it was a tournament-related issue they were supposed to call the client's representative. I also had the event coordinators and other event managers that were returning from the previous season share their experiences and best practices with the newcomers.

By early July, before all events started, I prepared an off-site coverage schedule that determined every event worker's responsibilities and assigned their daily location during the event. Event staff worked on a rotation (opening, mid-day, and closing) from place to place to ensure full coverage during the entire event. Throughout the events, I visited each venue regularly and addressed any issues that had occurred. Sometimes, it was merely bringing supplies and updates from the tournament headquarters, and other times there were issues that needed my attention on-site. Concurrently, I would begin paying venue rent and site director salaries for the events that were about to end.

By mid-August, when the last boys' basketball tournament was ending, I started reconciling each event and retrieving leftover equipment from each location. I would also send a "thank you" package (ours and our client's swag) to each off-site venue. Over the course of the summer, I had worked fifty-one days straight and driven 3,000 miles.

For any event manager, managing simultaneous events at a variety of facilities is a challenge. It is the good relationships that are cultivated that will allow event managers the flexibility to use off-site venues if the event outgrows existing space. Even with all of the hard work and long hours, watching events grow year after year and being able to provide opportunities for a large number of athletes to compete is a rewarding experience.

EQUIPMENT

Equipment can encompass a lot of different items in sport. Basketball goals, an award stand, and even a popcorn popper in concessions are all equipment. The role of event managers is to make sure the appropriate equipment is available, that it works correctly, and that back-up equipment is available for key functions. This all has to be accomplished within the budget. A list of common equipment needed to run an event is provided in Figure 14-1.

Capital Equipment

Capital equipment is generally considered to be any piece of equipment costing over $500 with a useful life of two or more years (Mull, Bayless & Jamieson, 2005). This type of equipment is likely owned by the facility and includes items such as basketball goals, portable flooring, staging, concessions equipment, and floor coverings. However, for events in non-traditional sport venues, such as road races, capital equipment may include scoreboards, timing equipment, and barricades. It is likely that a road race would need to rent this equipment unless it is owned by the host organization, city, or county.

Figure 14-1. Detailed List of Equipment

- Barricades
- Batteries (AA, AAA, and all the voltages)
- Bike rack
- Blowers
- Brooms, rakes, and/or squeegees
- "Buffy stakes" (the stakes that real estate professionals use for putting up yard signs)
- Bullhorns
- Bungee cords
- Cable cutters (small and large)
- Cable mats
- Cable ramps (Bumble Bees and Yellow Jackets)
- Cable ramps add-ons for ADA compliance (WASP ramps: Walkway Access for Special Purposes)
- Calculators
- Carpet (triathlon-specific, but could be used elsewhere, too)
- Cat litter (or VoBAN for spills)
- Chairs
- Clip boards
- Cinder blocks
- Computers
- Cones and/or delineator posts (w/bases)
- Coolers (for storage and for dispensing)
- Copier (high speed)
- Cork boards
- Cups
- Dry erase boards and markers
- Dumpsters
- Ear pieces and speaker mics for two-way radios
- Fax machines
- First aid kit
- Flags
- Flashlights
- Fuel for generators and/or golf carts
- Gator utility vehicles
- Generators

- Gloves (work gloves and rubber gloves)
- Golf carts (4-passenger, 8-passenger, flat-bed/utility)
- Greenery/plants
- Grommets and grommet maker
- Hand carts and/or flat-bed dollies
- Hand sanitizer
- Hand and foot warmers (disposable; for outdoor winter events)
- Hand wash stations
- Heat sheets
- Hoses—fire and garden (along with nozzles, hydrant connectors, and hydrant wrenches)
- Ice
- Laminator
- Lanyards (for credentials)
- L-Poles/signage poles
- Lightning detector (outdoor events)
- Linens (tablecloths, drapes, towels, etc.)
- Misting tents/machines (misters)
- "Office in a Box" (pens, pencils, binders, highlighters, labels, dividers, envelopes, receipt book, appropriate stamps, index cards, Sharpies/Marks-A-Lot [for body marking], 3-hole punch)
- Padlocks (combination so they can be opened even if the key is lost)
- Pallet jack
- Pallets
- Paper
- Pennants
- Phones (land line and cell)
- Pipe and drape
- Plywood
- Portable toilets (ADA and regular)
- Portable restroom trailers
- Power strips and industrial extension cords
- Printers
- Production manuals
- Radios (two-way/walkie-talkies)
- Rain ponchos/rain gear
- Results boards

- Risers
- Rope and/or twine
- Safety pins
- Sand bags
- Scanners
- Score cards
- Shovels
- Shrink wrap and dispensers
- Snow fence and/or scrim
- Sport-specific equipment (soccer balls and goals, tennis balls, etc.)
- Sports fence
- Spray adhesive
- Spray chalk
- Spray paint
- Stages
- Stop watches (minimum of 2)
- Storage boxes (plastic/waterproof)
- Storage trailers (sea containers)
- Surveyor's tape
- SWAG (Stuff We All Get)—gifts (T-shirts, hats, etc. for various parties)
- Tablecloths and table skirts
- Tables
- Tape (duct, masking, electrical, scotch, packing, etc.)
- Tents (pop-up and/or vendor-delivered)
- Toilet paper
- Tool kits
- Towels
- Tower lights
- Trailers (for on-site office space and/or storage)
- Trash and recycling bags
- Trash boxes (Duso boxes: foldable wax-coated garbage boxes)
- Trash cans
- Trays (coroplast or wax-coated cardboard sheets used for stacking water cups on tables)
- Umbrellas
- Utility cabinets

- Utility knives
- Velcro
- Visqueen (poly sheeting)—for rain cover
- Wet/dry vac
- Whistles
- Wire
- Wire cutters
- Zip ties (various lengths and widths)

Expendable Equipment

Expendable equipment is less expensive, less than $500, and has a useful life of less than two years (Mull, Bayless & Jamieson, 2005). Because of the shorter lifespan, this type of equipment is replaced as it wears out. Volleyballs, folding tables and chairs, and basketball goal safety padding are all considered expendable equipment. Facilities may or may not own the needed expendable equipment for a specific event. Any expendable equipment provided by the venue should be carefully examined to make sure it is safe, clean, and reliable. If the facility cannot provide the needed expendable equipment, event organizers will need to purchase or rent it.

Fixed Equipment

Fixed equipment is attached to the facility and could include spectator seating, scoreboards, and mechanical systems. Use of this equipment is part of using the venue. Often, fixed equipment is complex and requires someone specially trained to operate it. For example, scoreboard systems vary considerably from facility to facility. The scoreboard operator should be either provided by the facility, or training should be provided by the facility management to a member of the event management team.

Supplies

Supplies are items used on a regular basis that may or may not relate to the core activity of the event. Even if the event is a major football game, supplies such as paper, pens, credentials, and ticket stock will be needed to execute many event functions. Small items, such as greenery and temporary signage, would also fall into the supply category, as these help to create the event atmosphere.

Purchasing vs. Renting

Deciding whether to purchase or rent equipment is often a function of availability, price, and frequency of use. Once it is realized that equipment is needed, event managers should begin researching the equipment. The best scenario is to borrow the equipment from a local sports team or club that already owns the equipment. Another way to obtain equipment is to receive it as a "trade" for a sponsorship. If those are not options, then the cost of buying versus renting should be examined.

If the event is recurring in nature and there is a high likelihood that the equipment will be needed on a regular basis, often purchasing makes the most sense. Depending on the location of the event, some equipment might not be available for rent, or it is cost prohibitive to ship the items a great distance for a short rental period. However, in most cases, renting is less expensive than purchasing.

Equipment such as bike barricades (the heavy metal barricades that are used to separate participants from spectators or to create entrance gates) are expensive to purchase. However, because they are very heavy, they are also expensive to rent. Oftentimes, items like this are better to purchase for recurring events (e.g., a small college athletic department needs them for multiple sports and multiple events) because of the transportation costs associated with renting. For a traveling golf tournament, it might be necessary to set up temporary bleacher seating to accommodate the crowd. In this case, renting the seating is probably more appropriate than buying, since it will need to be constructed by representatives from the company and because there is no use for the seating after the event concludes.

Bidding

With respect to equipment, **bidding** refers to a competitive process in which companies are asked to provide service and price information based on criteria set by the event organizers. It is similar to bidding to host an event, but usually much less complex. Many public entities require that purchases/rentals over a certain cost be bid out. Whether it is required or not, bidding is a good practice because the event managers will be able to compare what companies can provide based on set criteria. Event managers need to be clear and detailed in the **request for bid (RFB)**, which is the letter seeking out prices on the equipment needed. If the equipment is complex and needs someone with special knowledge to set it up, then the setup should be part of the RFB. Any special costs the company charges for shipping, delivery, or pickup (in the case of a rental) should also be itemized. For equipment being purchased, there should be some expectation of a warranty written into the RFB. Event mangers can do research to see what a standard warranty is for that type of equipment. If the equipment purchased is so specialized that only the vendor selling it can service or repair it, be sure to request standard hourly rates for servicing and/or specific requirements related to service. Also, determining who pays for shipping of the equipment when servicing is needed, what the time needed for repair is, and the limits or exclusions to any warranty are important to know. If the equipment must be delivered on a certain day at a certain time, the RFB should be clear about that expectation. Upon delivery, all equipment needs to be inspected to ensure it is in good working order before delivery is accepted.

Let's use a fictitious youth soccer tournament for an example. The event managers recognize that, because of the location of the tournament and lack of existing restrooms, port-a-potties are needed for both spectators and participants. The event hosts certainly do not want to buy the port-a-potties, but they do need to rent them. A guideline ratio for port-a-potties is one per 75 people for regular port-a-potties, and one per 150 people for ADA units. With 200 participants, 300 spectators, and 50 volunteers, it is estimated that a total of 10 port-a-potties are needed. The regular and ADA units can be combined to arrive at the total needed, and the number of units should always be rounded up when in doubt. The event managers may decide to order six regular and four ADA compliant port-a-potties.

The event managers then write a letter that they will fax to all port-a-potty companies within 150 miles of the event. The letter is specific as to the number of units needed, the drop-off date and time, the location of the toilets, and the pick-up date and time. If it is a multi-day event, the letter will also need to request a cost to have the toilets serviced at the end or beginning of each day. The letter then asks interested companies to respond by a specific date and time with how much they would charge to provide the toilets. This letter is the RFB. The company that responds with the lowest price within the bid specifications then is awarded the job.

The benefit to bidding is that the companies involved know it is a competitive process and thus will submit the best price possible hoping to win the job. If event managers were to call the first company listed in the phone book, they do not have any leverage to lower the price.

Equipment Storage

The amount of equipment needed for the event will dictate storage needs. For smaller events it may be that storage is the trunk of a car or a small closet. For others, an entire warehouse might be required to accommodate all of the equipment and supplies. To try and manage storage needs, special attention should be paid to the specifics of delivery (and pickup, if rented) of equipment. Storage issues can be just as significant whether equipment arrives too early or too late. The challenges with equipment arriving too late are obvious. However, early-arriving equipment can create major storage problems. For most venues, storage is a concern on a daily basis, and the facilities do not have room to store extra equipment prior to an event.

For those events with significant storage needs, a rented warehouse or storage unit might be the answer. If the venue is being constructed for the event, there probably will not be any on-site storage. In this case, it is important that the storage is located in a convenient location to the event, is large enough, and is accessible 24 hours a day. Most, if not all, of the items stored will eventually need to be transported to the event location, so the closer it is to the event facility, the better. If large pieces of equipment will be required to be moved, then there needs to be access to a forklift (and forklift operator), pallet jack, or hand cart, depending on the size of the equipment.

Other temporary options for storage are sea containers and tents. Sea containers are large metal boxes traditionally used to transport materials on ships. They can then easily be transferred to the frame of a large truck for over-the-road transport. They can be placed on-site at temporary events. They have the advantage of being able to be locked, and some can include climate control. Tents are inexpensive and easy to use as storage, but have some disadvantages. They require security personnel on-site to ensure that the materials inside are not stolen. If the tent is set up on a soft surface, it may be necessary rent a temporary floor to keep materials from getting muddy if it rains.

Other Equipment Considerations

All equipment should be checked, double-checked, and then checked again immediately prior to use. Oftentimes, equipment will work perfectly when tested the day before the event, but then on event day a problem will occur. Or, the equipment works well in an empty stadium, but once 20,000 people arrive it fails. This is a common scenario with wireless microphones, headsets, and other communications equipment that is sensitive to interference.

Even if a piece of equipment seems to be functioning perfectly, back-up equipment is needed for critical operational functions. Anything related to timing and scoring is critical to event operations. Thus, portable shot clocks, play clocks, game clocks, manual scorecards, stopwatches, and paper and pens for hand scoring and statistics should be available quickly. Ideally, these crucial pieces of equipment and supplies are ready at the first sign of trouble. If the shot clocks go down in the middle of a nationally televised basketball game, the event manager should be able to get the back-up unit from around the corner of the primary space and have it hooked up and working in less time than it takes for a full commercial break. Being ready, staying calm, and handling these types of situations are the mark of great event managers.

Understanding the capital, fixed, and expendable equipment needs as well as the supplies required for the event should begin early in the planning process. Then, when the date of the event approaches, the event manager will check and double-check that the equipment has been bid out and ordered, that there is storage available, that the equipment has arrived intact and operable, that someone knows how to operate it, and that someone is available to fix it on-site if it is critical to the event function.

EVENT FLOW

The **event flow** takes into account the best traffic pattern for the event. Traffic patterns are the literal traffic of car and bus arrival, but also the foot traffic of all involved parties (i.e., spectators, participants, and officials). The concept of universal design introduced in Chapter 2, Event Feasibility, also applies here, as all of those that could possibly be involved in an event should have easy access and use of the facility. Keeping in mind those that might have disabilities, not speak the language, be illiterate, or have other characteristics different from the majority, should be part of the planning of event flow. Specifically, consideration and attention must be given to the following aspects of flow:

- Quickly getting vehicles to the location
- Getting people to the venue

- Emergency vehicle access

- Putting people in contact with the various areas that will bring in revenue (i.e., tickets, concessions, registration, merchandise)

- Moving people from parking to purchasing their tickets

- Smoothly purchasing concessions without missing the event

- Participant registration

- Merchandise sales

- Avoiding confusion, cross-traffic, and backtracking in all areas

One of the first questions event managers should ask themselves when reviewing an event is, what is the flow for the event? The flow should be a natural progression from beginning to end. Putting themselves in the place of the various represented groups is a good starting point for event managers. Pretend to be a spectator arriving by car. What is the first thing seen, what is the second? How do I know where to park? How do I know where to go when I exit my car? How do I remember where my car is parked? These are the types of questions that event managers start to ask as they visualize flow and conduct walk-thrus. The flow should be created from the perspective of someone who has never experienced this event before.

The easiest way to conceptualize flow is in a time sequence. Who will be arriving first and how? What happens next? And then what? Let's take the example of a marathon, because it is one of the most complex sports events encountered with respect to flow. For other events, the thought process is the same, it is just less complex. For the fictitious marathon which will be used to illustrate flow concepts in the following sections, a few assumptions will be made:

1) The start of the marathon is in a location relatively far away from participant arrival and there is no parking at the start.

2) It is a Point A to Point B race, rather than a Point A to Point A, or circuitous, race.

3) The organizers of the marathon will provide transportation to the start for the runners via motor coach.

4) The marathon is very popular, very large, and sold out.

Vehicular Flow

When examining how vehicles will arrive at an event, event managers need to take into consideration how many different types of vehicles are coming in, including emergency vehicles, deliveries, spectator vehicles, participant vehicles, and police, to name a few. How does each group get in and out, and what roadways are available?

Working Vehicles

In the case of the fictitious marathon, vehicles working the event will be taken into consideration first. What access points do they need? Where will they need to deliver equipment and supplies? Will they be coming into the same locations as spectators and participants? If these groups are arriving several hours earlier than spectators and participants it may not be an issue. However, if there is the possibility of any vehicles needing access while spectators are there, a specific plan for how they are going to enter, where, and what type of access control is at that location needs to be developed. As discussed previously, avoiding all vehicles within the event perimeter once the gates open is preferred. Questions such as what do to if the vehicle enters the wrong area, how do they turn around, and what type of space is available for parking for these vehicles if they need to stay should all be addressed.

A designated emergency lane is probably needed for large events. There may even be a need for multiple emergency access points. For the example marathon, there must be emergency access along the entire route to ensure an ambulance can reach an injured runner quickly. The emergency lane can even be a lane off the side of the road that is grass, but it has to be something that would enable an emergency vehicle to get through, and the emergency responders need to know and accept the plan. If the lane is grass, event mangers need to ensure it can withstand rain and still be passable.

Drop-Offs

In the case of cars dropping off people, a location or multiple locations should be designated where cars can easily get in and get back on the road without crossing traffic. In addition to cars dropping off people, runners are transported via bus to the starting line for the marathon in the example. So, the cars should not disrupt the flow pattern for the buses.

Motor coach buses generally seat anywhere from 44 to 54 passengers. These are quite large and require a good bit of room for maneuverability. What types of considerations should be taken into account as far as their movement? For safety reasons, the drop-off location for the bus should not require it to back up at any time. The bus should come in, drop people off, and then continue in the same forward direction on its way out of the area. Another consideration is to have the drop-off point so that the doors of the bus open towards the event entrance where, in this case, the staging area is for the start of the race. People should not have to get off the bus and go around the front, and definitely not the back, of the bus to get to the event entrance. That is dangerous, slows down egress from the bus, the buses overall, and movement into the staging area. For events with international participants where language might be a barrier, the more natural the flow, the better, so that participants exit the bus and directly continue walking to the next point.

In allowing for this, the event managers responsible for managing transportation may need to arrange for and manage what are called "contra lanes," contra meaning "against." **Contra lanes** are vehicle lanes in which vehicles travel opposite the normal direction of traffic. This may be necessary to keep the buses from turning around, so they can swiftly get back to the origination location and pick up additional participants. For example, if the event is near freeway exit ramps, buses could be allowed to drive up what would normally be a down ramp, across the overpass, and then get back onto the roadway in the normal direction via the opposite ramp. Event managers will have to work with the applicable municipal agencies in the event's jurisdiction that control those roads to set up and manage contra lanes. It will also be important to make sure the bus company has trained all of its drivers on the proper route, and that appropriate staff are on-site to direct the flow. Contra lanes could also be necessary for various work vehicles, such as supply and delivery trucks.

Driving In

For this fictitious marathon, participants and/or spectators will not be driving in, but for other events they will be. In that case, what does the parking flow look like? How are cars being parked? Is there parking staff helping people park? Giving people choices can be a bad thing in some cases. Think about large amusement parks. When cars pull in, people are directing them exactly where to park, all the way to the exact parking space. People are not given a choice. Cars go through systematically and it flows well. They may put 20–30 cars per minute through the toll plaza, and can park cars quickly and get people into the park to spend money that much sooner.

Event managers should make sure parking flows well and people know where to go based on being able to see staff directing them to park. From there, event managers want to take into consideration things like how are the cars being parked? Are they angle parking or straight-in parking? Which way causes the fewest potential problems for drivers? How are parking areas identified so people can find their car at the end of the event? Event managers also want to remember to take care of certain parking safety issues with flow. Staff can remind people to step in front of their cars and walk to the event to avoid the cars from behind that are continuing to park. From there, what is the flow to the next destination?

Other Vehicular Considerations

For the flow of staff and VIP vehicles, event managers should have very clear and specific directions written and diagrammed that these groups are aware of. Instructions should also include an early arrival time so they are not competing with spectators to enter the parking lots. Encourage staff to carpool or use public transportation as a strategy to eliminating parking issues.

Any security or agency representatives in the parking area need to know about staff and VIP parking. Go over the instructions (repeatedly) with staff and officials on-site. Make sure that everyone has the same, and most up-to-date, directions/maps that are available. It is also essential to generate and distribute parking passes, placards, or other identifiers to vehicles with special access.

No matter how well organized the event is, it is inevitable that there will be late arrivers. Late-arriving spectators are not a big deal; often they can just park themselves. However, late-arriving participants and deliveries are a bigger challenge. In the marathon example, there could be participants arriving late because they did not anticipate how long it would take to get there, or because they did not read all of the instructions provided to them. At this point, a bus transport might not make sense, so a few cars should be available to transport any late runners to the starting area. For deliveries, how are they going to get past the cars that are parking or the buses that are unloading if they arrive late? Is there another entrance? As discussed previously, these situations should be kept to an absolute minimum.

However, there may be times when the event cannot operate without the equipment or supplies that are arriving late. What if the bottled water distributor is late arriving for the marathon? The truck cannot be turned away, but the late arrival must be handled safely so that the driving route intersects participants and spectators as infrequently as possible. Crossing vehicle and pedestrian traffic is dangerous and causes further delay of the delivery and pedestrian movement. Depending on the size of the delivery, one strategy is to have flat-bed golf carts available to meet the truck at the event perimeter. Then, the equipment and supplies can be unloaded in smaller quantities, thus causing less disruption to the event flow.

Participant Flow

Participant flow is a major issue for an event such as the marathon in the example. However, for a recurring event such as a baseball game, participants know where they are supposed to be and when, and the flow for them is less of a concern.

For participant-driven events, there are likely two different categories of participants: those people who have registered and only need to pick up their information, and those who are registering on-site. They will all need to go through a registration area, but some may only need to pick up their packet because they registered online, via mail, and so forth. This process can be sped up by having a "packet pick-up only" line for people who have already registered. This will make their event experience begin on a positive note by not waiting in line with those who need to fill out forms and pay. For the fictitious marathon, since it is so large, packet pick-up would take place for several days before the event. No packet pick-up would be available on race day except for extreme circumstances, such as participant flight delays.

For events featuring children as participants, accommodations for parents as pseudo-participants should also be made. Parents will not want to drop their 7-year-olds off at an arena door and trust they find their way around. Parents should be able to stay with kids until the coach or team is in one place and is functioning as a participant in the event. Then, the parents will flow into the spectator area.

Staging Areas

In the marathon scenario, once participants are dropped off by the bus, the best-case scenario is for them to move into the staging area as quickly as possible to avoid a bottleneck at the entrance. The staging area should be a cordoned-off or fenced area where only athletes are allowed. Since this marathon is large and sold out, there may be bandit runners. **Bandit runners** are runners trying to sneak in to run who did not register or sign the waiver. As athletes move into the staging area, event staff should be at the entrance to verify that all runners are legitimate by viewing their bibs (the race numbers on runners' chests).

From a flow perspective, athletes should be encouraged to progress to the farthest point within the staging area. It is similar to the concept of efficiently loading a bus. In loading a bus, it is best if people move all the way to the back and then fill in the seats moving forward. When people stop at the first seats, others have to wait for them to take their seats in order to go by them. It is the same with a staging area. One way to help encourage runners to go to the back is to give them a reason to go there, such as placing service areas (e.g., refreshments, gear check, or entertainment) towards the back of the staging area. If these service areas are scattered throughout, those in the back should be opened first, and the ones nearer the entrance should have a delayed/rolling opening.

Once participants are in the staging area, they will eventually have to move and load into the start zone. The staging area should be designed to lead runners to the start without them having to go against the traffic or backtrack. Ideally, the flow should be continuous and move in one direction. Backflow will clog things up, aggravate the runners, and slow down the event.

In this scenario, spectators are not allowed at the start. If they were, event managers would need to determine specifically where they are allowed to go and what the flow would be. Should they be kept separate from the athletes? If so, how will they be kept separate and where? Where is the spectator viewing area for the start? What time will spectators be encouraged to move to that area? These additional questions would have to be answered if spectators were to be allowed at the start. Each small change in the event plan changes the flow throughout the event.

Spectator Flow

Spectator flow should be as simple and direct as possible by using straight lines. However, if a winding and bending flow is unavoidable, proper lines should be formed with rope and stanchions. If people start **queuing up**, or creating a line, on their own, they will likely start forming lines that will interfere with other aspects of event flow. Then, event managers will have to make them shift. Once people are already queued and then asked to move, it tends to frustrate and aggravate them. They do not understand why, and are irritated that the line was unanticipated by event management. Be prepared to set up lines and know in advance what type of queue might be needed (or automatically set it up in advance). If it is a long queue, place signs periodically along the way and/or have staff with bullhorns letting people know they are going in the right direction, what is waiting ahead, and how long the wait is.

Generating Revenue through Managing Flow

One of the great advantages of managing flow is that event managers can create the environment of what they want people to see and in what order. Disney is phenomenal at this. When exiting an attraction at a Disney theme park, the flow moves people directly into a merchandise shop. This is because Disney knows that people are more likely to purchase merchandise shortly after experiencing the attraction. If event managers can create this type of flow at their events, it will result in increased per cap for the event. **Per capita spending,** or "per cap," is the amount of money spent per person during the event.

Keeping Disney in mind, but allowing for the uniqueness of sports events, event managers can locate revenue-generating opportunities in a few prime locations. These areas create excitement because there are crowds, and when others see the crowds, they are naturally drawn to see what is going on. People do not like to feel like they are missing something. Placing revenue opportunities near entrances and exits to the venue will also allow for the event flow to push people to pass by. One cautionary note when placing points of sale near entrances and exits is that it can cause clogs in the flow of pedestrian traffic. By designing the area so that people are led slightly out of the way, congestion can be avoided.

For participants, event registration is the prime location. Every participant must register, so as they flow through registration, consider what the exit looks like. If event managers can get participants to exit through a merchandise location, it could result in more sales.

Signage

One of the considerations with any type of flow is what type of signage is needed. The location of signs is key; excellent information does no good if it is an area where no one will see it. Choosing a color theme for the event and integrating the colors and event logo into all signage will allow it to be easily identifiable to those at the event. As event managers are thinking about spectators, they need to put themselves in the place of a spectator that has never been to the venue before and is trying to park, walk to the entrance, buy a ticket, find his or her seat, buy concessions, and finally exit the facility.

Height and clarity of signs are very important. Are the signs visible from a distance? One of the keys to directional signage is height. A vertical height of eight to ten feet is easily visible from a car or for a pedestrian from a distance. If a sign is too low, people walking in front of the signs are going to block them from the view of others. If it is an event where people are going to be arriving at night, make sure the signage can be seen from a car, and that when headlights shine on it, it is clearly readable. Plus, any signs for pedestrians must be lit to be effective at night.

There are also safety precautions with signs. If it is a windy day, what has been done to ensure the sign does not blow down or blow away? Many sign companies have vandal-proof screws available for sign construction. Sports signage is a popular item to steal, and is often found in college residence hall rooms. Ensuring the base of the sign is secure and that vandal-proof screws are holding the sign to the base will act as a deterrent to theft.

Spectator Signage

Event managers anticipate that people will start to look for signs as they approach an event, whether approaching on foot, via car, or public transportation. To move people to the event location, reassure people as they go through signage indicators that they are headed in the correct direction. This will also keep them from stopping and creating problems with crowd movement. Once people enter the event, it is difficult to get them to read signs because their attention is being demanded by other things. However, if there are enough signs, the hope is that at least some of the people will see some of the signs.

Participant Signage

Within a confined space, such as the participant registration area, signs should be clear and plentiful. If there are separate lines for pre-registered participants and on-site registration, do the signs clearly indicate that? Event staff can also be assigned to this area to reinforce information on the signs. Staff can make sure participants know where they are supposed to go, and can speed up registration by reminding participants to "have your ID ready," "if you have already registered get in the line to your right," or "think about what size T-shirt you need."

Lighting

Adequate lighting for spectator and participant areas is a responsibility of the event managers and can impact flow. For events where people will be arriving or leaving in the dark, there will need to be tower lights to light the pedestrian areas and vehicle areas. This is a basic safety issue. Not only do people need to see where they are walking and what is around them, but they also need the signage lit so they can read it. If permanent lighting is inadequate, then renting lights is an option, and there are a variety of lighting setups that will ensure a safe environment.

Diagramming Flow

One of the easiest ways to conceptualize and communicate flow is to diagram it. If there is not an existing diagram of the area, make one, even if it is not to scale. Use the diagram to mark locations of staff, signage, where people will be directed, and so forth. Use different colors to indicate different types of personnel (e.g., police, staff, volunteers) and arrows to indicate movement direction. Computers make it easy to use different color lines/symbols/icons/objects to designate different groups and their traffic patterns. Or, if the flow changes depending on the time of day, different colors can represent different times of the day. Event managers can then use the diagram to see the traffic flow of the different groups and how the groups will interact with one another.

Once the diagram is created, event managers should walk the event areas repeatedly. Video can even be used to record specific areas if there is limited access pre-event. Walk-thrus are important to help make sure the event does not encounter a situation where the designed flow has to be changed because of unanticipated construction (or something else) that is going to impede the flow. No matter what the agencies/companies/groups say or confirm about the location, event managers should confirm it themselves. As the event gets closer, frequent reviews should take place to ensure that there are no surprises.

10 Event Operations Tips

The following list provides some guidelines to help event managers prepare for facility and equipment management during an event.

1. The event experience begins when spectators or participants leave their homes to attend the event, and ends when they return home. Everything possible should be done to make sure the experience is good during the entire event experience.

2. Remember that event teardown takes half as long as setup, and plan accordingly.

3. Make sure any necessary operating permits are available on-site in case they are requested by government officials.

4. Limit the number of people that have access (e.g., keys, credentials) for specific areas. The more access, the less secure the area is.

5. Keep rain gear, umbrellas, towels, squeegees, and snow shovels on-hand in case they are needed, and check the weather forecast frequently for outdoor events.

6. For venues without permanent restrooms, research the appropriate number of restrooms needed (include ADA restrooms). (General information can be found from the Federal Emergency Management Agency at http://www.americanrestroom.org/gov/fema/FEMA_SECP39_41.PDF).

7. Concessions should be provided at a ratio range of 1:120 (large concourses and crowded areas) to 1:250 (less crowded areas of the venue (Lamberth, n.d.).

8. Develop relationships with the Fire Marshal and Department of Health representatives prior to the event.

9. If the event will begin OR end when it is dark, provide adequate lighting for safety within the event perimeter as well as in parking and pedestrian areas outside of the event perimeter.

10. Integrate green practices into the event plan.

Determining the right flow becomes second nature to event managers with experience, and although flow seems like an abstract concept, it begins to make sense when thought of in relation to a specific event. The use of good staff placement, signage placement, point-of-sale locations, and appropriate lighting will all support the main event flow with proper planning.

SUMMARY

There are details related to facility and equipment operations that begin in the development phase of event management and become a reality during execution. On the event day, the event managers are the first ones on-site and the last ones to leave. The tasks associated with operations are not glamorous, but they are crucial to the event being a success. Hours of preparation occur before the event which allows the event managers to be knowledgeable about everything that has to get done on event day. There are facility walk-thrus, venue setup and teardown, field and facility maintenance, equipment management, and the overall flow of the event that all have to be completed. Most event managers learn about operations through their own mistakes and

Student Challenge

STUDENT CHALLENGE #14

In Challenge #14, work on the details of the event related to facility and equipment management and operations.

QUESTION 14-1

What equipment is needed for the event? List five pieces of equipment needed for the event that the facility *does not* own. Then, conduct research and decide whether the equipment should be purchased or rented. Discuss the rationale for either purchasing or renting each piece of equipment.

Equipment #1-

Equipment #2-

Equipment #3-

Equipment #4-

Equipment #5-

Student Challenge

QUESTION 14-2

Create an event day checklist for the set-up of the event. This list should include the primary and ancillary space set-up needs, as well as specifics as to what time each space should be completely set up. Refer to Chapter 12, Event Documents, for a reminder as to the format of a checklist.

Student Challenge

QUESTION 14-3

Describe the flow of the event. Choose either spectators or participants and discuss how an effective flow is ensured. What flow strategies can be used at the event to increase per cap spending?

CHAPTER 15

EVENT SETTLEMENT AND WRAP UP

John P. Tafaro and Heather Lawrence

Event settlement and wrap up are important concepts for event managers to understand. **Event settlement** is a specific process that occurs upon completion of all events. It is a financial transaction in nature, very similar to the closing on the purchase of real estate or the acquisition of a business. **Wrap up** is a general term referring to task completion that concludes the event management process, such as attending to any complaints received, generating sponsor reports, sending thank-you notes, debriefing and paying workers, and completing post-event recaps.

Event managers may or may not play a direct role in the settlement process, depending on the organizational structure of the facility, and whether they manage events as an employee of the venue or represent an outside organization hosting an event in the building. Commonly, settlement is the responsibility of the facility manager. If event managers are directly involved, it is likely they are the event representative settling with the building. Thus, it is imperative that event managers know what transpires during settlement. Regardless of whether or not the event managers are present at settlement, many of the financial components of the transaction are influenced, if not generated, by the work of the event managers.

The settlement process may be managed by the building manager, the facility's chief financial officer, business manager, or other person of authority. It is this person's responsibility to make sure that all financial consideration is accounted for and properly distributed. First and foremost, the responsible party has a duty to protect the financial interest of his or her facility and its owners, which could be a university or academic institution; a city, county, state or other governmental authority; a fair board; or a private corporation or enterprise. If the staffing model of the facility identifies a chief financial officer, director of finance, or comptroller as the party responsible for conducting the settlement, this individual is the point person in the settlement process, but the facility manager or chief executive is ultimately responsible for what transpires at settlement and should be involved in a supervisory role.

Wrap up may encompass different tasks depending on the event, organization, and people involved. However, differently from event settlement, the event managers will be the responsible party for this task. The overall goal of wrap up procedures is to create a comprehensive event file for the event and to thank all of those that spent time, effort, and money supporting the event. Once the event activities are complete, settlement has concluded, and teardown has finished, many event managers assume the event management process is over. But there are still some important tasks to complete. The importance of relationships is a consistent theme throughout the event management process, and through wrap up, relationships with participants, sponsors, fans, promoters, and the community can be strengthened.

BUILDING AGREEMENT

The settlement process begins with the written building agreement. All buildings have standard agreements or contracts that provide for the staging of an event. Some facilities call them the "Agreement," others are entitled "Contract," some can be termed a "Lease," while still more can be identified as a "License" or even a "Permit." The legal differences of each type of document are best left to another course and another book.

Regardless of any name on the top of these documents, they should all contain the same information and set forth the relative duties and responsibilities of each party, specifically, the building and the event sponsor or "promoter." Within this document should be clear direction as to how the revenues are shared and the expenses are divided (see Chapter 3 for detailed information on contracts). Since many events have common financial characteristics, a settlement template form can generally be established using Excel or other software programs capable of doing the required calculations. The specific line items, however, may vary by the type of event.

All events are different, and settlements are distinct and individual business transactions. Most events, however, fall into one of five general categories:

- Rentals
- Co-promotions
- Facility promotions
- Multiple performances/anchor tenants
- Non-traditional events

Rentals

A **rental event** is one where an outside presenter, sponsor, or promoter (let's use the term "promoter") is fully responsible for producing and staging the event in the venue (see Chapter 3, Figure 3-3, Ohio University Department of Intercollegiate Athletics Facility Rental Agreement). The facility negotiates a rental amount for the venue, which may or may not include building expenses such as staffing, clean up, box office or ticketing services, setup, utilities, and building rent. The building rent component can be a flat fee or a percentage of the gate (i.e., ticket receipts), with or without a guaranteed minimum and/or a cap or even a sliding scale percentage. Expenses can be quoted as extras, and again be either in the form of a flat fee, on a sliding scale (based on attendance), or at pre-determined rates with an overhead factor added or an administrative charge built in.

Be careful to avoid misrepresenting pass-through charges as actual costs. **Pass-through charges** are those expenses for which the facility pays a third party on behalf of the renter and then later charges to the renter. An example of a pass-through charge is when the promoter needs extra forklifts and operators to complete the setup for the event. The facility acquires the equipment and operators and then pays for the rental of the equipment, as well as the cost of the labor. At settlement, the facility might then add an additional 10% to the actual cost of the forklifts and operators when billing the renter. The 10% covers the cost and time associated with arranging for the forklifts, scheduling the labor, meeting the rental company for delivery of the forklifts, explaining to the operators what needed to be done, and ensuring the equipment was picked up as scheduled. It is well established in almost all businesses that the entity providing services and/or labor is entitled to a marked up or loaded rate to include the cost of recruiting, hiring, training, purchasing, supervising, and managing these assets, human or otherwise. Therefore, there is nothing wrong with marking up labor or services, provided the costs are represented accurately.

In all cases on a rental event, it is the building executive's responsibility that adequate rent is charged, regardless of how it is calculated or presented, to protect the financial interest of the venue by covering all expenses and providing a fair return on the investment of the building's owners. On a rental, there should be NO RISK for the venue.

Co-Promotions

In a **co-promotion**, the promoter is responsible for certain expenses usually associated with the production and staging of the event. This would include transportation, performers' payroll, equipment, costumes, depreciation on fixed assets, and all overhead for the attraction (see Chapter 3, Figure 3-2, Harlem Globetrotters Standard Co-Promotion Agreement).

The building is commonly responsible for the expense associated with running the facility during the co-promotion event or events. Typical building expenses could include ticket sellers, ticket takers, ushers, setup, teardown, security, clean-up, supervision, management, utilities, and overhead. Some items can be paid first, or "off the top." Commonly, this would include advertising expenses, perhaps union stagehands, and always includes taxes and any bond fee or facility debt retirement use charge.

After the off-the-top items are deducted, there is a negotiated split of remaining revenue. Splits can be fixed at any ratio, for example, 90/10; 80/20; 55/45; or any other combination that totals 100. Splits can also be on a sliding scale, with the bigger share amount often in favor of the party that has a higher cost of doing business, commonly the event, then shifting to a more level arrangement after the parties have recovered their respective costs. A co-promotion split arrangement can look like this: (i) advertising and taxes off the top; (ii) 70% to the promoter and 30% to the building on the first remaining $200,000; (iii) 60% to the promoter and 40% to the building on the next $200,000; and (iii) 50% each to the promoter and building on all remaining income.

Similarly, the nature of the split can be characterized in actual dollars, something like this: (i) promoter gets the first $50,000 (presumably, to cover the costs of the event); (ii) the building receives the next $35,000 (presumably, to pay for the operating costs incurred by the facility); (iii) promoter gets 80% and building gets 20% of the next $100,000; and (iv) the parties split evenly any remaining revenue.

Facility Promotions

With an event sponsored and staged by the facility, commonly called a **facility promotion**, the building or its owner acts as the promoter and takes all the risks, financial and otherwise. In a market where one or more promoters actively engage in the trade, the mere fact that an act or attraction is available to the facility should be a red flag that there is undue risk, as it is likely that one or more regular promoters have declined an offer to participate. Facility promotions should not be undertaken without substantial, current, and thorough research and a realistic assessment of the revenue potential of the event. Sales history for the contemplated event or similar events should be recent and independently verifiable to be valid.

In the case of a facility promotion, the settlement will be simpler, and encompass merely the payment of the talent fee to the act, attraction, talent broker, or show producer, which would have been determined well in advance of the event, but could be variable and based on final ticket sales. Other, subsequent accounting and the collection of revenue and disbursement of payments can occur at a later date, but should not be put off for too long. Often, an internal settlement will be conducted for purposes of interdepartmental accounting, budget reconciliation, or post-event evaluation and analysis. As in any case, the settlement of a facility promotion serves an important purpose in that it shows all income and expenses, so the facility can determine if the event is a financial success, break-even proposition, or an actual cost or losing venture.

Multiple Performances/Anchor Tenants

If a venue hosts a series of events of a similar nature, produced by the same entity and covered under a single rental agreement or contract, there may need to only be one final settlement, or a series of interim settlements may be conducted. Examples of this type of event could be a week-long engagement of a circus, rodeo, ice show or other family show, or a season-long relationship with a sports team (i.e., the anchor tenant) that calls the facility its "home court," "home field," or "home ice."

Regardless, the nature of the transaction is the same. First, all receipts are organized and identified, and all bills gathered with expenses itemized. Then, the balance is paid to the event sponsor, team, or promoter, or an invoice is generated should there be a shortfall in revenue held by the facility.

In the case of a national touring attraction, family show, or sports team, not all of the revenue to be divided may be in the hands of the facility. National or international shows may have sponsorship arrangements that fall outside the cash flow parameters of the event, yet the money generated is included in the event proceeds. Likewise, a sports team may control its season ticket sales, with the venue entitled to a portion of season ticket proceeds. While this situation is not preferred from the building perspective, it is sometimes unavoidable.

Non-Traditional Events

Non-traditional events may or may not occur at a venue, and may or may not include ticket sales as a component of the revenue stream. Instead, these events are participatory in nature, like marathons and other running events, triathlons, or even square-dance or bowling marathons. There is sometimes a charitable tie-in to the event with a recognized non-profit entity involved in one of many ways, usually as a beneficiary of the net proceeds, or a percentage of the gross revenue, or perhaps even as a commissioned sales agent on sponsorships, or any combination thereof.

With a non-traditional event, a settlement is still necessary and important. Revenues must be itemized and accounted for, and bills need to be paid. The settlement serves as the vehicle by which all such revenue and expenses are identified so that a final determination of profit or loss, or "the bottom-line," can be established. As in the case of a facility promotion, the settlement process for a non-traditional event may not be as time sensitive as for other events, but a speedy process results in more accuracy and quicker accountability from all involved.

Regardless of the type of event, the contractual agreement will set the stage for all that is to follow, including event settlement. The five types of building agreements discussed provide context as to the differences found in each; from those with limited or no risk to the facility, as in a rental agreement, to a facility promotion where the risk is solely on the building. Generalizations can be made about event settlement based on the type of building agreement, but specifics are limited only by being able to get both parties involved in the contract to agree upon the terms.

An Interview with Lynda Reinhart and Renee Musson

Director and Associate Director, Stephen C. O'Connell Center

Lynda Reinhart and Renee Musson are integral to the continued success of the Stephen C. O'Connell Center on the campus of the University of Florida. They work as a team, along with other O'Connell Center staff, to attract, execute, and settle the various entertainment events that perform in their building. Lynda and Renee provided some insight into the event settlement process.

So the readers understand your building setup, will you describe the Stephen C. O'Connell Center?

The Stephen C. O'Connell Center is a multi-purpose facility that is used for academic classes, recreation, sports, and entertainment events. The 12,000 seat main arena is the competitive home for the University of Florida Men's and Women's Basketball Teams, Women's Volleyball, Women's Gymnastics, and Men's and Women's Indoor Track and Field Teams. The perimeter of the building includes an Olympic-size competition venue that is the home of Men's and Women's Swimming and Diving. Also in the building are a dance studio, gymnastics practice facility, practice basketball court, classrooms, and a weight room.

What are some of the underlying principles by which you operate the building?

The primary use of the area space is varsity athletic events, but the entire staff is dedicated to fulfilling the mission of the building when attracting, booking, and executing events. The mission statement of the building is:

> The mission of the Stephen C. O'Connell Center is to serve as an academic, athletic, recreational and entertainment facility. In addition, we strive to provide superior service to guests and clients, and training for future leaders while operating the Center's auxiliary as a financially self-supporting entity.

Every decision we make comes back to this mission statement. Although we like to generate revenue through the events we have in the building, we are also aware that we provide a service and entertainment function for the community. So, we will occasionally book an event that will not generate a lot of revenue if it provides a service to the Gainesville area.

As a public state facility on a university campus, there are certain rules and regulations that we have to follow in everything we do. If those core principles are compromised by hosting an event, then we cannot host it. For example, we have a rule that prohibits mosh pits in the building. Therefore, if an artist who is known for moshing at their concerts wanted to play at our building, we could not book the performance.

What is the general process for booking events at the Stephen C. O'Connell Center?

The Stephen C. O'Connell Center's primary clients are the University of Florida and University Athletic Association, Inc. (the athletic department at the University of Florida). So concerts, family shows, and flat shows are all booked and scheduled after annual University events (i.e., commencement and career fairs) are scheduled and the athletic schedule is finalized. Sometimes promoters contact us and other times we go out looking for shows to bring to the building. In either case, there are three types of booking;

1) Rental: This is the least risky type of booking. The promoter/artist/performer rents the building and pays all the expenses. They also receive all of the revenue from the show.

2) Co-Promote: A co-promote agreement is where we share the risk with the artist/performer through a pre-defined split of the expenses and revenue.

3) Promote: A promote booking agreement is risky for us. In this case, we pay the artist/performer and all of the expenses for the show hoping that we sell a lot of tickets and make money through the popularity of the show.

As a side note, we have to be really careful what we book because of our geographic location and market. Located in North Central Florida, we cross markets with Jacksonville, Orlando, and even Tampa. Plus, with many of the potential ticket buyers being students, a lower price point is important to us.

How do you define event settlement?

For us, event settlement is the face-to-face process of accounting for, agreeing upon, negotiating expenses and revenues, and determining how much each party receives for an event.

When does event settlement occur?

Settlement usually begins immediately after the box office closes. So, depending on the show, this could be 30 minutes to an hour into the performance. Then the representative from the act meets with me (Renee) in the offices to go through the formal settlement negotiations. There is a lot of pressure to complete the necessary calculations quickly and accurately with the show representative looking over my shoulder.

Is the process generally cordial?

In most cases, settlements are quick and painless, as most of the negotiations and issues have been settled as the event day has progressed. However, if the show did not do well, there is more tension because of the possibility of taking a financial loss on the show. If there are disagreements on aspects of the settlement, then Lynda, as the building director, gets involved to resolve them. Good client service is always critical, but it becomes even more important when there is stress and pressure involved. The stronger the relationship is with the client, the easier these types of situations are to deal with.

What are some trends in event settlement?

Beyond the developments in the use of technology in the entire management of facilities, there are some other areas in which changes are occurring. Many of the trends are directly related to booking and negotiations and will ultimately impact settlement.

1) Merchandising: Traditionally, artists/performers have traveled with their own selling teams that handled merchandise sales. However, in recent years, more shows are trying to require that the building provide people to sell the merchandise. Often, they are also asking to keep more of the revenue.

2) Flat rate services: For a rental booking agreement, the largest portion of the cost to the show is the services provided by the building, and not the rent charged to be in the facility. The cost of security, event staff, forklift operators, and other services used to be charged at an hourly fee to the show. Many promoters are now pushing venues to provide these services at a flat rate versus an hourly rate. Since the venue then needs to be able to project accurately the cost of the services, it makes the deal more of a financial risk for the venue.

3) "All in" ticket pricing: Existing service, processing, and transaction fees now charged to ticket buyers when making a purchase may soon be invisible to the consumer. The charges will still be included in the price of the ticket, but the division of the charges will be done as part of settlement. When this becomes standard practice, venues will have one more complexity added to settlement, but they will also be more aware of how the fees are divided. In the current system, venues generally do not know how the service fees are split.

4) Cash handling: Large amounts of cash used to change hands at settlement. Today, with increased availability of electronic funds transfers, settlement is largely done via wire transfers.

What personal characteristics and skill sets should someone possess who is interested in working in event settlement?

Normally you would think someone like an accountant would be a good fit for event settlement, but it is more than just accounting skills that make someone successful at settlement. Bookkeeping, ticketing, and spreadsheet experience are also coveted. Maybe most importantly, the person doing settlement needs to know and understand facility operations. This ensures the building representative has a good understanding of industry terms, what goes on during an event, and can "speak the language" during settlement. Combine operations experience, good business knowledge, customer service skills, the ability to work under a deadline, and you have a great fit for event settlement.

What reports are generated post-event?

There are three categories of reports generated at settlement or after an event: internal reports, settlement reports, and public information. Internal reports contain information that is only for those working in the building or associated with its operations to see (i.e., building management and University governance). Settlement reports are those provided to the promoter at settlement and are also used internally by the venue. Public reports provide information that is shared with media and the public.

Internal Reports

Marketing staff reports: demographics of where tickets were sold and who buyers were.

Accounting reports: sales tax reports and other reports dictated by General Accounting Procedures.

Event summary/Board: provided to the governing board and includes a summary of the event in memo format.

Event summary/File: for the event file as a general record of the event, its characteristics, and those involved.

Settlement Reports

Ticket audit: indicates how many tickets were sold at each price point.

Financial spreadsheets: expenses and revenues by category and line item.

Building expenses: those expenses that were direct costs to the building.

Pass-through expenses: those expenses that the building paid for, but ultimately were charged to the promoter/agent.

Commissions: special reports are generated when the deal includes various commissions (i.e., group sales efforts are typically commissioned to cover the cost of those efforts).

Complimentary tickets: proof of how many free give-away tickets were used, who used them, and for what purpose.

Public Reports

Boxscore: used to report artist/event, venue, city/state, gross sales, attend/capacity, shows/sellouts, prices, and promoters in trade publications.

What else should event managers know and understand about settlement?

There are no secrets in event settlement these days. Promoters talk to each other, building operators talk to each other, and artists talk to each other. With the communication channels so open, it is important to treat each show individually.

It is imperative that up-front negotiations and contracts address everything and are solid agreements. This will lessen any disagreements at settlement. However, not every contingency can be covered, and whoever is sitting in settlement needs to have solid knowledge of both fiscal concerns and operational concerns surrounding an event, should the necessity arise to re-address contracted issues on the day of the event or during settlement.

Can you sum up settlement with five general rules for successful event settlement?

1. Be flexible.

2. Know and understand the mission of the building and why it exists.

3. Understand the industry.

4. Know what the cost to the building is to do the show.

5. Stand your ground and know when it is better to "shut it down" and not have a show than to compromise policy or public safety.

For more information on the Stephen C. O'Connell Center, please visit http://www.oconnellcenter.ufl.edu/.

MARSHALLING ALL REVENUE

Marshalling revenue refers to identifying, organizing, and accounting for everything related to revenue in an effective way. In the facility management industry there are very few absolutes, so the following presents ideal circumstances, but event managers and those responsible for settlement must be able to acknowledge when a variance from the standard operations will benefit all of those involved. Any variance is most likely to occur in a situation where there is a strong existing relationship with a promoter.

Security Deposit

A security deposit is among the first, and sometimes the most difficult, deal points to agree upon when negotiating a building contract. It operates the same way a security deposit functions in a commercial or even residential real estate setting. When renting or reserving a sports or entertainment facility, non-refundable money is collected to hold the date and is considered a **security deposit**. The deposit will compensate the building for (i) holding the date and foregoing other income-generating opportunities, public service options, or recreational functions; (ii) to cover all advance costs the building will incur in promoting, producing, and preparing for the event; and (iii) to pay for any and all potential costs should the event cancel, such as security to staff the building on the canceled date (in case fans arrive not knowing of the cancellation) and ticket refund expenses. (Note: Ticket monies held in trust are *not* available for this purpose.) Likewise, it is the duty of the facility manager to require and collect an adequate security deposit before an event can be announced or tickets can go on sale. Sometimes, less reputable and undercapitalized promoters will independently engage in a publicity campaign involving a speculative or tentative event merely to gauge customer response and potential market interest. Any promoter who announces an event prior to having a signed building agreement and funded security deposit should be avoided, and the facility should publicly deny the scheduling of any event until both the contract and deposit are in hand.

Sponsor Revenue

Some sponsorships are local, some are regional, and others are national. As discussed in detail in Chapter 7, Event Sponsorship, most include a cash component, but many can be in-kind arrangements where the sponsor supplies goods or services in support of the event with no actual money exchanging hands. A typical in-kind sponsorship can be with a media partner that provides advertising and marketing support for the event in exchange for any number of specific benefits. Benefits frequently include complimentary tickets and/or inclusion in the name or billing of the event. In some cases, the media outlet is promised a share of the event's advertising expenditures or even a percentage of gate receipts. Other in-kind arrangements can include the exchange of equipment, supplies, or other essential goods or services (like dirt for a rodeo or junk cars for a monster jam) for tickets, inclusion in advertising, on-site signage, or anything else of value.

When a sponsorship associated with an event includes a cash component, the final determination of who gets to keep what percentage of the cash needs to be determined at the contracting stage, not at settlement. A fair division of sponsorship proceeds will be determined by whose expenses have been reduced or offset because of the sponsorship and who delivered the sponsor.

Ticket Receipts

Ticket receipts are more often than not the single most significant revenue component of an event that is spectator driven. Therefore, ticket receipts are reported on a separate box office or ticket summary statement. The **box office statement** is often in the form of a computerized report prepared by a third-party ticketing vendor, such as TicketMaster, and will show all tickets sold at each ticket price, and specify the method by which they were sold (e.g., at remote outlets, via phone, on the Internet, etc.). Other valuable marketing reports may be available showing where the event's customers live or where individual tickets were purchased. These reports belong to the venue or client of the ticket company that generates them, and may or may not be shared with the promoter. In any case, beyond the box office statement, these additional marketing reports are outside the scope of the settlement process.

Participant Registration

For participant-driven events, registrations are similar to ticket receipts in that they may be the primary revenue generator. Depending on the type of building agreement, participant registrations may be in the hands of the event organization or the facility. In either case, a careful accounting of income from registrations is needed so that the facility and event managers know who registered, where they are from, and when they registered. A final report of registration numbers in addition to, or in lieu of, a ticket report is common.

Advertising

The building may or may not be involved in advertising the event. In the case of a co-promotion, the building is entitled to participate in and approve of all advertising. With a facility promotion, the building is completely responsible for advertising. In a building rental, the promoter may independently handle all advertising functions. Regardless of the type of event, the building has a vested interest in assuring that all media outlets are paid. Even though a promoter may bear full responsibility for the payment of advertising bills, if the show leaves town with invoices left unpaid, this casts a shadow on the building, reflects negatively on the business judgment of those involved, and could impair future relationships. It is important to let all media vendors know that invoices, memo-invoices (in the case where final invoices are unavailable), and/or final bills need to be presented to the venue prior to the event, or final performance in a multiple-performance event, so that money can be reserved for payment at the time of settlement.

Merchandise

Most, if not all, events bring an array of merchandise for sale to patrons consisting of T-shirts, sweatshirts, other apparel, programs, and perhaps additional novelty items. In exchange for the right to sell this merchandise on facility property, the promoter should be required to pay a fee. The building may or may not provide employees or independent contractors to sell this merchandise, but if labor is provided through the building, an add-on factor for payroll taxes and supervision is warranted. Employees or independent contractors can be paid on a flat rate, an hourly wage, or on commission. The building share of revenue can likewise be negotiated as a flat rate, a per capita fixed rate, or a percentage of sales. The merchandise settlement can be included as part of the overall settlement, or can be a separate and distinct transaction.

Food & Beverage/Parking

Historically, a building's food and beverage sales and parking receipts were not included in gross proceeds to be shared with a promoter; however, in recent days, promoters and major shows have been successful negotiating for a portion of this revenue. Anchor tenants, like sports teams playing a full slate of contests, will generally participate. If this revenue is included, it may require a separate settlement or a segregated line or two within the settlement, with different percentages applicable to distinct categories of product sales.

Media Rights

When an event is televised, additional costs will accrue, including higher utility bills and perhaps additional labor and/or security. Also, if television viewership will suppress attendance, and the building is receiving a share of ticket proceeds, then some payment should be required to make the building whole. This fee often called an **origination fee**. It should be included in the building contract and collected at settlement. The same concept could apply to radio broadcasts, but both the costs of hosting a radio production and its impact on attendance are generally less than television, and the origination fee, therefore, is proportionally smaller.

Taxes/Bond Debt Retirement/Facility Fees

Whether a facility is publicly or privately financed, the cost of construction and development is funded by debt, often in the form of bonds sold to institutional or private investors. Bondholders are generally entitled to some guaranteed revenue stream on all building income in the form of a percentage or fixed fee for each admission or ticket sold. This bond fee, which can sometimes be called an **admission tax**, **facility fee**, or **bond charge**, should be deducted from the price of each ticket and accounted for on the box office statement, which then yields a "net ticket sales" figure that is dropped into the revenue column of the settlement statement.

DISBURSEMENT OF EXPENSES

There are various categories of expense where the building has unlimited liability, and therefore must assure that these items are collected at settlement and paid either concurrently or at a later date. Payroll, payroll taxes, taxes, bond fees, and other governmental charges are examples.

Other expenses could fall outside the scope of the settlement; however, it is in the best interest of the building to make sure the promoter or attraction does not leave town with a host of unpaid bills and obligations.

Remember, when the show leaves, the promoter may be gone forever, but the building remains and must do business the next day with the same vendors who were left holding a worthless receivable. It is in the facility's best interest to seek out those ancillary vendors and protect them if they believe they are at risk for holding an uncollectible bill. These vendors will likely be permanent or long-term building sponsors and clients, such as the local media outlets (TV stations, radio stations, and newspapers), a local hotel, a printer (who may print a local program), a caterer, or even a limousine company. While the building has no obligation to act as a collection agent for these corollary businesses, the settlement process provides a vehicle to make sure local bills are paid. Make sure to alert the promoter or event sponsor in advance that (i) all local bills are to be paid; and (ii) the right to pay any local, uncontested bill at settlement from the settlement proceeds is reserved.

TICKET MONEY HELD IN TRUST

Ticket money held in trust is an essential concept and a vital consideration for all event managers. There are always occasions where a scheduled event will never take place. Sometimes inclement weather will force a cancellation. Illness of performers or technical difficulties pertaining to routing could be the cause of a postponement or cancellation. Unfortunately, poor ticket sales can sometimes result in cancellation of an event when the promoter recognizes the event is doomed to fail. When a patron purchases a ticket for an event, the purchase price is paid in exchange for the viewing and experience of attending that particular event. Until the event occurs, neither the facility nor the promoter has earned anything. The contract between the ticket buyer, the venue, and the attraction is not yet complete. Therefore, the entity holding the money paid by ticket purchasers is holding the money **in trust** for the customer, and is entitled to release these funds for the payment of expenses associated with the event or to the event promoter only after the event has occurred. If the event is cancelled or does not otherwise take place, the ticket purchaser is entitled to a full refund of the purchase price.

Generally, it is unwise to allow a promoter to use ticket trust money in lieu of a security deposit, and giving any promoter or event sponsor an advance on ticket money collected for an event that has not yet occurred is risky. Ultimately, the building is responsible to refund ticket sales to customers and will be liable to those customers regardless of the reason for the cancellation.

SECURITY INTEREST IN EVENT EQUIPMENT/FIXTURES

In a commercial lending transaction, a lender, typically a bank, will acquire a security interest in the equipment or fixtures purchased with the loan proceeds. This is known as a **purchase money security interest (PMSI)**. That security interest, however, can extend to other fixed assets beyond those acquired with the money borrowed through the loan. In other words, the borrower may need to add other collateral to induce the bank to make a loan.

The same concept can apply to a building rental. If the facility is unsure or insecure about the promoter's ability to pay its obligations, it can ask for a security interest in the attraction's assets. Exactly what needs to take place for a valid security interest to be a lien on personal property will vary from state to state and even county to county. An attorney should be engaged to draft the appropriate language for inclusion in the building contract and to advise on other steps required to properly record and protect such an interest. If a facility properly obtains a security interest, it has additional leverage at settlement time by having a legal claim, or encumbrance, on those assets.

Buildings that enter into multi-event agreements with anchor tenants such as arena football teams, for example, may consider requiring the grant of a security interest in the team's turf field. Minor League hockey teams could be asked for a security interest in the team's equipment or even intellectual property (e.g., the team's name), so if the team folds, the facility owns or at least has a claim against the property, and can use the uniforms, equipment, and team name as a head start in an effort to form a new team. Again, this should only be attempted with the assistance of a qualified attorney.

Other creative collection techniques, all employed to protect the building, include the requirement of a personal guarantee should there be a shortfall of funds available to pay all event obligations to the facility and/or an insecurity provision, which requires the promoter to increase the security deposit should the building reasonably believe there will be inadequate funds available to pay all obligations at settlement.

EVENT WRAP UP

As with event settlement, some aspects of wrap up may not be a direct event management responsibility. However, there certainly are scenarios when the event managers are responsible for all aspects of wrap up and need to be educated on what those components are. Common post-event wrap up tasks include: (i) completing payroll, (ii) debriefing staff, (iii) examining incident reports, (iv) addressing customer complaints, (v) generating sponsorship reports, (vi) sending thank-you notes and gathering customer information, and (vii) completing post-event recaps.

Payroll

In most circumstances, the event managers will not do payroll; in fact, it is recommended that a human resources specialist is involved with payroll for any event. Payroll is a complex process involving tax variables, the personal information of employees, and adherence to a variety of regulations. Employee hours worked should be certified by event managers or the specific supervisor responsible for each employee. Then, the time sheets will be submitted to human resources for accurate payment. Checks and balances should be in place at every step of the employee time-keeping and payroll process to ensure accuracy.

Debriefing

The debriefing of staff will be initiated by the event managers. A post-event meeting is an efficient way to share information from the different perspectives of all key staff involved in the event. Individuals serving in event day part-time positions will not be involved in this meeting, but supervisors will be. If any aspect of staffing is outsourced, the contact from the outsourcing agency should also be involved in post-event meetings. Topics of discussion should include details of what went right, what went wrong, what needs to be changed for the next event, and any specific occurrences during the event that warrant further discussion.

Incident Reports

Incident reports are simply a statement about anything related to a patron or staff member injury, illness, or any unusual occurrence during the event. Medical staff and EMTs will provide these to the event managers with details about the individual hurt and the nature of the injury or illness. Police and security are the other groups that will file incident reports, and most likely these will detail problems with patrons getting into fights or being unruly, and sometimes ultimately being ejected or arrested. All event staff should be encouraged to refer people that need assistance to the appropriate security or medical staff. This allows for proper reporting of the incident so it can be examined and documented after the event. Documentation is critical whenever an injury occurs at an event. The event managers must protect the organization from lawsuits by keeping accurate and detailed records of what happened.

Customer Complaints/Concerns

Unfortunately, happy customers generally do not call to thank the event or facility staff. However, those that have an unpleasant experience are not shy in sharing the trouble they experienced. Following an event, it is likely that there are some participant and/or spectator complaints that deserve follow-up. Event managers who are timely in responding and listening to these complaints and concerns are doing themselves, the event, and the venue a service. Many complaints are valid, and event managers can gather important information related to ways to improve the event experience. Additionally, the event managers can begin to rebuild relationships with the unhappy customers. Remember, unhappy customers will tell many others about their experience. For those complaints that are frivolous, event managers should still lend an ear and do their best to provide a positive response to the customer. By being responsive to complaints and concerns, the event and/or venue will be helping to mitigate public relations damage.

Sponsorship Reports and Acknowledgments

Each sponsor involved in the event should be acknowledged following the event. Depending on the type of event and type of sponsorship, along with the value of the sponsorship, the acknowledgement will vary. Some sponsorship contracts will require detailed return on investment (ROI) reports, while in other situations it may be sufficient to send a nice hand-written thank-you note.

For those sponsorships where a ROI report is generated, the details of what is needed will be discussed during the sponsorship contract negotiations because much of the data needed to calculate ROI needs to be gathered during the event. For example, if a sponsor has provided cash to the event in exchange for space in the program where the sponsor has printed a coupon for their business, they will want to know how many programs were sold, and then they can keep track of how many coupons were redeemed. This will all be included in a report so that the sponsor and the event can evaluate the effectiveness of the sponsorship as compared to the price paid by the sponsor. These reports can get very detailed, and the event managers may need to employ outside expertise to ensure that the information is accurate.

For smaller events where sponsors are involved as an act of goodwill, it may be sufficient to write a thank-you note or stop by in person to thank the sponsor and provide details of the success of the event. Providing photos to the sponsor of their logo integrated into the event is a nice touch that businesses appreciate.

Thank-You Notes and Customer Information Gathering

Everyone likes to be appreciated, so sending thank-you notes to those involved in the event is one way to accomplish this. It is critical to thank volunteer staff in as personal a way as possible. These individuals took time out of their lives to make the event a success and deserve a thank-you note, certificate of appreciation, or phone call from the event mangers. If the volunteer groups are very large, then sending a group thank you to the main contact is appropriate. Other staff also should be recognized for their efforts, but since they are paid for their time, the thank you can be less personal, such as an email to the entire group. It is not feasible for large events to deliver personalized hand-written notes to all participants, but even an email blast thanking participants will be noticed.

These communications are also one way to collect customer data and customer satisfaction information. By collecting as many email addresses as possible during ticket sales or participant registration, event managers can use that contact information for future marketing efforts or to ask for feedback. An online survey can be easily created and sent to various populations to assess the event. Again, this takes time and effort and may not make sense for every event, but surveys are a good way to get valuable information from customers.

Completing Post-Event Recaps

Just as event managers prepare documents when they are planning events, they should also create a recap of events that were just completed. This report is for internal use by management and future event managers of the event. Rather than relying on memory, post-event recaps will help in documenting details of the various areas. This is one of the first documents new event managers should read before beginning to work on an event. A post-event recap will include pieces from the other sections, such as debriefing and customer complaints, and will wrap up the overall picture of the event. It often includes, but is not limited to, summary sheets of budget numbers, staffing and volunteers, photographs of the event, complaints, incidents, successes, challenges, and suggested changes.

THE EVENT FILE

The event file is created so that all pertinent information is stored for future use in one location. The file might be hard copies of documents or electronic, but either way the same information should be included. All of the information needed to create the event file comes from either contracts (Chapter 3), event documents (Chapter 12), staffing (Chapter 13), event settlement, or wrap up. So, there is nothing new to do at this point except to organize and collect the existing information. The following should be included in the event file if appropriate for the event:

Contracts

Facility Rental/Promotion Contracts

Sponsorship Contracts

Game Contracts

Event Documents

Planning Timelines

Event Day Timelines

Checklists

Contact Sheets

Fast Facts

Staffing Positions/Call times

Diagrams/Maps/CADs/Google Earth

PA Scripts

Parking Pass

Credential /Ticket Samples

Meeting Agendas and Meeting Notes

Emergency plans

Event Settlement Documents

The Event Summary

Ticket and/or Participant Registration Reports

Financial Reports

Wrap Up Documents

Payroll Information

Sponsor ROI Reports

Incident Reports

Minutes from Debriefing Meetings

Incident Reports

Customer Complaints/Concerns

Post-Event Recap

Completing a thorough wrap up of the event will strengthen existing relationships, create new ones, and generate positive feelings towards the event. Time and effort spent on sponsor communications and ROI reports will help sponsors justify future involvement in the event or organization, and post-event communications with all personnel help with staff retention.

Having a complete and detailed event file will provide the documentation needed for the future. If the event returns to the facility, all of the finances of the event will be available for reference, ideas for improvement will be noted so they can be implemented, and mistakes are less likely since they will be recorded. Many events will not conduct follow up, therefore the event that does will also make a mark in the minds of all of those involved as a first-class operation.

SUMMARY

Event settlement is one of the crucial components of a successful sports or entertainment event hosted or staged at any facility. Primarily, the purpose of the settlement is to summarize all income from all sources, pay all legitimate expenses incurred by the event, and to divide any remaining proceeds pursuant to the original contract or lease agreement.

If all revenue and expense items are properly anticipated, accounted for, and verified, and a solid, clear, and executed agreement is in hand, the event settlement should be smooth and simple, with little or no anxiety, argument, or dispute. The parties will then leave the settlement table with a good feeling and be willing to do business together again another day.

Other wrap-up items may seem like common sense, but after a long event it is often a struggle to truly finish the event management process. However, there is significant long-term value in attention to detail in wrapping up the event. By taking time to communicate with sponsors, debrief staff, and create an event file, future events are sure to be improved because there are readily available notes of what went right, what went wrong, and which sponsors were involved. Additionally, all volunteer workers deserve to be thanked for their time, as they will feel valued by the organization and more likely to volunteer at future events. Payment should also be made promptly to staff that are compensated. The event is not truly over until settlement and wrap up are complete, and for many events this process just indicates the beginning of planning for the next event.

Student Challenge

STUDENT CHALLENGE #15

In Challenge #15, explore the event settlement and wrap up tasks associated with the event.

QUESTION 15-1

Which type of building agreement most closely resembles the contract for the event?

QUESTION 15-2

List and describe all disbursements for the event.

Student Challenge

QUESTION 15-3

List and describe event wrap up tasks for the event.

QUESTION 15-4

What is anticipated to be the most challenging aspect of event settlement or wrap up for the event? Why?

CHAPTER 16

INTERNATIONAL CONSIDERATIONS FOR EVENTS

Mike Rielly, Ming Li, and Jay Ogden

Sport and sports events have always had global appeal thanks to events such as the Olympics. But now, the emergence of global television coverage of major sporting events, as well as Internet technology, has made it easier for spectators to connect with events, athletes, and teams anywhere in the world. According to Plunkett Research (2008), "a reasonable estimate of the total U.S. sports market might be $425 to $450 billion yearly" (¶ 2). When examining sport beyond U.S. borders, there are no agreed-upon numbers as to the size of the global sports marketplace. It is clear, however, that the global sport industry is strong. For example, one estimate on global sport sponsorship spending is broken down by world region and indicates that North America spends $16.8 billion, Europe spends $11.7 billion, the Pacific Rim spends $9.5 billion, and Central/South America spends $3.5 billion (Ukman, 2008, p. 7).

The global sport industry is different from other industries in that it can, "stir up deep passion within spectators and players alike in countries around the world" (Plunkett, 2008, ¶1). In general, a vibrant sports industry will be found wherever there is a healthy economy. This chapter will provide a brief introduction to international sport, will discuss specific event considerations for events with international audiences and participants, and introduce special operational issues that need to be addressed for events with international participants.

INTERNATIONAL SPORTS

Emerging economies, like China, are experiencing sports booms. In fact, three of the largest sporting events or leagues in the world are international in nature: The Fédération Internationale de Football Association (FIFA) World Cup (soccer), the Union of European Football Associations (UEFA) Cup (soccer), and the Olympics (multi-sport). Additionally, the North American-based National Basketball Association (NBA) announced in 2008 a plan to expand the league to China.

By way of background, the FIFA World Cup has taken place every four years since its launch in 1930 and is for men's national teams who are members of FIFA, soccer's global governing body (FIFA, n.d.a). According to FIFA.com (n.d.b.), "The 2006 FIFA World Cup in Germany had a total cumulative television audience of 26.29 billion (24.2 billion in-home and 2.1 billion out-of-home viewers)" (¶ 2). FIFA also sponsors the Women's World Cup and men's and women's youth tournaments (FIFA, n.d.c). Although World Cup competition takes place in different countries, FIFA is based in Zurich, Switzerland (FIFA, n.d.d.).

The UEFA Champions League is a seasonal football competition for the most successful clubs in Europe. Since 1955, top clubs in this league have competed for the European Cup, one of the most important trophies in the sport (UEFA, n.d.a.). Historically, the most successful teams have been from England, Germany, Italy, and Spain, but all European teams have experienced success over the years (UEFA, n.d.a.). In addition to the Champions League, there are tournaments for women's and youth teams, and the UEFA supports grassroots efforts in Europe (UEFA, n.d.a). UEFA is also based in Switzerland (Nyon), although the competition moves around Europe each season (UEFA, n.d.b.).

The Olympic Games, of course, are the world's most important international multi-sport event and are governed by the International Olympic Committee (IOC). The (modern) Summer Olympic Games were launched in Greece in 1896, and the Winter Olympic Games were first held in France in 1924 (IOC, n.d.a.). The number of events and sports tends to increase with each Olympic Games to keep pace with advancements in sport. The 2008 Beijing Olympic Games, for example, featured approximately 10,500 athletes competing in 28 sports (IOC, n.d.b). The IOC, like FIFA and UEFA, is based in Switzerland (Lausanne) (IOC, n.d.c).

China has had the Chinese Basketball Association (CBA) since 1954 (China.org, n.d.), and the NBA has featured players from China for years. Recently, Yao Ming has sparked unparalleled in interest in the NBA among the Chinese. As a result of Yao Ming's impact, the 2008 Olympics in Beijing, new facility development in China, and the strength of the sport industry in China, the NBA has been exploring how to move into the Chinese market. In 2008, the NBA announced plans to expand into China with at least $253 million in backing from a variety of investors including ESPN (a division of The Walt Disney Company), Bank of China Group Investment, Legend Holdings Limited, Li Ka Shing Foundation, and China Merchants Investments (Plunkett, 2008). In what may be an effort by the CBA to keep the NBA out or an effort to work with them, new rules were passed for the 2008–2009 season which allows CBA teams to field up to two foreign players (Agency, 2009). Even with this new rule, former NBA players in China have to adjust to the different, less aggressive, playing style in China (Agency). It is clear that when the NBA does officially expand to China, it will have to work with the CBA to access facilities, leverage broadcasting relationships, and create buy-in from the Chinese.

The globalization of sport will continue to bring about the emergence of previously domestic leagues looking to enter the global marketplace. This trend will create opportunities for sports managers that are knowledgeable about international sport to manage events, facilities, teams, and even leagues around the world.

INTERNATIONAL CONSIDERATIONS

Sporting events can be local, regional, national, or international in scope. The continuum of international sporting events ranges from historically national events, which have developed an international strategy, to truly global events including those mentioned above, as well as World Championships, and international federation events in numerous sports. Managers of U.S. sporting events should be aware of numerous international considerations when planning their events.

Sponsors

Companies sponsor sports events for many reasons. For corporate awareness and branding, sports are ideal because they are TiVo proof and viewers cannot escape properly placed event signage. At non-speed events such as golf, tennis, and figure skating, sponsor signage can be seen for many minutes, if not hours. For example, at the 2007 International Skating Union (ISU) World Figure Skating Championships in Tokyo, the seven sponsors enjoyed a total of 272,688 seconds of global television exposure, with a gross media value of over $50 million.

At international championship events, it is not unusual to find a mix of national and global companies sponsoring the event. National companies are there to receive exposure in their home market, while global companies are trying to receive global exposure at less cost than a country-by-country media buy. With respect to national companies, it is interesting to note that often this revenue is left on the table by event managers unaware of this hidden revenue stream. For example, an international friendship soccer game held in Mexico City between the United States and Mexico has the potential to generate sponsor revenue from a cell phone provider in the United States and a cell phone provider in Mexico.

In other situations, the sponsor categories can be split several ways, as long as the products/services of sponsoring companies do not compete directly in their respective home markets. For example, a Chinese financial institution may have no problem sharing the financial institution category with a European financial institution if both institutions only do business in their home markets. In essence, the same sponsorship can be sold twice, resulting in additional revenue. Event managers then ensure through technology that the television viewing audience in Europe only sees the European company sponsor, and vice versa.

Media

Television coverage remains the key to a successful international event. For example, the UEFA Champions League has developed a very large television audience, not just in Europe, but also throughout the world. The first match, in 1956, was watched live only by 33,000 fans in the stadium (Harte, 2005). By 2005, the global television audience had grown to 200 million (Harte, 2005). In November 2008, UEFA announced its Chinese television partner, CCTV, would broadcast one live match and a highlights show each night of Champions League action (Associated Press, 2008; UEFA, 2008). CCTV reaches 350 million households in China alone, and more than doubles UEFA's global footprint when compared with 2005 (Associated Press, 2008; UEFA, 2008). Television is another area where events with international interest can generate more than one national broadcasting agreement. Using the international friendship soccer game referenced above, savvy event managers recognize the potential for broadcasting rights in both the United States and Mexico for greater exposure and, in turn, greater potential for revenue.

The Internet is becoming increasingly important for exposure to a younger audience, but data on a viable Internet financial formula is still lacking. In order to encourage online advertising at the Beijing Olympics, NBC bundled Web banner ads with its TV ads (Learmonth, 2008). Even without a set formula on the value of Internet broadcasting of sports events, the potential to expand the reach of an event is unlimited through providing access to events through the Internet. Whether or not to seek out Internet advertisers depends largely on the type of event, the event objectives, and the availability of technical personnel to ensure success. Currently, most advertisers have yet to fully embrace Internet advertising in sports. Until they are willing to pay for it, television coverage remains vital.

Participants

An event's success is often determined by the event participants and their performances. The Women's Tennis Association (WTA) and Association of Tennis Professionals (ATP) tennis events have been known to move around the world based on star player performances. Figure skating boomed in Germany in the early 1990s due to the success of German figure skater Katarina Witt. In 2007, Japan became the number one figure skating market in the world due to Miki Ando and Mao Asada from Japan, who finished first and second, respectively, at the International Skating Union (ISU) World Championships in Tokyo (ISU, 2007). Women's golf became an overnight sensation in Korea due to the success of Korean golfers, starting with Se Ri Pak. Today, there are 126 international Ladies Professional Golf Association (LPGA) players from 26 countries, and 45 of them are South Korean (Dorman, 2008; LPGA, 2008).

The world's best events attract the world's best players either by invitation, location, prestige, ranking points, or some combination thereof. However, the world's best events will often be found in those countries which have the stars of a particular sport. The stars attract a robust on-site audience and television viewership. This results in more revenue for the event. Over the last 25 years, the Fédération Internationale de Ski (FIS) World Alpine Ski Championships have only been held twice in the United States—1989 and 1999—when the Vail and Beaver Creek ski resorts in Colorado hosted this prestigious event (FIS, n.d.). The majority of alpine skiing stars are European grown, and every other World Championship over those 25 years was held in the traditionally strong alpine skiing countries of Europe. However, with the 2008 success of the U.S. stars, Bode Miller and Lindsey Vonn, it is anticipated that the World Championships will return to the United States soon.

Spectators

Closely tied to participant success is spectator interest. Tennis interest in the United States has suffered from the lack of U.S. male stars in recent years. Conversely, the "Tiger Woods effect" in golf is extraordinary, and this effect has been both national and international in terms of the spectator interest generated for events in which Tiger plays. The Frys.com Open, a 2008 PGA Tour event in Arizona, utilized the defending champion, Mike Weir, to attract residents of his native Canada. Tournament organizers created partnerships with Canadian travel companies and with the Canadian consulate in Phoenix to attract Canadian tourists to the event (Show, 2008). Generally speaking, spectators will support phenomenal athletes, and athletes with whom they have some affinity, including regional, racial, ethnic, and gender affinity. The challenge is in reaching these spectators.

Politics

The globalization of sports as illustrated by the Olympic Movement has had a positive effect on cultural and political differences among participants and spectators. The 2008 Beijing Olympic Games were a prime example of this. The Beijing Organizing Committee kept the focus on the competitions and the competitors, even with some trouble leading up to the Games.

During the Torch Relay, there were frequent political protests along the route as the Olympic Torch made its way to Beijing. The protestors, upset with China-Tibet relations, were able to make their point in front of a worldwide audience by interrupting the Torch Relay. Because of this, there were concerns before the Games about protestors disrupting events or even becoming a security threat. By the time the Olympics began, the eyes of the world were on the competitions, with little attention given to international politics.

Even a war between Russia and Georgia which began during the Games could not derail the competition. Prior to their match, Georgian and Russian volleyball players embraced each other, illustrating that sport does transcend politics (Xinhua, 2008). The Beijing Organizing Committee was able to produce an event that defied the odds and was a huge success for the Olympic Movement.

Budgets

Specific to international events, the budgeting may be complex in that exchange rates (which vary day by day) come into play, as do cultural issues related to conducting business. In-kind sponsorships can help defray the costs of doing business and can provide the event with a needed service. For example, if the event was being held in the United States and was looking to attract an international audience, the event organizers might look to well-known athletes from around the world to participate. Many of these athletes will expect that the event pay their expenses. However, if the event's budget does not allow that, maybe the event manager can secure a sponsor from each of the athletes' home countries willing to pay the travel for the athlete, in return for signage at the event that will be seen on television. Such arrangements can help an overall event budget stay on course.

As discussed previously in this book, contracts are the cornerstone to successful event management in the United States. However, many other countries use "handshake agreements" for some aspects of their business dealings. Event managers should not be surprised at resistance to contracts, as the verbal agreement in some cultures is common practice.

OPERATIONAL ISSUES

Operational issues at international events are similar to those faced by event managers at any event. There are some issues that are more apparent and more challenging when international athletes, spectators, and media are involved. Additionally, the operational issues at the FIS Alpine World Ski Championships are completely different from the ISU World Figure Skating Championships simply because of the differences in sports. However, some similarities exist in other areas of preparation such as event registrations, visa requirements, language services, media, food choices, interfaith services, temporary medical licenses, and national flags and anthems.

Registration

For participant-driven events such as the ING New York City Marathon, participants generally register themselves to enter the event. The Internet has enabled event organizers to avoid some issues previously encountered when participant entries had to be submitted through the mail (i.e. cost, not receiving entries, and late entries due to international mail service). Now, with effective use of the Internet, international athletes participating in events outside their home country are able to register for events as easily as their domestic counterparts.

Visa

All the international participants, including athletes, coaches, and other team officials are subject to the standard procedures for a visitor's stay in the United States. Visas are necessary for the international participants from nations that are subject to this requirement. To facilitate their entry into the United States, the event organizer will issue an official visa support form to the international participants once they have registered online.

International participants who will enter the United States in one of the following circumstances to compete and stay in the country temporarily can apply for a B-1 visa:

- A professional athlete, such as a golfer or tennis player, who receives no salary or payment other than prize money for his or her participation in a tournament or sporting event;

- An international athlete as a member of a foreign-based team;

- An amateur team sports player who is asked to join a professional team during the course of the regular professional season or playoffs for brief try-outs (Consulate General of the United States, n.d.).

The international participants must also be informed that they need to have a passport valid through at least six months after the event. Any difference between the information in the invitation and the passport may result in failing to get the visa.

Cultural Awareness Tips

Michelle Wells

It is common to interpret speaking the same language as having the same culture, when in fact, English-speaking countries may have very different expectations with respect to culture and business functions. Whether in a country that primarily speaks English or one that speaks another language, business cultures will vary between countries, even when on the face it seems that operations would be similar.

American culture sometimes varies on its deference to a person's status, but we often single out those in higher positions and publicly acknowledge those who have made accomplishments. In many other cultures, these practices may not be as acceptable. Whether referred to as the "tall poppy" syndrome or using the phrase "the nail that sticks up gets hammered down," specific individuals and individual achievements are often not recognized or appropriate to recognize in some countries. Instead, modesty, parity, and mutual respect are preferred.

Direct communication differs based on the part of the world in which one lives and/or works. Australians, for example, may jump quickly to using first names with business colleagues, whereas in China, this may not occur until colleagues know one another much better. In many Asian cultures, once the initial handshake has occurred, physical contact should not occur. One should not even put a hand on another's chair. During face-to-face conversations, the physical distance between speakers will vary around the world. Americans generally are comfortable with at least 18 to 24 inches between speakers. Other cultures space requirements vary significantly. It is important to read the signals of the other person. If she takes a step back, it may be an indication that her personal space is being invaded.

The pliable nature that some cultures have with time will generally not translate well to working situations in certain countries. Being late may convey the impression that people are unreliable or careless in their business to an American, but different cultures place different values on timeliness. The time needed to complete business transactions may vary, too. Americans generally have a "time is money" attitude and want business transactions to proceed and conclude quickly. In other locations, such as Asia and the Middle East, business dealings may take much longer than Americans are used to, often because it is important for people to get to know those with whom they will possibly be doing business. In the United States, it has become common for business colleagues to be available far beyond the standard 9 to 5 working hours with the advent of cell phones and email availability on cell phones. Some cultures do not "take work home with them" as many Americans tend to do. They may have set business hours and working and/or being available beyond those hours may not be reasonable to expect.

Hand gestures, such as a thumbs up or OK symbol may seem benign, but in fact, could be perceived as obscene in some cultures. The intention of the gesture and how it is received and interpreted could be on opposite ends of the spectrum. Body language is just as important as the actual words in international business. For example, making eye contact in many cultures is seen as a sign of respect and shows that a person is interested in what another has to say. Eye contact should be brief so that it does not suggest impoliteness or intimidation. If direct eye contact seems to be embarrassing for the other person, briefly break eye contact. Also, be cognizant of and avoid body language that may suggest boredom, such as slouching or yawning.

Communication across cultures can be difficult enough with all of the various aspects that come into consideration. To avoid adding undue challenges, avoid using jargon, slang, technical terms, and acronyms. Speak clearly, but not loudly. Raising the volume of one's voice will not increase understanding of the language or topic, but it will likely annoy people.

The best advice that can be given to event managers that will interact with event participants, media, spectators, or business partners from other countries is to understand the culture. Through basic Web research, reading travel books, and talking with colleagues, event managers should gain a good understanding of the culture to ensure they are respectful and have the best experience possible in their international interactions.

Language Services

The participation of international athletes in an event requires the event organizers to use a variety of measures to ensure that the international participants feel included throughout the event. The measures include the formation of an enthusiastic and friendly volunteer group whose members are proficient in the commonly used foreign languages, sensitive to cultural differences, and capable of handling conflicts. Event managers should also be prepared to disseminate all event-related information in multiple languages.

Media

The event organizers should expect and be prepared for international media. Volunteers with translation skills can be the key to foreign visitors feeling comfortable and being well informed. The fluid operation of media functions is a critical area. An event needs the technical infrastructure and staff to allow the media to tell the story of the event to a wide global audience.

Food

The event organizer should make a variety of ethnic food choices available to international participants to suit their special dietary requirements in the catering facility. For example, in addition to some traditional Chinese dishes and other Asian-influenced foods, the Beijing Olympic athletes were served with food from the Mediterranean, the Americas, the Caribbean, and Europe—a total of over 800 recipes—with a focus on lean meats and fish for protein, and a variety of fresh fruits, vegetables, and whole grains (Tsang & Newberry, 2008).

Interfaith Services

If an event lasts more than a couple of days, such as the Olympics, the World University Games, the Pan American Games, and other mega events, it is important for the event organizer to provide interfaith services for domestic and international participants alike. Often worship is extremely important to international competitors and spectators alike. To effectively handle various religious service-related issues, the event organizer should form an interfaith advisory council. Such a structure may (1) advise the event organizer on religious matters, and (2) help them in preparing for religious observances. The event organizer should identify appropriate facilities that conform to the religions requirements as venues for interfaith services.

Medical Services

While planning for an international event, the event manager should be prepared to handle a number of medical-related issues, one of which is: should foreign physicians coming along with participating teams be allowed to practice medicine in the United States? If yes, then the event organizer should develop a system to verify the qualification of foreign physicians so that they can be granted a temporary medical license and be allowed to provide care to their own participants. For example, the Chinese government required that all foreign team physicians register with the Beijing municipal health authorities before they were allowed to practice medicine in China during the 2008 Beijing Olympic Games.

National Anthem and National Flag

At the medal award ceremony, the gold medal winner's national anthem is played as his or her national flag is hoisted. So, it is important for the event organizer to require that all participating countries provide their national anthem and flag prior to the event. The size of the flag and the length of the anthem must be standard to allow for uniformity from country to country.

This is not an exhaustive list of possible operational issues event managers might face, but does begin to get the event manager thinking in terms of those areas that require extra attention.

EMERGING INTERNATIONAL SPORT: FORMULA DRIFT

The progressive event manger will also be educated and aware of emerging international sport trends. Not only do new sports provide an opportunity to create new events, but there are some sports that are popular internationally that have not caught on in the United States. There are also some popular sports in North America that have not yet translated to a large fan following internationally. Both of these situations provide opportunities for event managers looking for non-traditional opportunities in event management.

Formula Drift is a relatively new sport, appeals to the "tuner culture" (primarily males age 18–24), and is aggressively internationalizing its focus and operations. Drifting is a high-skill, high-powered motor sport that requires drivers to control a 200- to 400-horsepower car while it slides sideways at high speeds through a marked course. Drifting is judged on execution and style rather than who finishes the course the fastest (Formula DRIFT, n.d.a.). Drifting takes all the thrilling moments of traditional motor sports and packs it together into an intimate setting with non-stop action.

Drifting has been popular in Japan for at least 15 years, and is now among the most-attended motorsport events in Japan (Formula DRIFT, n.d.b.). In the 1980s and 1990s, the sport began to move to the United States, but only in very recent years has it evolved into what it is today as a powerful emerging sport. The Formula Drift Championship Series was created in the United States in 2003. This series features competition cars that are sold in the United States; aftermarket parts that are available in stores; and drivers with abilities and personalities to build the sport in the U.S. market. By 2007, Formula Drift was positioned at the forefront of this unique automotive culture which has been recognized as the fastest-growing segment in motor sports. The time was right to go global.

The Formula Drift organization in the United States established associations with other Drift organizers in Australia, Asia, continental Europe, and Scandinavia. A set of qualifying criteria was established for the first Formula Drift World Championships to be held in November 2008 in Long Beach, California. The World Championships will be televised in 40 countries and will give the sport the global exposure necessary for future growth.

As reported in Business Week, "...remember NASCAR started as a bunch of good 'ol boys running souped-up jalopies south of the Mason-Dixon line, and not so very long ago, tennis' Grand Slams tournaments were contested by amateurs"(Lehman, n.d., ¶ 2). In other words, emerging events and/or sports might be on the front pages of tomorrow's sports sections. With today's youth craving faster and novel sports, and thanks in large part to the mainstreaming of "action sports," participants, investors, and sponsors are moving into emerging sports and into international markets. The advice in this chapter, applied correctly, should help events secure national and/or international support.

An Interview with
Christine (Cusick) Moore

*Director, Torch Relays Promotions for the Vancouver 2010 Olympic and
Paralympic Games Organizing Committee (VANOC)*

This interview was conducted one year prior to the opening of the 2010 Winter Olympic Games in Vancouver, British Columbia, Canada.

What are your current responsibilities for 2010 Vancouver and the Torch Relay?

First of all, let me say that I think I have the greatest job ever. I work on the Vancouver 2010 Olympic Torch Relay. This is the type of project that connects the country and spreads the message of the Olympics far and wide. For the Torch Relay, we have three different divisions: Operations, Promotions, and Communications. I look after the Promotions Division, which has a variety of areas: marketing/sponsorship, community celebrations, torchbearer operations, aboriginal participation, as well as the Paralympic Torch Relay development. We work very closely with Communications and Operations teams in the overall delivery of the project.

Looking at the marketing and sponsorship side, we work closely with two presenting sponsors, Coca-Cola and RBC (Royal Bank of Canada), as well as the Government of Canada. Coca-Cola is a worldwide sponsor for the Olympic Games, and this is the eighth Torch Relay they've been part of. Coca-Cola has been involved in the Olympic Movement since 1928, and brings a great deal of experience in promoting the relay to all Canadians. We are really fortunate to have RBC involved, also. They are a respected Canadian company and have the "bricks and mortar" (physical locations) in the community. We are working with them on many community relations pieces. The Government of Canada has invested in the Olympic Games overall, and then specifically in the Torch Relay. They will assist the relay in reaching all Canadians, and will provide a considerable amount of support to the community celebrations. We have a few second-tier Olympic Torch Relay sponsors: Bombardier, who has designed the Olympic Torch; Hudson's Bay Company, who has designed the uniforms and will be outfitting all the torchbearers and staff; and Bell, who is the mobile services supplier. At one year to go to the Games, we announced our torch design and our uniform design for Relay runners.

The true event management area that is under my purview is Community Celebrations. We are working closely with the sponsors on how they will activate their sponsorship in the community celebrations and along the route. We will host nearly 200 community celebrations, from small towns such as Taber, Alberta, to large cities, like Toronto and Ottawa. Each celebration will be very different, with much of the programming being local, turning the spotlight on as many communities as possible across Canada. The Relay will be traveling 45,000 kilometers (nearly 28,000 miles) by plane, convoy segments, ferries, alternative modes of transport, (such as dogsled, snowmobile, ski, etc.), and of course by torchbearer running segments. We are running in over 1,020 communities and in the populated areas of Canada, while driving in between in order to reach as many people as possible.

We have appointed an agency to help us build out the celebrations platform. This agency is sourcing staff and stage trucks. Each stage truck will come fully equipped with lights, sound, video screens, all the banners, and all of the things that we need to take a rolling stage show across the Relay. For most of the relay, VANOC, along with Canadian communities, will host two celebrations per day—one around lunchtime and one in the evening. Each of the celebrations is about a six-hour operation. We have a couple of hours of setup, a couple of hours of testing and rehearsals with the communities, a couple of hours of performance, and finally about an hour-and-a-half of shut down/strike. Each one of those events is a lot to do in one day, and the event staff is doing it every day, six hours or more of operations every day for nearly 106 days. Plus, they will be driving long distances in order to get to the next destination and make sure that site is ready.

In mid-2008, we started the process to meet with nearly 200 celebrations communities, and all of them have welcomed us to their communities, signed agreements with us, and are helping us with city services and site selection. The communities are responsible for the majority of the entertainment on the stage and, in addition, will secure a lot of volunteers, help with security, and help with some setup. Of the over 100 crew who travel with us to put on the Relay overall, seven people for each stage are responsible for setup and strike every day. VANOC will run the different infrastructure pieces, bring an MC, and have all of the lights and sound, but the communities are responsible for the majority of the content. We will provide about 30–45 minutes of content with us every day that will contain 10–15 minutes of each presenting partner providing a performance or activation on the stage, followed by flame protocol programming. The flame protocol includes traditional speeches that need to be given by the sponsors, governments, and VANOC, as well as the final runner onto the stage to light the portable cauldron. We are in the process of programming that information now, and are also working with the communities on helping them program the time they are responsible for. Bottom line is we will create nearly 200 shows in the course of a three-month period.

Torchbearer operations are a critical area of the Relay as well. One of the key benefits for presenting partners Coca-Cola and RBC is that they can activate public outreach campaigns for the torchbearer program. Coke and RBC are the true way that people can become engaged with the Torch Relay and become a torchbearer. Coca-Cola and RBC are running promotional programs to encourage all Canadians to apply to be torchbearers through iCoke.ca and rbc.com/carrythetorch.

Vancouver is my forth international assignment. Other international assignments include: four years in Sydney, Australia (for the 2000 Olympic Games); two years in Manchester, England (2002 Commonwealth Games); and four months in Athens, Greece (2004 Olympic Games).

With your experience, what would you say are the biggest differences in working international events and domestic events?

The biggest difference, to me, is stakeholder management and stakeholder communications. With international events like the Olympics, there is a higher profile, and the event is under a bigger microscope. Each stakeholder, from sponsors, to communities, to governments, to suppliers, to just the general businesses with the host city, has some kind of investment in the project. And each stakeholder believes that their piece is the most important, most critical to delivering the event. And, quite honestly, they are all right! Events on the international stage could not be put on by just a few people. Each stakeholder investment (and this includes money, time, and emotional investments) is a critical piece in the success of the event. As the organizer of an event, it is our job to ensure that each stakeholder is recognized appropriately for what they are doing, as well as ensuring that stakeholder relationships and communications are solid. This ensures everyone is aligned and informed every step of the way.

In all events, there are a number of stakeholders that you need to look after. However, with events such as the Olympics, the stakeholders are all across the world, with time differences, language differences, and cultural differences, so the communication challenges are much greater.

What advice would you give to someone who wants to work in international events, and what skills do you think they should pick up?

There are two ways to look at this: (1) Try to secure a position within a company that has international business; and (2) secure your own visa/work permit.

First, starting young and networking are important. There a many companies out there that have international offices. If people get into an organization or agency that has an international arm, they should try to work their way into that international arm, even if it is freelancing or volunteering for a few projects. Those are all good ways to get involved, set targets, and put themselves in situations that will allow them to meet people, as well as perform duties or tasks that will put them in a position for an international assignment. Individuals have to be proactive, target organizations that have international offices, and if they have a country that they are targeting or trying to get access to, research and see what it takes to get their own work visa in that country.

Second, anyone who wants to work in international sports needs to be tenacious and do their own homework as far as permitting (work license/work visa) is concerned. I have been very lucky, because the companies I have worked for have always taken care of my visas because I was hired and then transferred, versus showing up in a country and needing to get the work visa. It is important that individuals take responsibility for their own permitting, which makes it easier for employers to hire them once they are in the country of choice.

If people want to work internationally, know right up front—it is going to be long hours. With international events, because of time zone differences, be prepared to take conference calls at 6:00 am or 9:00 pm, while working a full day in the office. My husband was working with the Beijing Olympics for a long period of time. He was on the phone many times at 9:00 pm for conference calls with China. When I lived in Sydney, I had a weekly conference call at 6:00 am with my team back in Atlanta and Lausanne (Switzerland). It is not a big deal, but it is one thing that I do not think people realize from the very beginning.

Last, it is important for people to do their homework and read books on the culture they are about to work in, and learn a language if possible. They need to understand cultural differences and be aware of and sensitive to them. Specifically, they should understand how they do business and how they manage their personal lives. I grew up in the Midwest of the United States, and even moving to Vancouver was very different. People should be patriotic about where they come from, but they also need to be open and mindful of what other cultures do and say and how they react. This is critical in order to live and work in another country.

ADVICE FROM THE INTERNATIONAL EXPERTS

Event managers with the ability to capitalize on international aspects of sport will find themselves in demand in the job market. It is the goal of the authors, who have been involved in many international events, to provide readers with some tips related to the planning and management of international events.

Tips

1. Identify sponsors with marketing objectives matching the profile of the sporting event, including the demographics of participants, spectators, and television audience. As sport is an increasingly global industry, determine whether there are international sponsors who may be interested in the event. Many global companies have U.S. representative offices (and budgets), while others require making contact with their global headquarters (and tapping into their global budgets).

2. Ideally, secure some kind of television coverage for the event. Simultaneously, in order to globalize the event, and to attract a younger audience, develop an Internet strategy, one that acts as a promotional arm and as primary or supplementary coverage for the event.

3. If the goal is a globally recognized event, attract a few of the best international competitors. Invite them directly, or through an intermediary, such as their national governing body. The event sanction becomes critical in this case due to rules and regulations surrounding competition eligibility of these competitors. In addition to any prize money the event offers, supplemental funding for travel expenses and other financial guarantees may need to be offered. All of this must, of course, be within the rules of the governing body.

4. Develop a strategy that targets supporters of the sport. For example, in order to attract international spectators, determine where the sport is followed internationally, and then target those particular expatriate communities and/or support clubs which exist in the community. Work closely with them to provide information, ticket promotions, and other creative proposals, including access to participants from their country. This will make attending the event attractive to their community.

5. In general, ramping up the event for international participants, spectators, sponsors, and media will lead to additional costs. Be aware of the budget consequences when globalizing the event, and make sure the benefits outweigh the costs. If globalizing the event is at the request of sponsors, or for the benefit of sponsors, consider asking the sponsor to provide additional financial support for the additional benefits they will receive.

SUMMARY

As economies around the world are emerging and strengthening, the sports business industry is also growing internationally. Sport is big business in the United States, and is becoming big business on a global scale. Thanks to the Olympic Movement, and the globalization of many sports including soccer, golf, tennis, figure skating, and, yes, Formula Drift, the sports industry is becoming a global community.

Whether the event is currently domestic or international in its focus, sport event managers should strive to be in tune with the needs and wants of spectators, participants, sponsors, and media. These needs and wants are increasingly international. Sport event managers should think beyond their borders and, where appropriate, reach out to international sponsors, media, participants, and spectators. There are indeed challenges and costs associated with going global; however, the immediate and long-term benefits can and should outweigh any such challenges and costs.

Student Challenge

STUDENT CHALLENGE #16

In Challenge #16, make the event international in nature. Apply some of the tips provided in Chapter 16 to the event.

QUESTION 16-1

What new group of international spectators should be targeted to view the event streaming online? Why?

QUESTION 16-2

How will the marketing and sponsorship strategies identified in Challenge #6 and Challenge #7 change to attract this new group of international spectators to view the event streaming online? Consider that international spectators would need to become aware of the event, sponsors are needed to cover the cost of streaming the event, and creativity is needed for it to be appealing to the international market.

REFERENCES

Agency. (2009, February 25). NBA veterans find culture class in China league. China Daily. Retrieved March 12, 2009, from http://www.chinadaily.com.cn/sports/2009-02/25/content_7511370_2.htm.

American Airlines Center. (n.d.). Standard operating procedures. Unpublished document.

Ammon, R., & Stotlar, D. K. (2003). Sport facility and event management. In J. B. Parks, & J. Quarterman (Eds.), (2nd ed., pp. 255). Champaign, IL: Human Kinetics.

Arbitron Inc. (2009). Radio stations: Terms of the trade. Retrieved on April 14, 2009, from http://www.arbitron.com/radio_stations/tradeterms.htm.

Associated Press. (2008, November 17). UEFA sells Champions League TV rights in China. Retrieved December 1, 2008, from http://msn.foxsports.com/soccer/story/8807816/UEFA-sells-Champions-League-TV-rights-in-China.

Athletic Business. (n.d.). Facility specifications. Retrieved January 22, 2009, from http://www.athleticbusiness.com/specifications.

Baseball Writers' of America. (2008). Constitution. Retrieved December 5, 2008, from http://www.baseballwriters.org/constitution.html.

BC 2010 Olympic bid. (n.d.). Retrieved December 4, 2008, from http://www.mapleleafweb.com/old/education/spotlight/issue_28/olympic.html.

Beck, H. (2008, 19 November). The real O'Neal puts his cyber foot down. The New York Times. Retrieved on March 24, 2009, from http://www.nytimes.com.

Cecil Soccer. (n.d.). Cecil soccer links page—soccer field measurements. Retrieved January 20, 2009, from http://www.cecilsoccer.org/links.htm.

China.org. (n.d.). Chinese basketball association (CBA). Retrieved March 12, 2008, from http://www.china.org.cn/english/features/2004-2005cba/118959.htm.

City of Cincinnati Task Force on Crowd Control and Safety. (1980). Crowd management: Report of the task force on crowd control and safety. Retrieved April 8, 2009, from http://www.crowdsafe.com/taskrpt/chpt1.html.

Communicaid Group, Ltd. (2007). Doing Business in Australia. Retrieved March 18, 2009, from http://www.communicaid.com/access/pdf/library/culture/doing-business-in/Doing%20Business%20in%20Australia.pdf.

Consulate General of the United States. (n.d.). Non-immigrant frequently asked questions performers/athletes. Retrieved March 10, 2009, from http://amsterdam.usconsulate.gov/niv_perf_athl.html.

Corriher, K. (2007, December 6). NCAA volleyball tourney a win for the local economy. Retrieved December 5, 2008, from http://ohiobobcats.cstv.com/sports/w-volley/spec-rel/120607aaa.html.

Cotten, D. (2003). Which parties are liable? In D. Cotton, & J. Wolohan (Eds.), Law for recreation and sport managers (3rd ed., pp. 66–77). Dubuque, IA: Kendall Hunt.

Cotten, D. (2007). Waivers and releases. In D. Cotten & J. Wolohan (Eds.), Law for recreation and sport managers, (4th ed., p. 85). Dubuque, IA: Kendall Hunt

Crews, D., & Zavotka, S. (2006). Aging, disability, and frailty: Implications for universal design. Journal of Physiological Anthropology, 25, 113–118.

Deeson, Mike. (n.d.). Economist says 2009 super bowl will have little economic impact on Tampa. Retrieved April 5, 2009, from http://www.wtsp.com/news/local/story.aspx?storyid=73176.

DiRocco, M. (2009, April 1). Numbers don't add up to shift Florida-Georgia game: Some think the annual game ought to be in Georgia despite the tradition. Florida Times Union. Retrieved April 5, 2009, from http://www.jacksonville.com/news/metro/2009-04-01/story/numbers_dont_add_up_to_shift_uf-uga_game.

Dorman, L. (2008, August 26). LPGA players required to learn English. Retrieved October 24, 2008, from http://www.mercurynews.com/golf/ci_10310954.

Epstien, A. (2003). *Sports Law*. West Legal Studies. Clifton Park, NY: Thompson Delmar Learning.

EventManagerBlog. (2008, June 15). Top 5 qualities of the successful event manager. Message posted to http://www.eventmanagerblog.com/2008/04/top-5-qualities.html.

EventManager. (2009a). Home. Retrieved on March 30, 2009, from http://www.sbdatabases.com.

EventManager. (2009b). Download. Retrieved on March 30, 2009, from http://www.sbdatabases.com/event-manager-software.html.

Federal Emergency Management Agency. (2005, March). Special events contingency planning. Retrieved, January 27, 2009, from http://www.americanrestroom.org/gov/fema/FEMA_SECP39_41.PDF.

Fédération Internationale de Football Association. (n.d.a.). *Previous FIFA worldcups*. Retrieved October 29, 2008, from http://www.fifa.com/worldcup/archive/index.html.

Fédération Internationale de Football Association. (n.d.b.). *TV data*. Retrieved October 13, 2008, from http://www.fifa.com/aboutfifa/marketingtv/factsfigures/tvdata.html.

Fédération Internationale de Football Association. (n.d.c.). *Tournaments*. Retrieved October 29, 2008, from http://www.fifa.com/tournaments/index.html.

Fédération Internationale de Football Association. (n.d.d.). *Contact FIFA*. Retrieved October 29, 2008, from http://www.fifa.com/contact/index.html.

Fédération Internationale de Ski (n.d.). FIS world ski championships. Retrieved December 2, 2008, from http://www.fis-ski.com/uk/majorevents/fisworldskichampionships.html.

Flash Seats. (2009). FAQS. Retrieved on March 28, 2009, from www.flashseats.com.

Formula DRIFT. (n.d.a.). Formula DRIFT info. Retrieved November 4, 2008, from http://formulad.com/general-info/formula-drift-info.html.

Formula DRIFT. (n.d.b.). Formula DRIFT history. Retrieved November 4, 2008, from http://formulad.com/general-info/formula-drift-history.html.

Free Teleconferencing and Conference Call. (2009). Retrieved on April 1, 2009, from http://www.freeconferencecall.com/prodfreeconferencecall.asp.

Fried, G. (2005). *Managing sport facilities*. Champaign, IL: Human Kinetics.

Green Events Group (n.d.). News. Retrieved on April 14, 2009, from http://www.greeneventsgroup.com/news.htm.

Harte, A. (2005, May 26). The game that had it all. Retrieved December 1, 2008, from http://www.uefa.com/competitions/ucl/news/kind=8192/newsid=304666.html.

Helitzer, M. (1999). *The dream job: Sports publicity, promotion and marketing* (3rd ed.). Athens, OH: Ohio University Press.

Humphreys, J.M., & Plummer, M.K. (1995). *The economic impact on the State of Georgia of hosting the 1996 Summer Olympic Games*. Report prepared for the Atlanta Committee for the Olympic Games.

Hums, M. A., & MacLean, J. C. (2004). *Governance and policy in sport organizations*. Scottsdale, AZ: Holcomb Hathaway Publishers.

International Olympic Committee. (2007a, September 14). Seven applicant NOCs/cities for the 2016 games. Retrieved November 24, 2008, from http://www.olympic.org/uk/news/olympic_news/full_story_uk.asp?id=2318.

International Olympic Committee. (2007b, May 16). *IOC launches 2016 bid process*. Retrieved November 24, 2008, from http://www.olympic.org/uk/games/torino2006/presscenter/mediapress_uk.asp?id=2162.

International Olympic Committee. (2007c). *Candidature Acceptance Procedure and Questionnaire*. [electronic version]. International Olympic Committee, Lausanne; Switzerland.

International Olympic Committee. (n.d.a.). *The Olympic games.* Retrieved October 31, 2008, from http://www.olympic.org/uk/games/index_uk.asp.

International Olympic Committee. (n.d.b.). Beijing 2008: games programme finalized. Retrieved October 29, 2008, from http://www.olympic.org/uk/organisation/commissions/programme/full_story_uk.asp?id=1797.

International Olympic Committee. (n.d.c.). *The Olympic movement.* Retrieved October 31, 2008, from http://www.olympic.org/uk/organisation/index_uk.asp.

International Skating Union. (2007). ISU world figure skating championships 2007. Retrieved October 30, 2008, from http://www.isufs.org/results/wc2007/CAT002RS.HTM.

Josephson Institute. (2009). The six pillars of character. Retrieved June 22, 2008, from http://josephsoninstitute.org/sixpillars.html.

Kladko, B. (2008, July 10). "Show me the money" colleges produce would-be Borases. Bloomberg.com. Retrieved July 11, 2008, from http://www.bloomberg.com/apps/news?pid=20601109&sid=avpkYOse_uc4&refer=exclusive.

Krause, P. (2008, 1 October). Ticketmaster defeats Cleveland Cavaliers in suit over ticket resale. Cleveland.com. Retrieved March 28, 2009, from http://blog.cleveland.com/metro/2008/10/ticketmaster_defeats_cleveland.html.

Kraus, R., & Curtis, J. (2000). *Creative management in recreation, parks and leisure service.* Dubuque, IA: McGraw-Hill Higher Education.

Ladies Professional Golf Association. (2008). Players. Retrieved October 30, 2008, from http://www.lpga.com/players_index.aspx.

Lamberth, C. R. (2005). Trends in stadium design: A whole new game. *Implications.*[Electronic version]. 4 (6). Retrieved January 27, 2009, from http://www.informedesign.umn.edu/_news/jun_v04r-p.pdf.

LaRue, R.J., Sawyer, T.H., & LaRue, D.A. (2005). Landscape design, sports turf, and parking. In Sawyer, T.H. (Ed.), *Facility design and management for health, fitness, physical activity, recreation, and sports facility development* (11th ed., pp. 220–233). Champaign, IL: Sagamore.

Lawrence H. J., Contorno, R. T., Kutz, E., Hendrickson, H., & Dorsey, W. (2007, May 15), "Premium seating survey," working paper. Athens, OH: Ohio University Center for Sports Administration.

Learmonth, M. (2008, July 21). NBC hedges its Olympic bets: Buy a TV ad, get a Web banner, too. *Silicon Alley Insider.* Retrieved August 3, 2008, from http://www.alleyinsider.com/2008/7/nbc-hedges-its-olympic-bets-buy-a-tv-ad-get-a-web-banner-too.

Lehman, P. (n.d.). The wide world of emerging sports. *Business Week.* Retrieved December 2, 2008, from http://images.businessweek.com/ss/07/08/0823_emerging_sports/index_01.htm?sub=travel.

Little League. (n.d.). Structure of little league baseball and softball. Retrieved March 1, 2009, from http: //www.littleleague.org/Learn_More/About_Our_Organization/structure.htm.

McCarthy, M. (2008, December 18). A security tool or the "rat line"? NFL targeting the unruly fan. Retrieved March 23, 2008, from http://www.usatoday.com/sports/football/nfl/2008-12-18-fan-conduct-cover_N.htm.

McMillen, J.D. (2003). Game, event, and sponsorship contracts. In D. Cotton, & J. Wolohan (Eds.), *Law for recreation and sport managers* (3rd ed., pp. 414–424). Dubuque, IA: Kendall Hunt.

Miller, L.K. (1997). *Sport business management.* Gaithersburg, MD: Aspen Publishing, Inc.

Montreal Canadiens. (2009). Contact us. Retrieved on March 20, 2009, from http://canadiens.nhl.com/team/app/?service=page&page=NHLPage&id=16746.

Moorman, A. M. (2007). Defamation. In D. J. Cotton and J. T. Wolohan (Eds.), *Law for recreation and sport managers* (4th ed., p. 518). Dubuque, IA: Kendall/Hunt Publishing Company.

Mull, R. F, Bayless, K. G., & Jamieson, L. M. (2005). *Recreational sport management.* Champaign, IL: Human Kinetics.

Mulrooney, A. L., & Farmer, P.J. (2005). Risk management in public assembly facilties. In H. Appenzeller (Ed.), *Risk management in sport: issues and strategies* (pp. 303–316). Durham, NC: Carolina Academic Press.

National Cable & Telecommunications Association. (2008). 2008 Industry Overview. Retrieved on April 14, 2009, from http://www.ncta.com/MediaCenter/MediaCenter/MediaResources.aspx?ki=y.

National Collegiate Athletic Association. (n.d.a.). Composition & sport sponsorship of the NCAA. Retrieved March 1, 2009, from http://www.ncaa.org/wps/ncaa?ContentID=811.

National Collegiate Athletic Association. (2009). I chose division II: division II strategic plan January 2009 through January 2012. [Electronic Version]. Retrieved April 26, 2009, from www.ncaa.org/wps/wcm/connect/resources/file/eb41164f99948fb/Final%2009-12%20Division%20II%20Strategic%20Plan.pdf?

National Collegiate Athletic Association. (n.d.b.). *NCAA toolbox—conducting a meeting.* Indianapolis: NCAA.

National Federation of State High School Associations. (n.d.). About us. Retrieved June 23, 2008, from http://www.nfhs.org/web/2006/08/about_us.aspx.

National Labor Relations Board, (n.d). Workplace rights. Retrieved April 21, 2009, from http://www.nlrb.gov/Workplace_Rights/i_am_new_to_this_website/what_is_the_national_labor_relations_act.aspx.

New York State Department of Health. (2008, August). Fact sheet: crumb-rubber infilled synthetic turf athletic fields. Retrieved January 27, 2009, from http://www.health.state.ny.us/environmental/outdoors/synthetic_turf/crumb-rubber_infilled/fact_sheet.htm.

Nielsen. (2009). Profile. Retrieved on April 14, 2009, from http://en-us.nielsen.com/main/about/Profile.

North American Society for Sport Management. (n.d.). Sport management programs United States. Retrieved July 15, 2008, from http://www.nassm.com/InfoAbout/SportMgmtPrograms/United_States.

NYC.gov. (2007). Mayor Bloomberg and MLB Commissioner Selig announce 2008 MLB all-star game will be played in historic Yankee stadium in its final season. Retrieved April 5, 2009, from http://www.nyc.gov/portal/site/nycgov/menuitem.c0935b9a57bb4ef3daf2f1c701c789a0/index.jsp?pageID=mayor_press_release&catID=1194&doc_name=http%3A%2F%2Fwww.nyc.gov%2Fhtml%2Fom%2Fhtml%2F2007a%2Fpr032-07.html&cc=unused1978&rc=1194&ndi=1.

Official Site of the 2008 Superbowl. (n.d.). Superbowl faq's. Retrieved December 5, 2008, from http://www.azsuperbowl.com/super_bowl_faqs.aspx#1.

Phoenix Suns. (2009). Media center: An online resource for Phoenix Suns media partners. Retrieved on March 20, 2009, from http://www.nba.com/suns/news/media_center.html.

Plunkett Research, Ltd. (2008). *Introduction to the Sports Industry.* Retrieved March 12, 2009, from the Plunkett Research, Ltd. Database.

Plunkett Research, Ltd. (2008). *NASCAR* weathers rising costs. Retrieved March 12, 2009, from Plunkett Research, Ltd. Database.

Prosser, A., & Rutledge, A. (2003). *Special events and festivals: how to plan, organize and implement.* State College, PA: Venture Publishing.

Quinn, J. (2008, November 13). UK minister's Olympic bid comments cause uproar. Retrieved November 24, 2008, from http://ap.google.com/article/ALeqM5hi_0zkCuloKBOlvRjX0ISqV9Z92wD94E84U00.

Research Director. (n.d.). Glossary. Retrieved July 17, 2009, from http://www.researchdirectorinc.com/Glossary.htm.

Rob, P., Coronel, C., & Crockett, K. (2008). *Database systems: Design, implementation, & management.* International Edition. Retrieved on March 30, 2009, from http://books.google.com.

Salt Lake Organizing Committee. (2000). Team 2002 in training. Salt Lake, Utah.

Show, J. (2008, September 8). Events add spice to fall series. *Sports Business Journal,* 11(19),8.

Schaber, G., & Rohwer, C. (1984). *Contracts,* (2nd ed.). St. Paul, MN: West Nutshell Series.

Sharp, L. (2003). Contract essentials. In D. Cotten, & J. Wolohan (Eds.), *Law for recreation and sport managers,* (3rd ed., pp. 384–392). Dubuque, IA: Kendall Hunt.

Silvers, J. R. (2003). Event management body of knowledge project. Retrieved July 8, 2008, from http://www.juliasilvers.com/embok.htm#The_Definition_of_Event_Management.

Solomon, J. (2002). *An insider's guide to managing sporting events.* Chicago, IL: Human Kinetics.

Sports Business Daily (2008). Sports Business Daily September 12, 2008: NBC touts sale of 85% of Super Bowl XLIII ad inventory. Retrieved on March 19, 2009, from www.sportsbusinessdaily.com/article/123957.

Stadium Managers Association. (n.d.). About SMA. Retrieved July 9, 2008, from http://www.stadiummanagers.org/about/.

Techniques for Effective Alcohol Management Coalition. (n.d.). Techniques for effective alcohol management. Retrieved March 25, 2009, from http://www.teamcoalition.org/about/about.asp.

The Baseball Tomorrow Fund. (n.d.). *Baseball field maintenance: A general guide for fields of all levels.* Retrieved January 23, 2008, from http://mlb.mlb.com/mlb/downloads/btf_field_maintenance_guide.pdf.

The Center for Universal Design. (1997). *The principles of universal design, version 2.0.* Raleigh, NC: North Carolina State University. Retrieved March 17, 2008, from http://www.design.ncsu.edu/cud/about_ud/udprinciples.htm.

The New York City Sports Commission. (2008). Annual events. Retrieved April 5, 2009, from http://www.nyc.gov/html/sports/html/nyc_marathon.html.

The Real Shaq. (2009). The real Shaq. Retrieved on March 28, 2009, from http://twitter.com/the_real_shaq.

Ticketing. (2009). Cleveland Cavaliers. Retrieved on March 30, 2009, from http://www.nba.com/cavaliers/tickets/ticketplans.html.

Tsang, G., & Newberry, C. (2008). What do high performance athletes eat for their Olympics diet? Retrieved March 7, 2009, from http://www.healthcastle.com/sports_olympics_diet.shtml.

Ukman, L. (2008). *IEG's guide to sponsorship: everything you need to know about sports, arts, event, entertainment, and cause marketing.* Chicago, IL: IEG, LLC.

United States Department of Justice. (n.d.). Americans with Disabilities Act questions and answers. Retrieved April 21, 2009, from http://www.ada.gov/q%26aeng02.htm.

United States Department of Labor. (n.d.). The Fair Labor Standards Act. Retrieved April 21, 2009, from http://www.dol.gov/compliance/laws/comp-flsa.htm.

United States Equal Employment Opportunity Commission. (n.d.). Sexual harassment. Retrieved April 21, 2009, from http://www.eeoc.gov/types/sexual_harassment.html.

Union of European Football Associations. (n.d.a.). *History.* Retrieved October 29, 2008, from http://www.uefa.com/competitions/uefacup/history/index.html.

Union of European Football Associations. (n.d.b.). *UEFA organization.* Retrieved October 29, 2008, from http://www.uefa.com/uefa/contacts.html.

Union of European Football Associations. (2008, November 18). China 2009-12 media rights. Retrieved December 1, 2008, from http://www.uefa.com/uefa/keytopics/kind=131072/newsid=775377.html.

University of Florida Athletics. (2008, June 26). Gator athletics program finishes sixth in nation. Retrieved June 27, 2008, from http://www.gatorzone.com/story.php?id=14131.

USA Diving. (2007). *USA diving competitive & technical rules.* [Electronic version]. Retrieved December 4, 2008, from http://www.usadiving.org/05redesign/resources/rulebook.htm.

USA Track and Field. (n.d.). USATF Course Certification. Retrieved January 22, 2009, from http://www.usatf.org/events/courses/certification/.

USA Triathlon. (2006). USAT event sanctioning. Retrieved June 22, 2008, from http://rankings.usatriathlon.org/Event_Sanctioning/Event_Sanctioning.htm.

Vodafone McLaren Mercedes. (2009). Media centre. Retrieved on March 20, 2009, from http://www.mclaren.com/mediaroom/media-login.php.

Xinhua. (2008, August 13). Georgian, Russian volleyballers embrace at Beijing Olympics. *Chinaview.* Retrieved November 4, 2008, from http://news.xinhuanet.com/english/2008-08/13/content_9267520.htm.

Zullo, R. (2005, August/September). The right moves. *Athletic management.* Retrieved December 4, 2008, from http://www.momentummedia.com/articles/am/am1705/rightmoves.htm.

EVENT MANAGEMENT PROFESSIONAL ORGANIZATIONS AND RELATED RESOURCES

The organizations and companies listed here are merely examples. The authors do not necessarily endorse any of the organizations or companies listed.

Concessions

National Association of Concessionaires (NAC)

http://www.naconline.org

Conventions & Exhibits

Association for Convention Operations Management

http://www.acomonline.org

Association for Convention Sales and Marketing Executives

http://www.acmenet.org/

Convention Industry Council

http://www.conventionindustry.org/

Destination Marketing Association International

http://www.destinationmarketing.org/

Exhibit Designers and Producers Association

http://www.edpa.com

International Association of Conference Centers

http://www.iacconline.org

International Association of Exhibits and Events (IAEE)

http://www.iaee.com/

Professional Convention Management Association (PCMA)

http://www.pcma.org/

Trade Show Exhibitors Association

http://www.tsea.org

Entertainment & Technology

Entertainment Services and Technology Association

http://www.esta.org

infoComm International, the Audiovisual Association

http://www.infocomm.org/

Information Display and Entertainment Association (IDEA)

http://www.ideaontheweb.org/

Hospitality

Hospitality Sales and Marketing Association International (HSMAI)

http://www.hsmai.org

Safety and Security

Federal Emergency Management Agency

www.fema.gov

International Association of Campus Law Enforcement Administrators (IACLEA)

www.iaclea.org

National Fire Protection Association

www.nfpa.org/Research/NFPAFactSheets/NFPAFactSheets.asp

Venue Risk Self-Assessment Tool (RSAT)

http:\\www.rsat.iac.anl.gov\register

Marketing & Sponsorships

Corporate Event Marketing Association (CEMA)

http://www.cemaonline.com

Direct Marketing Association

http://www.the-dma.org

Promotional Products Association International

http://www.ppa.org

National Association of Collegiate Marketing Administrators (NACMA)

http://www.nacda.com/nacma/nacda-nacma.html

Rights Holders

Amateur Athletic Union (AAU)

http://www.aausports.org/default.asp

General Association of International Sports Federations

http://www.agfisonline.com/

International Olympic Committee (IOC)

http://www.olympic.org/uk/index_uk.asp

National Collegiate Athletic Association (NCAA)

http://www.ncaa.org

United States Olympic Committee (USOC)

http://www.usoc.com/

United States Specialty Sports Association (USSSA)

http://www.usssa.com/sports/

Facility Management

APPA: The Association for Higher Education Facilities Officers

http://www.appa.org

Association of Luxury Suite Directors (ASLD)
http://www.alsd.com/

Collegiate Event and Facility Management Association (CEFMA)
http://nacda.cstv.com/cefma/nacda-cefma.html

Club Managers Association of America (golf)
http://www.cmaa.org/

International Facility Management Association (IFMA)
http://www.ifma.org

International Association of Assembly Managers (IAAM)
http://www.iaam.org/

National Recreation and Park Association (NRPA)
www.nrpa.org

Sports Turf Managers Association (STMA)
http://www.stma.org/

Stadium Managers Association (SMA)
http://www.stadiummanagers.org/

Special Events

International Special Events Society (ISES)
http://www.ises.com

Meeting Professionals International (MPI)
http://www.mpiweb.org

National Association of Sports Commissions
http://www.sportscommissions.org/Home

Travel, Events and Management in Sports (TEAMS)
http://www.teamsconference.com/

Ticketing

Better Ticketing Association (BTA)
http://www.betterticketing.com

International Ticketing Association (INTIX)
http://www.intix.org/

National Association of Ticket Brokers
http://www.natb.org

Transportation & Logistics

International Transportation Management Association
http://itma-houston.org/

Other Resources - Trade Publications

Billboard
http://www.billboard.com/bbcom/index.jsp

BizBash

http://www.bizbash.com

Event Marketer Magazine

http://www.eventmarketermag.com

Facility Manager Magazine

https://www.iaam.org/Facility_manager/Pages/Facility_Issues.htm

Special Events Magazine

http://www.specialevents.com

Sports Business Journal

http://www.sportsbusinessjournal.com/

SportsTravel Magazine

http://www.sportstravelmagazine.com/

Stadium and Arena Management Magazine

http://www.sam.uk.com/sam_magazine/index.asp

Venue Safety and Security Magazine

https://www.iaam.org/vss/pages/issues.htm

Other Resources- Miscellaneous

AgendaOnline

http://agendaonline.com

Ballparks

http://www.ballparks.com/

Ballparks of Baseball

http://www.ballparksofbaseball.com/

Federal Emergency Management Agency - Emergency Response Training
http://training.fema.gov

Game Entertainment and Operations

www.Gameops.com

Golf Tournament template

http://www.reach.ca/building/annex11.htm

Guide to NFL Stadiums

http://www.stadiumsofnfl.com/

National Intramural-Recreational Sports Association (NIRSA)

www.nirsa.org

Road Runners Club of America

http://www.rrca.org

World Stadiums

http://www.worldstadiums.com/

EVENT RESOURCES (EXAMPLES)

The companies listed here are merely examples. The authors do not necessarily endorse any of the companies listed. Many vendors in these industries are regional, and event managers should search their local area for companies to provide some of these services.

Audio/Video Providers

ACE Communications (www.aceav.com)

Daktronics (www.daktronics.com)

Smart Source (www.smartsourcerentals.com)

Bus Services

Event Transportation Associates, Inc. (www.eventtransportation.com)

Gameday Management Group (www.gamedaymanagementgroup.com)

Mears Transportation (www.mearstransportation.com)

Contest Insurance

K & K Insurance (www.kandkinsurance.com)

SCA Promotions (www.scapromotions.com)

Hole in One, International (www.holeinoneinternational.com)

Event Equipment Suppliers (tables, tents, chairs...)

PTG Event Services (Parties To Go) (www.partiestogo.com)

ConTent Party Rentals, Inc. (www.contentpartyrentals.com)

Bedrock Party Rentals, LTD. (www.bedrockpartyrentals.com)

The Tent Rental Company (www.thetentrentalcompany.com)

Event Promotions Management

LEJ Sports Group (www.lejsports.com)

Eventage Event Production (www.eventage.net)

Event Signage

EPS Doublet (www.eps-doublet.com)

APCG Productions (phone: 917-405-4045)

Omni Promotional, LLC (www.omnipromo.com)

Experiential/Live Event Marketing

GMR Marketing (www.gmrlive.com)

Octagon (www.octagon.com)

Relay Worldwide (www.relayworldwide.com)

Velocity Sports and Entertainment (www.teamvelocity.com)

Field Maintenance

Carolina Green Corp. (www.cgcfields.com)

Burnside Services Inc. (www.burnside-services.com)

Labor (Part-time/event day)

Craig's List (www.craigslist.com)

Lighting Services

United Rentals (www.ur.com)

On-Site Energy (www.onsite-energy.com)

Musco Lighting (www.musco.com)

Media and Marketing Research

Artibron (www.arbitron.com)

Nielsen (www.nielsen.com)

Scarborough Research (www.scarborough.com)

Turnkey Sports and Entertainment (www.turnkeyse.com)

Sports Business Research Network (www.sbrnet.com)

Plunkett Research, Ltd. (www.plunkettresearch.com)

Team Marketing Report (www.teammarketing.com)

Merchandise Sales

Zazzle (www.zazzle.com)

CafePress (www.cafepress.com)

Miscellaneous

Bag Tags Inc. (www.bagtagsinc.com)

Event Credentials, LLC (www.eventcredentials.com)

Grainger (www.grainger.com)

Wiki Spaces (www.wikispaces.com)

Online Registration

Active (www.active.com)

Cashnet (www.cashnet.com)

Sports Signup (www.sportsignup.com)

Photography

Brightroom (www.brightroom.com)

Action Sports International (www.asiorders.com)

MarathonFoto (www.marathonfoto.com)

Portable Restrooms

National Construction Rentals (www.rentnational.com)

Mesa Waste Services (www.mesawasteservices.com)

A Royal Flush, Inc. (www.aroyalflush.com)

Promotional Products

Brand Marketing Works (www.brandmarketingworks.com)

Barker Specialty Company (www.barkerspecialty.com)

Radios and Wireless Communication

Bearcom (www.bearcom.com)

Event Radio Rentals (www.eventradiorentals.com)

Event Communications, Inc. (www.eventcomm.net)

Road Race/Triathlon Management

New York Road Runners (www.nyrr.org)

Premier Event Management, LLC (www.pem-usa.com)

Track Shack (www.trackshack.com)

Sponsorship Organizations

IEG International Events Group (www.sponsorship.com)

ISP (www.ispsports.com)

Learfield (www.learfield.com)

IMG (www.imgworld.com)

Sports Team Travel

Anthony Travel Inc. (www.anthonytravel.com)

American Tours & Travels, Inc. (www.travelgroups.com)

Ticketing Software Programs

TicketBiscuit, LLC (www.ticketbiscuit.com)

Ticketmaster Entertainment, Inc. (www.ticketmaster.com)

Tickets.com (www.tickets.com)

Trophies and Medals

Midwest Trophy (www.mwtrophy.com)

Trophy Depot (www.trophydepot.com)

Wilson Trophy Company (www.wilsontrophy.com)

EVENT MANAGEMENT CHECKLIST
Multipurpose

David Miller

The following list provides an outline for areas that need attention for many events. Depending on the type, size, and purpose of the event, specific requirements will vary. However, event mangers should review this list to ensure attention is given to all of the appropriate areas.

I. Bid process

II. Date and time of event
- Facility and/or grounds availability
- Weather forecast
- Possible conflicting/competing events

III. Game/event staff
- Manager(s)
- Coordinator(s)
- Ticket operations
- Medical
- Support
  - Maintenance
  - Electrical
  - Plumbing
  - Custodial
  - Technology
- Police/security
- Ushers
- Table/scoreboard/timer
- Sports information/media services

IV. Important phone numbers
- Police
- Fire
- Key game/event managers, supervisors, and workers
- Local businesses who provide logistical support
- Vendors supplying equipment/services for the event

V. Rights holders/coordinating groups
- Local organizing committee
- Rights holders needs
- Sanction

VI. Visiting team(s)/participants
- Locker room assignment(s)
- Practice(s)
- Lodging/team headquarters
- Meals
- Transportation
- Activities
- Information packet
- Game/event guarantee(s)
- Waivers
- Registration/check-in

VII. Officials
- Locker room assignment(s)
- Security and escorts
- Meeting space
- Lodging
- Meals
- Transportation
- Activities
- Information package
- Contract
- Compensation
- Arrival time at event

VIII. Contracts/Financial arrangements
- Entry fees
- Event budget
- Contracts
  - Teams
  - Officials
  - Facility and/or grounds
  - Sponsorship
  - Concessions
  - Parking
  - Ticketing
  - Custodial
  - Event-day staff
  - Police/security
  - Ushers
  - Medical
  - Vendors
  - Transportation
  - Logistical

IX. Event setup and teardown
- Diagrams
- Supervisor(s) and workers
- Date(s) and time(s)
- Equipment required (see Chapter 14 for detailed equipment list)
  - Sport specific
- Misc. items/equipment list
  - Drills

- Hand tools
- Nails, bolts, etc.
- Electrical cord
- Bunting/skirts/flags

X. Ticket operations
- Reserved and/or general admission
- Total capacity
- Ticket cost(s)
- Printing
- Staffing
  - Sellers
  - Takers
- VIP seating
- Sample board

XI. Credentials
- Design
- Distribution
  - Media
  - Participants, team, coaches, and staff
  - Event staff
  - Vendors and contractors
- Sample board
- Access map/diagram

XII. Communication
- Public Address system
- CD/MP3s/iPod
  - National anthem(s)
  - School/team song(s)
  - Warm-up, half-time, etc.
- Communications/radios/cell phones
  - Programming of channels
  - Assignment of channels
  - Individual assignments
  - Call sign list
  - Headset/field phones/ear pieces/batteries
- Internet/streaming video/live stats

XIII. Police/security/safety
- Date(s), time(s), location(s)
- Expectations
- Number of officers required/requested
- Estimated attendance
- Anticipated crowd attitude
- Team and officials security
- Information sheets/fast facts
  - Locker room assignments
  - Fast facts
  - Countdown information
  - Restricted areas
- Point of contract

- Crowd management policies
- Keys
- Agencies
  - Campus/university
  - Local
  - County
  - Highway patrol
- Emergency preparedness plan
- Patron screening

XIV. Custodial support
- Date(s), time(s), location(s)
- Staffing requirements
- Expectations
- Materials required
- Estimated attendance
- Crowd attitude

XV. Parking and traffic control
- Date(s), time(s), location(s)
- Staffing requirements
- Expectations
- Estimated number of vehicles
- Signs needed
- Cost of parking
- Starting cash
- Receipts
- VIP, officials, staff, participant parking
- Bus and motor home parking
- Type of surface parking will be on/materials for grass lots in case of rain
- Sample board

XVI. Media services/sports information
- TV coverage
  - Parking and power
  - Camera locations
  - Electrical limitations
- Radio coverage
  - Phone lines
- Print media
- Photographer(s)
- Press conference/interview room
- Event point of contact
- Media working room
  - Internet
  - Phone lines
  - Fax capability
  - Copy capability
  - Adequate number of power outlets
  - Food/drinks
  - SWAG
  - Media guides (and/or other print materials)

XVII. Activities
- Banquets
- Hospitality room
- VIP area
- Sponsor activations
- Pre-event/game
- Half-time/intermission
- Post event/game
- Band
- Cheerleaders and/or dance team
- Sponsor promotions

XVIII. Vendor(s)
- Date(s), time(s), location(s)
- Contract(s)
- Contact(s)
- Delivery schedule
- Estimated attendance
- Weather forecast
- Procedure to keep cash secure

XIX. Awards
- Ceremony
- Music
- Number and type of awards
- Award stand and backdrop
- Presenter(s)
- Table(s) to place awards before ceremony
- Photography bullpen

XX. Insurance
- Liability and property insurance
- Waivers
- Contest/promotions insurance
- Weather insurance
- Event cancellation

XXI. Test condition and readiness
- Communications equipment
- Headsets/field phone/ear pieces
- Audio/P.A./music
- Electrical
- Lighting

XXII. Call time/pre-event meeting
- Review items on event day checklist
- Review all aspects and sequence of event/game/post-game
- Cover all questions and concerns
- Distribute uniforms
- Hand out important information
  - Fast facts
  - Passes and credentials

XXIII. Fast Facts Sheet should review
- Parking
- Tickets
- Seating
- General schedule
- Rain policy/cancellation policy
- Merchandise sale locations
- Medical services
- Policy and procedures
- Smoking policy
- Lost children
- Lost & Found
- Location of rest rooms
- Concessions
- Locker room assignments
- Diagrams and venue layouts
- Emergency procedures

XXIV. Event/Game book for event managers
- Fast facts
- Event day timeline
- Event day checklists
- Contact Sheet
- Diagrams and layouts
- Rule books
- Correspondence and memos
- Contracts
- Vendor list

XXV. Weather forecast
- Snow removal from parking lots, walkways, seats
- Cover playing surface
- Lightning policy
- Heat precautions

XXVI. Event wrap-up
- Review all aspect of game/event both good and bad
- Event summary
- Lessons learned
- Create event file
- Payroll information
- Sponsor ROI reports
- Incident reports
- Minutes from debriefing meetings
- Customer complaints/concerns
- Ticket and/or participant registration reports
- Financial reports
- Post-event recap

RATIOS

Beginning event managers may have a fairly sound grasp of *what* needs to be budgeted just from having attended events in the past. It is often more difficult for beginning event managers to figure out *how many/how much* to budget. Following are some ratios to use as guidelines when evaluating equipment needs. These are guidelines only, and are not set in stone.

TOILETS AND HAND WASH STATIONS

Some toilet rental companies also rent portable hand wash stations. A ratio is provided below for those that do. More common, though, is a hand sanitizer dispenser inside each portable toilet. The ratio provided for toilets is low compared to what some events use, but inadequate toilet accessibility is an area that can cause dissatisfaction for participants and spectators. It is often better to budget the extra dollars as a relatively low-cost way to keep people happy. Toilets may be spread out in various "banks" around the event site or all of them put in one central location, depending on the site layout. Event managers also need to budget for daily servicing of the toilets if the event is a multi-day event. The toilet paper will have to be replaced throughout the day if it is an all-day event, as may the hand sanitizer.

Portable toilets	1 per 75 people
ADA compliant portable toilets	1 per 150 people
Portable hand wash station	1 per 300 people

These numbers for toilets may be combined or used separately to get the number of toilets needed. For example, if an event will have 5,000 people (total) in attendance, the ratios suggest that the event should have 67 toilets (5000/75). The number of ADA toilets needed is 33 (5000/150). The event organizers may decide, then, to rent 34 regular toilets and 33 ADA toilets to get to the total of 67. They may also decide to combine the number for a total of 100 toilets, or to have the number fall somewhere in between, with at least 33 of them being ADA toilets. This lowers the actual ratio of people to toilet. Again, these toilets will be used throughout the event location.

The ratio may need to be adjusted depending on the makeup of the event, too. If the majority of participants and spectators are women, the event should budget more toilets simply based on the fact that the average time it takes women to use a facility is going to be greater than the average time for men. The ratio needs to be significantly lower (1:50) if the event is an all women's event, such as a women's only half marathon or triathlon. Remember, these numbers are for the entire event.

WATER AND ISOTONIC DRINK

Ratios for water and isotonic drink are dependent upon the type of event. **Isotonic drink** is a sports drink used to replace fluid and electrolytes lost during prolonged exercise. Since the main example provided in this text is a marathon, let's look at ratios for water stations. The assumption should be made that each runner will stop at each fluid station provided along the course. The temperatures are going to be relative to what the normal temperature is for the location where the race is being held. Another factor that will come into consideration is the number of total fluid stations along the course. If the fluid stations are spread out beyond very 1–1.5 miles, the numbers may need to be increased. If runners know that they will come upon another fluid station relatively soon, they may not feel the need to take as many cups.

Cold Temperature Day

Cups of water per water station	1–1.5 cups per runner
Cups of isotonic drink per fluid station	1 cup per runner

On a cold day, many runners will not stop at every fluid station.

Average Temperature Day

Cups of water per water station	1.5 cups per runner
Cups of isotonic drink per fluid station	1–1.5 cups per runner

High Temperature Day

Cups of water per water station	2 cups per runner
Cups of isotonic drink per fluid station	1.5–2 cups per runner

6′ tables for cups	approximately 200 cups/table layer

Cups can be stacked on a table three levels high without much difficulty or risk of falling over. Each level will fit approximately 200 cups, which means that a table with cups stacked three levels high will hold 600 cups. The trays used to stack the cups are usually coroplast (corrugated plastic) or wax coated cardboard and are often cut into 2′ x 3′ pieces.

Many runners will take fluid to pour on them as a coolant, and these ratios account for that. Still, this can make it difficult for staff at the water stations to keep up with the number of cups needed to meet the demand of the runners passing the station. One way to alleviate this is by providing misting stations that runners can pass through to cool themselves. A misting station can be as simple as a hose hooked up to a potable water source (low cost) or as intricate as equipment designed specifically as a mister for road races (higher cost). Any misting stations should be set up so that runners pass under/through them before the water station to help reduce the number of runners taking water to pour on themselves.

Races may be provided free cups with a sponsor's logo for water, isotonic drink, or both. In this situation, event managers may be able to request cup sizes, but they may have to take what they can get. Generally, though, water cups are usually six ounce or eight ounce cups. They should be filled half to three-quarters full. For isotonic drink, if a sponsor has provided the cups, they may be a bigger size, twelve ounces, for example, so that the logo is more visible to runners (and the cameras, both still photo and broadcast if the race is televised). Why are these details important? Sponsors may agree to provide water and/or isotonic drinks, but it may not be an unlimited supply. They will need to know from the event managers what amount of product is required. If no sponsors are providing these items, then the event has to budget for them. Event managers have to be able to calculate how much water and isotonic drink are needed to know what to request. Do not skimp in this area. With something like this that can impact the health and safety of athletes, it is always better to have an overage than a shortage. Cups, water, and isotonic drink are very inexpensive relative to athlete safety. Dumping out extra water and isotonic drink left on fluid station tables and having cups and isotonic drink left over is always preferable to not having enough available for runners who need it. Event managers should allot the money in their event budgets for the worst-case scenario of the amount needed.

For a team sport event such as a soccer, basketball, or volleyball tournament, it is usually enough to budget one cooler (usually 5 gallons) per team bench with the appropriate amount of water to fill it between each game or every other game. If athletes are filling their personal water bottles from the coolers rather than drinking fountains, event managers may need to set up additional coolers near the field of play for this purpose to prevent the coolers on the field of play getting empty as quickly. For a larger team sport, such as football, more coolers may be needed.

CORRAL SPACE

Road races often stage runners into a corral system before the start of the race. With regard to road races, a **corral** is a cordoned-off holding zone in which a predetermined number of runners is assigned to stage before the start of the race. Corrals may be assigned based on runners' predicted finish times, randomly, a mix of the two, or some other factor determined by the race organizers. The things that obviously need to be budgeted are the number of corrals and the cost of the temporary fencing method and staff needed to control access to the corrals.

Corral	approximately 2 sq. ft. per runner
Access Control Staff	2–4 per corral

All of these ratios should be used as guidelines, or a starting point, and not as definitive rules. As event managers become more familiar with the specific details of their respective sport(s) and geographic location(s), they may need to adapt these ratios accordingly.

GLOSSARY OF TERMS

Acceptance: Consenting to receive the terms of the offer for the purposes of fulfilling a contract.

Accounting codes (also: chart of accounts): Identification numbers assigned to specific categories (accounts) of revenues and expenses used for record keeping.

Admission tax (also: bond charge or facility fee): Whether a facility is publicly or privately financed, the cost of construction and development is funded by debt, often in the form of bonds sold to institutional or private investors. Bondholders are generally entitled to some guaranteed revenue stream on all building income in the form of a percentage or fixed fee for each admission or ticket sold. This bond fee should be deducted from the price of each ticket and accounted for on the box office statement, which then yields a "net ticket sales" figure that is dropped into the revenue column of the settlement statement.

Advertising campaign: A plan that can utilize all forms of media, including, but not limited to, television, radio, newspaper, outdoor, direct mail, and online advertising to promote ticket sales and/or entry for an event.

Ancillary events: Events that supplement and surround the pre-defined core sports events. Examples include a carbohydrate loading dinner the night before a marathon, a tailgate party before the Super Bowl, or a concert after a baseball game.

Ancillary spaces: All of the areas that support the primary space. Examples include the locker rooms, concourses, storage areas, lobbies, press areas, loading docks, offices, restrooms, security areas, merchandise shops, etc.

Attrition: The shrinkage or reduction in number of hotel rooms to be used. Attrition is different from cancellation, which is the complete annulment of the event or contract. Most hotel contracts have different clauses and terms for these two situations.

Back of house: Roles in which employees do not regularly engage in face-to face contact with the public, such as the public address announcer, the scoreboard operator, operations personnel, truck dock employees, and even set-up and teardown employees.

Bandit runners: Runners trying to sneak in to run a race for which they did not register or sign the waiver.

Base: As outlined in the facility's standard operating procedure, base references a person or small group of personnel who field all medical calls at the command center and disseminate information during an event.

Baseline staffing: The bare minimum of staff required to accomplish the management of the event. This baseline number of staff is where all staffing plans begin and then are built up from there.

Basic provisions: The section of the contract that lists the fundamental areas for which each party will be responsible.

Bidding: A competitive process in which companies are asked to provide service and price information based on criteria set by the event organizers.

Biometric scanning: Technology that uses individual physiological characteristics such as fingerprints, face recognition, and/or iris recognition to allow or not allow access to an area.

Boilerplate: Detailed standard wording (e.g., insurance, warranty, rules, and regulations) in a contract that remains the same for all clients unless all parties agree to specific changes. Boilerplate can also refer to any section of writing that can be used repeatedly without change. Another example is the company/organization description at the end of a press release.

Bond charge: See admission tax.

Box office statement: A report, often computerized, prepared by a third-party ticketing vendor that will show all tickets sold at each ticket price, and specify the method by which they were sold (e.g., at remote outlets, via phone, on the Internet, etc.)

Breach of contract: When certain aspects of the contract are not completed, whether intentional or not.

Breakage: The difference in the amount that the customer pays and the amount they actually spend on any packaged purchase (e.g., concessions, parking, merchandise credit, and two tickets).

Budget summary: A one page synopsis showing the total from each segment of the budget (e.g., equipment, labor, marketing) and the grand total of those segments for both revenues and expenses.

Budgeted amount: The expenses and revenues that the event managers project the event will have.

CADs (computer-aided design/drawing): Diagrams created using computer software to show event setup and details in a to-scale depiction.

Call sign list (also: contact list): A record of all parties relevant to the event and all of their contact phone numbers.

Call time: The time that staff are expected to be on site and signed in ready to go to work.

Call time meeting: A pre-event meeting with staff in which event managers review general information about the event, key issues they foresee that might come up and discuss how to handle the issues, and answer any questions workers have.

Capacity: The notion that the parties involved in the contract have the legal right to enter into that contract.

Capital equipment: Any piece of equipment costing over $500 with a useful life of two or more years.

Changeover: The process by which the primary space in the venue is converted from functioning for one purpose to another (e.g., flat exhibit space to basketball).

Chart of accounts: See accounting code.

Co-promotion: A contract for an event in which the venue and the promoter share the risk associated with the event and are both responsible for certain expenses usually associated with the production and staging of the event.

Command centers: Essentially the building's "nerve center," bringing the use of security-related technologies to a central location.

Contact list: See call sign list.

Contract: A legally binding agreement or a way to enforce a promise made as a bargained exchange (Epstien, 2003; Schaber & Rohwer, 1984).

Consideration: The details of the contract. Consideration is necessary for the formation and validity of the contract.

Contingency account: Money set aside in a budget to cover costs that may arise due to an unexpected event or circumstance.

Contra lanes: Traffic lanes closed to allow vehicles to travel opposite the normal direction of traffic in order to speed up the movement of vehicles.

Convention and Visitors Bureau (CVB): An organization, usually non-profit, that represents an area or destination to promote it and assist in attracting a variety of events, tourism, and business to the local area.

Corkage fee: A charge exacted at a hotel/venue/restaurant for every bottle of beverage (liquor, water, soda, isotonic drink, juice, etc.) served that was not bought on the premises.

Cost Per Rating Point (CPP): The cost of reaching one percent of the target population. CPP is calculated by dividing the cost of the schedule by the gross rating points. National and regional advertising buyers frequently use this cost efficiency measure since it can be applied across all media.

Cost Per Thousand (CPM): The relative cost of a schedule of announcements. CPM is calculated by dividing the cost of the schedule by the sum of the average quarter-hour audiences of the announcements purchased.

Database: "A shared, integrated computer structure that stores a collection of end-user data. . . metadata, or data about data through which the end-user data are integrated and managed" (Rob, Coronel, & Crockett, 2008, p. 7).

Day of event timeline: A document created to note and track details of the event day schedule such as time, task, functional area, task owner, and notes/comments.

Defensible space: Using architectural design to diminish or mitigate any tendency toward negative behaviors.

Delivery schedule: A document that includes the date, time, company, the driver's name, contact phone numbers, vehicle description, and the license plate number of each expected delivery.

Design issues: With regard to Web sites, the areas of the Web site evaluated for ease of use and usefulness to visitors, including aesthetics, data collection points, multimedia usage, sponsor images, languages, and user accessibility.

Drayage: The monetary charge for pickup and hauling of containers.

Earned media: Media exposure not paid for by the event organizers and that has gone through an independent editorial source before it reaches the intended audience.

Economic impact: The new money entering a region resulting in a change in regional output, earnings, and employment (Humphreys & Plummer, 1995).

Emergency preparedness plan (EPP): A document that articulates the policies guiding emergency management and how the organization functions given a specific type of emergency.

Entertainment and education: The concept that the event planners provide additional experiential opportunities surrounding the event through the use of different technologies, but mainly the Web site.

Event contracts: Similar to game contracts in that the time and place is paramount. Event contracts differ from game contracts in that they often include ancillary event stipulations. An event, in a sporting context, can include a contest, a single special event like the Super Bowl, or multiple events like the Olympics or AAU, Inc. Junior Olympics.

Event management: Event management is the process by which an event is planned, prepared, and produced. As with any other form of management, it encompasses the assessment, definition, acquisition, allocation, direction, control, and analysis of time, finances, people, products, services, and other resources to achieve objectives (Silvers, 2003, ¶ 2).

Event management software: A package that facilitates different aspects of the event planning process, depending upon the nature of the software.

Event manager: The individual responsible for making the event "come to life," from conceptualization through execution.

Event sanctions: An official approval for the event granted by the governing body associated with the sport (Solomon, 2002).

Event settlement: A specific process that occurs upon completion of all events. It is a financial transaction in nature, very similar to the closing on the purchase of real estate or the acquisition of a business.

Event theme: An idea or topic that helps establish an identity people will associate with the event, and should be a part of every aspect of the event.

Expendable equipment: Equipment that is less expensive than capital equipment (less than $500) and has a useful life of less than two years.

Experiential marketing: An atmosphere at the event that allows attendees to interact with a sponsor's product or service, creating a unique encounter for the sponsor which traditional advertising cannot deliver.

Expo: A sponsor and/or vendor display that often ties into a larger event.

External relations: The management process concerning the creation and communication of information through media (both earned and paid) to intended audiences (publics).

Facility contract: See venue contract.

Facility fee: See admission tax.

Event flow: The traffic pattern (people and/or cars) for the event.

Facility promotion: The building or its owner acts as the promoter for an event and takes all the risks, financial and otherwise.

Fair Labor Standards Act (FLSA): A law that restricts the employment of child workers. "Child labor provisions under FLSA are designed to protect the educational opportunities of youth and prohibit their employment in jobs that are detrimental to their health and safety. FLSA restricts the hours that youth under 16 years of age can work and lists hazardous occupations too dangerous for young workers to perform" (United States Department of Labor, n.d., ¶ 1).

Fast facts: A document for staff and volunteers that contains pertinent facts about an event and will list questions that participants and spectators are likely to ask about an event.

Feasibility: Evaluating whether or not the event can be produced successfully.

Features: A form of earned media centered on human-interest stories that somehow link back to the event through personalities or elements of the event that are the focus of the story.

Festival seating: Ticketing process where no seats are assigned and people stand to experience the event in a large open area.

Fixed equipment: Equipment that is part of the facility and could include spectator seating, scoreboards, and mechanical systems.

Flat fee agreement: The facility or city charges the event a set fee for the right to set up and sell products.

Forecast: Showing any positive or negative variances from the original budgeted amount.

Format: Programming of a radio station aimed at a specific audience such as Country, Adult Contemporary, Urban, Rock, etc.

Frequency: The average number of exposures to the commercial or song heard by the average listener, or a frequency distribution revealing the number of persons estimated to have heard the commercial or song one time, two times, three times, four times, etc.

Frequently Asked Questions (FAQ's): The most common questions that people will have about an event. FAQ's are often listed in a specific section of an event or organization's Web site.

Front of house: Event staff with face-to-face contact with the public, such as ticket office, ticket takers, parking attendants, ushers, concession, and merchandise staff.

Game contract: A contractual agreement that arranges a contest or contests between two organizations.

Game guarantee: Payment for one team to play another team.

General admission: Seating is open and patrons with a ticket are able to sit in any unoccupied seat, but they are guaranteed a seat.

Governing bodies: Organizations charged with setting the rules for the sports they oversee.

Guerrilla marketing: An aggressive way to market an event that could best be defined as "taking the message to the streets."

Grassroots marketing: Marketing an event on a local and personal level, and a way to get the word out on the event by using a street team or group of volunteers to help promote the event.

Hard ticketing: All tickets for an event are printed in advance.

In trust: Money that is held by the organization, generally ticket money in a sport context, and not spent by the organization. If an event is cancelled, this money is available for customer refunds.

Incident reports: A written statement about anything related to a patron or staff member injury, illness, or any unusual occurrence during the event. Medical staff and EMTs will provide these to the event managers with details about the individual affected and the nature of the injury or illness. Police and security are the other groups that will file incident reports, and most likely these will detail problems with patrons getting into fights or being unruly and sometimes ultimately being ejected or arrested.

Incremental revenue: Revenue that is generated through "up selling," such as sending a loyal fan a $5 coupon for the merchandise store knowing that the cheapest item in the store is $20.

Independent contractors: People or businesses that provide products or services to another person or business based on the terms of a contract.

Information dissemination: The ways in which different technologies can help to promote an event and its message (e.g., marketing plan), in addition to sponsors, partners, and other aspects planners want people to know about their events.

Information management: All of the back-end technology employed to plan an event. Examples include the internal work applications, event management software, database structure to handle the information gathered from the event registration section, questions and comments submitted to the staff, and the server that holds the Web site and other event-based information and the benefits of a near-paperless planning process.

Infrastructure: Refers to the aspects of the venue that are at the core of its operation, such as the structure, roadways, access ways, lighting, and utilities associated with the venue.

In-kind advertising: See trade advertising.

Instant messaging (IM): A near-real-time information exchange on a computer or device with Internet access. Organizations can create an IM interface on their Web sites and have staff monitor it, allowing customers to ask questions or even buy tickets.

Jump teams: Squads of event-day workers that are available to fill in at a variety of staffing positions throughout the event day.

Killed seat: A seat that is removed from the ticket inventory for the event, usually because of an obstructed view.

Legal representation: Internal General Counsel or an outside legal firm that represents an organization's interests.

Legality: See capacity.

Marshalling revenue: Marshalling revenue refers to identifying, organizing, and accounting for everything related to revenue in an effective way.

Media audit: The process of determining the content, format, deadlines, and contacts at the entire population of outlets that are active in the media market where the group, and/or the event, takes place.

Media center: A special section on the Web site and a centrally located physical site at an event that seeks to provide maximum information to all members of the media.

Mega events: The most complex category of events that often take years of planning prior to the event taking place. Mega events are often international in nature (whether through media exposure, participation, or location) and are easily identifiable to sport consumers because the event is a brand in itself. These events become stand-alone business ventures since many of them have organizing committees composed of full- and part-time personnel dedicated solely to the execution of the event.

Monetization: Describes the efforts made to utilize Web site space for revenue generation, even if the revenues are not for profit purposes.

National Governing Body (NGB): Recognized by the United States Olympic Committee (USOC) or an international governing organization to oversee a particular sport. Most amateur sports in the United States have an NGB (e.g., USA Volleyball, USA Swimming, and USA Table Tennis).

National Labor Relations Act: A law that restricts an employer's ability to interfere with employees in the execution of their job duties by offering coercive incentives such as higher pay, better work conditions, or a more comprehensive benefits package in order to sway an employee away from joining a union.

News items: A form of earned media that normally surround the event itself and include coverage of what happens at the event, previews of the event, and announcements that the event is going to happen—often by covering a smaller ancillary event related to the main one (e.g., a press conference).

Offer: The proposal that forms the contract. It is a promise to do something or refrain from doing something.

On-sale date: The date the tickets are available for purchase.

Organizing committees: These groups play a large role in the bidding, obtaining, and hosting of some events as the local group that puts on the event.

Origination fee: When an event is televised, additional costs will accrue, including higher utility bills and perhaps additional labor and/or security. Also, if television viewership will suppress attendance, and the building is receiving a share of ticket proceeds, then this type of fee may be required to make the building whole.

PA script: Includes the specific details of what is being said when by announcers.

Package-to-compete: Event entry strategy where event organizers group the entry fee to the event with theme park tickets, hotel room nights, or special events tickets and require that an individual or team purchase the package in order to enter the event.

Page view counts: The number of times Internet content is loaded into a browser, which can be tracked by the page's publisher.

Paid advertising: Any time cash is spent in return for the specified form of advertising.

Paid media: Advertising, sponsorship, and activation marketing that event organizers pay for and therefore retain control over the message.

Participant: Anyone taking part in a sports event. This includes everyone associated with a team taking part in a sports event who will be on the field of play (including, but not limited to, players, coaches, statisticians, athletic trainers, managers); volunteers; participants in promotions; etc.

Participant registration: The act of providing information and/or payment to an event with the expectation of participation and access to all of the rights and benefits associated with event participation.

Partner: Can be a sponsor, but the relationship to the event might be over a longer period of time, carry a higher monetary value, or might just be named differently.

Partnership: Used as a synonym for sponsorship, in that an event organizer should treat a sponsor like a true partner where together both parties can benefit from a successful event.

Pass-through charges: Those expenses for which the facility pays a third party on behalf of the renter and then later charges to the renter.

Peak times: Periods in which specific areas will have a surge in spectator/participant traffic. For example, sports that have a half time will see a surge to concessions during this time.

Per cap: See per capita spending.

Per capita spending (also: per cap): The amount of money spent per person during the event. For example, the per cap for merchandise spending is calculated by taking the total revenue for merchandise divided by the total number of people in attendance.

Per-person fee agreement: Used mostly in merchandise and concession contracts, the event is charged an amount for each person in attendance.

Percentage of gross sales agreement: The event splits its gross revenue with the venue (or city in the case of many nontraditional venues).

Permits: Permission from a city, county, or national governing agency to allow an event to occur. Events that are held outside of a traditional venue will most likely need a permit.

Planning timelines: Documents used to set up and track detailed tasks by functional area. They ensure that event managers can account for each detailed item, who is responsible for specific items, and whether the event is on schedule.

Premium seating: Encompasses a variety of seats such as luxury suites, party suites, club seats, loge boxes, field-level seats in baseball, courtside seats in basketball, and any other special section of tickets with enhanced amenities.

Primary space: The area of the venue where the main activity takes place.

Processing fee: The amount charged to participants for the right to enter the lottery or other selection process associated with the event. This fee covers the costs to the organization in managing the lottery and entry procedures.

Production binder: A book or collection of detailed information (e.g., parking maps, event-day checklists, fast facts, staffing positions, maps and diagrams, etc.) about the event that can be carried with event staff during the event.

Promotional campaign: Special discounts, giveaways, theme nights, and other publicity strategies that are sponsored by a media outlet and not a part of the paid advertising campaign.

Publicity: Any news coverage for the event that is generated with some type of announcement or interview and is not paid for by the event.

Purchase Money Security Interest (PMSI): In a commercial lending transaction, a lender, typically a bank, will acquire a security interest in the equipment or fixtures purchased with the loan proceeds.

Purpose statement: A short, to-the-point acknowledgment of the overall motivation for holding the event.

Queuing up: When people at an event create a line on their own, often interfering with other aspects of event flow.

Question and answer availability: The different ways in which questions and concerns can be directed to event planning staff, including, but not limited to, information on Web sites, instant messaging, text messaging, and Twitter.

Quid pro quo: A Latin phrase that literally means "this for that." A sponsor will give money, product, and/or services, but expects something in return to benefit the company and provide an effective ROI (Return on Investment) (McMillen, 2003).

Radio repeater: Radio transmission equipment that receives a low-level signal and retransmits it at a higher power, increasing the distance the signal can effectively cover. A repeater will most likely be needed for golf events, road races, or just to maintain communication within the locale if staff is driving out of the immediate event range.

Rate card: The retail price that a media outlet charges for its commercial time. The rates charged vary depending on the time of day or the specific programming on the station. Related to venues, a rate card can also be the rates charged by a venue for rental of its equipment and/or services by a third party.

Rating: The percentage of the population listening to a given radio station during a day part. Ratings apply to both average quarter-hour and cumulative audiences.

Reach: The total number of different persons exposed to a commercial or song during a specified day part. Reach can be calculated using a computer for a single station, multiple stations, or across media using formulas generally accepted by the advertising industry.

Recurring event: An event that happens on a regular basis (e.g., university basketball game or youth soccer game).

Registration fee: The monetary amount that participants pay to enter a competition.

Release of liability: See waiver.

Rental event: An event where an outside presenter, sponsor, or promoter is fully responsible for producing and staging the event in the venue.

Request For Bid (RFB): The letter sent by the event manager to potential vendors seeking out prices on the equipment needed.

Reserved seating: The ticket holder is assigned, or chooses, a specific seat in the venue for the event.

Revocable permit: The organization reserves the right to take the ticket back from the purchaser (usually with a refund).

Rights fee: The payment made by an entity to a rights holder to legally associate with the event.

Rights holders: Organizations or businesses that control and own the entitlement to an event.

Risk: A hazard or the possibility of danger or harm.

Risk management: The entire process of evaluating risk and using cost-effective strategies to reduce and treat risk.

Room nights: The number of total nights' stay sold for an event.

RSS feeds: Web feeds that allow people to create links to information sources (e.g., other Web sites) on their Web browser or computer desktop. Whenever an organization or individual adds new content pertaining to that link to a Web site, a hyperlink is created at the individual's browser or desktop indicating new information has arrived.

Sample boards: Displays of exact replicas of credentials, tickets, and/or parking passes used as an easy reference guide for staff.

Secondary ticket market: The reselling of tickets after the first purchase.

Secure event: An event in a venue (traditional or non-traditional) with an enhanced atmosphere for patrons and participants while providing a certain level of safety and an efficient, direct, and unobtrusive emergency response. For the patrons, the feeling is positive and they feel well attended-to, while the level of security intervention will be minimized. The measures required to sustain a safe venue will be focused from a patron service rather than a punitive environment.

Security deposit: Non-refundable money collected to hold the date when renting or reserving a sports or entertainment facility.

Setup: The process of preparing the venue for the event.

Share: The percentage of people listening to a specific radio station in a particular day part compared to all those listening to radio in that day part. Share answers the question: "What percentage of the radio audience is listening to a specific station at a particular time?"

Shared network drives: Common storage areas that allow individuals to post documents and have them accessed by others who have access to the drive.

Site context: Refers to whether or not the venue site and immediate areas convey a sense of welcoming, safety, and control. To create a welcoming feel, designers should conceive a site in the context of surrounding neighborhoods, whether they are urban, suburban, or a college/university campus.

Site setback: The distance between the spectator venue and other structures and/or public right of ways.

Sponsor: An entity that provides cash or in-kind products or services in exchange for an association with or presence within the event.

Sponsorship: A cash and/or in-kind fee paid to a property (typically in sports, arts, entertainment, or causes) in return for access to the exploitable commercial potential associated with that property.

Sponsorship contract: A legal agreement that binds two or more parties to agreed-upon obligations.

Sports commission: An organization, often non-profit, that exists specifically to attract sports events to an area and assist in hosting those events.

Sport governance: "The exercise of power and authority in sport organizations, including policy making, to determine organizational mission, membership, eligibility, and regulatory power, with the organization's appropriate local, national or international scope" (Hums & McLean 2008, p. 4).

Standing Room Only (SRO): Tickets to enter the venue with access to specific areas where there are not seats, but where the event can still be viewed.

Supplies: Items used on a regular basis that may or may not relate to the core activity of the event (e.g., paper, pens, credentials, ticket stock).

Trade advertising (also: in-kind advertising): Any advertising that is secured in exchange on a dollar-for-dollar trade with tickets or something else of value to the event.

Teardown: The process of returning the venue to the pre-event condition.

Terms and conditions: In a contract, the specific details not spelled out in the General Provisions.

Ticket as a limited contract: The ticket buyer receives the right to attend the event and the organization has an obligation to provide the event as advertised and promoted.

Ticket manifest: A representation of the venue layout needed for all ticketed events. The ticket manifest identifies how many seats are in each row and section of the venue.

Time Spent Listening (TSL): The amount of time the average listener spent listening to a radio station during a day part. The estimate may be expressed in number of quarter hours or in hours/minutes. TSL answers the question: "How much time does the average listener spend with this station?"

Trained crowd manager: Someone who has been educated in crowd management techniques, the responsibilities of their job, as well as emergency procedures.

Traveling event: An event that does not occur on a regular basis at a consistent location, but may either occur on a regular basis or at a set location.

Universal design: "The design of products and environments to be usable by all people, to the greatest extent possible, without the need for adaptation or specialized design" (The Center for Universal Design, 1997, ¶ 1).

User Generated Content (UGC): refers to pictures, video, podcasts, and text (e.g., blogs) contributed by individuals for others to see regarding their experiences associated with an event.

Venue contract (also: facility contract): A rental agreement for use of a venue/facility that must be in writing.

Waiver: Is "a contract in which the participant or user of a service agrees to relinquish the right to pursue legal action against the service provider in the event that the ordinary negligence of the provider results in an injury to the participant" (Cotten, 2007, p. 85).

Walk-thru: A literal walk around the building or site examining, in detail, how everything will look, function, and flow for the event.

Wayfinding: The ease at which visitors find their way throughout the venue. Well placed, visible entries help people to navigate into the building efficiently.

Wrap up: A general term referring to task completion that concludes the event management process, such as attending to any complaints received, generating sponsor reports, sending thank you notes, debriefing and paying workers, and completing post-event recaps.